Housing Policy at a Crossroads

Housing Policy at a Crossroads

The Why, How, and Who
of Assistance Programs

John C. Weicher

The AEI Press

Publisher for the American Enterprise Institute

WASHINGTON, D.C.

Distributed by arrangement with the Rowman & Littlefield Publishing Group, 4501 Forbes Boulevard, Suite 200, Lanham, Maryland 20706. To order, call toll free 1-800-462-6420 or 1-717-794-3800. For all other inquiries, please contact AEI Press, 1150 Seventeenth Street, N.W., Washington, D.C. 20036, or call 1-800-862-5801.

Library of Congress Cataloging-in-Publication Data

Weicher, John C.
  Housing policy at a crossroads : the why, how, and who of assistance programs / John C. Weicher.
     p. cm.
  Includes bibliographical references and index.
  ISBN-13: 978-0-8447-4258-8
  ISBN-10: 0-8447-4258-9
  1. Housing policy—United States. 2. Low-income housing—United States. 3. Housing subsidies—United States. I. Title.
  HD7293.W362 2010
  363.5'80973—dc22

                                                          2010000106

Printed in the United States of America

To Alice, who married me just before
I unexpectedly became involved in housing
policy, and has been my companion
and advisor ever since.

Contents

List of Tables

Preface

About thirty years ago, I wrote a book on housing policy in the United States (*Housing: Federal Policies and Programs,* American Enterprise Institute, 1980). The book described the main objectives of federal policy, and explained how the various programs served, or did not serve, those objectives. It drew on my experiences at the Department of Housing and Urban Development during the mid-1970s, when the department confronted both scandals and high costs in some of the subsidy programs, and as a result implemented major—and controversial—policy changes.

The book was intended for an audience of policymakers and citizens concerned with housing issues. To my surprise, however, it found another audience—in the academic world, and specifically in the fields of real estate economics, public policy, and urban planning. As an academic friend told me, "It explains to our students how economists think about these issues, in nontechnical terms, and they need to know that." Over the next decade or more, scholars in these fields still used the book, even as it became increasingly out of date. Indeed, during my service at HUD as Federal Housing Administration commissioner and assistant secretary for housing, I was more than once referred to my own 1980 book when I asked academic friends for nontechnical explanations of housing policies and programs that HUD colleagues might find useful.

That book, of course, is now almost completely out of date. Some programs that were very active in the late 1970s have been terminated; others have been substantially revamped. New programs have been created, sometimes embodying new forms of subsidy. Housing policy and housing programs have remained controversial, as evidenced most dramatically by a radical proposal by President Clinton in 1995 to "reinvent" HUD, to say nothing of occasional proposals to abolish the department. The interests of policymakers have changed; they now seek to use housing programs for different purposes than their predecessors.

Most importantly, a very large body of research about and relevant to assisted housing programs has developed in the years since my book appeared. To a large extent, this work has been sponsored by HUD's Office of Policy Development and Research, which (despite an 80 percent reduction in real research funding since the mid-1970s) has worked consistently to illuminate major policy issues, evaluate the effectiveness of individual programs, and provide a context for housing policy by tracking the broader changes in the housing market.

In short, much has changed since my earlier book, and I am grateful to the National Research Initiative, under the leadership of Kim Dennis and Henry Olsen, and to the American Enterprise Institute and its former president Chris DeMuth, for offering me this opportunity to revisit the subject of housing policy.

Two recent books have reviewed assisted housing policy and programs: *A Primer on U.S. Housing Markets and Housing Policy,* by Richard K. Green and Stephen Malpezzi (Washington, DC: Urban Institute Press, 2003), and *Housing Policy in the United States: Second Edition,* by Alex F. Schwartz (New York: Routledge, 2010). These excellent books overlap with mine, but differ from it in important respects. As their title implies, Green and Malpezzi have a broad focus, and their discussion of assisted housing is relatively brief. Schwartz is more narrowly though not exclusively concerned with assisted housing programs, but he does not write from an economist's perspective. Readers of my book will benefit by reading both of these; it is my hope that readers of these books will find mine useful as well.

A substantial number of people have helped me in writing this book. Much of what I know about assisted housing I have learned during various terms of public service at HUD, the first one beginning in 1973 and the last one ending in 2005. I have benefited greatly from the insights and suggestions of a number of former HUD colleagues. They are far too numerous to list, but I would like to thank especially Robert W. Gray, Jill Khadduri, Kathryn P. Nelson, James W. Stimpson, and Margaret Young.

I have also benefited from the good work of a series of research assistants and associates, listed here in chronological order: Theresa Firestine, Philip Schuster, Richard Goggins, Richard Jacobson, Megan Dorman,

Margaret Mailander, Van T. Nguyen, Brett McCully, David M. Block, and Akshay Bajaj. Daniel Broxterman, my colleague at the Center for Housing and Financial Markets at Hudson Institute, was especially helpful in organizing program data. Edgar Olsen, whom I first met and worked with at HUD many years ago, read early versions of several chapters and offered useful comments. I am grateful to all of these former colleagues and associates. The photograph of the subsidized housing project on the cover was taken by Philip Ross. Samuel Thernstrom and Laura Harbold (formerly of AEI Press), Martin Morse Wooster, and Anne Himmelfarb carefully and conscientiously edited the manuscript for publication, strengthening and clarifying it in the process.

I remain fully responsible for any errors and for all conclusions and interpretations.

Introduction

Ever since the New Deal, the goal of American housing policy has been to provide decent housing for the poor. The social benefits deriving from this purpose, and the efficacy of the programs created to achieve it, are both open to question. The federal government spends large sums directly on housing assistance—on projects owned by local government agencies, on projects owned by private developers, and on houses and apartments chosen by lower-income households. It also spends large sums to honor guarantees on loans to build privately owned subsidized projects, and it spends indirectly in the form of tax credits to finance the construction of privately owned projects. The federal government spends about as much on housing assistance as it does on Medicaid for each assisted person. Some major housing programs cost much more than Medicaid. Housing assistance costs less than Medicaid in the aggregate only because it is not an entitlement.

Neither the public nor policymakers have ever been fully satisfied with governmental housing programs. Quite a few programs have been abolished over the years—in some cases replaced by other programs that have been abolished in their turn. Construction programs have been partially superseded by vouchers, and vouchers partially superseded by tax credits; now construction programs may be making a comeback. Various Congresses and administrations have even considered abolishing the agency that administers most U.S. housing programs, the Department of Housing and Urban Development (HUD). (No administration has ever actually proposed to abolish HUD, however, and while such legislation has been introduced in Congress—most recently by Republicans in the mids-1990s—no bill has ever made it out of committee.) Dramatic program changes have been proposed about once a decade, most notably the introduction of housing vouchers in 1974 and the Clinton administration's proposals to "reinvent" HUD in the mid-1990s. Meanwhile the federal government wrestles with the unexpected results of its past actions, including periodic scandals involving private firms and individuals, local government employees, and HUD staff. Long before the current subprime mortgage predicament, "housing crisis" had almost become one word in discussions of U.S. housing policy.

This book describes and analyzes the policies and programs that have been created to provide housing assistance for low-income families and individuals. In my view, it is not possible to understand contemporary housing policy issues and housing programs without understanding how these programs have developed over time. For that reason, the book puts current programs and issues into historical context, and describes how programs have evolved. This approach is useful also because many current policy proposals are essentially revivals or variants of programs that have been tried, and usually found wanting, in the past.

The book is about policies and programs, not personalities, but it necessarily also discusses HUD, where I served in four different administrations between 1973 and 2005. This is a book by an economist, giving primary attention to the economic issues that arise in housing programs, but as a former policy official within HUD I have also been concerned with social and technical aspects of programs, and administrative matters as well.

This book's primary focus is on urban housing, particularly in its analysis of federal housing programs. There is no discussion here of the rural housing programs administered by the U.S. Department of Agriculture, of military housing, or of the many housing programs of other federal government agencies.[1] The book also does not address broader urban issues or urban programs. It largely ignores community development activities, including the community development programs within HUD, except when these programs affect the housing programs discussed here. Nor is this a book about mortgages or other aspects of the U.S. housing finance system; the problems with subprime mortgages that have become evident since 2007 are not related to housing policies or programs for lower-income renters.

This book concentrates instead on federal housing policy since its inception, specifically the extent to which this policy has succeeded or failed in meeting its stated goals, and the reasons for this success or failure. It is at once a history of housing policy, a guide to the issues confronting policymakers, and an argument about the proper direction that housing policy should take. It begins by explaining the original reasons why the federal government began subsidizing housing for the poor (chapter 1). It next offers an account of housing conditions in the past and today (chapter 2). The remainder of the book describes and analyzes the range of federal housing programs for lower-income households; specifically, it looks at public housing and subsidies to build privately owned projects, vouchers to allow families to choose their own housing, tax credits to developers to build projects, block grants to state and local governments, and the newest subsidies for privately owned projects. Chapter 3 describes these programs and traces their development over time. Chapter 4 presents quantitative information on the programs to provide an overall picture of assisted housing, including both the number of households and housing units receiving subsidies and the total cost of housing assistance. The next two chapters summarize the pertinent research on the effects of the various programs on housing and on neighborhoods in order to compare the two main approaches to housing assistance, production, and vouchers. They are followed by comparisons of the costs and cost-effectiveness of the various programs (chapters 7 and 8), and finally by an analysis of the issue of housing availability for the poor (chapter 9).

Much of the data on housing conditions and programs ends with the year 2009. The information on housing conditions, particularly in chapter 2, is largely drawn from the American Housing Survey, conducted biennially for the Census Bureau by HUD; the most recent published AHS is for 2009. Also, the most recent information on a number of the housing programs described in chapters 3 and 4 is for fiscal year 2009. Available later data are presented in the relevant tables, marked as "estimated" where appropriate, but most of the analysis employs 2009 data.

The book reaches three general conclusions: vouchers have been shown to provide the greatest choice to the poor at the lowest cost to the taxpayer; vouchers address affordability—a key housing issue for the poor—most directly and effectively, while enabling the poor to improve the quality of their housing; and future housing programs should seek to help the very poorest members of society rather than those substantially above the poverty line.

1

Housing Assistance and the Problems of Poverty

American housing policy, like so much domestic policy, dates back to the New Deal. The first mention of housing in a national party platform came in the 1936 Democratic platform; in 1940 housing was featured in the platforms of both parties. The milieu of the Great Depression provided the basic rationales both for housing assistance as a public policy and for the form of housing assistance. These rationales concerned the relationships between housing and the overall economy and society; the belief was that good housing for the poor would eliminate or ameliorate crime, unemployment, and poor health. Thus housing mattered not so much for its own sake as for its effect on social welfare and economic well-being in general.

These assumptions have had consequences for generations, but as this chapter will show, they have been borne out by neither direct observation nor academic research. Moreover, evidence to support other rationales for federal aid to housing—that it revitalizes poor neighborhoods, that it stimulates the economy generally—is at best mixed.

Subsidized Housing as Social Welfare Policy

The concerns that the federal government sought to address in the 1930s were largely those of the urban reformers of that day. To them, urban social problems were caused primarily by poor housing. At least as far back as the turn of the last century, reformers were pointing to slums as the home of all the ills of urban society. Slums were considered the breeding ground for crime, delinquency, disease, mental illness, and even death. Living in the slums kept people from becoming productive members of society. These views were buttressed by many studies showing that medical problems and social pathologies were much more common in the slums than elsewhere.[1] The reformers concluded that the slums should be razed and replaced with decent housing.

Reformers also believed that the cost of housing was high—both in the slums and elsewhere—and that the private sector simply did not provide decent housing for lower-income people. Such data as were available supported the view that much of the housing stock did not meet the desired standards. They blamed the landlords for charging rents much beyond the cost of building and maintaining the housing, and for reaping excessive profits from substandard housing. They believed that decent housing could be built and operated at reasonable cost if the profits were eliminated. This view dovetailed with their concern about the social costs of slum housing. If the slums were eliminated, they believed, government would need to spend much less money dealing with crime and disease.

When the U.S. Housing Act, which created public housing, was being considered in Congress in 1937, urban reformers and experts were among many witnesses who argued for a program of slum clearance and publicly owned housing. Opponents of public housing, who advocated as an alternative that poor people be given cash assistance to enable them to afford decent, privately owned housing, were outnumbered. A Senate committee report accompanying the bill accurately describes the conventional wisdom of the day:

> The acute shortage of decent, safe, and sanitary dwellings within the financial reach of families of low income is inimical to the general welfare of the Nation by:
>
> (a) encouraging the spread of disease and lowering the level of health, morale, and vitality of large portions of the American people;
>
> (b) increasing the hazards of fire, accidents, and natural calamities;
>
> (c) subjecting the moral standards of the young to bad influences;

(d) impairing industrial and agricultural productive efficiency;

(e) increasing the violation of the criminal laws of the United States and of the several states;

(f) lowering the standards of living of large portions of the American people;

(g) necessitating a vast and extraordinary expenditure of public funds, Federal, State and local, for crime prevention, punishment, and correction, fire protection, public-health service, and relief.[2]

Similar statements can be found in later legislation, such as the Housing Act of 1949, where Congress invoked welfare, security, and mental and physical health benefits as the reasons for establishing a national housing goal of "a decent home and a suitable living environment for every American family."[3]

It is not too much to say that housing was seen as a war on poverty, all by itself. Indeed, when Congress enacted the public housing program in 1937, housing was separate from the welfare system, and was provided to families on a different basis from cash relief. Relief was limited to the unemployed and widows with children (who were expected to be out of the labor force), but subsidized housing was available to the working poor as well.

The Logic of the Rationale

Housing reformers clearly believed that the residents of slum housing were themselves harmed by their housing conditions, and would benefit if they were able to live in better housing. This view is certainly reasonable, but it does not necessarily imply that better housing should be provided directly by the government. Economists in particular typically find arguments of this nature inadequate as a justification for specific benefits in kind, such as housing subsidies. It is true that the poor will be made better off by being given the opportunity to live in decent housing, but they can also be made better off by being given assistance in other forms as well.

Indeed, if individuals are considered to be the best judges of their own well-being, cash assistance will help them more than housing assistance or any other in-kind benefit having the same dollar cost. They can choose to spend the money as they wish, rather than as somebody else thinks they should. They may wish to spend all of it on housing, although it is highly unlikely they will; but even if they do, they are as well off as if they received housing assistance.

Economists have generally seen housing assistance as a form of income redistribution. In contrast to the urban reformers who argued that assistance should be given in the form of housing rather than cash because housing was especially important to the well-being of the poor, most economists have argued that the poor can make that judgment themselves. The poor person's choice may not always seem rational or desirable, but the government cannot know the individual's full circumstances and preferences.[4] The view that consumers are best able to maximize their own utility blends with the view that citizens can best decide what public policies are in their own interest.

Housing or Cash? This theoretical economic argument was given little weight in housing policy until the 1970s, but has been one of the key elements of policy debates ever since. Critics of cash assistance offer two arguments. The first is that individuals do not always know what is in their own best interests—for instance, if they do not know that inadequate housing causes health problems, they may act against their own interests and not make decent housing a priority.

The second argument is that housing markets don't work—that is, individuals will not be able to find decent housing even if they are given money to pay for it because there is something in the housing market itself that prevents them from satisfying their desires. This was part of the case for public housing construction in the 1930s, when much of the housing stock was considered inadequate in quality and unlikely to be brought up to standard. A modern variant is that housing for low- and moderate-income households is not available in tight markets and that it is therefore more effective to provide housing than cash, which would simply be dissipated in higher rents without improving housing quality or increasing the housing stock.

One particular market imperfection which has attracted special interest is discrimination, particularly on racial or ethnic grounds. If a private landlord is unwilling to make housing available to members of minority groups, or charges them much higher rents, then the only way they can obtain decent housing is if the government provides it. This argument about race, it should be noted, does not apply only to the poor or residents of slums, unless they are the only members of the minority groups who suffer from discrimination, and of course laws to prevent housing discrimination are intended to protect all members of minority groups, not only the poor.

Externalities. A different argument for housing subsidies can be inferred from some of the items on the Senate committee's list above. Not all the benefits of decent housing accrue to the poor themselves. If improved housing checks the spread of disease, for example, or lessens the risk of fires, then such housing benefits not only the poor but other residents of the community as well.

Community residents may also benefit financially from improved housing for poor neighbors. They may pay less in taxes if crime rates are lower or there are fewer fires. They may also be better off if the value of their homes rises when nearby slum housing is torn down. (This externality is widely believed to exist, as witness the real estate adage that the three most important factors in the market are "location, location, and location.") To the extent that the value of one house depends on the quality of other houses in the neighborhood, there is an economic argument for subsidizing housing specifically. This argument applies in general not simply to the poor or even to slum residents, but to all residents of urban areas. It may have a special application in low-income neighborhoods, however; subsidized housing may help to revitalize or stabilize such a neighborhood, whereas the original housing stock may be seen as an indication that the neighborhood is not worth investing in.

To the extent that these rationales are valid, they justify housing subsidies as serving more purposes than just income redistribution. Assistance in the form of housing is warranted if it overcomes market imperfections—even if the household would from its own standpoint be better off with cash instead. Conversely, if the rationales are not valid, the case for housing assistance collapses into the general case for income redistribution, and there is no reason specifically to give assistance in the form of housing.

Subsequent Evidence

To what extent have these rationales for housing assistance been borne out by the record of the housing subsidy programs—how well have they stood the test of experience? There are two kinds of relevant evidence: direct observation of what has happened in subsidized housing projects, and academic research on the relationship between housing conditions and social or medical problems. Neither kind, it turns out, provides much support for most of the rationales for housing assistance.

Direct observation of housing programs offers less conclusive evidence than systematic analysis, but is perhaps more powerful in the political arena because policymakers and program administrators are confronted with this sort of evidence every day. It has been clear for many years that subsidized housing projects have not solved the problems of slum residents—the problems of poverty. By the late 1950s, Daniel Seligman could write of "the enduring slums" and quote disillusioned erstwhile supporters of public housing as its bitter critics.[5] By 1961, Jane Jacobs could refer matter-of-factly to "low-income projects that have become worse centers of delinquency, vandalism and general social hopelessness than the slums they were supposed to replace"—and draw little criticism.[6]

By that time, also, policymakers were looking for alternatives to public housing, and President Kennedy proposed what became the first of a series of programs to subsidize the construction of privately owned projects for low-income families and individuals. These proved unsatisfactory; they were expensive and prone to financial failure and mismanagement; in some instances contracts were awarded in return for payments by the winning bidders. By 1974 policymakers were willing to provide low-income families with cash assistance (in the form of a voucher) to find decent housing of their own choosing on the private market. By 1983 cash assistance became the preferred subsidy program.[7] Policymakers were no longer inclined to put much stock in the original rationale for public housing, and few believed that public housing in and of itself would end poverty or the problems of poverty.

Meanwhile, a host of academic studies in a variety of disciplines was providing scholarly explanations for the failure of subsidized housing to solve the social problems of the slums. The general conclusion can be stated succinctly: slum housing was a less important cause of social ills than such personal attributes as lack of education or low income. Most slum residents were poor and poorly educated, in addition to living in poor housing.

Separating these contributing factors and evaluating their relative importance became possible with the development of research computers and their use by social scientists and public health researchers after World War II. Thus in 1962 a longitudinal study of public housing residents in Baltimore, conducted by Daniel Wilner of Johns Hopkins University and several associates, found that residents' health was no better after moving into public housing than the health of a similar control group who remained in private unsubsidized housing over the same period. There was also no difference in mortality rates.[8] Ten years later, after reviewing 178 studies of the relationship between housing and health, epidemiologist Stanislav Kasl concluded that

> the link between parameters of housing and indices of physical health has not been well supported by the reviewed evidence, at least not in any direct sense. . . . The association between housing and mental health (excluding housing satisfaction) is supported only by the weakest, most ambiguous studies. . . . The best designed studies do not demonstrate any mental health benefits, and it now appears that some of our most cherished hopes—such as raising educational and occupational aspirations by moving people out of slums—never will be realized.[9]

Economists who studied housing reached the conclusion that the social and health problems of the poor were generally due to their poverty rather than their housing. Richard Muth characterized "most arguments which seek to establish a causal connection between poor housing, on the one hand, and crime and poor health, on the other," as "tenuous at best."[10] Edwin Mills made a similar point:

> It is often claimed that underinvestment in slum housing breeds crime, alienation, drug abuse, and other ills. Undoubtedly, the important causes of these problems are poverty, racial conflict, etc., none of which represent housing market failure.[11]

These conclusions relate primarily to the claim that the problems of the poor are caused by bad housing and that the poor themselves benefit from improved housing. The rationale that better housing generates externalities for neighbors and other residents of the community—that it brings crime rates down and property values up—is more difficult to analyze and has received less attention. But available evidence indicates little external benefit to neighborhoods or the city generally from replacing slums with subsidized housing projects.[12] If crime, delinquency, and poor educational performance stem more from the characteristics of the individual than from his or her housing, then expenditures on public services such as the police force or public schools will not drop if housing for the poor becomes better. Nor did analysts find much evidence that subsidized housing raised property values or contributed to revitalizing low-income neighborhoods.[13]

These conclusions are based on studies conducted in the first twenty-five years or so after World War II. Later research, particularly among public health analysts, confirms them. A 2001 analysis of a British longitudinal data set, which included information on the housing of children in the late 1930s and their death rates over the next decade, found "relatively weak" effects from major housing deficiencies, taking account of socioeconomic status: "Associations between housing conditions in childhood and mortality from common diseases in adulthood are not strong, but are in some respects distinguishable from those of social deprivation."[14] This study addresses some of the same outcomes as the Baltimore study by Wilner and his colleagues, with similar results.

In general, the recent public health literature has tended to focus on specific environmental hazards such as lead-based paint, asbestos, and vermin, rather than "housing quality," broadly defined. These hazards are often found in housing that is in good condition generally, and while separating housing quality from socioeconomic status is necessary for housing policy purposes, the problem of disentangling the effects of poverty from those of housing conditions has remained serious.[15] Most of these hazards have been identified relatively recently; indeed, lead-based paint and asbestos were considered to improve the quality of housing when they were in common use in the 1950s and 1960s. The exception is the presence of vermin, which has been a concern for a much longer period and is part of the standard

HUD definition of "severely inadequate" housing (see the next chapter). It is not a common problem.[16]

Lead-based paint is perhaps the best-known environmental hazard in housing, and exemplifies the analytical complications. Exposure to lead paint is related to high blood lead levels in children, which in turn are related to physical and mental health problems; in extreme cases, ingestion of lead paint chips causes death. Reducing the incidence of lead paint in housing has been a policy goal since 1972. Before 1979, when its use was finally prohibited, lead paint was widely used in housing of all qualities, and it is still quite commonly found in older housing. A study by HUD in 1990 found that 57 million housing units probably had lead paint, out of a total of 77 million built before 1979, and out of a total housing stock of 92 million occupied units. Lead paint was about equally pervasive for higher-income and lower-income households, and in houses of all rents and prices.[17]

These data also illustrate the policy complications of addressing environmental hazards. The pervasiveness of lead paint provides little guidance for low-income housing policy. As of 2009, there were still 70 million occupied units built in 1979 or earlier. While poor households are slightly more likely to live in older housing (72 percent compared to 61 percent of those above the poverty line), providing housing assistance to the poor would clearly not address most of the problem.[18] Instead, public policy has aimed to remove or, more often, encapsulate lead-based paint as a specific remediation technique, rather than build new homes to replace the ones where lead paint was used.

Much of the more recent research on environmental health hazards and other health problems is confronted with the same problem as the earlier research—identifying a causal relationship between housing quality and health while disentangling the effects of poverty and housing conditions. Having reviewed the literature, Gary W. Evans and Elyse Kantrowitz conclude that "it is difficult to draw definitive conclusions" because of the difficulty of separating housing quality from income or socioeconomic status. They believe that "the preponderance of evidence" does suggest some relationships between housing quality and health, but their focus is on housing and neighborhood quality (among other factors) as manifestations of poverty, rather than as independent causes of health problems.[19]

Evans and Kantrowitz also review the literature on mental health and conclude that "work investigating a possible link between housing and mental health is more controversial. The findings are less numerous and consistent than the physical health research."[20] Evans subsequently reviewed some 157 studies of housing and mental health, mostly conducted in the previous thirty years, subsequent to the literature review by Kasl, finding some evidence that housing quality contributes to psychological distress, but again finding the same methodological difficulties in identifying causal relationships.[21] Evans suggests that there is perhaps more evidence of a relationship between the quality of the neighborhood and the mental health of residents, despite the methodological problems.

In an extensive review of this literature, Sandra J. Newman describes the studies of health benefits from better housing as "suggestive" but also "insufficient" and concludes that "evaluating current housing assistance policy with the yardstick of research findings to date is perilous." Her only policy recommendation is for minimum quality standards in assisted housing programs.[22]

The evidence finally does not seem strong enough to support a policy of assistance specifically for housing, rather than general income support.

Secretary Kemp's "New War on Poverty"

The original rationale for subsidized housing production, as stated in the 1937 Senate committee list, no longer has many adherents. During the 1970s and 1980s, it received little attention from policymakers. In 1989, however, when Rep. Jack Kemp (R–NY) became secretary of HUD, he launched a "new war on poverty" that represented a return to the original purpose of low-income housing programs: housing policy would combat the problems of the poor and help the poor to become productive members of society. At the same time, Kemp did not want to rely exclusively on housing programs to fight poverty, recognizing that such a strategy had not been successful over the course of half a century. Instead, he wanted to combine housing assistance with other programs, particularly those that promoted "human capital formation," such as education, job training, and medical care (particularly for the homeless), and also child care and social services.[23]

Kemp's approach, combined with the welfare reforms of the 1990s, led to several demonstrations and program experiments combining housing assistance with services in an effort to promote labor force participation and raise earnings for assisted households. The results of these efforts, discussed in detail in chapter 5, have been somewhat mixed, and the measured effects are often small. There is some evidence from these demonstrations that the initial effect has been to reduce labor force participation, but this effect may disappear over time. This effect is perhaps not surprising, since programs to encourage work face a fundamental problem: assisted households are in general less likely to work, because their rent is usually fixed at 30 percent of their income, which in effect means that these tenants have a marginal tax rate of 30 percent on their earnings, in addition to whatever income tax rate they may be subject to. On the positive side, there were some improvements in mental health for adults and for girls (but not boys).[24]

It is important to keep in mind that these demonstrations include social services as well as housing. Kemp supported the original purpose of housing programs but did not believe that housing programs alone could constitute an effective antipoverty program, and the evaluations of these demonstrations provide no evidence that housing by itself results in better economic circumstances for assisted households.

Subsidized Housing as Community Development

The related but broader argument that subsidized housing improves neighborhoods also has its roots in the urban environments of the Great Depression. Slums were thought to breed crime and disease, and they certainly were unattractive places to live. Replacing a slum with new housing seemed likely to benefit the neighborhood as a whole.

Over time, however, the new housing itself aged, and deteriorating housing built for low-income families became less attractive to its neighbors. Jane Jacobs's description of decaying public housing, quoted above, came fifteen to twenty-five years after the projects were built. In a Pulitzer Prize–winning book about Boston during the 1960s and early 1970s, J. Anthony Lukas describes a similar trajectory of decline in a subsidized Boston project, from a church's plan in 1965 to raze several blocks of urban blight and build attractive duplexes, through a fractious construction process lasting until 1971. By 1973 the project, known as Methunion Manor, faced foreclosure as a result of severe financial and management problems, and by 1974 it was being called an example of "disastrous failures of public policy . . . destined to spawn social problems."[25] More recently, several local governments have sought to have twenty- to thirty-year-old privately owned subsidized projects demolished, because the projects are inhibiting the locality's community redevelopment plans.[26]

The research evidence on subsidized housing as a community development tool is limited, and evaluations are at best mixed. Partly this is because it is hard to measure how subsidized housing enhances "community development." There is some research on the narrower question of whether subsidized housing increases nearby property values. The impact appears to depend on the neighborhood. Subsidized housing is more likely to have a positive impact on property values in better neighborhoods and in neighborhoods that do not have many subsidized projects.[27] Overall, subsidized housing is not likely to help in revitalizing low-income neighborhoods; its impact is frequently negative. Research on the effects of programs intended to provide subsidized homeownership has also produced mixed results.[28]

An additional limitation to the research on the relation between subsidized housing and community development is that it has generally focused on atypical subsidy programs. These programs either provide "mixed-income" housing, that is, housing for unsubsidized or moderate-income households as well as for lower-income subsidy recipients, or they provide homeownership opportunities for lower-income families.

Subsidized projects have historically been limited to lower-income residents, but encouraging a mix of incomes within projects has been a federal housing policy objective since at least 1974. Although there were probably over 1,000 mixed-income projects with perhaps close to 100,000 apartments built during the 1970s and early 1980s, there is very little evidence about the efficacy of mixed-income housing as a tool for neighborhood revitalization.[29] The research question is simply not asked in a way that would provide such evidence. The most relevant evidence concerns the extent of improvements in the lives of the lower-income residents within the mixed-income project, a measure of direct benefit to residents rather than external or community benefit. Even on this issue, the evidence is limited and inconclusive.[30] Mixed-income projects have been located predominantly in low-poverty neighborhoods, where they do not particularly contribute to the development of the community, but rather are much like the private housing in the area. Some projects have been built in lower-income neighborhoods; these are successful only in markets where the demand for housing is strong enough that middle-income families are willing to live among poor neighbors.

Generally similar findings are reported in the most extensive evaluation of the Low-Income Housing Tax Credit (LIHTC), covering the first ten years of the program (1987–1996). Tax credit projects are intended to serve both households that need subsidy and those with moderate incomes. They are located mostly in low- and moderate-income areas, and thus can contribute to revitalizing their neighborhoods, but income limits on residents place an upper bound on the possible effect on community development. The tax credit can be part of a revitalization strategy, but not the only component, if the intention is to encourage middle-income households to live in the neighborhood.[31]

Since 1992, much of the worst public housing in America has been replaced with mixed-income housing in a program known as HOPE VI. This program is discussed in more detail in later chapters. Here it is important to note that the HOPE VI projects require low-income residents to leave while the project is razed or renovated; that the new project nearly always has a smaller number of units, only some of which are available to the former residents or other low-income households; and that the others are reserved for middle-income residents. Implicitly if not explicitly, this program design is based on a recognition that subsidized housing hinders community development. Early research finds dramatic improvement in living conditions and resident satisfaction in many (though not all) HOPE VI neighborhoods, but researchers have not been able to measure the extent to which the HOPE VI project itself, as opposed to other changes, can be said to have caused the improvement.[32]

Jill Khadduri, a senior career HUD official who has been concerned with subsidized housing both as analyst and participant in policy development, has concluded that "the production of housing units for low-income occupancy has an ambiguous record of accomplishments as a developmental program."[33] Overall, the limited research evidence on subsidized housing as a community development tool finds that improved housing at best is only partially responsible for making communities better. Housing is perhaps the most visible manifestation of neighborhood conditions, but it is not the most important factor in generating neighborhood improvements; indeed, better housing cannot in and of itself improve a neighborhood.

In the view of Anthony Downs, a senior fellow at the Brookings Institution, "place-based tactics . . . cannot work effectively without simultaneously carrying out the person-based strategies that are being neglected."[34] Place-based tactics include attracting more business, enhancing the physical environment, and improving schools, police protection, and other public services, as well as housing development; person-based strategies aid the residents instead of the neighborhood, and include improving education, linking residents to jobs outside the neighborhood, and changing resident behavior patterns. Downs believes both person-based and place-based strategies are necessary and desirable.

Subsidized Housing as Macroeconomic Stimulus

Housing reformers originally had a third rationale for subsidizing housing: stimulating the economy. During the Depression, the federal government attempted to stimulate the economy in part by stimulating the production of housing. Subsidized housing was seen as a tool of macroeconomic policy; public housing was part of a more general program of public works.

This rationale has some appeal because the housing industry as a whole has historically been somewhat countercyclical. Construction has usually risen during recessions and fallen during booms. The reason is that housing demand is sensitive to interest rates, which rise when the economy is expanding and fall when it is contracting. If the government supports construction of subsidized housing when the economy as a whole is weak, the thinking goes, it may be able to generate employment for workers who have lost jobs in other industries.

In reality, however, subsidized housing has done little to stimulate the economy. Constructing a project takes a long time; by the time the housing is being built, the economy is already pulling out of the recession and the stimulative effect is no longer needed. Such was the case even during the Great Depression, when President Franklin D. Roosevelt transferred funds that had been appropriated to build low-income housing to other public works, because public housing took longer and he wanted jobs created as quickly as possible.[35] Housing production programs that were created during several recessions failed to have much effect until the recovery was well under way. This happened in 1961, when the Section 221(d)(3) subsidized housing program was enacted; the economy was in its third year of expansion before the program could produce 15,000 units per year, less than 1 percent of the 1.5 million total new housing units being built annually. It took another three years before the program could produce 20,000 units per year. In 1974 the Section 8 New Construction program was enacted about eight months before the trough of the recession (April 1975); although production under this program was more rapid, the recovery was two years old before a substantial number of units was produced. Public housing projects have typically taken a long time as well, with at least a year of planning and processing before site acquisition can begin, and still longer until construction is in progress. Indeed, it has been a common criticism of subsidized housing production programs that they take too long to produce housing.[36] The Obama administration's large economic stimulus program, the American Recovery and Reinvestment Act of 2009 included $4 billion for public housing, but the money was allocated to rehabilitating already-existing public housing projects and retrofitting them for energy conservation, rather than for new public housing. It did not provide funding for any new program.[37] Historically, when subsidized housing projects have been authorized in the expectation that they will put the unemployed to work during recessions, they have proved a disappointment; projects were not built until economic recovery was well under way.

A more recent and narrower variant of the macroeconomic rationale is the claim that subsidized housing production increases the overall supply of housing, or the supply for low-income households. It thus lowers their housing cost and gives them the opportunity to live in decent housing, even if they do not themselves directly receive assistance.

Again, the research evidence is mixed. Perhaps the best summary statement is that subsidized production of privately owned lower-income housing projects appears to be in large part, if not entirely, a substitute for unsubsidized housing production that would probably have occurred in any case. There may be some difference by program; public housing may not crowd out private housing, at least not to the same extent as privately owned subsidized projects.

Two recent papers have investigated the question on a cross-sectional basis. Stephen Malpezzi and Kerry Vandell analyzed the effect of the Low-Income Housing Tax Credit across states as of 2000.[38] Their best estimates are that the tax credit did not result in an increase in the total housing stock. The same result obtains for all project-based housing units combined and all tenant-based units combined. But the standard errors are so large that it is not possible to reject the hypothesis that each subsidized program or group of programs simply adds to the housing stock, without any substitution for unsubsidized housing.

Another analysis, by Todd M. Sinai and Joel Waldfogel, relates the total number of subsidized housing units in all programs as of 1996 to the total housing stock as of 1990, by place.[39] The authors find that for every three subsidized units in a place, there are two fewer private units. However, when they disaggregate into project-based and tenant-based assistance, they find a larger effect on the total stock for the tenant-based programs, which seems unlikely.

As their authors recognize, both studies are limited by the fact that they do not use the most appropriate geography. The best approximation to a local housing market is the metropolitan area; the state is too large, the city or town too small, to be considered a housing market. The Sinai-Waldfogel result for tenant-based assistance may be explained by this fact. Tenant-based assistance may lead property owners to keep units in the housing stock for a longer time, while places where fewer vouchers are used may experience the withdrawal of some low-rent units as the buildings are converted into other uses or demolished. More importantly, what happens in one municipality is only part of the picture; there may be offsetting withdrawals in other parts of the larger metropolitan area. Statewide data are in one sense preferable; the effect in one market may be independent of the effect in others. At the same time, state-level data introduce imprecision into the analysis, and some large metropolitan areas, particularly in the Northeast and Midwest, cross state lines.[40]

There have also been several time-series analyses examining the relation of subsidized housing to the overall supply of housing. In the most recent of these, Michael Murray concludes that in fact the privately owned subsidized projects have completely crowded out the production of privately owned unsubsidized housing.[41] Murray's analysis covers the period 1960 to 1987, which is also the entire history of these programs from Section 221(d)(3) (BMIR) through Section 8 New Construction, with the exception of some Section 8 projects that were funded by 1983 but not built until after 1987. These results are similar to those in earlier research by Murray and by Craig Swan covering the years between 1961 and 1977, and thus including Section 221(d)(3)(BMIR) and Section 236, but not Section 8.[42]

In both of his articles, Murray separated public housing from privately owned projects. In the more recent, he concludes that public housing does not crowd out private housing, but instead that construction of public housing increases the overall housing stock. He suggests that public housing may increase the number of households because it enables poor elderly individuals and poor single-parent families to live in their own households rather than with relatives or friends.

John C. Weicher and Thomas G. Thibodeau took a different approach, with some similar results. They looked at the effect of private and subsidized housing production on the extent of low-quality housing on a cross-sectional basis and found that public housing construction may result in an improvement in housing at the bottom of the quality distribution, while production of privately owned subsidized projects does not.[43]

An implication of these findings is that, to the extent that public housing or other subsidized housing results in a larger housing stock, it also results in a larger number of households. This suggests that there are fewer multigenerational households. Public housing may allow elderly individuals to live apart from their adult children, or enable young single parents or couples to move away from their own parents.

The effect of subsidized production on the housing stock is certainly relevant to evaluating the effects of housing programs, but it concerns a narrower issue than the original rationale.

The Remaining Rationale

The national housing goal of "a decent home" remains in law, and policymakers continue to be concerned about the specific effect of programs on the housing conditions of their beneficiaries. But the idea that housing is especially important for social and economic purposes has fallen out of public policy discussions in the light of both practical experience and systematic research. What is left from the original social welfare rationale is mainly the arguments that housing markets don't work well for poor people: that there is not enough decent housing available in the private market, that it will not be produced even if the poor are given enough money to pay for it, that the government should provide housing in tight markets, and that it is necessary to provide housing directly to those who suffer discrimination. Similarly, what is left from the original macroeconomic rationale is that housing subsidies may affect the housing market, especially the housing of low-income families who do not receive assistance.

But these are all statements about the housing consequences of specific housing programs and the workings of the housing market; they are not statements about the relationships between housing and other aspects of individual well-being or public policy. Put differently, they concern whether income should be transferred to the poor as housing rather than as cash—whether there is some reason why low-income households cannot obtain decent housing if they are given the ability to pay for it, or whether their housing circumstances will be affected by housing programs that directly benefit other people.

These are the issues on which subsidized housing policy now turns, and they will be discussed at length in later chapters. Chapter 3 looks in detail at the history and structure of current housing programs, and chapter 4 presents data on their size and funding levels. These chapters serve as background to the discussion in chapter 5 that compares how effectively these programs redistribute income, change housing quality, and address housing market problems, and the discussion in chapter 6 about the effects of subsidy programs on neighborhoods. Some basic information about current housing conditions and trends is necessary to provide context for these discussions; this information is provided in chapter 2.

2

Housing Conditions and Problems

In presenting some basic information about American housing conditions, this chapter supplies a necessary background for evaluating housing policy and programs. The context of this review of housing conditions is provided by the stated goals of American low-income housing policy, which concern the people to be served and the housing problems to be addressed. Since the first federal housing legislation in the 1930s, policy has been based on the presumption that not every family needs assistance. Because housing assistance has never been an entitlement—unlike, for example, Medicaid and (until its termination in 1996) Aid to Families with Dependent Children—it is necessary to determine which people and what problems should be given priority. Generally, housing assistance has been limited to renters, with occasional exceptions. Homeowners are considered to be able to address their housing concerns within their own financial resources; to the extent they cannot, the mechanisms for helping them are very different from those that provide housing assistance to renters.[1] Within the renter population, assistance has been limited to certain categories of lower-income households; and within those categories, not all renters have received assistance. Congress has never been willing to appropriate sufficient funds to assist every eligible household, or more precisely has preferred to provide a relatively large amount to a subset of eligible households rather than a smaller amount for everyone.

The National Housing Goal

To understand what sorts of problems and households are targeted by housing policy, it is appropriate to begin with the national housing goal.

Most recently enunciated and modified in 1990, the goal is "that every American family be able to afford a decent home in a suitable environment."[2] This broad statement is an elaboration of the national housing goal established in 1949, "the realization as soon as feasible of the goal of a decent home and a suitable living environment for every American family."[3] In 1979 and 1983 Congress directed that priority for rental housing assistance should be given to very low-income households that live in substandard housing, that pay more than 50 percent of their income for rent, or that have been involuntarily displaced. These rules were implemented by regulation in 1988.[4]

In the Senate committee report accompanying the 1991 HUD appropriations act, HUD was directed to prepare an annual report on "worst case housing needs," defined as "the number of families and individuals whose incomes fall 50 percent below an area's median income, who either pay 50 percent of more of their monthly income for rent, or who live in substandard housing."[5] The concept of worst-case housing needs had developed during the early 1980s out of discussions between HUD, the Office of Management and Budget, and the Senate appropriations subcommittee staff.[6] The first HUD report on worst-case needs was issued in 1991, and reports have been issued regularly since; the thirteenth and most recent national report appeared in February 2011, based on data for 2009.[7] (The report has not been prepared annually because the basic data source, the American Housing Survey, is biennial.) Because these reports are the most extensive analysis of housing conditions among lower-income households, the discussion in this chapter usually is based on data for 2009.

The national housing goal as revised in 1990 has two elements: affordability and quality. Each of these requires some elaboration.

Affordability

Affordability is defined in terms of the income of the household and the cost of its housing. Income in turn is defined in relation to the local income distribution, since housing costs vary between local markets, and costs are higher in markets where household incomes are higher. This definition differs from the official measure of "poverty" and the income criteria for some other programs, which are set nationally rather than locally. "Affordability" can thus vary substantially from region to region. The median incomes reported by HUD in 2009 ranged from $19,000 in Buffalo County, South

Dakota, to $122,300 in the Stamford-Norwalk metropolitan area in Connecticut.[8] The median for the U.S. is calculated at $49,800.

For program purposes, HUD median incomes and income limits are calculated by household size, using the medians for families of four as the common base measure. Incomes for larger or smaller households are calculated as fractions of the income for four-person families. Panel A of table 2-1, on the following page, reports the income limits by household size as percentages of the four-person base. For comparison, the panel also reports the poverty thresholds by household size. The adjustments for household size are smaller for the HUD income limits than for the poverty thresholds, so the latter are lower than the HUD income limits for smaller households and higher for larger households. Panel A also shows the relationship of actual median incomes across households of different sizes; these are consistently lower, relative to the four-person household base, than the HUD income limit ratios, particularly for single-person households and for households with five or more persons. While both the HUD income limits and the poverty thresholds are intended to measure the cost of achieving a given standard of living and therefore increase with household size, actual incomes do not increase with household size, above four persons.[9]

The actual incomes corresponding to these limits, shown in panel B, give a different picture, however. The HUD income measure for a four-person household at 50 percent of area median is more than $10,000 above the poverty threshold (almost 50 percent higher), and the HUD limits range from more than double the poverty line for single-person households to almost 15 percent above the poverty line for eight-person households. At the same time, the actual four-person median household income in 2009 was over $73,000, so 50 percent of the actual median was about $4,500 (about 15 percent) above the HUD income limit. Fifty percent of the actual median was also above the HUD limits for the two-person, three-person, and five-person households. These comparisons show that HUD reaches farther up in the income distribution for single-person households, which comprised about 27 percent of all households in 2009, and for large households, which comprised about 4 percent, than for the typical households that are used as the basis of analysis and program design. The same relationships generally hold for earlier years in the decade.

TABLE 2-1
INCOME LIMITS AND INCOME BY HOUSEHOLD SIZE, 2009

Household Size
Panel A – Relative to 4-Person Base

	1 person	2 persons	3 persons	4 persons	5 persons	6 persons	7 persons	8 persons
HUD Very Low Income	70%	80%	90%	100% (base)	108%	116%	124%	132%
Poverty Threshold	50%	64%	78%	100% (base)	118%	134%	152%	170%
Actual Income of Household	36%	73%	85%	100% (base)	95%	86%	88%[b]	88%[b]

Panel B – Actual Income

	1 person	2 persons	3 persons	4 persons	5 persons	6 persons	7 persons	8 persons
HUD Very Low Income	$22,400	$25,600	$28,800	$32,000	$34,560	$37,120	$39,680	$42,240
Poverty Threshold	$10,956	$13,991	$17,098	$21,554	$25,991	$29,405	$33,372	$37,252
Actual Income of Household[a]	$13,040	$26,838	$31,236	$36,536	$34,840	$31,373	$32,334[b]	$32,334[b]

SOURCES: U.S. Department of Housing and Urban Development, Office of Policy Development and Research, "FY 2009 HUD Income Limits: Briefing Material," April 20, 2009, at http://www.huduser. org/portal/datasets/il/il09/IncomeLimitsBriefingMaterial_FY09.pdf; U.S. Bureau of the Census, *Income, Poverty, and Health Insurance Coverage in the United States: 2009,* Report P60-238, September 2010, 55; U.S. Bureau of the Census, "Selected Characteristics of Households by Total Money Income in 2009," table HINC-1, at http://www.census.gov/hhes/www/cpstables/032010/hhinc/new01_001.htm.
NOTES: a = Calculated at 50 percent of median for given size of household. b = Income is reported for households of seven or more persons.

These calculated medians are important because they become the bases for determining eligibility for housing assistance. The special approach to determining the income limits for housing assistance in relation to local income levels has led to the development of a specialized terminology, which has gradually become standardized. The official income categories are described in exhibit 2-1 (see page 54). Because the terminology has evolved over a number of years, the qualitative labels such as "low income" are less useful than the quantitative percentages relating income to the median income of an area. The percentages are also useful for defining subcategories; for example, "between 51 and 80 percent of area median" is clearer than "low but not very low" income.

Special mention should be made of the concept of "low and moderate income," probably the oldest term in housing policy discussions and the one used in the most senses. In an extended review of low-income housing programs up to 1973, four experienced housing lawyers noted that "as matters now stand, 'families of low and moderate income' has become standard, all-but-universal usage . . . The phrase has no defined meaning, however."[10] Whether despite or because of the lack of definite meaning, a survey taken for HUD at about the same time found a large majority of the public favoring government housing assistance for low-income families, and a large majority rejecting assistance for moderate-income families.

The housing policy concept of "extremely low income"—30 percent or less of the area median—comes closest to corresponding to what is generally understood as "poverty." For a family of four, "extremely low income" in 2009 was $19,200, about 11 percent lower than the poverty threshold of $21,554. For renters as a whole, about 81 percent of those below the poverty line also had "extremely low income," and about 84 percent of those with "extremely low income" were also below the poverty line.[11]

Within the eligible income groups, the criterion for affordability is based on the share of the household's income devoted to housing. Such cost-income ratios have served as financial management guides for household budgets, guidelines for mortgage lenders in evaluating applications for home mortgages, and requirements for household rental payments in housing subsidy programs. A household that spends 50 percent of income on rent is considered to be a low-income household with "worst-case needs." That is well above the limit of 30 percent of income that has been the standard requirement in subsidized housing programs since 1981. Persons who pay 31 to 50 percent of their income in rent are regarded as having housing problems that are less serious than worst-case needs.

Quality

The criterion for housing quality is more complicated. It is derived from data collected in the American Housing Survey (AHS), conducted for HUD by the Census Bureau every two years. The AHS samples over 50,000 households and asks more than thirty questions about housing. These questions refer to the physical condition of the structure and the housing unit within the structure, and also ask about the existence and functioning of various systems—for example, whether the household has complete plumbing and a heating system and how often the plumbing or heating system breaks down. The questions are grouped by category, and units are ranked as "adequate," "moderately inadequate," or "severely inadequate" (alternatively, as having "moderate physical problems" or "severe physical problems"). The complete definitions appear in exhibit 2-2 (see page 55). Essentially the same definitions have been used in the AHS published volumes from 1985 to 2005, and in HUD's worst-case needs reports from the first one for 1989 to the eleventh one for 2005, with minor changes to reflect changes in the wording of the AHS questionnaire.[12] For the 2007 and 2009 surveys, however, most of the questions concerning one category, "hallways," were dropped, and the criteria for "severely inadequate" and "moderately inadequate" were revised to eliminate problems with hallways.

The criteria are based on research conducted by HUD, the Congressional Budget Office (CBO), and various independent analysts during the 1970s and 1980s.

The category of "severely inadequate" is used in the HUD worst-case needs reports to Congress as equivalent to "substandard."

The Housing Situation of Lower-Income Renters

Table 2-2 reports on the housing conditions of very low-income renters as of 2009. Most lower-income renters face a range of housing problems, having either "worst-case needs" or less serious problems of affordability and quality. Few of those who do not receive assistance have no significant problems. Over 55 percent of unassisted very low-income renters have problems that give them priority for housing assistance. Nearly all of these worst-case needs households live in physically adequate housing. Out of 7.1 million with priority problems, 6.9 million are paying more than half their income for rent; of these, 6.2 million have only a high rent burden. About 450,000 live in housing with severe physical problems (about 6 percent of those with worst-case needs); of these, 240,000 also have a high rent burden. Most households with less serious problems, like most households

TABLE 2-2
HOUSEHOLDS WITH PRIORITY HOUSING PROBLEMS, 2009
("WORST-CASE NEEDS")

Housing Condition	(Very Low-Income Renters)		
	Households (1,000s)	Percentage of All Households	Percentage of Very Low-Income Renters
All Very Low-Income Renters	17,118	15.3	100.0
"Worst Case Needs" (Unassisted)	7,095	6.3	41.4
Severe Physical Problems	443	0.4	2.6
Rent Burden Above 50%	6,892	6.2	40.3
Rent Burden Only	6,197	5.5	36.2
Also Severe Physical Problems	241	0.2	1.4
Also Less Serious Problems	657	0.6	3.8
Less Serious Problems Only (Unassisted)	3,850	3.4	23.5
Rent Burden of 31-50%	3,516	3.1	20.5
Moderate Physical Problems	540	0.5	3.2
Crowded (More Than 1 Person per Room)	412	0.4	2.4
Unassisted, with No Problem	1,899	1.7	11.1
Receiving Housing Assistance	4,274	3.8	25.0

SOURCE: U.S. Department of Housing and Urban Development, Office of Policy Development and Research, *Worst Case Housing Needs 2009: Report to Congress,* Washington, DC, February 2011, tables A-1a, A-3, A-7.

with worst-case needs, have a rent burden, and most have only a rent burden.[13] Fewer than 1 million households have either moderate physical problems or are living in crowded housing, which is defined as housing having more than one person per room. Crowding has been recognized as a housing problem at least as far back as the first Census of Housing in 1940, but has been regarded as less serious than living in inadequate housing or being unable to afford decent housing.

The data on priority housing problems in table 2-2 are limited to households that are not receiving housing assistance. This reporting practice developed from the purpose of the worst-case needs reports, which was to identify households that might need housing assistance. But problems exist among those living in assisted rental housing as well as among unassisted very low-income renters. Table 2-3 reports information on problems for assisted households, similar to the data in table 2-2.

The data reported in table 2-3 have some limitations. The assisted households shown in the table are households included in the AHS who are also identified in HUD administrative program data as receiving assistance. While AHS respondents are asked directly whether they receive assistance, and the responses are used in the worst-case needs reports, the answers have not been considered satisfactory. Respondents to the AHS survey may not know whether the household is receiving a subsidy, or what the nature of the subsidy is.[14] Another way of identifying assisted households is by matching the addresses of units in the AHS sample with the addresses of assisted units in HUD program data. The HUD administrative database also has limitations; it may contain errors such as incorrect addresses, or the assisted unit may be in an apartment building with two or more entrances; more importantly, not all public housing authorities (PHAs) are required to report program data to HUD. There are twenty-three such PHAs, including those in such large cities as Chicago, Philadelphia, Washington, and Atlanta; together they do not report on 99,000 public housing units and 112,000 vouchers—about 9 percent of all public housing units and 6 percent of all vouchers.[15] To match the weighted number of assisted units by program to the known total number of assisted units, HUD reweights the AHS respondents. Despite these limitations, the administrative database appears to be more accurate than the AHS responses.[16]

Table 2-3 compares these two sets of data as of 2003 (the most recent administrative database comparison). The number of self-identified households receiving assistance is almost two million higher than the number identified in the administrative database; however, the number of self-identified assisted households with very low incomes is almost the same as the number in the administrative database. For all three groups, the number of households with priority problems is similar, for both the total and individual categories. Even though the AHS reports almost 2 million assisted households with incomes above 50 percent of the area median, few of these households have priority problems. Over 400,000 of these households, however, do have less serious problems, in particular a rent burden between 31 and 50 percent of income. In each group, a remarkably large number of assisted households reports a high rent burden. Between 18 and

TABLE 2-3

HOUSING PROBLEMS FOR HOUSEHOLDS LIVING IN ASSISTED HOUSING, 2003

(1,000s of Households)

Identified as Assisted:

| Housing Conditions | by AHS respondents | | in HUD Program Data |
	All	Very Low Income	All
All Assisted Renters	6,211	4,256	4,279
Priority Problems	1,386	1,305	1,158
Severe Physical Problems	222	170	141
Rent Burden Above 50%	1,222	1,191	1,050
Rent Burden >100%	538	NA	474
Rent Burden Only	1,164	1,135	1,017
Less Serious Problems Only	1,828	1,389	1,376
Moderate Physical Problems	327	193	236
Rent Burden 31-50%	1,498	1,232	1,073
Crowded	198	128	143

SOURCES: U.S. Department of Housing and Urban Development, Office of Policy Development and Research, *Affordable Housing Needs: A Report to Congress on the Significant Need for Housing*, Washington, DC, 2006, tables A-1a, A-3; U.S. Department of Housing and Urban Development, Office of Policy Development and Research, and U.S. Census Bureau, *American Housing Survey for the United States: 2003*, Washington, DC, September 2004, tables 4-12, 4-19; U.S. Department of Housing and Urban Development, Office of Policy Development and Research, *Characteristics of HUD-Assisted Renters and Their Units in 2003*, Washington, DC, May 2008.
NOTE: NA = not available.

27 percent report a rent burden of 50 percent or more; between 45 and 55 percent report a rent burden above 30 percent. The proportions vary by HUD program, according to the administrative data: about one-third of those receiving vouchers, 15 percent of those in public housing, and 20 percent of those in other HUD programs spend half or more of their income for rent (this is not shown in the table). Another 20 percent of those receiving vouchers and those living in public housing, and 30 percent of those in other programs, spend at least 30 percent of their income on rent.[17]

This is surprising because, in public housing and nearly all other HUD-subsidized housing except the voucher program, program rules require that assisted tenants should pay no more than 30 percent of their income for rent. Voucher recipients may spend more than that share, although the subsidy is calculated on the basis of a 30 percent rent-income ratio. It seems odd that so many assisted households would actually spend more than they are required to spend.[18] A further oddity is that some households report spending 100 percent or more of their income on housing; the proportion ranges from 7 percent of those living in public housing to 15 percent of voucher recipients. Such an expenditure pattern is certainly not sustainable, and indeed the Census Bureau adds this footnote: "may reflect a temporary situation, living off savings, or response error."[19]

In contrast, a much smaller number of households in each group have physical problems or live in crowded conditions. Between 3 and 4 percent have severe physical problems; between 4 and 7 percent have moderate problems; and about 3 percent are crowded. Unassisted very-low-income households have higher incidences of these problems than do assisted households overall: 4 percent have severe physical problems, 9.2 percent have moderate physical problems, and 7.5 percent are crowded. Unassisted households also have a consistently higher incidence of these problems than do assisted households in each program, with one exception: public housing residents have a relatively high incidence of severe physical problems—4.6 percent. The most common severe physical problem in all programs, and also for unassisted very-low-income renters, is the absence of complete plumbing, and the second most common source of problems is heating equipment.

Two conclusions can usefully be drawn from all these data. First, housing assistance in any form does not necessarily solve all important housing problems. Second, the official data on worst-case needs may understate the number of households with priority problems because the data may overstate the number receiving assistance, but they do not misstate the composition of those problems: rent burden is much the more common problem, and physically inadequate housing is relatively infrequent.

Priority Problems by Household Category

Housing policy has long been concerned with the distribution as well as the level of worst-case needs and other housing problems. In general, problems are distributed fairly evenly across the population.

Demographics and Location. Table 2-4 disaggregates the national data on worst-case needs by race and ethnicity, household composition, region,

TABLE 2-4
HOUSEHOLDS WITH PRIORITY PROBLEMS, 2009

(Numbers in 1,000s)

Category	Unassisted Very Low Income Households	Worst-Case Needs	Percentage with Worst-Case Needs
White[a]	6,445	3,436	53.3
Black[a]	2,783	1,640	58.9
Hispanic	2,821	1,582	56.1
Other[a]	795	437	55.0
Elderly	2,320	1,328	57.2
Families with Children	5,067	2,734	54.0
Other[b]	5,358	3,034	56.1
Northeast	2,514	1,415	56.3
Midwest	2,642	1,410	53.3
South	4,574	2,479	54.2
West	3,113	1,791	57.5
Central City	5,796	3,344	57.8
Suburb	4,816	2,632	54.7
Nonmetropolitan	2,237	1,119	50.0
Disabled[c]	2,583	986	38.2

SOURCES: U.S. Department of Housing and Urban Development, Office of Policy Development and Research, *Worst Case Housing Needs 2009: Report to Congress,* February 2011, exhibit 1-3, tables A-6a, A-9, A-10, A-11; U.S. Department of Housing and Urban Development, Office of Policy Development and Research, *2009 Worst Case Housing Needs of People with Disabilities,* March 2011.
NOTES: a = Non-Hispanic households. b = Households with a nonelderly householder and no children in which at least one person is related to the householder by birth, marriage, or adoption; or households with a single nonelderly person living alone or only with nonrelatives. c = Households with at least one nonelderly person with any of six types of disabilities.

and metropolitan location, all of which have been of concern to policy-makers. In 2009, when the overall incidence of worst-case needs was 55.2 percent among unassisted very-low-income households, the incidence for virtually every group was between 50 and 60 percent. The exception is the category of disabled households, at 38 percent, but it should be noted that the share of disabled households receiving assistance is relatively large. It is noteworthy that women head over two-thirds of the families with children having worst-case needs, and 20 percent of all female-headed families with children have priority housing problems.[20]

It is also noteworthy that for each household type, very few households are living in units with severe physical problems. As noted in table 2-2, nationally, about 6 percent of households with worst-case needs live in such units. The incidences for the household type groups in table 2-4 are generally close to the national incidence. The highest is 10 percent, for households living in the Northeast. No group has a particularly high incidence of severe physical problems.[21]

To summarize, about half of all unassisted very low-income renters have worst-case needs, and this proportion is about the same for all households by demographic category and geographic location; in addition, nearly all of them have a severe rent burden rather than severe physical problems in their housing unit, which is also true for every type of household.

Housing Problems by Income. The choice of 50 percent of area median income as the cutoff for worst-case needs, and formerly for priority for housing assistance, is an arbitrary one. Other points in the income distribution could be used, and several are or have been used. Tables 2-5 and 2-6 present the incidence of priority housing problems by income category. They show that the incidence of these problems drops sharply as income rises. Almost two-thirds of extremely low-income renters have priority problems, compared to 30 percent of renters with incomes between 31 and 50 percent of the area median (who between 1988 and 1996 had equal priority for housing assistance with extremely low-income renters), and less than 10 percent of higher-income renters (including those with an income of 51 to 80 percent of area median, who are still considered "low income" and are still eligible for housing assistance). It is worth noting, however, that the proportion of households actually receiving assistance also declines sharply with income. About one-third of extremely low-income renters receives assistance, compared to about 12 percent of renters with incomes between 31 and 50 percent of the area median, and about 4 percent of those with incomes between 51 and 80 percent.

Table 2-5 shows that in each income category, including the lowest, few unassisted households have homes with severe physical problems; here also the proportion declines with income. While 4.2 percent of the

TABLE 2-5

HOUSING PROBLEMS BY INCOME FOR RENTERS, 2009

(Numbers in 1,000s)

	Extremely Low Income (<30% of Area Median)		31–50% of Area Median		51–80% of Area Median		81–120% of Area Median		>120% of Area Median	
	Number	Percentage	Number	Percentage	Number	Percentage	Number	Percentage	Number	Percentage
All renters	9,961		7,157		7,128		5,658		5,452	
Priority Problems	6,536	65.6	2,139	29.9	662	9.2	208	4.0	144	2.6
Unassisted renters	6,661		6,223		6,814		5,512		5,355	
Priority Problems	5,069	76.6	2,026	32.6	644	9.5	203	4.0	143	2.7
Rent Burden	4,996	75.5	1,896	30.4	469	6.9	97	1.8	41	0.9
Severe Physical Problems	278	4.2	165	2.6	186	2.7	107	1.9	101	1.9

SOURCE: U.S. Department of Housing and Urban Development, Office of Policy Development and Research, *Worst Case Housing Needs 2009: Report to Congress*, February 2011, tables A-1a, A-3.

renters with extremely low income reported physical problems with their homes, just over 2.5 percent did so in each of the next two income categories, and only 2.0 percent of renters with incomes above 80 percent of the area median did so.

Owner-occupied housing is outside the scope of this study, but similar patterns exist among owners: priority problems decline sharply by income, and few in any income bracket have severe physical problems. The incidence of severe physical problems among homeowners is half or less the incidence among renters.

The Housing of the Poor. It bears repeating that the category of "very low income" used in housing policy and programs does not correspond conceptually or quantitatively to the term "poverty," which is commonly considered to be a broad gauge of economic well-being and used in other social welfare programs such as Medicaid and Food Stamps (now the Supplemental Nutrition Assistance Program). The very low-income cutoff in 2009 for a family of four was $32,000, while the poverty threshold for the same four-person family was $21,554 (see table 2-1). As noted previously, the poverty threshold is much closer to the category of "extremely low income," less than 30 percent of area median income, which was $19,200 nationally in 2009. There are important conceptual differences between "extremely low income" and "poverty": (1) because housing income limits are calculated in terms of local median incomes rather than nationally, a higher proportion of households in the large metropolitan areas in the North and West, and a smaller proportion of households in nonmetropolitan areas, are classified as extremely low income; (2) adjustments for household size rise more sharply for the poverty thresholds, so "extremely low income" includes proportionately more small households and fewer large ones.

However, there are strong similarities between poor renter households and extremely-low-income renters, as shown in table 2-6. The total number of households is close; there are about 7 percent fewer poor renter households. Housing conditions for the two groups are almost identical. About two-thirds of the households in each group pay more than 50 percent of their income for housing, and fewer than 4 percent in each group say their homes have severe physical problems.

TABLE 2-6

HOUSING PROBLEMS OF POOR RENTERS COMPARED
TO EXTREMELY LOW-INCOME RENTERS, 2009

| | (Numbers in 1,000s) | | | |
| | Extremely Low-Income Renters | | Poor Renters | |
	Number	Percentage	Number	Percentage
All Households	9,961		9,334	
Rent or Cost Burden	6,407	64.3	5,578	67.7[a]
Severe Physical Problems	387	3.9	348	3.7

SOURCES: U.S. Department of Housing and Urban Development, Office of Policy Development and Research, *Worst Case Housing Needs 2009: A Report to Congress,* February 2011, table A-1a; U.S. Department of Housing and Urban Development, Office of Policy Development and Research, and U.S. Census Bureau, *American Housing Survey for the United States: 2009,* Washington, DC, March 2011, tables 4-7, 4-13.
NOTE: a = Calculated by excluding households with zero or negative income.

Trends in Housing Conditions

To get a fuller picture of the housing problems of low-income renters, the data for 2009 should be put in historical perspective. Table 2-7 reports the trends in priority problems, overall and by type of problem, going back to 1978. The years shown in the table have been selected partly because they represent different phases of the economic cycles during the period, and partly because the AHS questions on housing quality are similar enough to provide a consistent measure of inadequate housing. Recessions occurred in 1980 and 1981–1982 (bracketed by the AHS data for 1978 and 1983), in 1990–1991 (bracketed by 1989 and 1993), and from March to November 2001 (bracketed by 1999 and 2003). The long expansions of the 1980s and 1990s are approximately measured by the 1983–1989 and 1993–1999 intervals in the table.

The data show some cyclical patterns, with an increase in worst-case needs and severe rent burden during 1978–1983, when there was unprecedented peacetime inflation as well as two recessions; an improvement during the long expansion of 1983–1989; stability or slight deterioration during the recessionary period 1989–1993; further improvement during

TABLE 2-7
"WORST CASE NEEDS" AND OTHER PROBLEMS, 1978–2009

(as percentage of very low-income renter households)

	1978	1983	1989	1993	1999	2003	2005	2007	2009
Worst Case Needs	37	42	36	36	33	33	37	37	41
Severely Inadequate	9	7	5	3	3	3	3	3	3
Rent-Income Ratio above 50%	30	38	33	34	31	31	36	36	40
Rent Burden Only	24	30	25	28	25	28	31	32	36
Problems other than/ besides Rent-Income Ratio above 50%[a]	13	12	11	8	8	5	6	5	5
Less Serious Problems	29	23	25	25	26	24	22	24	22
Rent-Income Ratio between 30% and 50%	23	19	21	22	22	17	20	21	21
Moderately Inadequate	6	4	5	3	5	4	3	3	3
Crowded	6	4	4	3	4	3	3	3	3
No Problems	14	12	13	13	12	14	12	12	12
Receiving Housing Assistance	20	23	26	26	29	27	28	27	25

SOURCES: U.S. Department of Housing and Urban Development, Office of Policy Development and Research, *Rental Housing Assistance at a Crossroads: A Report to Congress on Worst Case Housing Needs,* March 1996, table A-4; U.S. Department of Housing and Urban Development, Office of Policy Development and Research, *Trends in Worst Case Needs for Housing 1978–1999: A Report to Congress on Worst Case Housing Needs,* December 2003, table A-4; U.S. Department of Housing and Urban Development, Office of Policy Development and Research, *Affordable Housing Needs: A Report to Congress on the Significant Need for Housing,* December 2005, tables A-1a, A-3, A-7a; U.S. Department of Housing and Urban Development, Office of Policy Development and Research, *Worst Case Housing Needs 2007: A Report to Congress,* May 2010, tables A-1a, A-3, A-7; U.S. Department of Housing and Urban Development, Office of Policy Development and Research, *Worst Case Housing Needs 2009: Report to Congress,* February 2011, tables A-1a, A-3, A-7.
NOTES: a = Includes severely inadequate, moderately inadequate, and/or crowded.

1993–1999; and then a dip and recovery to about the 1999 level by 2003. The increase in worst-case needs between 2003 and 2005, which consists entirely of an increase in households with high rent burdens, is anomalous in that it occurred during an economic expansion. The increase between 2007 and 2009 again coincides with a recession.

Whether there is a secular trend in the overall level of worst-case needs depends on the time period under consideration. As table 2-7 shows, the incidence was the same in both 1978 and 2007. But from 1983 to 2003 there was a pronounced downward trend. The sharp increases during 1978–1983 and 2003–2005 offset the two decades in between. The movements in rent burden account for this pattern. Indeed, the incidence of rent burden in 2009 was higher than in 1978 because of the large increases during the recessions. In contrast, the incidence of severely inadequate housing declined steadily from 1978 to 1993, through recession and expansion, and has remained stable at about 3 percent since then.[22] Thus the composition of worst-case needs has been changing. In 1978 there were just under four million households with priority problems, of whom just under one million lived in housing with severe physical problems. By 2009, there were seven million households with priority problems, but fewer than 500,000 with severe physical problems.[23]

Long-Term Trends in Housing Quality

Because the common housing criteria dealt only with quality and not affordability before the 1980s, it is convenient to separate quality from affordability in discussing longer-term trends in housing problems, and in analyzing the reasons for the trends.[24] This section looks at housing quality, which has been studied far longer than affordability has. For convenience in measuring long-term changes, the section includes summary information on quality since 1970 as well as earlier.

The Problem of Measurement. Until Congress amended it in 1990, the national housing goal had only one criterion: housing quality. But the problem of measuring housing quality, and of consistency among changing criteria, is a long-standing one. The National Housing Act of 1949 did not define "decent" housing (or, for that matter, either "suitable" or "living environment"), but in 1948 the Joint Committee on Housing offered as a criterion "the number of nonfarm units shown by the reports of the Census Bureau to be in need of major repairs, together with all units in urban areas which lack private inside bath and toilet."[25] This definition, as the committee implied, is derived from the data collected in the 1940 census, which included the first Census of Housing. The Census Bureau asked whether a housing unit had complete plumbing and whether the unit was in sound physical condition. Units lacking complete plumbing, or classified as "needing major repairs" ("dilapidated" in 1950 and later) were considered substandard.[26] The census also reported on crowding.

From 1940 to 1970 the Census of Housing provided almost the only housing data for the country, although there were occasional special surveys for various purposes. The Joint Committee on Housing, as well as other agencies and independent analysts, thus had only one source for the data they analyzed.

In planning the 1970 census, the Census Bureau decided to discontinue collecting data on structural soundness, partly because the census would be conducted largely by mail for the first time. In 1940, 1950, and 1960, the determination of housing quality was made by enumerators who visited the house and conducted a personal interview; in a mail census, the household would have to rate its own housing quality. An evaluation of the 1960 census had concluded that there was an unacceptably high degree of error by interviewers in assessing housing quality, but city governments objected strongly to the Census Bureau's proposal because they relied on the quality data for planning purposes, and the Census Bureau finally decided to collect data on quality as part of a smaller postcensus survey, the Components of Inventory Change. This survey provided data on a national basis, for the four census regions and the fifteen largest metropolitan areas.[27]

The decennial Census of Housing was to a substantial extent superseded by the American Housing Survey, originally the Annual Housing Survey. The AHS contains questions on about thirty specific aspects of housing quality, as well as questions on the presence and functioning of various systems. The AHS has never included the question about overall structural housing quality used in the 1940 to 1970 decennial censuses, however.

Once the AHS data became available, analysts in several government agencies and private institutions began using it to construct new measures of housing quality. These standards were quite diverse, but typically they rated housing quality on several dimensions and classified a unit as inadequate if it failed to meet criteria in a certain number of those dimensions. Efforts to identify a single criterion as a substitute for the "dilapidated" census measure proved unsatisfactory. The details of these new quality measures are less important now than the fact that all set a higher standard for adequacy than the previous census definition, so that many more inadequate units were reported in 1974 and subsequently than the census classified as substandard or dilapidated for 1970.[28] But from 1974 onward, the AHS has showed a steady fall in the number of units with severe problems. This continues the downward trend shown by the decennial census before 1970.[29]

Quality Changes since 1974. Table 2-8 reports the incidence of housing with severe physical problems, and also the incidence of crowding, for all households and for various groups of special policy interest. The table differs from earlier tables in this chapter because it presents data for all households, rather than those with worst-case needs, to be consistent with the data from the decennial censuses between 1940 and 1970. The improvement in housing quality for very-low-income renters since the 1970s is part of a trend among all households. As panel A shows, the incidence of severely inadequate housing has been more than cut in half over the last thirty years. Nearly all of that reduction occurred between 1974 and 1993; since then, around 2 percent of the occupied housing stock has been severely inadequate, with a further decline in 2007. Crowding (more than one person per room living in the housing unit) has also been more than cut in half since 1974, and again nearly all of the reduction occurred by 1993; there has been a further modest decline since 2001.

Panels B and C of table 2-8 make clear that the amount of crowding and severely inadequate housing has fallen in both urban and rural areas. Minority groups have also reported improved housing, with a particularly noticeable improvement among African American households (panel D).[30] In 1974, the incidence of severely inadequate housing was more than twice as high for African American households as for Hispanic households; by 1993 they were about the same. Since 1999 the incidence has declined more for Hispanic households than for African Americans, but the difference is much smaller than it was in 1974 (panels D and E). Both live in inadequate housing to a greater extent than white households, and both are more often crowded than white households, but the differences have been narrowing. Hispanic households live in crowded conditions much more often than the other two groups, which may reflect the fact that so many are relatively recent immigrants. The continuing high rate of immigration would be expected to push up the incidence of housing problems among Hispanic households (as has been true historically for immigrants in general), but this effect has been overshadowed by other factors, most probably the economic gains of

TABLE 2-8
HOUSING QUALITY, 1974–2009

(Percentage of Occupied Units)

	1974	1978	1983	1989	1991	1993	1999	2001	2003	2007	2009
Panel A: All Households											
Severely Inadequate	4.2	3.6	3.4	3.4	3.1	2.0	2.0	2.0	1.9	1.6	1.7
Crowded	5.3	4.2	3.5	2.9	2.7	2.5	2.5	2.5	2.4	2.3	2.2
Panel B: Urban Households											
Severely Inadequate	NA	NA	NA	3.2	2.9	2.0	2.2	2.2	2.0	1.7	NA
Crowded	4.9	4.0	3.5	3.1	3.0	2.9	2.9	2.8	2.8	2.6	NA
Panel C: Rural Households											
Severely Inadequate	NA	NA	NA	3.8	3.5	1.9	1.5	1.6	1.5	1.4	NA
Crowded	6.6	4.7	3.5	2.2	1.9	1.5	1.5	1.7	1.4	1.4	NA
Panel D: Black, Non-Hispanic Households											
Severely Inadequate	12.5[a]	9.3	7.2	5.7	4.9	3.4	3.4	3.5	3.3	2.8	2.8
Crowded	12.6	10.1	7.5	5.0	5.2	3.9	3.3	3.3	3.1	2.9	2.6
Panel E: Hispanic Households											
Severely Inadequate	5.9[a]	4.9	4.7	4.5	4.3	3.3	3.8	3.2	2.9	2.2	2.3
Crowded	19.3	18.5	16.0	14.6	14.7	13.8	13.0	12.8	12.2	10.2	10.2

SOURCES: U.S. Department of Housing and Urban Development and U.S. Census Bureau, *Annual Housing Survey*, various years through 1983; U.S. Department of Housing and Urban Development and U.S. Census Bureau, *American Housing Survey*, various years beginning in 1985.

NOTES: NA = not available. a = Data are for 1975.

previous Hispanic immigrants and those whose ancestors have been in the United States for many generations.

Housing Quality before 1974. Even taking into account the discontinuity in the data between 1970 and 1974, the evidence suggests that the trend toward better housing is a continuation of the improvement reported in the decennial Census of Housing between 1940 and 1970.

A summary of relevant census data appears in table 2-9. It illustrates how dramatically different American housing quality was some seventy years ago. Almost half of the occupied housing stock then was "substandard," mostly because it did not have complete plumbing facilities. In part this was because so much of America was still rural; many Americans still lived on farms and in small towns. In urban areas, as panel B shows, housing quality was substantially better. The proportion of households in rural areas without complete plumbing was 75 percent, compared to 23 percent in urban areas. Historically, urban households have lived in higher-quality, less crowded housing than rural households; the reversal of this pattern since 1989, as reported in table 2-8, is a notable change.

Table 2-9 shows that housing quality improved steadily; the share of substandard units was cut in half during the 1950s and again during the 1960s, as complete plumbing became nearly universal.

Table 2-9 also reports the trend in crowding from 1940 to 1970, showing that the number of crowded homes declined steadily. The proportion of households in which the number of people exceeded the number of rooms (excluding bathrooms) fell steadily over the entire period from 1940 to about 1990, as new housing units became steadily larger and households became steadily smaller. In the immediate postwar period, the United States was generally believed to suffer from a housing shortage (after fifteen years of low housing production), and many returning servicemen moved with their families into a parent's home. The best indication of the extent of improvement is the fact that the standard itself changed. In 1940, units were commonly considered "crowded" if they had more than 1.5 persons per room; today the figure is more than 1 person per room. Unlike the data on physical condition, the data on crowding have been collected on a consistent basis since 1940, and they show crowding declining from 1940 to 1974, as well as since 1974.

TABLE 2-9
HOUSING QUALITY, 1940–1970

(Percentage of Occupied Units)				
	1940	1950	1960	1970
Panel A - All Households				
Substandard[a]	48.6	35.4	16.0	8.3
Lacking Complete Plumbing	44.6	34.0	14.7	5.9
Dilapidated[b]	18.1	9.1	4.3	2.4
Crowded[c]	20.2	15.7	11.5	8.2
Panel B - Urban Households				
Substandard[a]	28.4	21.9	9.6	5.5
Lacking Complete Plumbing	23.1	20.2	6.8	3.1
Dilapidated[b]	11.3	6.3	3.1	2.4
Crowded[c]	15.9	13.3	10.2	7.6
Panel C - Rural Households				
Substandard[a]	77.0	62.4	40.0	16.9
Lacking Complete Plumbing	74.8	61.7	35.0	14.5
Dilapidated[b]	27.7	14.5	7.5	2.4
Crowded[c]	26.5	20.6	15.1	10.1
Panel D - Non-White Households[#]				
Substandard[a]	82.7	73.2	44.0	23.2
Lacking Complete Plumbing	79.5	70.5	32.7	17.0
Dilapidated[b]	35.1	33.4	16.8	6.2
Crowded[c]	39.9	NA	28.3	19.9
Panel E - Very-Low-Income Households[##]				
Substandard[a]	NA	52.1	35.8	NA
Lacking Complete Plumbing	NA	50.2	21.6	13.0
Dilapidated[b]	NA	16.9	9.9	NA
Crowded[c]	NA	16.6	12.1	8.3

SOURCES: *Sixteenth Census of the United States: 1940, Housing*, vol. 2, part 1; *1950 Census of Housing*, vol. 1, part 1; *1960 Census of Housing*, vol. 2, part 1, vol. VI; *1970 Census of Housing*, vol. 1, part 1; *1970 Census of Housing: Components of Inventory Change*, HC (4)-1; *1970 Census of Housing: Plumbing Facilities and Estimates of "Dilapidated" Housing*, HC (6). All are publications of the U.S. Bureau of the Census.

NOTES: NA = not available. a = Either lacking complete plumbing or dilapidated. b = "Needing Major Repairs" in 1940. c = More than 1 person per room. # = Black in 1970 (Negroes comprised over 90 percent of nonwhites in each previous Census). ## = Below $2,000 in 1950, $3,000 in 1960, $5,000 in 1970 (approximately 50 percent of median household income in each year).

In addition to data for all households, table 2-9 shows corresponding data for various population categories of special importance for housing policy. These data are not as complete, as they have a number of gaps and some changes in coverage, but the trends are parallel to those for the population as a whole. Minority households (panel D) lived in much worse housing than whites throughout the period, but their homes steadily improved. Housing also improved for very-low-income households (panel E), beginning in 1950 (data on housing conditions by income were not tabulated in 1940). The income levels shown in the table are the closest approximations available to 50 percent of median income on a national basis, without interpolating within the income brackets reported in the decennial censuses.

The data in table 2-9 may seem to be ancient history, but they are relevant both as a measure of long-term progress and as a reminder that American housing policy was formulated in the context of housing conditions during the 1930s and 1940s. Our oldest low-income housing programs date back to a time when about half the housing stock in the country was inadequate.

Why Has Housing Quality Improved?

Explaining these improvements in housing quality, particularly for low-income households, is an important task for public policy. It is also a difficult one. Evidence to answer it comes from analyses of available data, including time-series data, cross-sectional studies, and formal models of the housing market; these are considered below. But it remains the case that more and better research is required.

Time-Series Analysis. Time-series analysis is hampered by the limited information on housing quality. Over the last six decades and more, there are only the four decennial censuses of 1940 through 1970, the four AHS surveys (1974, 1978, 1983, and 1989) that asked about housing quality in a consistent enough manner to measure housing units with severe physical problems between 1974 and 1989, and the biennial surveys since then, which are generally but not entirely consistent with earlier surveys. And of course the data from the census and the AHS are incommensurate.

Given these limitations, about all that can be inferred is that housing quality improvement was more rapid during the first half of the postwar period, when income growth was also much greater. From 1947 to 1973, real median family income increased at an annual rate of about 5.5 percent; since 1973 , it has increased at only about 0.2 to 0.3 percent. It is evident that there was a sharper drop in "substandard" housing between 1950 and 1970 (panel A of table 2-9) than in "severely inadequate" housing after 1974 (panel A of table 2-8). But given that there was much more room for improvement during the earlier period, comparisons between the 1940–1970 period and the period from 1974 to today are not by themselves very meaningful.

The impact of housing policy over the period is also hard to ascertain. There were about 750,000 subsidized rental units and 500,000 subsidized single-family homes built between 1950 and 1970; an additional 1 million were built between 1970 and 1974, during the period of the discontinuity in data on housing conditions; about 1.5 million subsidized rental units have been built since 1974, and another 2 million existing housing units have received rental subsidies, as well.[31]

Cross-Sectional Studies. There is much more cross-sectional data on housing quality, though studies using these data turn out to be only slightly more informative. The decennial censuses of 1950 and 1960 reported on substandard housing for all metropolitan areas and indeed for all census tracts, and some analysts made use of these data for 1950 and 1960 to compare inadequacy across cities either at a given time or from one census to the next. The general conclusion in this literature was that rising real income is the most important factor in explaining housing quality improvements.[32] These studies, however, seldom included subsidized housing production as a possible alternative explanation for housing improvements, and they were conducted mainly during the earlier postwar period when incomes were rising rapidly. Cross-sectional studies began to die out when the decennial census dropped the question about housing conditions in 1970, just before the beginning of the period of lower income growth.[33] The number of metropolitan areas surveyed in the AHS has been declining steadily, from sixty areas on a three-year cycle to seven each in 2007 and 2009. Some slightly more recent work does make use of the AHS and finds a strong relationship between income and quality.[34]

Economic Models of the Housing Market and the Filtering Hypothesis.
Beginning with the "commodity hierarchy" model of James Sweeney, several
formal economic models of the housing market have been constructed to
analyze the implications of various housing policies. These models typically
analyze the housing market as a set of related submarkets differentiated by
quality; units are constructed at high quality levels and gradually deteriorate
through lower levels. One purpose has been to investigate the possible effect
of subsidized production on the price and/or quantity of lower-quality housing. These models have diverse results with respect to the effect of subsidized
production. Sweeney and Lawrence Schall have concluded that public housing construction results in lower rents for all low-quality housing (including unsubsidized units with market rents), while James Ohls reached the
opposite conclusion.[35] This approach has also been used to analyze the effect
of income transfers on housing quality for lower-income households. Most
relevant is the work of Ralph Braid, who has modeled a variety of housing
allowances, finding for example that transfer payments to the poorest households result in improved housing quality for them. Braid appears to be more
concerned about housing policies than are the builders of other formal models, but he has not modeled actual housing subsidy programs, and has not
performed empirical tests to see if existing housing subsidy programs work.[36]

These formal models have been particularly concerned with the concept of "filtering" in housing markets—that is, with the relationship, if
any, between unsubsidized private housing and the cost and quality of the
housing occupied by the poor.[37] The theory of the filtering mechanism is
that, when new housing is built for well-to-do households, they sell their
former homes to households that are slightly less well off. These families in
their turn sell their homes to households that are slightly worse off again,
and so on down through the income distribution and the distribution of
housing quality. At the bottom end of the market, some households move
from inadequate to adequate housing, and the inadequate housing becomes
vacant and eventually ceases to be part of the housing stock. This complex
filtering process involves changes in the price of housing of different quality
levels as the supply and demand for those quality levels change.

The most recent published model, by Alex Anas and Richard J. Arnott,
concludes that filtering does occur, and that lower-income families benefit
from the construction of high-quality housing.[38]

As a policy issue, the filtering hypothesis is controversial because it implies that government assistance to build high-priced homes will improve the quality of housing occupied by poor people—if the government assistance actually increases the supply of housing (a question which remains open, with varied findings by researchers). It is certainly distasteful to subsidize the rich on the grounds that the subsidies will flow to the poor. But the filtering hypothesis can be accepted as a description of how the housing market works, without adopting any housing policy in consequence. Its most relevant implication is that economic growth results in housing improvement for the poor, indirectly through filtering as well as directly as the incomes of poor people rise.

Ultimately, more empirical evidence is needed to judge the validity of these economic models. The most systematic research, by Weicher and Thibodeau, finds that quality improvement does occur for low-income households in response to new construction for higher-income households, and that the effect is substantial.[39] They find no direct effect on housing quality from either subsidized production or income growth, but suggest that the effect of income may be captured in several demographic variables that are included in the analysis. Similar results with respect to subsidized housing production have been found in earlier studies.[40]

The Trend in Rent Burdens

As housing has improved, rent burdens have become greater. As rents rise, concern mounts about the affordability of housing. This concern is reflected in the restatement of the national housing goal in the 1990 National Affordable Housing Act as "a decent home that every American family can afford." Indeed, rent increases have been a matter of national policy concern since the President's Commission on Housing in 1981–1982.

Rent-Income Ratios. Rent-income ratios provide a useful way of describing rent burdens. As a guideline for household rental payments in housing subsidy programs, they have varied over time. The earliest requirement in public housing was that a household should not have to pay more than 20 percent of its income to cover housing costs. This had become 25 percent by the late 1960s. It was raised to 30 percent in 1981 (phased in for households already being subsidized), and the 30 percent level remains the standard for household contributions in subsidized housing. The increases in the rent-income ratio paralleled increases in the ratios used by private lenders, and reflected the rise in housing costs, relative to both household income and the general price level, that had been occurring over the previous few years. These increases make it clear that such guides are essentially rules of thumb, useful in some circumstances, but not immutable.

Table 2-10 reports the incidence of households with high rent burdens since 1960. Such data were not collected in the 1940 census, and the limited 1950 data were not reported in the same categories as later years. The introduction of the 50 percent threshold in 1978—households paying half their income in rent—is an indication that rent levels (and concern over them) have been growing over time. The highest category that has been reported consistently since 1960 is the number of households paying more than 25 percent of their income in rent. The share of renters in this category has grown fairly steadily from 35 percent in 1960 to 72 percent in 2009. Data for other high rent levels have been available only since the 1970s. They show substantial increases since 1978, and an upward trend since 1999 or 2001. The share of households paying more than half their income in rent has risen from 14 percent to 25 percent, while the share paying between 31 and 50 percent of income in rent has risen from 18 to 23 percent. Since 1978, the percentage of households paying over 30 percent of their income in rent has risen from 31 to 48 percent.

Limitations of the Rent-Income Ratio as a Measure of Rent Burden. The rent-income ratio is a simple concept, easy to construct and report and seemingly obvious to interpret. But it is actually the result of a complex of factors that affect the housing consumption decision of a household, and it remains an imperfect measure of rent burden and an imperfect yardstick for housing policy. If the share of income devoted to rent is high and rising over time, then it is easy to assume that the cost of housing is high and rising, or alternatively that income is low and falling. Empirically, some of the data support these assumptions. Rent-income ratios are higher for lower-income households, as shown in table 2-5, and ratios tend to be high in markets where the cost of housing is high; households have to spend a larger share

TABLE 2-10
RENT BURDEN, 1960–2009

(Percentage and Number of Renter Households with High Rent-Income Ratios)

	% Rent-Income Ratio >25%	% Rent-Income Ratio 31–50%	Total (number in 1,000s)	% Rent-Income Ratio >50%	Total (number in 1,000s)
1960	35.3				
1970	39.3				
1978	51.2	17.7	4,765	13.6	3,661
1983	57.9	18.9	5,661	18.3	5,461
1989	56.1	20.7	6,983	15.4	5,187
1993	60.4	21.4	7,163	17.8	5,958
1999	57.6	21.0	7,141	18.5	6,291
2001	59.5	19.7	6,916	19.0	6,412
2003	62.0	21.4	7,468	19.3	6,477
2005	65.4	22.1	7,502	23.2	7,891
2007	68.1	23.8	8,340	22.2	7,793
2009	72.4	22.5	7,981	25.4	9,000

SOURCES: *1960 Census of Housing,* vol. 2, part 1; *1970 Census of Housing,* vol. 1, part 1; *Annual Housing Survey,* various years through 1983; *American Housing Survey,* various years beginning in 1985; U.S. Department of Housing and Urban Development, Office of Policy Development and Research, *Rental Housing Assistance at a Crossroads: A Report to Congress on Worst Case Housing Needs,* Washington, DC, March 1996; U.S. Department of Housing and Urban Development, Office of Policy Development and Research, *Affordable Housing Needs: A Report to Congress on the Significant Need for Housing,* Washington, DC, December 2005; U.S. Department of Housing and Urban Development, Office of Policy Development and Research, *Worst Case Housing Needs 2007: A Report to Congress,* Washington, DC, May 2010; U.S. Department of Housing and Urban Development, Office of Policy Development and Research, *Worst Case Housing Needs 2009: Report to Congress,* Washington, DC, February 2011. NOTE: After 1970, excludes households reporting zero/negative income or no cash rent.

of their income on housing in order to live in housing that meets their desires for space and quality.[41]

Changes in incomes and housing prices are not the only reasons for changing rent burdens, however. The rent-income ratio is also subject to changes in personal preferences and social trends that may have tended to result in rent increases, such as declining household size and the growing numbers of single individuals, especially elderly, who if they are renters are likely to spend a larger share of income on housing than are families that rent.[42]

Finally, it should be mentioned that low-income people receive many in-kind benefits, such as food stamps, Medicaid, and Medicare, which allow the household to spend more of its cash income on housing. Poor people who receive subsidies for their groceries and health care can afford to pay more of their incomes for housing.

There is also the fundamental question of the appropriate concept of "income." In 1957 Milton Friedman developed the concept of "permanent income," a household's expectation of its normal, long-run income, in contrast to current income; Friedman argued that household decisions about consumption were based on this normal long-run income, rather than on short-term, fluctuating income.[43] The concept of permanent income is particularly relevant to housing, which is purchased infrequently and used for a long period of time. It helps explain why a household whose income is temporarily low because of a layoff or illness may prefer to stay in the same place and pay the rent by cutting back on other purchases, by borrowing from family or friends, or by drawing on savings, rather than move twice. Thus it is reasonable to expect that a household's rent will be fairly stable as its income fluctuates. This suggests that the cyclical fluctuations in rent burden shown by AHS data may result at least in part from cyclical fluctuations in income, with the household borrowing or using its savings during a period of unemployment. Such an interpretation is the more likely because the AHS is a longitudinal survey, visiting the same housing units every two years.

It therefore seems likely that a rising average rent-income ratio partly reflects undesirable changes in the housing market from the household's point of view, and partly reflects changes that are desirable. The average ratio rises when incomes fall or house prices rise (and to that extent is an indicator of possible problems for policymakers). But it also rises when in-kind transfers to the poor increase, even though the transfers increase both the overall well-being of the recipients and their ability to afford decent housing. In addition, it has probably been pushed up by the rise in single-person households, which reflects changing preferences in American society, such as elderly individuals deciding to live apart from their adult children.

The Real Cost of Housing. There exist alternative measures of housing costs that are more meaningful conceptually than rent-income ratio. The most useful concept for tracking trends is the real cost of housing, and the

best available measure of this concept for rental housing is the rent component of the Consumer Price Index (CPI), which is calculated on the basis
of changes in rents for a sample of apartments from month to month and
year to year. Table 2-11 compares the change in the rent component of the
CPI with the changes in the overall CPI, to measure the relative price of
rental housing; and it compares the change in the rent component of the
CPI with the changes in median family income and the median income of
renter households, to measure the affordability of rental housing, over the
intervals between the years reported in table 2-10.[44]

Table 2-11 shows that trends are not consistent over the entire postwar period, for either comparison. From 1950 to 1978, the overall CPI
increased more rapidly than rents did, meaning that rental housing became
relatively cheaper than other consumer goods. From 1978 to 1993, the
overall CPI rose faster than the rent component during the recessions, and
more slowly during the economic expansion of the 1980s; over the full
fifteen years, both indices grew at almost exactly the same rate. Since 1993,
the rent component has consistently increased more rapidly.

Similarly, from 1950 to 1978, median family income grew at twice the
rate of rents.[45] Over the thirty-one years since then, however, incomes and
rents have grown at almost exactly the same rate. There is a pronounced
cyclical pattern: during economic expansions, median family income has
risen more rapidly than the CPI rent component, but this pattern has been
reversed during recessions. Median renter income has shown the same
cyclical pattern, and over the full period since 1978 it has also increased
at about the same rate as rents. Since 1999, however, rents have increased
faster than the income of renters.

This general pattern is consistent with the permanent income hypothesis.
These comparisons imply that rental housing has become more affordable,
rather than less, over the postwar period. One implication is that the typical
household could have maintained the same rent-income ratio as its income
changed. Rent-income ratios have increased since 1978 in part because people have preferred to pay more and live in better housing as their resources
increased, not because housing has become increasingly unaffordable.

A different, more complicated approach to measuring housing costs
was developed a number of years ago by Anthony Yezer. This approach
involves calculating the cost of adequate housing from information on rents

TABLE 2-11
CHANGES IN RENTS AND INCOMES, 1950–2009

(annual average percentage changes)

	Consumer Price Index	Rent Component of Consumer Price Index	Median Family Income	Median Renter Income
1950–1960	+2.1	+2.7	+5.4	NA
1960–1970	+2.7	+1.9	+5.8	+6.8
1970–1978	+6.7	+5.1	+7.5	+5.0
1978–1983	+8.8	+7.6	+6.9	+5.9
1983–1989	+3.7	+4.8	+5.7	+7.7
1989–1993	+3.9	+3.1	+1.9	+1.6
1993–1999	+2.4	+2.8	+4.8	+3.0
1999–2003	+2.5	+3.7	+1.9	+2.2
2003–2007	+3.0	+3.4	+3.9	+1.9
2007–2009	+1.7	+2.1	−1.0	−0.9
1950–1978	+3.6	+3.1	+6.1	NA
1960–1978	+4.5	+3.3	+6.6	+4.6
1978–1993	+5.4	+5.7	+5.1	+5.4
1993–2009	+2.5	+3.1	+3.1	+2.0
1978–2009	+3.9	+4.4	+4.0	+3.6

SOURCES: U.S. Department of Labor, Bureau of Labor Statistics, at http://data.bls.gov/PDQ/servlet/ SurveyOutputServlet (Series CUSR0000SEHA, CPI for all urban consumers, for rent of primary residence, U.S. city average, not seasonally adjusted); U.S. Bureau of the Census, *1960 Census of Housing,* vol. 2, part 1; *American Housing Survey,* various years beginning in 1978.
NOTE: NA = not available.

and attributes such as space and quality dimensions. The cost of adequate housing is then compared to the income of the household.[46] Households that would have to spend "too much" of their income to afford adequate housing—measured as higher than 30 percent or some other appropriate fraction of their income—are considered to have a housing cost problem. This sort of analysis is particularly useful for assessing the housing cost problem of low-income households. It can be performed for households of different sizes and other attributes, and for households in different areas around the country. Yezer used the AHS for 1975–1977 and found that 27 percent of renters could not have afforded decent housing without spending 25 percent or more of their income for rent, and 22 percent would have had to spend 30 percent or more.[47] Unfortunately, because of the complexity of the analysis, it has not been repeated. Table 2-11 indicates that, since the late 1970s, rents have risen about as rapidly as incomes, so the proportion with a rent burden by this measure may be about the same as that determined by more conventional measures.

Conclusion

Two broad conclusions can be drawn from this large volume of data on American housing. First, there has been a major change in our housing stock since housing first became a concern of the federal government. Originally, the problem for poor people was the quality of their housing; at the beginning of World War II, close to half of all American households lived in housing that was officially "substandard." Now, very few households live in such housing—fewer than 2 percent.[48] Similarly, there was originally a serious space problem: about one-fifth of all American households were crowded in 1940, but now less than 2.5 percent are.

Second, the major American housing problem now is the ability of the poor to afford decent housing with enough money left over for the other necessities of life. Affordability in this sense is arguably a growing problem, or at least a problem that public policy is not making much progress in resolving.

EXHIBIT 2-1

INCOME CATEGORIES USED IN FEDERAL HOUSING PROGRAMS

100 percent of area median income—defined as "low and moderate income" and also as "moderate income" by the Federal Housing Enterprises Financial Safety and Soundness Act of 1992 for purposes of establishing one of the housing goals which the government-sponsored enterprises, Fannie Mae and Freddie Mac, were required to meet each year. (This category is not used in HUD's housing assistance programs, but is included here for completeness and to avoid confusion with the similarly named assistance categories.)

80 percent of area median income—defined as "lower income" by the U.S. Housing Act of 1937, as amended, and used as the upper income limit for housing assistance in many programs.

60 percent of area median income—no special name; used to determine household eligibility in the Low-Income Housing Tax Credit program and the HOME program.

50 percent of area median income—defined as "very low income" by the U.S. Housing Act of 1937, as amended, and used from 1988 to 1996 to establish priority for housing assistance in many programs, and used since 1989 to calculate the number of households with priority housing problems for reporting to Congress ("worst-case needs").

30 percent of area median income—defined as "extremely low income" by the Quality Housing and Work Responsibility Act of 1998, which requires that a minimum share of entrants in each rental housing assistance program have extremely low incomes.

SOURCES: U.S. Department of Housing and Urban Development, *Rental Housing Assistance— The Worsening Crisis: A Report to Congress on Worst Case Housing Needs*, Washington, DC, March 2000, 5; Federal Housing Enterprises Financial Safety and Soundness Act of 1992, Public Law 102-550, 12 USC 4501, secs. 1303 (10), 1332.

EXHIBIT 2-2
DEFINITIONS OF INADEQUATE HOUSING

A. "Severely Inadequate" A housing unit is defined as severely inadequate if it meets any of the following five conditions:
Plumbing. Lacking hot piped water or a flush toilet, or lacking both bathtub and shower, all for the exclusive use of the unit.
Heating. Having been uncomfortably cold last winter, for twenty-four hours or more, or three times for at least six hours each, due to broken-down heating equipment.
Electric. Having no electricity or having all of the following three electrical problems: exposed wiring; a room with no working wall outlet; and three blown fuses or tripped circuit breakers in the last ninety days.
Upkeep. Having any five of the following six maintenance problems: leaks from outdoors; leaks from indoors; holes in the floor; holes or open cracks in the walls or ceilings; more than a square foot of peeling paint or plaster; or rats in the last ninety days.
Hallways. Having all of the following four problems in public areas: no working light fixtures; loose or missing steps; loose or missing railings; and no elevator.
B. "Moderately Inadequate" A housing unit is defined as moderately inadequate if it meets any of the following five conditions, but none of the conditions listed under the definition of "severely inadequate":
Plumbing. Having the toilets all break down simultaneously at least three times in the last three months, for at least six hours each time.
Heating. Having unvented gas, oil, or kerosene heaters as the main source of heat (because these heaters may produce unsafe fumes and unhealthy levels of moisture).
Upkeep. Having any three of the six upkeep problems listed under the definition of "severely inadequate."
Hallways. Having any three of the four hallways problems listed under the definition of "severely inadequate."
Kitchen. Lacking a sink, range, or refrigerator for the exclusive use of the unit.

SOURCE: U.S. Department of Housing and Urban Development, Office of Policy Development and Research, *Affordable Housing Needs: A Report to Congress on the Significant Need for Housing,* Washington, DC, December 2005, 79–80, appendix B.
NOTE: In 2007 most of the AHS questions concerning "hallways" were dropped, and the "hallways" criteria were deleted from the definitions of "severely adequate" and "moderately adequate." The number of inadequate units was not recalculated for previous years, however.

3

Housing Assistance Programs: Taxonomy and History

Subsidized housing is not an entitlement. Until the welfare reform of 1996, it was the only major federal low-income benefit program which was not. This is a consequence of the original view in the Depression that public housing was part of public works. The number of subsidized households has always been limited; at present about one-third of eligible households receive assistance. Among other things, this means that households receiving assistance under existing programs do not automatically transfer into newly created programs; usually they continue to receive assistance under the original program. The long-lived nature of housing also means that units built under a program remain in existence, and continue to receive subsidies, after the program has been "terminated"—that is, after the federal government no longer is making commitments to provide additional units under the program. Thus very different housing programs exist side by side.

This chapter offers a detailed account, both structural and historical, of these different programs. It looks first at the three major types of federal programs that subsidize housing for low-income households: public housing; privately owned projects, whose owners have received subsidies to build or rehabilitate the projects and usually continue to receive subsidies to operate them; and housing vouchers, which are given to individual households to use in privately owned existing housing of their own choosing. It looks also at two other types of programs that have come into being in the last twenty years: cash block grants and federal income tax credits. Finally, it discusses a newly created block grant and production program authorized by Congress in 2008 but not yet funded. The subsidy mechanisms of all these programs are different, and they need to be understood before the outcomes and effectiveness of the programs are compared in later chapters.

It might be helpful to understand at the start how big a share each program has in the government's efforts to offer housing assistance. As of 2009, there were about 1.129 million public housing units, 1.511 million units in privately owned subsidized projects, and 2.112 million units receiving vouchers—a total of about 4.741 million receiving subsidies from HUD.[1] (In 1996 there were about 4.483 million subsidized units, split fairly evenly among the three categories: 1.394 million in public housing, 1.743 million in privately owned projects, and 1.346 million receiving certificates and vouchers.[2]) About 1.785 million units have been subsidized under the Low-Income Housing Tax Credit, but some have received other subsidies in addition to the tax credit (as discussed later in this chapter and chapter 4), including project-based assistance and also vouchers from HUD.[3] The HOME block grant provides funds for both owner-occupied and rental housing; through June 2009 it funded the construction or rehabilitation of about 388,000 lower-income rental units, and about 210,000 units in tenant-based assistance programs akin to vouchers.[4]

Public Housing

Public housing is the oldest subsidy program, dating back to the U.S. Housing Act of 1937, and it is probably what most people have in mind when they think of subsidized housing.[5] About 1.5 million public housing units have been built since 1937. Over one million were built between 1950 and 1975, particularly during the Truman, Kennedy, and Johnson administrations; some 200,000 were built before 1950. The program was suspended in 1973 and reactivated in 1976. Few units have been built since the mid-1980s. Half the units now standing were built before 1965.[6]

The subsidy is "project based," meaning that the federal government makes a commitment to give subsidies to the owner of the housing rather than the tenant. The tenant's rent is set at 30 percent of his or her income; the federal government pays the rest of the cost of building and operating the unit. Residents receive the benefit of the subsidy as long as they live in the housing unit, but if they move out, the benefit of the subsidy goes instead to the next occupant of the unit.

Public housing projects are owned by local government agencies, or in some cases state agencies, which are known as public housing authorities or PHAs. The PHAs do not pay for the housing, however. The federal government has always paid the cost of construction.

The forms of federal subsidy have changed over the years. There are three categories: construction cost, operating cost, and rehabilitation (termed "modernization").

Subsidies for Construction Costs. Originally, the federal government paid the construction costs by paying the principal and interest on forty-year bonds issued by PHAs. (Technically, the federal government gave the money to the PHAs, which then made the payments.) The bonds were tax exempt and federally guaranteed. This shifted part of the construction cost from a budget outlay to a forgone tax revenue and created an additional subsidy for public housing in the process. Various studies in the 1970s and early 1980s estimated that the tax exemption added between 25 percent and 100 percent to the direct construction cost.[7]

In 1974, the federal government decided not to issue long-term bonds, because long-term interest rates were high by historical standards; instead, the government financed public housing by issuing short-term debt and rolling it over, waiting for interest rates to come down. As it happened, rates went up rather than down, and the government's outlays were higher than if it had issued the forty-year bonds to begin with; but it continued to finance each year's additional public housing construction with short-term debt. In 1985, the government stopped rolling over the debt and instead paid the construction cost of all projects since 1974 in full. At the same time, it switched to a policy of paying the full cost of public housing projects when they were built, instead of financing them through debt in any form. Coincidentally, interest rates came down after 1985.

Subsidies for Operating Costs. Originally the tenant was expected to pay the cost of operating and maintaining the project. Income limits for eligibility were set at five times the tenant's rent—that is, five times the operating costs. The fact that tenants had to pay the operating costs meant that in most cases the poorest people could not afford to live in public housing, even though the U.S. Housing Act defined the eligible population as "families who are in the lowest income group." As the bill's chief sponsor, Sen. Robert Wagner (D–NY), observed, "Obviously this bill cannot provide housing for those who cannot pay the rent minus the subsidy allowed."[8] In practice, public housing was housing for the working poor; in World War II, it was intended to be housing for war workers. It was not within reach of the unemployed or what today is often termed the "underclass," insofar as it existed at the time.

Congress gave the PHAs the right to set their own income limits and rents in 1959, and PHAs generally set rents high enough to cover operating costs. As inflation began to drive up operating costs faster than tenant incomes after 1965, it became harder for the tenants to afford to live in public housing. At about this time also, court decisions were limiting the ability of PHAs to select their tenants from among eligible applicants, requiring them instead to take those who were at the top of the waiting lists. Thus PHAs could not choose tenants who were best able to pay the operating costs from their own income. In response to the problems of rising costs and a growing number of tenants who could not pay the full operating costs, Congress passed the Brooke Amendment and the federal government began to pay part of the operating costs of public housing in 1969. This law also changed the nature of the subsidy by limiting the tenant's payment to 25 percent of household income.

The result of these changes was that public housing became available to a lower-income population. From 1967 to 1979, the median real income of public housing tenants fell by about 25 percent, and the proportion with a worker in the family fell from about half to about one-third.[9] By 1989, the median real income had fallen another 10 percent, while the proportion with a worker in the family was about the same.[10] As of 2003, however, the proportion with a worker had risen to about 45 percent, though the median real income was about the same as in 1989.[11] The changing composition of public housing and the changing nature of the subsidy led to federally established income limits. Since 1981, rules have required that at least 85 percent of the units in the program must be occupied by very low-income families, with a lower minimum—75 percent—for projects built before that date.

Subsidies for Modernization and HOPE VI. A further type of subsidy was added to public housing in 1967—"modernization" of older projects that had begun to deteriorate and needed renovation if they were to continue to provide decent housing. Originally modernization was funded through twenty-year bonds, following the precedent of the construction bonds. In 1987, the government began to fund modernization on a cash basis, as it had begun to do with construction in 1985. In 1998 funding for construction and modernization was combined in a single capital fund for public housing.

Despite modernization funding, some public housing projects deteriorated badly as they aged. Indeed, some became bywords for blight and slums. In 1989 Congress established a National Commission on Severely Distressed Public Housing, and the commission's 1992 report estimated that about 86,000 public housing units—about 6 percent of the 1.3 million units then in existence—were in fact severely distressed. The commission recommended a ten-year program to address the problems in these projects: the program would raze and replace the units, or rehabilitate them; revitalize the neighborhoods in which they were located; and provide supportive services to the project residents.[12] Congress enacted the commission's recommendations in 1992 as the HOPE VI program.

In the course of the next decade, most of the original recommendations of the commission were put in place. Between 1993 and 1996, HUD made 287 grants to demolish public housing, razing 57,000 units. Between 1993 and 2007, HUD made 240 revitalization grants to rehabilitate or replace projects; plans for these projects called for razing 96,000 units and replacing them with 112,000 units. Of the new units, 53,000 would be public housing units for low-income households and would receive funding under annual contributions contracts. This implies a reduction by 100,000 in the number of units for low-income households.[13] An evaluation by the Urban Institute and the Brookings Institution, however, calculated that about one-third of the razed units were vacant and uninhabitable, implying a net reduction by 49,000 in the number of units effectively available to low-income households.[14] These data indicate that HOPE VI is more a community development program than a low-income housing program. In this respect it revives the original purpose of public housing, but with an important difference. Originally, public housing for the poor was expected to revitalize neighborhoods; under HOPE VI, the revitalization occurs because much of the new housing is not for the poor, but for middle-income households.

In its FY2004 budget, the Bush administration proposed to terminate HOPE VI, arguing that it had achieved its original objective (though also noting that construction of approved projects was proceeding slowly). Congress did not approve termination, and continued to vote funds for additional projects, though at a much lower annual level. In its FY2010 budget, the Obama administration also proposed to terminate HOPE VI, but then to replace it with an expanded program including construction of mixed-income housing and purchases of unsubsidized, privately owned rental housing that would be renovated or replaced. The new program is named "Choice Neighborhoods," and the proposed funding level was doubled from $120 million to $250 million.[15] These changes would shift the emphasis further from housing assistance to community development. Congress approved the new program but did not terminate HOPE VI; $65 million in funding for Choice Neighborhoods was provided as a setaside within HOPE VI. The administration has repeated its proposals in its 2011 and 2012 budgets.

Privately Owned Projects

In 1961 a new type of subsidized housing program was created. This involved private ownership of projects built with federal government subsidies and having mortgages insured by the federal government. During the postwar period, the federal government had become active in multifamily housing and began insuring mortgages on apartment buildings through the Federal Housing Administration (FHA).[16] FHA collected a mortgage insurance premium from the project developer, which was supposed to cover the cost of claims arising from default and foreclosure, and in turn guaranteed the payment of the outstanding principal balance if the project defaulted and the lender foreclosed. These apartment projects were intended to provide housing for middle-income families who could afford to pay the rents without direct subsidies. In fact, the projects were indirectly subsidized, because the federally backed loans carried lower interest rates than developers would have paid if they had received funding through the private market. Other than these federally guaranteed loans, the projects did not receive any federal subsidies.

The new approach combined FHA insurance with direct subsidies on privately owned projects. It was employed in what turned out to be several successive programs, each terminated within a few years: Section 221(d) (3)(BMIR)—enacted 1961, terminated 1968; Section 236—enacted 1968, terminated 1974; and Section 8 New Construction—enacted 1974; terminated 1983. The main difference between these programs was the subsidy mechanism; in other respects they were generally similar, and the high cost of each program contributed substantially to the decision to terminate it. All of the projects in Section 221(d)(3)(BMIR) were insured by FHA; about 80 percent of the Section 236 projects and about half of the Section 8 New Construction units were also insured. Most of the others were built by state or local housing agencies without FHA insurance and were financed by tax-exempt bonds or by the U.S. Department of Agriculture's Section 515 loan program. Altogether, about 75 percent of the units in these programs were insured by FHA as well as assisted by HUD. Such projects are known as the "insured assisted inventory."[17]

For analytical purposes it is often convenient to divide the projects subsidized under these programs into two categories: "older assisted" and "newer assisted." The former consists of projects subsidized under Section 221(d)(3)(BMIR) or Section 236 Rent Supplement projects, or projects insured under Section (221)(d)(3) and bearing a market interest rate that subsequently received subsidy under several programs designed to avoid default on the project mortgage. The latter consists of Section 8 projects. As of 2009, "older assisted" projects are generally thirty to forty-five years old, and "newer assisted" between twenty-five and thirty-five years old. The overlap occurs because the categorization applies to programs rather than year of construction, and the latest Section 236 projects were completed after the earliest Section 8 projects. The distinction matters because different programs to prevent default and maintain the projects in decent condition have been developed for the two different types of projects.

Section 221(d)(3)(BMIR). The complicated name of this program occurs because Section 221(d) of the National Housing Act authorizes FHA mortgage insurance for several types of housing, and Section 221(d)(3) authorizes insurance for both "market-rate" and "below-market interest rate" (BMIR) multifamily projects. (The projects are colloquially known simply as "BMIRs.") The interest rate on the mortgages for these projects was brought down by the government's buying the mortgage at its face value (through the Federal National Mortgage Association, FNMA or Fannie Mae, then a part of the government). For example, the government would pay $100,000 for a $100,000 mortgage for forty years with a 3 percent interest rate, at a time when the market interest rate was 6 percent. At 3 percent, the project developer's monthly payment would be $357.99, which would have a present value of $65,063 at the market interest rate of 6 percent. The government would sell the mortgage for this amount to a private investor; the difference of $34,937 was the cost to the government. It was also the present value of the monthly subsidy to the project owner, whose monthly payment of $357.99 would enable him to obtain a loan for $100,000 through the government, whereas his monthly payment on a $100,000 loan at 6 percent would be $550.22. The lower monthly mortgage payment made it possible to charge a lower rent on the unit, and thus serve a household with a substantially lower income; owners were required to set rents that reflected the 3 percent mortgage rate, and to rent to households with incomes below 95 percent of the local median.[18]

Like public housing at that time, the program at first provided no subsidies for the cost of operation. Tenants were expected to pay the operating and maintenance costs out of their own income. The program was intended to serve families that could not afford "market-rate" housing but were above the income limits for public housing. In the words of the Douglas Commission in 1968, "public housing was to assist the poorest quarter of urban families while Section 221(d)(3) would assist the next quarter."[19] Limits on the dollar value of the mortgage per apartment were written into the program in an effort to ensure that it served the desired income group.

Some 192,000 units were subsidized under this program, of which 173,000 were new construction. Only 80,000 were subsidized in the first seven years, however—a low rate of production which contributed to the program's demise. The peak year for the program, at 49,000 units, was 1968, which was also the program's last year. Over 60,000 units were completed after that date.[20]

Even though production levels were low, the cost of this program was very large in terms of the federal budget, because under the budget scoring rules of the time, each mortgage purchased by the federal government counted as an outlay to the full amount of the mortgage. The payments of principal and interest over the life of the mortgage counted as offsetting receipts only when they actually occurred, over the ensuing forty years. Under today's budget rules for federal credit programs, the outlay would be measured as only the difference between the present value of the mortgage payments capitalized at 3 percent and their present value capitalized at the market rate of interest—the difference between $100,000 and $65,063, in the example above. Thus the budgetary cost of the program was about three times its actual cost to the government, in present value terms.

Rent Supplement. Because of the high cost of the BMIR program, in 1965 the Johnson administration proposed a less expensive and novel form of subsidy, under which the federal government could make rental payments on behalf of tenants to sponsors of unsubsidized or "market rate" projects that were insured under Section 221(d)(3).[21] This was the Rent Supplement program. It was much less expensive per unit because the subsidies did not have to cover the full cost of construction, and the tenant's rent payment offset part of the cost. This was the first subsidy to be based on income; the federal government paid the difference between 25 percent of the tenant's income and the rent. (The Brooke Amendment, under which the government began to pay part of the operating costs of public housing, was not enacted until 1969.) Controversy developed over the administration's proposal to provide subsidies based on income for families whose incomes were well above those of families being served by public housing, and well above the incomes of many households that were receiving no housing assistance. The program as approved by Congress was limited to those eligible for public housing, rather than those being served by Section 221(d)(3)(BMIR).[22] About 180,000 units were receiving rent supplements by 1977, the peak year of the program.[23]

Rent Supplement was suspended in 1973, and no further commitments were made under the program, with the exception of projects financed by state housing agencies. As of 2009, about 15,000 state-agency units were still receiving assistance. All other Rent Supplement projects were converted to other programs, particularly Section 8, in the 1980s.

Section 236. Section 236 succeeded section 221(d)(3)(BMIR) in 1968. This program provided a mortgage interest rate subsidy in a different form. Projects were underwritten and mortgages were issued at market interest rates, but the federal government paid part of each month's mortgage payment. The maximum subsidy was the difference between the monthly payment necessary to amortize the mortgage at the market rate and the payment necessary to amortize it at an interest rate of 1 percent. The mortgage payment was thus reduced by close to 50 percent—more, as interest rates rose in the late 1960s and early 1970s.[24] Following the precedent of the Rent Supplement program, the subsidy amount also depended on the income of the tenant. It was smaller if the tenant's income was sufficient to support a mortgage at a rate above 1 percent. This subsidy was not expected to be enough for the poorest households to afford the rents, and the Rent Supplement program was made available for 20 percent of the units in Section 236.

The subsidy formula proved to be one of the weaknesses of the program. Tenants had to pay either 25 percent of their income or a "basic rent" consisting of operating costs and the amount needed to amortize the mortgage at 1 percent, whichever was higher. When operating costs increased, those paying the basic rent had to meet the higher operating costs out of their own pocket. These were the poorest tenants, those for whom the basic rent exceeded 25 percent of their income to begin with. Those paying 25 percent of their income would not have to pay any operating cost increases from their own resources until the basic rent rose above that level. This meant that the tenants with the highest incomes would be the last to feel the effects of operating cost increases, a perverse outcome for a housing subsidy program.

Section 236 quickly became a large program. It provided subsidies for 437,000 units, of which 388,000 were new. Over 300,000 were subsidized in the first four years.[25] Yet despite—or perhaps because of—the large volume of production, Section 236 had a shorter life than its predecessor. The per-unit subsidies were much smaller in the first year of the project, but they were larger in each succeeding year as operating costs rose, and they cumulated to large numbers as the number of units in the program increased. By 1972 there was bipartisan concern in Congress about the cost of the program and about other problems; in January 1973 President Nixon suspended it (at the same time as public housing, mentioned previously). It was terminated in 1974.

Program termination, however, applies to commitments to subsidize additional projects; assistance continues for projects which already have assistance contracts (or which had received a commitment prior to the program termination). As of 2009, about 265,000 units were still receiving subsidies under Section 236.[26] The number is projected to decline by about 20,000 units annually over the next few years, as projects reach the end of their contract.

Section 8 New Construction. After a six-month study (known as the National Housing Policy Review), President Nixon recommended a new program to replace Section 236, which Congress enacted in 1974. This was the Section 8 New Construction program, added as an amendment to the U.S. Housing Act of 1937 in the Housing and Urban Development Act of 1974.[27] Under Section 8, the subsidy mechanism was explicitly based on the household's income rather than the cost of construction. Families were expected to contribute 25 percent of their income as their rental payment. The federal government paid the difference between that amount and the Fair Market Rent (FMR) of the unit. The FMR was calculated for each metropolitan area or nonmetropolitan county as the cost of decent, modest housing in that market. Most such housing was not new and rented for much less than the amount needed to support a newly built project, so HUD based FMRs on the rents in recently constructed unsubsidized apartment projects of modest design—using what was known as the "rent reasonableness" test. Various adjustments to project costs were also allowed, each adding 5 to 10 percent, and virtually every project qualified for at least one adjustment. Subsidies could be raised from year to year as market rents increased.

Unlike its predecessors, Section 8 was intended to serve low-income households as a substitute for public housing; the 1973 suspension of public housing continued during the first two years of the program. Since 1981, Section 8 New Construction has had the same income limits as public housing.

The largest of the programs to build privately subsidized projects, Section 8 New Construction eventually subsidized the construction of about 700,000 units.[28] Another 200,000 were built under the Section 202 program for the elderly (discussed later in this chapter) and assisted through Section 8; these are often counted simply as Section 8 projects. Another 350,000 received Section 8 subsidies after being built under other programs (such as Section 236), and 100,000 were subsidized under the Moderate Rehabilitation program. As of 2009, about 1.3 million units were being subsidized in the program.[29] About 500,000 carry FHA insurance.[30]

By 1980, it was clear that Section 8 was a very expensive program, about as expensive per unit per year as Section 236 with Rent Supplement.[31] By that year, 208,000 units were completed, and another 273,000 were under construction. Under the Substantial Rehabilitation program, which had the same subsidy mechanism, 27,000 units were completed and another 60,000 were rehabilitated, though not all were insured by FHA. In the last year of the Carter administration, budget commitments for additional Section 8 units were cut by about 25 percent. President Reagan proposed sharp further reductions in his budgets for FY1981 and 1982, to less than a quarter of the 1979 level. He also established the President's Commission on Housing within a few months of taking office. The commission recommended terminating the Section 8 New Construction and Substantial Rehabilitation programs, and Congress did so in 1983.[32]

Tax Benefits. Common to all these programs was the notion that profit was a large component of the cost of housing. Projects were therefore to be developed and owned by nonprofit sponsors or limited-dividend corporations, or in the case of Section 8 by state housing finance agencies, and rents could be lower because these entities did not need to make profits.

To attract private investors, the programs offered favorable tax treatment. Investors could depreciate the project more rapidly for tax purposes than its actual decline in economic value, and deduct the accelerated depreciation from other income for tax purposes. The excess depreciation was subject to recapture when the project was sold, but if it was owned for ten years, the excess depreciation was taxed as capital gains rather than ordinary income, even though the accelerated depreciation had originally sheltered ordinary income from tax at the higher rate.

During the 1960s and 1970s, the tax rate on capital gains was half that on ordinary income. Individuals in limited partnerships could benefit further from the fact that most of the money for the project was borrowed; they could deduct depreciation based on their share of the equity in the project, not on their share of the cost of the project. If 90 percent of the cost was borrowed, the individual could deduct depreciation based on 10 times the amount he or she had invested in the project.[33] This increased investors' willingness to put money into a project, and transferred part of the cost from the direct appropriation for housing to the Treasury in the form of forgone tax revenue, much like the tax exemption for public housing bonds. A further tax advantage was conferred on Section 236 projects in 1969, when accelerated depreciation was reduced for investments other than housing. The total volume of real estate tax shelters tripled in value from 1970 to 1972. In addition, depreciation schedules for subsidized housing were more favorable than for unsubsidized housing. This was the first time that the tax laws favored subsidized housing projects over unsubsidized housing. One consequence was that investors in subsidized housing could anticipate recouping their investment in a much shorter period, about five to ten years, and thus were less concerned about the long-run viability of the projects.

The Consequences of Combining Insurance and Subsidy. Programs under which housing is privately owned are more complicated than public housing programs because of the interactions between FHA insurance and the subsidies. They are also more difficult to manage. Underwriting mortgages on multifamily properties is complicated and difficult to begin with. Every project is unique, and underwriting is very staff-intensive. As of 2005, two-thirds of FHA's staff—roughly 1,800 people—was devoted to multifamily mortgage insurance, but its multifamily portfolio accounted for only 10 percent of its business. When projects are subsidized as well as insured, the difficulties are compounded. At the beginning of the development process, there is always pressure to underwrite the projects generously in order "to make the program work." Then there is pressure to provide generous subsidies in order to support the mortgage. The complications of multifamily mortgage underwriting also increase the potential for fraud, and the need "to make the program work" reduces the effectiveness of management protections against both honest and dishonest overvaluation.

Despite the generous underwriting, many projects in these programs have run into financial difficulties and have had trouble making their mortgage payments. Privately owned projects can default on their mortgages (unlike public housing, where the federal government directly paid the bondholders). Since the projects carried FHA mortgage insurance, lenders could foreclose on them if they went into default, forcing FHA to pay the outstanding principal balance and take over the project. Defaults became a problem in both Section 236 and the Section 221(d)(3) market rate program. In 1973, the National Housing Policy Review reported that Section 236, then only five years old, was not actuarially sound; the losses on the defaulted projects would exceed the mortgage insurance premiums. It estimated that 20 percent of projects would fail in the first ten years of the program.[34] (In fact, as of 1979, about 17 percent had defaulted, so this prediction turned out to be reasonably accurate.) It further concluded that the Rent Supplement program, then eight years old, was also not actuarially sound.[35]

The combination of insurance and subsidy complicates the federal government's reaction to a probable default. FHA's incentive is to avoid foreclosure in order to avoid paying an insurance claim. It also does not want to take responsibility for managing a project, which it must do between foreclosure and resale. Because project owners know that FHA does not want to foreclose, they have the upper hand in any dispute over meeting their contractual obligations. If, for example, HUD tries to impose sanctions on an owner because a project is in poor physical condition, the owner can walk away from the project. Thus HUD's role as insurer obstructs its role as provider of housing assistance for poor people.

The consequences of default are unattractive. FHA either acquires the mortgage from the lender, paying the outstanding balance and effectively becoming the lender itself, or it pays the insurance claim and takes title to the project. FHA then tries to sell the mortgage or the project. Selling defaulted mortgages or projects was a problem for FHA before the subsidy programs were established, but the problem became much more acute for the subsidized projects. Through 1967, FHA had acquired projects with 87,000 units, and mortgages on properties containing 104,000 units—a total of 191,000 units; it sold or otherwise disposed of the majority of these but in 1967 still owned projects with 26,000 units and held mortgages on properties with 46,000 units. By 1979, cumulative defaults had nearly tripled; the total number of units in projects acquired by FHA was now 186,000, and the number of units in properties with acquired mortgages was 367,000—meaning that through defaults a total of 553,000 units had passed into the hands of FHA. The subsidy programs accounted for half of the increase; defaults in Section 221(d)(3)(BMIR) amounted to 81,000 of the units acquired, and defaults in Section 236 amounted to another 86,000. In 1979, after selling or otherwise disposing of these defaulted properties, FHA still owned subsidized projects with 21,000 units, and held the mortgages on properties with another 84,000 units.[36] FHA had to manage these projects while it was trying to sell them, which was expensive and sometimes difficult. Moreover, because a deteriorating project was often a problem for the neighborhood in which it was located, FHA had to deal with residents'—and sometimes neighbors'—complaints.[37]

Additional Subsidies to Avoid Default. From the federal government's standpoint, the alternative to foreclosing or acquiring a mortgage is providing additional subsidies to forestall default. These can take two forms: either lump-sum payments for repairs or mortgage writedowns, or annual payments to supplement the tenants' rent. There has been a long series of such programs. The first of them, Loan Management (LM), later known as Loan Management Set-Aside (LMSA), was enacted in 1976; it provided subsidies to projects in the "older assisted" programs, based on the income of the resident, in addition to the original interest rate subsidies.[38] In 1979 a new Flexible Subsidy program (originally the Troubled Projects program) was created for the older assisted projects; it provided low-interest loans for deferred maintenance and capital improvements to projects that had trouble meeting their debt service and operating expenses. By 1989, 31 percent of the projects in the older assisted inventory had received assistance under Section 8 LMSA, and 14 percent had received assistance under Flexible Subsidy. Nearly all of the latter (82 percent) received subsidies between 1980 and 1985.[39] Flexible Subsidy was discontinued in 1996.

The effectiveness of these subsidies has not been systematically studied. An assessment of the FHA-insured portfolio as of 1992 found that subsidized projects were typically in worse physical and financial condition than unsubsidized, but this finding does not prove that the subsidies were responsible.[40] It is certainly clear that the subsidies have not prevented further defaults or continuing physical and financial problems in the projects that have received them. Some of the privately owned projects are in very poor condition, as bad as the worst of the public housing projects.

The physical and financial problems are more serious in the insured older assisted inventory than in Section 8, but they have become more evident in the newer program as well. In 1992 HUD concluded that about 6 percent of the older projects, and 3 percent of the Section 8 projects, were financially "distressed," meaning that they needed at least $6,000 worth of renovation per unit without any prospect of obtaining the necessary funds.[41] A subsequent analysis found that as of 1995, 32 percent of the older projects and 15 percent of the Section 8 projects were "distressed," defined as having an annual cash-flow deficit of $250 per unit after taking account of both net cash flow and the annual cost of remedying the backlog of physical needs.[42] These data are certainly out of date; the Mark-to-Market Program enacted in 1997 has provided funding for rehabilitation and capital replacement of about one-third of all FHA-insured Section 8 projects, although the program includes more than New Construction and Substantial Rehabilitation projects.[43] HUD has also created a Real Estate Assessment Center, which conducts periodic reviews of the physical quality of assisted housing; it reports that over 90 percent of privately owned assisted projects meet the established physical standards.[44] There has been no more recent analysis of the overall inventory, however, along the lines of the studies in the early 1990s.

Determining how much subsidy is needed poses the same kind of underwriting problems as the original mortgage insurance commitment. Subsidies often turn out to be more generous than needed to keep the projects operating, especially when they are piled on top of other subsidies. This situation invites corruption. In the late 1980s, for example, subsidies to rehabilitate Section 8 projects were made available under a limited congressional appropriation. To obtain these subsidies, project owners found it useful to hire well-placed consultants and to make contributions to certain charities. The subsidies were generous enough that project owners could pay the consultants and make the charitable contributions from the subsidy grant, and still have enough money to rehabilitate the project. This dubious activity in the Section 8 Moderate Rehabilitation program led to sensational hearings involving former secretary of the interior James Watt, former senator Edward Brooke, and former Kentucky governor Louie Nunn, among others, and to the appointment of a special prosecutor to investigate then HUD secretary Samuel Pierce (who was never charged).

The worst HUD scandals have occurred in programs that combine subsidy and mortgage insurance.

Flexible Subsidy and Section 8 Loan Management can be regarded as successors to Rent Supplement and somewhat analogous to operating subsidies and modernization for public housing. The privately owned assisted projects have come to receive the same kinds of subsidies as public housing: subsidies for the initial construction, subsidies to cover increases in operating costs, and subsidies for renovation. When the programs were created, they included only the construction subsidies—also like public housing when it was created. In both kinds of programs, projects become steadily more expensive as they age; the initial costs almost always substantially understate the eventual cost as new forms of subsidy are considered necessary to keep the projects operating.

Prepayment Problems. Not all the problems with privately owned projects involve financial difficulties or poor housing quality. Problems also arise for projects at the other end of the quality or financial spectrum. Owners of desirable projects in desirable neighborhoods often want to prepay their mortgages and convert their projects to market-rent housing. Prepayment and conversion reduces the stock of subsidized lower-income housing, and presents the project residents with the unpleasant alternatives of paying higher rents or moving. Prepayment has therefore become as big a policy concern as default.

Under the terms of the original mortgage insurance contract, project owners had an opportunity to prepay after twenty years, halfway through the forty-year contract term. Thus the policy issue became important in the late 1980s, when the BMIR projects that had received LMSA subsidy contracts began to approach the 15-year term of the contract, and loomed even larger on the political horizon as the projects in the much larger Section 236 and Section 8 programs approached their twentieth anniversaries.

Prepayment has in fact been about as big a risk as default. The National Low Income Housing Preservation Commission, an ad hoc bipartisan group created with the support of both congressional housing subcommittees to analyze the viability of Section 221(d)(3)(BMIR) and Section 236 projects, estimated in 1988 that about 47 percent of the inventory would default and about 37 percent would prepay over the next fifteen years, absent some policy change.[45] Some projects were not eligible to prepay, including those which had received Flexible Subsidy or had Rent Supplement contracts, those which were sponsored by limited-dividend corporations, and—in the case of Section 236—those which were financed by state housing agencies. The Congressional Budget Office estimated in 1987 that only about 48 percent of projects were eligible.[46]

The first congressional response was to impose a moratorium on prepayments in the Emergency Low Income Housing Preservation Act of 1987, until "the interests of owners, tenants, and the communities most affected by the consequences of prepayment" could be reconciled.[47] After the moratorium had been in effect for three years, Congress addressed the prepayment problem with the Low Income Housing Preservation and Resident Homeownership Act of 1990 (LIHPRHA). Its purpose was to preserve the housing in question for its intended beneficiaries, while guaranteeing the owners a fair and reasonable return on their investment. Under LIHPRHA, owners who agreed to keep the project as low-income housing for another thirty years could receive subsidies up to 120 percent of the FMR for their market area, or more if the project was located in a high-rent neighborhood; owners could also receive FHA-insured loans so they could take out part of their equity in the project. Those wishing to sell their projects had to give rights of first refusal for fifteen months to entities that were willing to operate the project as subsidized housing. In the words of its authors, the legislation "recognizes that some prepayments may need to occur,"[48] but in practice it discouraged prepayment: the secretary of HUD had to certify that prepayment would not create hardship for current tenants or materially affect the supply of low-income housing in the market; in addition, tenants had to receive vouchers or certificates, and owners had to pay half their moving expenses, offer three-year lease extensions for the elderly and members of other groups designated as having special needs, and accept tenants with certificates or vouchers. In the view of at least one advocate, LIHPHRA "effectively prohibited subsidized mortgage prepayments."[49]

Within four years of LIHPRHA's passage, the Clinton administration found it unsatisfactory, concluding that "preservation [had] been achieved at very high cost to the government"—an average of $17,500 per unit ($25,300 in 2009 dollars)—and that it imposed "excessive administrative burdens on participants and the Department."[50] After a year of policy debate, Congress restored the project owner's right to prepay the mortgage and terminate the subsidy contract. Tenants were protected by a new type of voucher, the "enhanced voucher," which paid the difference between 30 percent of the tenant's income and the market rent of the unit occupied by the tenant as long as the tenant stayed in the project; if the tenant moved, the voucher would pay only the difference between 30 percent of the tenant's income and the FMR. Enhanced vouchers essentially solved the major political problem with prepayment.

Nonetheless, preservation efforts continued. In 1999 Congress provided additional incentives to retain Section 236 projects as subsidized housing. Owners were allowed to refinance the mortgage, terminating the FHA mortgage and mortgage insurance; at the same time, they continued to receive the interest reduction payment from the original contract. In return, the project had to remain as low-income housing for the term of the original contract, plus five years. Refinancing the mortgage and "decoupling" the mortgage and interest reduction payment were intended to let owners receive a cash return on their investment in addition to the interest subsidy.

When Section 8 projects began to reach the twenty-year milestone, the Clinton administration and Congress faced a new problem. They wanted to preserve the projects as subsidized housing, but also wanted to reduce the continuing subsidies arising from the fact that the FMRs on new construction projects had been set to cover construction costs rather than to match market rents. Reducing subsidies to market-rent levels might set off a wave of defaults; leaving subsidies at above-market levels would be a substantial budget drain. The proposed solution was the Mark-to-Market Program, enacted by Congress in 1997.[51] Originally, the program was scheduled to expire in 2002, but it has been extended three times, most recently to 2015.

Under the program, which applies to FHA-insured Section 8 projects, including older Section 221(d)(3)(BMIR) and Section 236 projects that had subsequently received Section 8 subsidies through LMSA or other arrangements, project rents were reduced to the market rents in the neighborhood of the project, and the mortgage principal amount was reduced to a level that could be supported by the new rents. The rest of the outstanding principal was placed in a second mortgage, to be held by the federal government; the project owner was not required to pay any interest or principal on this "silent second" unless the project revenues exceeded the amount needed to cover the first mortgage and operating costs, or unless the project was sold. The first mortgage also was set at a level that provided funds for major repairs and project improvements. In some cases, project rents were reduced without restructuring the mortgage, because the market rents were high enough to cover the original mortgage amount. Through November 2011, about 3,400 projects had completed the Mark-to-Market process; of these, about 2,500 (containing about 183,000 assisted units) had their mortgages restructured and about 900 (containing about 74,000 assisted units) had their rent levels reduced without restructuring.[52] The program also allowed owners to opt out of the Section 8 program, rejecting restructuring. As with Section 236, enhanced vouchers were provided to residents of such projects. This expansion of the original enhanced voucher was enacted in 1999.

This program saves money in the sense that annual budget outlays are reduced, but it achieves these savings only by converting part of the principal into a second mortgage. If the reduction in principal were simply forgiven and written off, the amount would be counted in the federal budget as an expenditure, and the savings would not occur. Since it is not likely that the government will receive much back on the second mortgages, the ultimate fiscal effect is nearly the same as a write-off.

Mark-to-Market is winding down. As mentioned above, the program's authority is scheduled to be terminated on October 1, 2011, although projects in the pipeline at that date can be restructured. About 600 projects were processed from the program's beginning in 1997 through the year 2000; another 1,700 were processed through 2004; and another 1,100 through June 2009. Fewer than one hundred had been processed between June 2009 and November 2011 (the latest data available), and the active pipeline included about 100 more projects at that time.

While Mark-to-Market is designed to lower rent subsidies on Section 8 projects, another program, Mark-Up-To-Market, raises subsidies in order to forestall prepayment. For projects in desirable neighborhoods, where market rents exceed project rents, the Mark-Up-To-Market program allows increases in subsidies up to 150 percent of the FMR, or even higher with HUD approval. (The FMR is calculated for the overall metropolitan market; rents in neighborhoods within the metropolitan market may be generally higher or lower.) The program is available to Section 221(d)(3)(BMIR) and

Section 236 projects that have received further assistance such as Flexible Subsidy or Section 8 LMSA and are therefore covered by a Section 8 contract, as well as Section 8 projects. In return for the higher rents, the project must be kept as subsidized housing for an additional five years. Mark-Up-To-Market is available to for-profit project owners; a companion program, Mark-Up-To-Budget, is available to nonprofit owners and to nonprofits wanting to buy subsidized projects.[53]

In all, prepayments and opt-outs have probably affected between 300,000 and 400,000 units. The number is uncertain because there is no single program data source, and independent studies using the available data have somewhat different calculations.

According to HUD budget data, the number of assisted units in Section 8 and Section 236 fell by 380,000 between 1997 and 2010.[54] This is conceptually an upper bound, because not all of these units are prepayments or opt-outs. They include units in foreclosed properties, whose owners have been unable to meet their mortgage obligations; after foreclosure, the new owner may not be required to maintain the project as assisted housing. They also include projects with serious physical deficiencies, where HUD may have terminated the subsidy contract. Collectively, these are termed "enforcement actions."

The number of tenant protection vouchers provides another measure of prepayments and opt-outs. Over the same 1997–2010 period, HUD has funded 317,000 tenant protection vouchers. It is tempting to treat this figure as a lower bound, because not all units are occupied at the time of prepayment or opt-out, and not all residents of these projects receive tenant protection vouchers. However, vouchers are also provided to residents of foreclosed projects and projects with terminated subsidy contracts.

Two independent studies have calculated prepayments and opt-outs over shorter periods. The National Housing Trust, which has been interested in preservation for many years, conducted a study for the period 1995–2003 and found a reduction of 244,000 units, including enforcement actions.[55] Over the same period, HUD budget data show a reduction of 225,000. Combining the National Housing Trust figures through 2003 with HUD budget data for later years, the total is 388,000. A study for HUD conducted by Econometrica, Inc., and Abt Associates, Inc., calculated 121,000 prepayments and opt-outs between 1998 and 2004. Over the same period,

HUD budget data show a reduction of 191,000. Combining the study figures with HUD budget data for earlier and later years, the total is 332,000. The Econometrica/Abt Associates study differs from the others because it separated prepayment and opt-outs from foreclosures and other enforcement actions, using detailed HUD program data.[56] The study calculated that enforcement actions totaled 182,000 units during the period, including projects with the possibility of foreclosure as well as actual foreclosures and projects that were subject to enforcement actions but might remain in the program. It thus has a lower figure than either the HUD budget or the National Housing Trust if foreclosures and enforcements are excluded, and a higher figure if they are included.

Using a round number of 400,000 as an upper bound, I calculate that prepayments and opt-outs amount to 22 percent of the 1996 total number of units in privately owned projects (1.830 million, also as reported in the HUD budget). Over the same period, the total number of assisted households increased by 55,000 from 4.683 million to 4.738 million, as I discuss in chapter 4. All these figures combine Section 236 prepayments and Section 8 opt-outs. The different data sources have very different figures for the separate programs; HUD budget data have substantially more prepayments and fewer opt-outs than either study. The aggregate figure is probably more reliable; Section 236 projects which have subsequently received a Section 8 subsidy contract can be counted in either program. Further, Section 236 is both an insurance program and a subsidy program (unlike Section 8, in which projects are insured under other sections of the National Housing Act or not insured by FHA, and subsidized under Section 8); decoupling removes the Section 236 insurance while continuing the interest reduction payment subsidy, and permits subsidies from other sources after decoupling; it is thus more difficult to track the status of these projects.

In addition to calculating the number of prepayments and opt-outs, the Econometrica/Abt Associates study analyzed the differences between properties that prepaid or opted out and those that continued in the subsidy programs. Prepayment and opting out were more likely for properties located in markets with rents below the local market rent, and for properties in "better" neighborhoods—with higher median incomes and lower poverty and vacancy rates. They were also more likely for projects whose residents were families, and less likely for projects serving the elderly. For-profit owners were more likely to prepay or opt out than nonprofit owners. These findings indicate that owners who anticipated higher economic returns from prepaying or opting out were more likely to do so. The various programs to provide financial incentives to property owners have been directed at the right objective.

Default and prepayment on privately owned subsidized projects have been arguably the most perplexing policy problems at HUD in recent decades.[57] The complicated financial arrangements now in place have involved substantial expenditures beyond those originally envisioned when the programs were created, despite bipartisan recognition that the subsidies on Section 8 New Construction at least are excessive. It does not seem likely that any new approach will be simpler or less expensive.

Section 202. One program to subsidize privately owned projects still survives. This is the Section 202 program for the elderly, enacted in 1959, before any of the programs described above. Under the original subsidy mechanism for Section 202, nonprofit sponsors, typically churches and synagogues, borrowed directly from the U.S. Treasury to finance project development. The Treasury loans carried a lower interest rate than privately financed mortgages, including those insured by FHA. At first, the interest rate was based on the average Treasury long-term borrowing rate during the previous year; later, as rates increased, it was set at 3 percent.

This interest rate subsidy was not enough to bring the Section 202 projects within reach of the low-income or even the typical elderly household or individual; additional subsidies were necessary. After Section 8 New Construction was created, HUD began to provide Section 8 subsidies for all Section 202 projects, with Section 202 taking priority over other Section 8 projects.

Section 202 is not a large program, but it is extremely popular and has survived proposals to terminate or restructure it in several administrations. In 1981 the Reagan administration left it untouched as it proposed to terminate Section 8 New Construction, an indication of its political popularity. Between 1959 and 1972 some 45,000 units were built under this program.[58] After Section 8 subsidies were provided, another 207,000 units were funded as "Section 202/8" through 1990.[59]

In 1990, Section 202 was changed from a loan to a grant program, with funds appropriated in the HUD budget each year for some projected number of units. Unlike the other production programs, this program saw project sponsors using other sources of funding in combination with the federal grant, enabling more units to be built but complicating the development process. A companion program for the disabled, Section 811, was enacted in 1990, and the two programs are commonly combined in policy discussions. As of 2010, there were 114,000 Section 202 units funded by direct appropriations, 32,000 units in Section 811 projects, and 15,000 disabled individuals receiving "mainstream vouchers" under Section 811.[60]

Tenant-Based Assistance: Section 8 Existing Housing

Section 8 created more than a new construction program. It also created the third major type of housing assistance: subsidies given directly to families, who could then choose their own housing. Because families can take the subsidy with them to a new apartment if they move, this form of subsidy is termed "tenant-based" assistance, in contrast to the "project-based" assistance provided by public housing and privately owned projects. These two approaches are also known more widely but less accurately as "demand-side" and "supply-side" programs, respectively.[61]

The subsidy formula is basically the same as in Section 8 New Construction, and for that reason the programs could be created in the same section of the act—indeed, in the same sentence. The program became known as Section 8 Existing Housing, following the custom of naming programs by the section number of the act that created them. The fact that the two programs have the same section number in their names has become a source of endless confusion; for example, program expenditures have commonly been reported on a combined basis in many official government documents, including the HUD budget until FY2005. Because the programs are so different, it is more useful to refer to Section 8 Existing Housing as "tenant-based assistance."

Certificates, Vouchers, and the Housing Choice Voucher. As in the New Construction program, tenant-based assistance offers a subsidy consisting of the difference between the FMR and 30 percent of the tenant's income.

Two variants on this formula were enacted at different times, resulting in two different existing housing programs under Section 8—"certificates" and "vouchers." Certificates were the first program, enacted in 1974 at the urging of President Nixon; vouchers were enacted in 1983 as a proposal by President Reagan. In 1998, the two programs were merged into a single program, the Housing Choice Voucher, combining features from both.

The most important differences between the programs concern the maximum rent for an assisted unit and the subsidy formula. In the certificate program, the FMR is the maximum rent allowed on a unit in the program; in the voucher program and the Housing Choice Voucher, the FMR is a payment standard for the maximum subsidy amount, and the family is able to rent a unit costing more than the FMR if it is willing to spend its own money to make up the difference. Thus if the FMR is $500 and the family's contribution is $300 (30 percent of $12,000 annual income), the family in the voucher and Housing Choice Voucher programs can rent an apartment costing $525 if it is willing to spend $25 of its own money; but it cannot rent the unit at all in the certificate program because the rent is above the FMR.

The basic difference in the subsidy formulas is that in the certificate program, the tenant's contribution toward the rent is fixed and the subsidy amount varies, while in the voucher program the reverse is true.[62] The Housing Choice Voucher uses the certificate model. In the certificate program, the FMR is the maximum subsidy as well as the maximum rent; the tenant pays 30 percent of income toward the rent, and the program pays the rest.[63] The tenant's payment is thus determined by the tenant's income and does not vary with the rent of the unit; if the unit rents for less than the FMR, the subsidy is lower. In the voucher program, the payment standard is the maximum subsidy, and the assistance payment is the difference between the payment standard and 30 percent of the tenant's income. The assistance payment is a fixed amount, regardless of the actual rent. The tenant's payment thus varies with the rent of the unit.

To understand the difference, assume an FMR of $1,000 and a household with monthly income of $2,000. In the certificate program, the tenant's payment toward the rent is $600, regardless of whether the unit rents for $601 or $1,000 (rents above $1,000 disqualify apartments for the certificate program). In the voucher program, the program assistance payment is $400 (the difference between the FMR or payment standard and 30 percent of the tenant's income); the tenant receives a voucher worth $400 whether the unit rents for $601, $1,000, or $1,500. The tenant's payment and the subsidy are the same in both programs only for units renting for the FMR.[64] For units renting for less, the tenant's payment is higher and the subsidy is lower in the certificate program; for units renting for more, the tenant can still rent the unit in the voucher program, at a higher cost to the tenant, but cannot rent the unit in the certificate program. As mentioned, with a Housing Choice Voucher, the tenant's payment is the same as with a certificate, and is thus higher than with a voucher for units renting for less than the FMR.

Another way of describing the difference is that in the voucher program, the family has a "shopping incentive," while in the certificate and Housing Choice Voucher programs, it does not. Under the voucher program, a family finding a unit renting for less than the FMR can keep all of the savings; it keeps none of the difference under the certificate program or the Housing Choice Voucher.

When the Housing Choice Voucher replaced both the certificate and voucher programs, both certificate and voucher holders received Housing Choice Vouchers instead. This would have meant that voucher holders renting units at less than the FMR incurred a reduction in assistance and a rent increase. Instead, these families were allowed to keep their existing subsidies without reduction, as long as they remained in the unit they were renting at the time of conversion to the Housing Choice Voucher.[65]

In other major respects the programs were essentially the same. At the time they were combined in the Housing Choice Voucher, about 1.1 million households were receiving certificates, and about 400,000 were receiving vouchers. As of 2009, the total number of vouchers distributed under the Housing Choice Voucher program was reported as 2.098 million.[66]

Although the subsidy formula is the same, certificates and vouchers are much less expensive than Section 8 New Construction. This is because the FMRs are different. The FMRs in the existing housing programs are calculated from the distribution of rents paid for decent existing rental housing by new tenants; they are about half as much for the certificate program as for the New Construction program. Subsidy costs per unit, net of the family's income, are also about half as high. As in the New Construction program, exceptions to local FMRs can be granted for a variety of purposes. The tenant-based programs have the same income limits as public housing and Section 8 New Construction.

The Section 811 "mainstream" vouchers, mentioned in the previous section, serve the same purpose of allowing lower-income disabled individuals to find privately owned housing of their own choice. The fact that Section 811, a small program to begin with, includes both projects and vouchers reflects a split among organizations representing the disabled in housing policy preferences.

The Experimental Housing Allowance Program. Experience with providing housing assistance through the existing stock antedates Section 8 by almost a decade. In 1965, PHAs were allowed to lease existing units from private landlords, with the federal government making the same subsidy payments as for new units. This was the Section 23 leased housing program. Then in 1968 the President's Committee on Urban Housing (the Kaiser Committee) recommended that HUD conduct an experiment to study the feasibility of making greater use of the existing stock to provide housing assistance, and in 1970 a housing allowance experiment was authorized. The Experimental Housing Allowance Program (EHAP) began in 1973 and concluded in 1979. It included 20,000 households in twelve different communities around the country. There were three components: (1) the Demand Experiment, testing different assistance formulas in two locations (Pittsburgh and Phoenix); (2) the Supply Experiment, giving assistance for up to ten years as an entitlement to every eligible family in two locations (Green Bay and South Bend);[67] and (3) the Administrative Agency Experiment, analyzing the costs and problems of using different administrative structures in eight locations, including two rural areas.

These experiments were underway but not near completion in late 1973, and Section 8 was proposed by President Nixon pending more information. In his message to Congress, he termed housing allowances "the most promising way to achieve decent housing for all of our families at an acceptable cost,"[68] and indicated that he expected to recommend a housing allowance program by early 1975. By that time, of course, he had resigned, EHAP was still continuing, and Section 8 itself was a new program just getting started (it was approved in August 1974), so President Ford did not present a new proposal for a housing allowance.

Vouchers and certificates are thus unique among housing programs. They were extensively analyzed on an experimental and demonstration basis before they became settled housing policy. Indeed, the voucher was not formally established as a regular program (as opposed to a demonstration) until 1987. Nonetheless, first certificates and then vouchers have been the preferred approach to providing incremental housing assistance for five of the six administrations between 1974 and 2008, the exception being the Carter administration. (The proposals of the Obama administration will be discussed later in this chapter.)

Project-Based Vouchers. The certificate program from its inception included an option for public housing authorities to attach 15 percent of their certificates to specific units, rather than offering them to households to find their own housing in the private market. As originally enacted, the subsidy was purely project based. Assistance was limited to projects that were newly constructed or rehabilitated. The PHA could enter into a contract with the owner for a period of two to five years, and the subsidy remained with the unit for that period. A household receiving a project-based voucher would lose it and receive no assistance if it moved out of the unit.

As part of the Housing Choice Voucher program, the project-based certificate was converted to a project-based voucher, with some changes. The term of contract with the owner could be up to ten years, but the household could move out after a year and would then receive a tenant-based voucher. The share of vouchers that could be project based was increased from 15 to 20 percent. To promote deconcentration of assisted households, no more than 25 percent of the units in a building could receive project-based vouchers. The requirement that a unit be newly built or rehabilitated to receive a project-based voucher was eliminated.[69]

As of 2008, about 26,000 units were being subsidized under the project-based voucher program. This is a little more than 1 percent of households receiving vouchers through the Housing Choice Vouchers program.[70]

Housing Block Grants: The HOME Program

In 1990 a completely different mechanism for providing housing subsidies was enacted, the culmination of almost twenty years of discussion and occasional proposals. This mechanism is a block grant for housing assistance. Federal funds are given to state and local governments on a formula basis with broad discretion as to how the money should be spent.[71] The logic behind a block grant is that decisions on housing assistance should be made at the local level, because housing markets are local markets and vary across the country, and because local preferences can be taken into account in developing programs. Its most important drawback is that housing assistance may not go to those who most need it. Housing subsidies are essentially income redistribution, and redistribution can be better handled on the federal level.

The new block grant, entitled HOME, was part of a political compromise between the Bush administration and the Democratic Congress. The administration wanted HUD secretary Jack Kemp's HOPE program (an acronym for Homeownership and Opportunity for People Everywhere) to let tenants buy public housing and privately owned projects; Congress wanted a low-income housing construction program in return.

HOME consolidated half a dozen small programs that provided subsidies for both rental housing and lower-income homeownership. One of these programs, Section 8 Moderate Rehabilitation, provided continuing subsidies for a period of years within the context of the Section 8 program; it had been created in 1978, and was terminated as a separate program in 1990 in the aftermath of the scandals involving favoritism in awarding contracts. The others provided subsidies to build, rehabilitate, or buy housing, but the subsidies did not continue during the subsequent life of the house or apartment project. These programs were the Rental Rehabilitation program, which provided grants by formula to state and local government to upgrade rental properties not receiving subsidies, in the hope that the rehabilitated properties would attract Section 8 certificate and voucher holders; the Housing Development Grant program, which supported construction and substantial rehabilitation of rental housing; Section 312, which provided acquisition and rehabilitation loans for both rental and owner-occupied properties; the Nehemiah program, which funded new construction of lower-income units intended for sale; and Urban Homesteading, which provided funds for selling federally owned homes at a discount, in distressed neighborhoods, to buyers who would rehabilitate and occupy them.[72]

As this list shows, the programs that were folded into HOME supported both homeownership and rental housing, and HOME itself was also expected to support both. The formula to allocate the funds, however, included four factors specifically concerned with the number and type of renters in a region, and two factors based on the number and income of poor people in a given area.[73] Thus more weight was given to the number and condition of rental units than to owner-occupied housing.

As passed in 1990, HOME required local governments to match the federal funds, and had different local matching requirements for different types of housing assistance. The highest local match of 50 percent was required for new construction; a 33 percent local match was required for substantial rehabilitation; and 25 percent matches were required for moderate rehabilitation and for programs similar to vouchers and certificates. In 1991, however, Congress reduced the amount of matching local funds for all programs to 25 percent.[74] There is still an implicit trade-off within the block grant funds, because each dollar spent on one kind of housing assistance cannot be spent on another kind. This forces local governments to make decisions based on the full costs of different types of assistance, although the choice may be conditioned by other programs or funding sources which change the relative cost of different programs as faced by the local government.[75]

The match can include cash or bond proceeds but can also consist of a wide variety of in-kind contributions: forgone taxes, land, infrastructure improvements, site preparation and construction materials, voluntary labor or sweat equity, supportive services to residents, or counseling.

HOME Program Activity. The first congressional appropriation for HOME was $1.5 billion in FY1992. Subsequent appropriations have varied between $1.2 and $2.0 billion, except for FY2009, when a supplemental appropriation of $2.25 billion was enacted as part of the American Recovery and Reinvestment Act, making the total for that year $4.071 billion. Through FY2009, total appropriations amounted to about $32 billion (about $38 billion in 2009 dollars), and about $24 billion (about $29 billion in 2009 dollars) had actually been spent.[76]

As mentioned, HOME funds can be used for either rental or owner-occupied housing. Slightly more than half have consistently been spent for rental housing. Through the end of 2008, the shares of cumulative spending have been 53 percent for rental development, 3 percent for tenant-based assistance, 27 percent for homeownership, and 17 percent for rehabilitation.[77] This pattern of distribution has been generally the same since the program was established.[78] Activity measured by household is very different, however, because the cost of tenant-based assistance is so much less than the other activities. Of the 1.16 million households receiving HOME funding, rental development and home purchase each account for about 33 percent (388,000 and 377,000 households, respectively), homeowner assistance for 16 percent (184,000), and tenant-based rental assistance for 19 percent (210,000). Tenant-based assistance costs about $3,000 per household, compared to about $8,000 for home purchase, and between $20,000 and $30,000 per unit in each of the other categories.[79]

In important respects, HOME is a successor to the terminated programs to build private projects, including Section 8 New Construction and its predecessors. HOME projects can receive FHA insurance; indeed, making FHA insurance available again for subsidized projects was one of the major attractions of HOME to its supporters. The record of past programs suggests that the projects subsidized under HOME will not be able to serve poor people without additional subsidies to bring the rents within their reach. The income limits in the program reflect this; all units must be occupied by families with incomes below 80 percent of the area median, and 90 percent of rental units must be occupied by families with incomes below 60 percent of the median. Unlike the older subsidized programs, HOME does not require that priority go to very low-income families (those with incomes below 50 percent of the median), but in fact most units, both project based and tenant based, are occupied by such families. Tenant-based assistance has gone primarily to extremely low-income households. As of 2002, after ten years of program activity, about 40 percent of rental development project units funded by HOME were occupied by extremely low-income households; another 40 percent by those with very low incomes (between 31 and 50 percent of the local median); and 15 percent by households with incomes between 50 and 60 percent of the local median. About 80 percent of tenant-based assistance has gone to extremely low-income households, and another 17 percent to those with very low incomes. Single-person households, which are most likely to be elderly, occupy half of the production units; most tenant-based assistance has gone to families.[80]

HOME differs from both project-based and tenant-based subsidy programs in that it establishes maximum rents for assisted units, but it does not directly provide any subsidy for households that cannot afford these rents. The program requires that all units have rents below the FMR for the Housing Choice Voucher, and there is a further requirement that 20 percent of units must have rents affordable for tenants with 30 percent to 50 percent of area median income; in other words, they must be within reach of very low-income renters. But this does not bring the units within reach of extremely low-income households unless the rents are still lower, or unless the households receive other subsidies, as a substantial minority do. As of 1998, 22 percent of HOME rental units were occupied by households receiving assistance through Housing Choice Vouchers; 10 percent were receiving Section 8 project-based assistance; and 8 percent were receiving other subsidies. These households experienced lower rent burdens than unassisted households, but the average rent burden was high for both groups. Extremely low-income households receiving subsidies still paid 40 percent of their income for rent; those not receiving subsidies paid 69 percent. The average rent burden for all extremely low-income households was 53 percent of their income. For households with incomes between 30 percent and 50 percent of the median, the average burden was 34 percent. Over two-thirds of these households had a rent burden above 30 percent of their income.[81]

The past record of new construction and substantial rehabilitation programs in subsidizing very low-income households suggests strongly that the upfront subsidies to the owners are not likely to be enough to maintain the housing in decent condition. The monthly income-related subsidies will help to maintain the projects, but nonetheless state and local governments may in a few years be asking the federal government for a new version of operating subsidies or Flexible Subsidy to support the projects on an ongoing basis; and for those projects with FHA insurance, HUD may then be confronting the risk of defaults similar to those it has experienced under Section 221(d)(3)BMIR and Section 236.

Earlier Interest in Housing Block Grants. A housing block grant was first proposed in 1973 by congressional Democrats with responsibility for housing policy; it was meant as a replacement for the suspended subsidy programs, but the idea was ultimately rejected by President Nixon in favor of Section 8.[82] Three years later the block grant was proposed by President Ford as a replacement for Section 8, but it was rejected by the incoming Carter administration. In 1981 President Reagan expressed support for the concept of a housing block grant, but ultimately decided in favor of the voucher program. Thus there has been bipartisan political support for a housing block grant, but until 1990, block grants could not get the support of both the executive and legislative branches at the same time.

A major problem with the block grant concept until 1985 was that housing production programs were funded by twenty- to forty-year commitments to pay principal and interest on long-term bonds or mortgages, while the certificate program was then funded by five-year commitments, and could in principle have been funded one year at a time (as it in fact has been in recent years). Block grant funding is typically annual; it is discretionary in the federal budget. It could be used to support construction of privately owned projects only if these projects were paid for in full as they were built. This problem was removed in 1985 when the federal government shifted to paying the cost of public housing at the time of construction, but in the 1970s and early 1980s bond and mortgage finance was much preferred by policymakers: paying the cost upfront seemed prohibitive and limited the number of units that could be built with each year's appropriation, while tenant rental assistance needed to be funded only one year at a time, so more families could be helped with a given year's appropriation.[83]

The Low-Income Housing Tax Credit

The Low-Income Housing Tax Credit, like the HOME block grant, also gives federal resources to lower levels of government, but only to state governments and only for a specific form of assistance. Since it was enacted as part of the Tax Reform Act of 1986, it has become the largest active lower-income housing assistance program.[84]

The Tax Reform Act of 1986 reduced individual and corporate tax rates and eliminated most tax shelters, including accelerated depreciation and other benefits for low-income rental housing projects. The LIHTC was intended as a replacement for these provisions. It operates as much like a housing subsidy program as possible within the tax code.[85] For qualifying housing projects, investors are allowed a tax credit annually for ten years; the present value of the stream of benefits is expected to be either 30 percent or 70 percent of project costs, depending on whether the project is federally subsidized or not.[86] Both construction and rehabilitation are eligible for the credit.

The right to allocate tax credits to housing projects is given to the states. Each state receives an annual credit allocation amount on a per capita basis. Originally the annual credit allocation was $1.25 for each resident of the state ($12.50 over ten years), and the total credit allocated per year was $3 billion. In 2001 the credit amount was increased by statute to $1.50 per capita for 2001, $1.75 for 2002, and then adjusted for inflation beginning in 2003; a further increase of 20 cents per capita was enacted in 2008. The total credit per year was over $7 billion as of 2009. These credits are applicable over the first ten years of the project, so the present value of the $3 billion or $7 billion is substantially less.

An eligible LIHTC project must have 40 percent of its units occupied by families with incomes below 60 percent of the area median, or alternatively 20 percent occupied by families with incomes below 50 percent of median (the income limit for public housing, vouchers, and certificates). Project developers have annually elected the 60 percent criterion for over 90 percent of units, but in practice nearly all projects serve low-income households almost exclusively.[87]

Projects must make a commitment to remain in low-income use for thirty years (originally fifteen) to be eligible for the credit. An individual investor can claim a maximum credit of $7,000 per year, which is equivalent to between $17,000 and $25,000 in deductions, depending on the investor's marginal tax rate.

In 1989 Congress changed the law to provide more generous credits for housing located in low-income areas (known as Qualified Census Tracts) or metropolitan areas with high housing costs relative to income (Difficult to Develop Areas). The amount of the per-unit credit is increased by 30 percent in these locations.

Scope of the Tax Credit. The LIHTC is a large program. Between 1987 and 2009, over 33,000 projects, involving a total of close to 2 million units, received tax credits. About 1.75 million, over 90 percent, qualify as low-income. Annual average activity has been about 1,450 projects with 85,000 units.[88]

The LIHTC can be and has been combined with a wide variety of other housing subsidies. It can be yet another form of subsidy with Section 236 and Section 221(d)(3) projects needing rehabilitation; some of these projects also receive Section 8 project-based assistance. It has been used with HOPE VI. A detailed analysis of a sample of projects placed in service between 1992 and 1994 found that 31 percent of tax credit residents were in units receiving Section 8 project-based assistance.[89] The LIHTC database, however, indicates that only about 5 percent of LIHTC units have received project-based assistance from HUD. It can also be used in conjunction with the housing programs of the Department of Agriculture. About 125,000 units, about 6 percent of the total, have been financed through the Rural Housing Service's Section 515 program to subsidize the production of rental housing. Over 500,000 units have received tax-exempt bond financing through the state governments which allocate the credit. This is over a quarter of all tax credit units and about 30 percent of the low-income units. About 100,000 low-income units have received HOME funds as well as the tax credit, and about 25,000 have received both CDBG funds and tax credits. The tax credit can also be used with tenant-based assistance. The most recent analysis uses two techniques to estimate the number of tax credit units occupied by households with vouchers; one method yields an estimate of 140,000 and the other 280,000.[90] The difference is certainly large, but either number is larger than any reported combination of the tax credit with other subsidies, except for state-issued tax exempt bonds.

Most vouchers are tenant based, so there is no guarantee that any given project will have households with vouchers. Projects therefore cannot be underwritten on the assumption that vouchers will provide some or all of the project's rental income. By contrast, projects can be underwritten on the basis of commitments for Section 515 or HOME funding, or other project-based subsidies. However, state allocating authorities often favor projects that are intended for very low-income renters, and such projects, if awarded tax credits, have incentives to appeal to households with vouchers.[91]

Differences from Other Subsidy Programs. Offsetting the flexibility of the LIHTC are some complications which arise because it differs from other subsidy programs in important ways.

The tax credit does not cover the full cost of the project. It is therefore necessary for a developer to combine the tax credit with other sources of funding. These include first mortgages from private lenders or state or local government agencies; other loans, beyond the first mortgage, from state or local government agencies, nonprofit organizations, or private lenders (termed "gap financing"); and in some cases grants. Both first mortgages and gap financing may carry below-market interest rates, down to and including zero percent. These loans help to hold down the cost of the project, but the need to find additional financing takes time and resources.

In addition, the developer does not use the tax credit to reduce his or her own taxes, but instead sells the tax credit to an investor, who uses it to reduce tax liability over the next ten years. The proceeds from the sale become part of the funds for the project. In a Section 8 or Section 236 project, the subsidy commitment is given to the developer in the expectation that the developer will be the direct beneficiary for the term of the commitment; with the tax credit, neither the federal nor the state government has any particular interest in who ultimately uses the credit. The process by which tax credits for future years are converted into funds that can be used now to develop a project is called "syndication." Among other activities, syndicators pool several projects into a single fund, protecting investors from the risk of loss on particular projects.

Thus there is a market for tax credits, as there is not for subsidy contracts or FHA mortgage commitments. The market price has varied. The earliest tax credit projects received less than fifty cents on the dollar; by 1995, the yield was about fifty-five cents.[92] Proceeds have increased since then, to about eighty cents as of 2001, and to a dollar by 2006.[93] In 2007, however, the market demand for tax credits began to decline, and the decline accelerated sharply in 2008. Corporations buy most tax credits, because the "passive loss" limitations in the federal income tax law generally prohibit individuals from using the credit to offset tax liability. The economic downturn in 2008 reduced corporate profits, and thus the value of tax credits. In particular, Fannie Mae and Freddie Mac, substantial buyers of tax credits, found that credits were not useful, as they incurred large and unexpected losses beginning in late 2007. Indeed, the two government-sponsored enterprises (GSEs) wrote off substantial amounts of tax credits in 2008—$21.4 billion in the case of Fannie Mae, and $22.6 billion in the case of Freddie Mac—which contributed to their reported losses; as of the end of that year, their holdings of unused tax credits amounted to only $6.3 and $10.5 billion, respectively, and they were no longer active buyers.[94] In this situation, developers found themselves unable to sell tax credits for the amounts they had anticipated, and therefore unable to develop their projects.[95]

The American Recovery and Reinvestment Act of 2009 allows states to turn in part of their 2008 and 2009 LIHTC allocations to the Treasury Department, in exchange for cash, at the rate of 85 cents per dollar of tax credit, and then use the cash to finance previously approved projects. The act also includes an appropriation of $2.25 billion in additional HOME funds to provide gap financing for tax credit projects. While these measures may result in development of the projects affected by the economic downturn and the GSEs' financial problems, they certainly add to the overall cost of the projects and the program.

The Housing Trust Fund

The newest low-income housing program is the Housing Trust Fund. First introduced in Congress in 2000, it was enacted in 2008, as Section 1131 of the Housing and Economic Recovery Act to address the mortgage and financial problems that became acute that summer.[96]

The National Low Income Housing Coalition (NLIHC), which has been a vigorous advocate of the trust fund, describes it as "the first new federal housing production program since the HOME program was created in 1990 and the first new production program specifically targeted to extremely low-income households since the Section 8 program was created in 1974." According to the NLIHC, the trust fund's goal is to produce or preserve 1.5 million units of low-income housing over ten years. This would be a large program.

Conceptually, the trust fund is a grant program to states for the purpose of producing lower-income rental housing. It is thus similar to the HOME block grant but has a narrower focus: whereas HOME funds can be spent for tenant-based assistance and for homeownership, the trust fund is specifically for the production of new housing, and the preservation and rehabilitation of existing housing that is affordable to lower-income households.[97]

The trust fund differs from HOME further in that it is a categorical program: states choose which projects to fund, and must report to HUD on their activities in more detail than they provide on HOME.

The trust's unique feature—at least as envisioned by advocates—is the funding source. Rather than being funded by annual appropriations, it is meant to have a dedicated source of revenue, similar to the federal gasoline tax that provides resources for the highway trust fund. Advocates have also sought a revenue source that is off budget: in the language of the federal budget process, the trust fund would not "score."

Precisely what this dedicated, off-budget revenue source would be has proved problematic. In 1999, Senator John Kerry (D–MA) called for funding the trust by using the reserves of the Federal Housing Administration's Mutual Mortgage Insurance Fund (MMIF), which consists of home mortgage insurance premiums from FHA's basic homeownership program, Section 203(b) of the National Housing Act. By 2004, the MMIF's net worth was more than two and a half times the statutory minimum ratio of 2 percent of mortgage insurance in force (5.5 percent).[98] Yet this funding source posed several problems. First, FHA is part of the federal government, and the reserves of the MMIF are part of the federal budget. An increase in reserves counts as a negative outlay (an offsetting receipt). Correspondingly a reduction in reserves, including a withdrawal for other purposes, counts as an outlay, or "scores"; it is not free money.[99] Second, the reserves are just that—reserves, to be drawn on should FHA defaults exceed expectations and the cost of insurance claims exceed the premium income, as happened following Hurricane Katrina and during the mortgage market problems that began in 2007. FHA's reserves were in fact reduced almost by half between 2004 and the end of FY 2008, to a net worth of 3.0 percent.[100]

A third problem with this funding source is perhaps most fundamental; it would provide subsidized rental housing by raising the cost of homeownership for young middle-income families. Section 203(b) is the federal government's primary program for promoting homeownership, which is a public policy goal that has as long a history as the goal of decent housing for everyone. Homebuyers who use FHA loans are typically young families with limited resources buying their first home. Between 1996 and 2004, between 30 and 40 percent of these FHA loan recipients were members of minority groups.[101] It is dubious public policy to tax these middle-income families through unnecessarily high mortgage insurance premiums in order to subsidize rental housing construction for lower-income families already decently housed. (In the year 2000, the typical FHA homebuyer had a median income of $49,000, slightly below the overall family median income of $51,000.) The Housing Trust Fund would fund one public purpose at the expense of another—providing subsidized rental housing by raising the cost of homeownership for young families trying to buy their first home.

More recently, supporters of the trust looked to the housing GSEs, Fannie Mae and Freddie Mac, as a funding source. Language to create the trust and fund it from GSE profits was attached to a GSE reform bill (S. 1508) in 2004, but the bill was not considered by the Senate. As enacted in 2008, the trust is to be funded by a charge levied against the mortgage purchases by the GSEs, rather than profits, at a rate of 4.2 basis points (0.042 percent of purchases). Allocation to the fund would have been $556 million out of the GSEs' business in 2007, the most recent year for which data were available when the fund was created. At the national average development cost for new public housing units in 2008 ($169,000), this would have funded about 3,500 units.

At that time, the GSEs' activities were not part of the federal budget, so the Housing Trust Fund would not have appeared in the federal budget. Within six weeks of passage, however, the GSEs had been placed in conservatorship, and their rapidly rising losses were being paid by the U.S. Treasury Department. The conservator suspended payments into the trust fund (before any had been made) for an indefinite term, as permitted under the statute. This left the housing trust fund with no source of revenue. Some initial funding—$1 billion—was called for in President Obama's proposed 2010 budget, released in February 2009, but no source was specified, and Congress did not approve any funds.[102] The proposal was repeated in the president's 2011 and 2012 proposals, again without specifying a source; again Congress did not approve funds. Since 2009, several bills have been introduced in Congress that would allocate $1 billion from the Troubled Asset Relief Program (TARP), in one way or another: as a direct allocation of TARP funds, from the repayment of TARP funds, or from the sale of warrants acquired by the federal government under TARP. The most recent such legislation has 14 Senate sponsors.[103]

Funding through TARP would be quite different from the funding sources originally envisioned. Funds would be appropriated only for the current year; future funding would have to be appropriated in future years, probably from different sources.[104] Unless a dedicated funding source is established, the most important feature of the trust does not come into play, and the program would be subject to appropriation by Congress each year—like Section 8 New Construction, HOME, or any other housing subsidy program. Also, like those programs, the trust could be terminated by Congress, just as Congress has terminated the earlier programs to build privately owned projects for lower-income families. Indeed, legislation has been introduced in the House of Representatives that would repeal the trust fund.[105]

The trust does have the merit of being targeted toward the poor. All of the funds for rental housing must serve very low-income households (those with incomes below 50 percent of area median), and 75 percent of the funds must serve extremely-low-income households (incomes below 30 percent of median, approximating to households in poverty). This is better targeting than the LIHTC, HOME, or the earlier production programs.

The trust has a faulty fund allocation formula, however. The legislation specifies that funds should be allocated to states with relative shortages of lower-rent housing, and with high construction costs. Thus, rather than distributing funds in proportion to a state's total population or poor population, the trust would be targeted to states with tight housing markets and relatively expensive housing, which are concentrated on the coasts. Under a proposed formula developed by HUD, California, with about 12 percent of the population, would receive about 17 percent of the trust funds; New York, with between 6 and 7 percent, would receive about 12 percent. Smaller states such as Massachusetts and New Jersey, and also the District of Columbia, would be similarly favored. On the other hand, Texas, with 8 percent of the population, would receive less than 6 percent of the funds; most of the other southern states, and several of the larger states in the Midwest, such as Michigan and Indiana, would also have smaller shares than their share of the population.[106]

The favored states with tight markets are also states with substantial regulatory barriers to affordable housing.[107] They have chosen to have expensive housing, and funding from the trust would reinforce their choice.

It would also run counter to efforts by HUD secretaries of both parties, dating back to Patricia Roberts Harris in the Carter administration, to cajole or coerce local governments to reduce their barriers. If the Housing Trust Fund offers more money to states where local jurisdictions have erected barriers, and less to states where local jurisdictions have not, there is no incentive for states and localities to lift them.

What's Wrong with the Programs?

Although several housing programs have been terminated, there are still five major HUD programs that provide low-income housing subsidies, offering essentially the same services to more or less the same clientele, with the Housing Trust Fund perhaps to become the sixth, if it is funded. Why are there so many? Part of the answer is that none of the programs has been considered satisfactory by policymakers and interested groups—all appear to have flaws, at least in the eyes of some of those concerned with housing policy. The perceived flaws in each program stimulate efforts to develop programs without those flaws, and the new programs are in turn perceived to have flaws of their own.

The problems commonly cited with the three oldest major HUD program categories are briefly considered here.

Public Housing. The most fundamental problem with public housing is that it has not worked, in the sense that it has not achieved its original objectives. Living in public housing has not solved the economic and social problems of the poor, contrary to what the early urban reformers had anticipated. Indeed, it can plausibly be argued that the concentration of poor families in large projects has exacerbated these problems, and as Jane Jacobs said fifty years ago, public housing projects have often provided worse living environments than the slums they replaced.[108] No one now claims that public housing is an effective "war on poverty" by itself, and it may seem quaint to hearken back to the claims of its original advocates, but public housing's failure in this regard is the most basic reason why housing policy and programs have changed so frequently. Had it worked as intended, there would not have been the continuing search for alternatives.

It is not coincidental that criticism of public housing was growing in the years immediately before the creation of Section 221(d)(3)(BMIR), the first program of privately owned subsidized projects.[109]

Second is the fact that some projects do not achieve even the more limited objective of providing decent housing. In many of the largest cities there are large projects which are locally notorious as terrible places to live.[110] Concomitantly, some PHAs, notably those in the largest cities, do not manage their housing well. (New York City is the major exception.) About 175 public housing authorities were officially classified as "troubled" by HUD as of April 2009, and 61 have been cited by HUD at least three times since 2004 for mishandling government funds.[111] Of the troubled PHAs, 172 received stimulus funds from the American Recovery and Reinvestment Act. Troubled PHAs were relatively slow to obligate these funds.[112] Five have been identified as lacking the capacity to manage the funds.[113] Some are incompetent; a few are corrupt. In 1995, HUD took over the Chicago PHA because of its management problems; in the early 1990s, there were scandals in Philadelphia and Passaic.[114]

Public housing generally can be faulted for location and design. Projects are often located in low-income and minority neighborhoods, thus increasing residential segregation and the concentration of poverty. Their design, particularly in high-rise projects, facilitates vandalism and crime.[115]

Finally, the cost of public housing is high and rising.[116] As the projects age, their modernization and repair needs increase. Modernization in particular sometimes seems to be a bottomless pit; expenditures have been increasing for years, but modernization needs seem to be increasing faster. At the same time, public housing is criticized for being "Spartan" and "shoddy."[117]

Privately Owned Projects. The problems in public housing became apparent over a twenty-year period. In contrast, the problems of privately owned projects became apparent in just a few years, so that each program was terminated in less than a decade. The major reason for terminating programs was cost. Each was quickly seen as costing more than Congresses and administrations of both parties were willing to pay. Section 8 was particularly expensive, with costs well above those of unsubsidized private rental housing,[118] and Section 221(d)(3)(BMIR) and

Section 236 were plagued by defaults within just a few years, in spite of their high costs.[119]

There has also been concern about the equity of all of these programs. They provide large subsidies for some families who are not poor, while many poor families receive no housing assistance at all. Inequity was considered particularly objectionable in the older programs, but Section 8 was also criticized, at least initially, for serving primarily white elderly households in suburban areas.[120] There have also been management concerns; private owners have a diminishing financial incentive to manage the properties in the interests of providing decent housing, while nonprofit owners often lack the capacity to manage properties and have experienced a disproportionate share of the defaults.[121]

Tenant-Based Assistance. The most basic concern about tenant-based housing assistance is that certificates and vouchers do not result in better housing for their recipients. This is claimed to be true not just for some recipients, as in the case of the worst public housing and privately owned projects, but for most. An important corollary, which has been widely asserted since the first housing allowance experiments, is that tenant-based assistance merely drives up rents, particularly for those who receive subsidies, but also for other low-income households that are not receiving any assistance.[122]

Other concerns about the housing market effects of tenant-based assistance have been raised. In recent years, critics have maintained that vouchers do not work in tight markets. This usually refers to markets with low vacancy rates, where voucher recipients are thought to have difficulty finding acceptable housing costing no more than the local FMR.[123]

Finally, there are two opposite concerns about the ability of minority households to use tenant-based assistance. The first is that they will be unable to find private rental housing because of discrimination in the market.[124] The second is that they will be all too successful in finding private housing, and in moving from inner-city minority to suburban white communities, they will destabilize neighborhoods and create new concentrations of the poor.[125] Criticisms of the cost of tenant-based assistance have not been common, but they have been raised in the past, and the programs have complicated the budget process of the federal government.

Conclusion

These concerns are not all consistent with each other and cannot all be true at once; clearly there is considerable confusion and disagreement about the facts. Moreover, the various problems carry different weight in the opinions of different individuals and groups. Thus even if there were agreement about the facts concerning each program—its accomplishments and its problems—there would still be room for disagreement about the programs' relative merits. But it is certainly worth trying to identify and limit factual disagreements. Housing policy discussions are much simplified if the participants are operating on the basis of the same, accurate, information.

Along with controversies over program outcomes, there have been controversies about the magnitude of the financial resources devoted to housing assistance. The next chapter therefore revisits the history of housing policy from a quantitative perspective (involving budgets and housing units). It addresses some areas of disagreement about the facts of housing policy and seeks to establish what is known for sure about the various programs. The subsequent five chapters examine the evidence about the effectiveness of the various programs in several respects: how well they provide decent housing, where the housing is located, how it affects the neighborhood in which it is located, and how the cost of the housing compares in the different programs.

Indeed, much of the remainder of this book constitutes an effort to examine to what extent concerns about each program have a factual basis; the findings thus provide a foundation for policy recommendations. The focus is largely on the older major housing programs, because there has been little analysis of the two newest programs, LIHTC and HOME. However, it is important to put these relatively new programs in historical perspective and to suggest that the subsidies in the LIHTC and the HOME block grant are a throwback to the earliest versions of public housing and Section 221(d)(3)BMIR. That is, both the LIHTC and HOME provide subsidies to build or rehabilitate housing, but not subsidies for ongoing operations and maintenance. Like public housing as it was originally enacted, the LIHTC and HOME do not produce housing that is within reach of the poorest families and individuals in America.[126] In the case of the LIHTC, as noted above, further subsidies are already being provided so that poor families can afford to live in some of these projects. From a housing policy standpoint, the return to the earlier subsidy mechanism is ominous, since each of the major subsidized production programs has eventually needed additional subsidies—usually multiple additional subsidies—for operations, maintenance, and rehabilitation.

Makers of housing policy would do well to keep this history in mind; the problems in some of the older programs may foreshadow problems still to come in the newer programs.

4

Program Activity and Costs in the Aggregate

This chapter brings together information on all of the programs to provide an overall picture of assisted housing, in terms of both the number of households and housing units receiving subsidies, and the total cost of housing assistance. It describes the budgetary treatment of housing programs, and then uses aggregate budget and program data going back to the mid-1970s, and in some cases back to the 1940s, to trace trends in federal spending on subsidized housing and trends in the number of households receiving assistance.

These data are of more than just historical interest. They help to resolve one of the most commonly debated issues in housing policy: whether the overall budget for housing assistance is increasing or decreasing. This question has been raised virtually every year since the early 1980s, especially when the federal budget is published. A closely related question is whether the number of households receiving assistance is rising or falling. The chapter concludes that expenditures on housing assistance have been steadily increasing over the last three decades, and that the number of assisted households was growing until quite recently. But it is also true that commitments to subsidize additional households, beyond those already receiving assistance, reached a peak around 1980, and for that reason program advocates sometimes speak of a decline in the federal government's support for assisted housing, even though the number of assisted households has continued to grow.

Budgetary Cost Concepts and Basic Financing Practices

HUD's budget is complicated and trends are hard to measure, both because of policy changes (as the government has shifted from project-based to tenant-based programs) and because of changes in the budgetary treatment

101

of individual programs. It is therefore necessary to begin by defining the basic concepts used in federal budgeting. Budget authority is the authorization by Congress for the federal government to purchase some commodity or pay for some service; it establishes the maximum amount that an agency can spend on a particular program or other activity over a period of years. The maximum amount that HUD agrees to pay each year under its contractual commitment to subsidize a housing unit is known as "contract authority"; this concept mattered particularly for public housing and other subsidized projects which were financed by tax-exempt bonds or subsidized mortgages. Outlays are the actual expenditures made by the government in a given year. Both budget authority and outlays are routinely reported in the federal budget and other budget documents— usually in adjacent rows or columns as "BA" and "O" for each item in the budget—and congressional appropriations are measured in both ways.

Budget authority must be enacted before an expenditure can be made. The expenditure can occur in a different year from the budget authorization. This gap is quite common for government purchases of defense equipment or for public works, which can take a long time to build. The distinction between budget authority and outlays is important in assisted housing as well, for several reasons involving both the time lag and the conceptual difference between the two terms. Historically, the construction of subsidized housing projects was financed in the same way as private housing, with long-term bonds or mortgages—bonds in the case of public housing, mortgages for the privately owned projects. Thus when Congress approved construction of a unit in a particular year's appropriation bill, it had to authorize HUD to pay the full cost that the government would incur, including the payment of principal and interest on the bonds or the mortgages for their full term—between twenty and forty years, depending on the program. The budget authority was therefore large relative to the cost of developing the unit. In public housing, for instance, where forty-year tax-exempt bond financing was used, the total amount spent by the federal government on a particular project over the forty years would be double the development cost or more, depending on the interest rate. In Section 8 New Construction, interest rates were higher, because the interest on the mortgage was taxable to the lender; in these cases budget authority might be triple the development cost.[1]

This financing practice was changed in 1985 when the government began to pay cash for the development cost of public housing construction. (Section 8 New Construction had been terminated in 1983.) The budget authority for the unit was thus much smaller. At the same time, however, the outlay for the unit was much larger during the years that it was built. For example, the development cost of a new public housing unit was reported as $83,340 for 1995 in the FY1997 HUD budget.[2] This is the budget authority. Outlays for public housing construction were generally very small in the year the unit was authorized and then were about one-third of the total development cost for each of the next three years as the unit was built: as an approximation, perhaps $3,000 in 1995 and $27,000 in each of the next three years. Under the pre-1985 financing system, the budget authority would have been about $193,000, assuming a 5 percent interest rate on a forty-year bond, and the annual outlay would have been about $4,800; assuming a 3 percent interest rate, the budget authority would have been about $143,000, and the annual outlays about $3,600.[3]

There have been several major changes in budget authority accounting for individual housing programs, and these affect the overall amount authorized for housing assistance:

(1) The most important change is the shift in FY1985 from financing public housing with forty-year bonds to paying the cost of development in cash when the project is built. This shift also entailed paying the cost of projects authorized since 1974, which had been financed by rolling over one-year borrowings while waiting for interest rates to come down, as discussed in chapter 3.

(2) A parallel shift occurred in FY1987, when payment for public housing modernization began to be made in cash rather than in twenty-year bonds.

(3) The term of subsidy commitment has been shortened in tenant-based assistance programs. Originally, when the certificate program was enacted, subsidy commitments were made to each household for a term of fifteen years. Subsequently the term was shortened to five years, then to three years, then to

two years, and finally in 1997 to one year as successive Congresses wrestled with the need for additional budget authority to renew long-standing commitments that were expiring.

(4) In 1996, the budget authority for tenant-based assistance ceased to be calculated on the assumption that the recipient made no payment toward the rent—in effect, that he or she had no income. This calculation had been used because it was necessary to authorize the maximum amount that the government might have to spend over the life of the commitment, and that maximum is determined by the Fair Market Rent in the case of a household with no income. In reality, subsidy recipients typically pay about 30 percent of the rent from their own income, so the federal outlay is about 70 percent of the authorized amount.[4] In this respect, budget practices for existing housing differed from those for public housing operating subsidies, which are authorized as the difference between projected operating costs and expected rent payments by tenants.

(5) Between 1975 and 1991, Section 202 was financed with direct federal government loans for construction, coupled with twenty-year commitments of Section 8 rental assistance to pay the loan. Since 1991, Section 202 has been financed with grants to pay the construction costs, and shorter (and smaller) Project Rental Assistance Contracts, which are analogous to operating subsidies in public housing, to pay the amount of operating costs that exceed the tenant's rent payment.[5]

How Much and How Many? Dollars and Housing Units

With an understanding of the various budget concepts and the changes in accounting practices, it is possible to describe and reach some conclusions about the trends in federal government expenditures on housing.

Budget Authority. Table 4-1 reports budget authority for housing assistance provided by HUD annually since 1977, adjusted for inflation. The table covers the years between 1977 and 2010 because the former is the

TABLE 4-1
BUDGET AUTHORITY FOR LOW-INCOME HOUSING, 1977–2010

	(Millions of 2010 Dollars)		
Year	HUD Programs	LIHTC	Combined
1977	105,892	--	105,892
1978	110,287	--	110,287
1979	76,340	--	76,340
1980	75,739	--	75,739
1981	66,166	--	66,166
1982	34,308	--	34,308
1983	23,831	--	23,831
1984	28,607	--	28,607
1985	54,576	--	54,576
1986	24,042	--	24,042
1987	19,960	6,009	25,969
1988	18,857	5,743	24,600
1989	16,972	5,528	22,500
1990	18,651	5,302	23,953
1991	31,060	5,034	36,094
1992	29,356	4,969	34,325
1993	30,402	4,880	35,282
1994	29,808	4,810	34,618
1995	19,176	4,721	23,897
1996	20,586	4,587	25,173
1997	13,448	4,563	18,011
1998	20,864	4,534	25,398
1999	23,790	4,487	28,277
2000	19,931	4,380	24,311
2001	27,194	5,403	32,597
2002	28,566	6,229	34,795
2003	30,861	6,167	37,028
2004	30,122	6,226	36,348
2005	29,359	6,248	35,607
2006	30,610	7,301	37,911
2007	31,938	7,431	39,369
2008	31,747	6,891	38,638
2009	43,658	7,286	50,944
2010	36,849	NA	NA

SOURCES: HUD programs—Office of Management and Budget, "Budget Authority," in Public Budget Database, Budget of the United States Government, Fiscal Year 2012, http://www.whitehouse.gov/sites/default/files/omb/budget/fy2012/assets/outlays.xls, as reported in the appendix to this chapter. LIHTC—National Council of State Housing Agencies, "Housing Credit Utilization Charts," http://www.ncsha.org/resource/housing-credit-utilization-charts.
NOTE: NA = not available.

first fiscal year on the October-to-September calendar, and the latter is the most recent year for which the actual appropriation has been published as part of the president's budget.[6] Several of the changes in budget authority accounting mentioned above are manifest in the table.

As table 4-1 shows, budget authority for assisted housing was cut sharply between 1977 and 1980. In 1977 and 1978, budget authority was over $100 billion annually (measured in 2010 dollars); by 1980 it was about $75 billion. Even steeper cuts followed in the early 1980s; by 1983, budget authority was less than $25 billion. For the next twenty years, with the exception of 1985, it fluctuated between $15 billion and $30 billion. The low was $13.4 billion in 1997, and the high was $31.1 billion in 1991. Beginning in 2003, it was about $30 billion annually, until a sharp increase in 2009. The decline of more than 75 percent between 1977 and 1983 partly reflects a policy shift from building subsidized housing projects in the public housing and Section 8 programs to providing rental assistance in the form of housing certificates so families could live in existing housing of their own choice. The term of the budget authority was forty years for the production programs and only fifteen years for the certificates; in addition, the annual per-unit cost was lower for the certificate, an important point to which the chapter will return.

The 1985 spike to over $54 billion reflects the policy decision to pay the full cost of building public housing projects that had been authorized between 1974 and 1984. The 1991–1994 levels reflect multiple-year renewals of expiring Section 8 contracts from the early years of the program; for the renewal, the term was shortened from fifteen years for the original contract to five years, thus reducing the required budget authority in a given year by two-thirds. The increase after 2000 reflects authorization of additional vouchers through Housing Choice Vouchers in the first two years, and then contract renewals in the Section 8 and voucher programs.

Table 4-1 also reports "budget authority" for the LIHTC. This is listed separately because it is not part of the HUD budget, and more fundamentally because it is not an appropriation. The tax credit does not appear in the federal budget except as a "tax expenditure," and the amount so reported is less than the amount of the credit.[7] The data in table 4-1 are the amounts allocated each year to the states, as authorized by the legislation. The credit was fixed in nominal dollars during the 1990s; in 2000 it was increased and indexed for inflation, effective in 2003. From 2001 to 2008, it represented about 15 to 20 percent of the annual appropriation for housing assistance, and total federal resources fluctuated between $30 billion and $40 billion, consistently higher than in nearly every year since 1985. The increase in 2009 primarily reflects the stimulus legislation; increases in public housing modernization and the HOME block grant, which were reversed in 2010.

Incremental Assistance: The Number of Additional Subsidized Units. As this discussion implies, historically the most important use of budget authority has been to provide funding for additional units of assisted housing, beyond the number already being funded from budget authority enacted in past years; the incremental units require additional resources. Table 4-2 reports the number of incremental units authorized in the HUD budget for each year between 1977 and 2009. As with budget authority, there was a sharp decline from 1977 to 1980, from 367,000 units annually to 173,000 units, followed by a further and sharper decline to 54,000 in 1983. This is a 53 percent reduction in the first three years, and a further reduction of 69 percent in the next three.

The table also separates incremental units into those that are new construction or substantial rehabilitation (essentially, those receiving project-based assistance) and those that provide subsidies for families to live in existing housing (tenant-based). Between 1977 and 1980 the number of incremental new construction units was cut by 43 percent; over the next three years new construction was cut to zero. Section 8 New Construction was terminated in 1983 and the statutory authority repealed. The approximately 20,000 incremental new units in 1983 and succeeding years consisted mainly of some new public housing and the Section 202 and 811 programs. During the three-year period between 1977 and 1980, the number of incremental existing units was cut by 69 percent. The number of incremental certificates rebounded from a low point of 22,000 in 1982. With the creation of the voucher, the number of incremental exist units rose to 75,000 by 1985 and remained above 40,000 annually until 1995.

As table 4-2 shows, the sharp reductions began in FY1980, the last full year of the Carter administration; this was also the first year when the president's budget included the full cost of Section 8 New Construction and housing certificates on a comparable basis. The further reductions in

TABLE 4-2

INCREMENTAL SUBSIDIZED HOUSING UNITS, 1977–2010

Year	In New HUD Projects	HOPE VI	Total in New HUD	Tenant-Based	Total HUD Assisted	% New
1977	226,832		226,832	140,480	367,312	62
1978	190,584		190,584	98,300	288,884	66
1979	200,406		200,406	86,653	287,059	70
1980	129,490		129,490	43,116	172,606	75
1981	110,231		110,231	53,947	164,178	67
1982	39,109		39,109	21,908	61,017	64
1983	17,906		17,906	36,147	54,053	33
1984	22,251		22,251	67,939	90,190	25
1985	20,265		20,265	74,877	95,142	21
1986	17,586		17,586	66,110	83,696	21
1987	22,351		22,351	57,859	80,210	28
1988	21,919		21,919	55,155	77,074	28
1989	15,897		15,897	66,287	82,184	19
1990	9,251		9,251	52,454	61,705	15
1991	14,124		14,124	43,712	57,836	24
1992	23,537		23,537	48,398	71,935	33
1993	23,586	4,871	28,457	42,276	70,733	40
1994	19,946	4,843	24,789	47,306	72,095	34
1995	16,587	5,360	21,947	29,833	51,780	42
1996	1,438	4,637	6,075	27,128	33,203	18
1997	12,449	3,699	16,148	9,229	25,377	64
1998	17,675	5,890	23,565	18,376	41,941	56
1999	11,060	3,406	14,466	16,225	30,691	47
2000	9,556	3,800	13,356	121,951	135,307	10
2001	7,611	4,631	12,242	85,720	97,962	12
2002	8,689	3,705	12,394	25,900	38,294	32
2003	7,464	3,500	10,964	19,265	30,229	36
2004	7,243	1,434	8,677	20,363	29,040	30
2005	5,892	1,782	7,674	23,813	31,487	24
2006	5,305	685	5,990	25,781	31,771	19
2007	4,866	698	5,564	20,922	26,486	21
2008	4,704	1,867	6,571	25,292	31,863	21
2009	4,627	1,268	5,895	21,098	26,993	22
2010	4,446	NA	NA	17,728	NA	NA

SOURCES: Unpublished table prepared by the HUD Budget Office (provided by Robert Gray) (1977–1996),U.S. Department of Housing and Urban Development, "Congressional Justifications for (Year)

(continued)

TABLE 4-2
INCREMENTAL SUBSIDIZED HOUSING UNITS, 1977–2010 (*continued*)

Estimates" (1997–2008), available at http://www.hud.gov/offices/cfo/reports/cforept.cfm (budgets for FY2003–2012, with data for 2001–2010); specific program information taken from the sections on "Housing Certificate Fund" (budgets for 1999–2006), "Tenant-Based Rental Assistance" (for 2007–2012), "Housing for Special Populations" (for 1999–2003), "Housing for the Elderly (Section 202)" (for 2004–2012), and "Housing for Persons with Disabilities (Section 811)" (for 2004–2012); Henry G. Cisneros and Laura Engdahl, eds., *From Despair to Hope: HOPE VI and the New Promise of Public Housing in America's Cities* (Washington, DC: Brookings Institution Press, 2009), Appendix B (HOPE VI units).
NOTES: NA = HOPE VI units not available for 2010.

the early 1980s reflected both the cost of new construction and the political commitment to vouchers.

Table 4-2 also includes imputed incremental units for HOPE VI.[8] The budget authority for HOPE VI is not matched with a specific number of units to be built; the funds are used for demolition, new construction, rehabilitation, and vouchers for displaced project residents. The numbers shown in the table are taken from a HUD database of HOPE VI projects which reports the number of units intended for occupancy as public housing. They are not large, and declined after 2003, when the Bush administration sought to terminate the program.

The table does, however, exclude the LIHTC, even though it is a much larger program. From its first year in FY1987 it has funded more new units in nearly every year than all the new construction programs in the HUD budget combined; from its third year it has funded more incremental units than all HUD programs, tenant-based and project-based, in nearly every year. The reason for excluding it is that the LIHTC is often used in conjunction with other housing programs. Some units in LIHTC projects are not designated as low-income units and therefore the units are not eligible for the credit, and some projects are supported by the Rural Housing Service Section 515 program, rather than HUD. In addition, some HUD-funded privately-owned projects receive tax credits as part of rehabilitation or preservation of the project. Further, tax credits are used in combination with CDBG or HOME block grant funds in some projects, and some tax credit units are occupied by families with vouchers. Finally, some tax credit projects are funded with state tax-exempt bonds. It is not possible to ascertain how many of the units receiving these additional subsidies are in fact incremental. Moreover, as noted in chapter 3, there are no annual data on voucher holders in tax credit projects. Thus, it is accurate to include the tax credit as a separate funding source in Table 4-1, because the dollars from the tax credit and the HUD budget are separate; but it is not accurate to include all of the units funded with the tax credit as different from those funded by the HUD budget, because some units are funded from both sources. The LIHTC is therefore discussed separately, later in this chapter.

Budget authority is required for more than incremental assisted units. It is also required to renew commitments and provide additional subsidies to units already built and already being subsidized. Over the years, these additional subsidies have absorbed a steadily larger share of HUD's budget authority. Table 4-3 separates budget authority for selected years into these two different categories—authority for incremental units and authority for units already built—and shows that over time, the shares have essentially been reversed. In 1977, budget authority for incremental units was almost 95 percent of the total; since 2001, it has been 10 percent or less, consisting of "enhanced" vouchers (formally, tenant protection vouchers), Section 202, Section 811, HOPE VI, about half of the HOME block grant, and almost half of the small Native American Housing Block Grant.[9] A sharp increase in nonincremental budget authority in 2009 (not shown in Table 4-3) occurred because of increased funding from the American Recovery and Reinvestment Act of 2009 for modernization of public housing and rehabilitation of privately owned subsidized projects. The figure for 2010 is more normal. In both nominal and real dollars, nonincremental authority has grown steadily. The growth of nonincremental authority also explains why the decline in incremental units between the late 1970s and early 1980s was larger than the decline in total budget authority; budget authority for incremental units and the number of additional units declined at about the same rate. The increase in nonincremental budget authority between 1990 and 1991 is accounted for by the renewal of expiring Section 8 contracts. There was no change in policy, just a continuation of older policies—but the continuation required the new budget authority.[10]

Outlays. In contrast to budget authority, actual outlays for assisted housing have been growing steadily. Table 4-4 reports outlays in constant dollars since 1977; it parallels table 4-1 for budget authority. Between 1977 and

TABLE 4-3
INCREMENTAL AND NONINCREMENTAL HUD BUDGET AUTHORITY
FOR ASSISTED HOUSING, 1977–2010

(Millions of 2010 Dollars)

Year	Incremental	Nonincremental	Total Authority	% Incremental
1977	$95,062	$6,548	$101,609	94%
1980	$62,636	$11,143	$73,778	85%
1983	$14,665	$16,148	$30,813	48%
1986	$14,302	$7,891	$22,193	64%
1991	$4,897	$22,713	$27,610	18%
2001	$4,273	$27,191	$31,365	14%
2010	$2,243	$32,854	$35,097	6%

SOURCES: Congressional Budget Office, *The Challenges Facing Federal Assistance Programs*, Washington, DC, December 1994, Table A-2; U.S. Department of Housing and Urban Development, Chief Financial Officer, "Budget Authority by Program, Comparative Summary, Fiscal Years 2001–2003," Congressional Justifications for 2003 Estimates, http://archives.hud.gov/budget/fy03/cjs/part_1/summary/budgetauthority.pdf; U.S. Department of Housing and Urban Development, Chief Financial Officer, "Budget Authority by Program, Comparative Summary, Fiscal Years 2010-2012," Congressional Justifications for 2010 Estimates, http://portal.hud.gov/hudportal/documents/huddoc?id=budget_authority_2012.pdf.

2007, real outlays almost quadrupled. Through 1995, there was a steady growth from year to year, with few exceptions. The most notable are the 1985 public housing spike and its aftermath and the efforts by Congress to contain the cost of subsidy programs by reducing the rents on Section 8 projects, which are reflected in the reduction between 1995 and 2001. Table 4-4 also includes imputed LIHTC outlays, which occur only during the first ten years of a project, so that beginning in 1997 some projects were entering their eleventh year, and the termination of imputed outlays for those projects partly offset the outlays for new projects coming into operation.[11]

The Total Number of Assisted Households. Outlays have increased in part because the number of assisted households has increased. Table 4-5 shows the total number of assisted households annually since 1975, and also for selected years back to 1941. Through 1965, public housing was the only subsidy program, and in 1970 it still accounted for over 95 percent of assisted units; Rent Supplement (about 30,000 units) and the first Section 236 projects (about 5,000 units) accounted for the rest.[12] Rapid growth and

TABLE 4-4

OUTLAYS FOR LOW-INCOME HOUSING, 1977–2010

(Millions of 2010 Dollars)			
Year	HUD Outlays	LIHTC	Combined Outlays
1977	10,481	--	10,481
1978	12,660	--	12,660
1979	14,191	--	14,191
1980	16,626	--	16,626
1981	20,232	--	20,232
1982	21,090	--	21,090
1983	23,387	--	23,387
1984	24,961	--	24,961
1985	51,785	--	51,785
1986	13,351	--	13,351
1987	25,081	80	25,161
1988	26,145	335	26,480
1989	26,643	680	27,323
1990	27,101	882	27,983
1991	28,120	1,273	29,393
1992	29,178	1,567	30,745
1993	31,570	1,926	33,496
1994	33,951	2,338	36,289
1995	37,730	2,722	40,452
1996	35,268	3,078	38,346
1997	35,693	3,387	39,080
1998	35,951	3,570	39,521
1999	33,387	3,645	37,032
2000	33,588	3,759	37,347
2001	33,959	3,808	37,767
2002	36,731	4,035	40,766
2003	38,421	4,227	42,648
2004	38,346	4,354	42,700
2005	38,943	4,480	43,423
2006	38,629	4,740	43,369
2007	37,793	5,017	42,810
2008[a]	42,793	NA	NA
2009[a]	43,045	NA	NA
2010[a]	41,770	NA	NA

SOURCES: HUD programs—Office of Management and Budget, "Outlays," in Public Budget Database, Budget of the United States Government Fiscal Year 2012, http://www.whitehouse.gov/sites/default/files/omb/budget/fy2012/assets/outlays.xls, as reported in the appendix to this chapter.

(continued)

TABLE 4-4
OUTLAYS FOR LOW-INCOME HOUSING, 1977–2010 (*continued*)

LIHTC—National Council of State Housing Agencies, "Housing Credit Utilization Charts," http://www.ncsha.org/resource/housing-credit-utilization-charts; Carissa Climaco et al., *Updating the Low-Income Housing Tax Credit (LIHTC) Database: Projects Placed in Service Through 2006* (Washington, DC: U.S. Department of Housing and Urban Development, 2009; and Abt Associates, Inc., *Updating the National Low-Income Housing Tax Credit Database: Projects Placed in Service Through 2007* (Washington, DC: U.S. Department of Housing and Urban Development, 2010) http://huduser.org/Datasets/lihtc/tables9507.pdf.
NOTE: a = LIHTC data for Section 515 (Rural Housing Service of U.S. Department of Agriculture) project share of utilization not yet available for years after 2007.

change commenced in the early 1970s, and by 1975 there were 400,000 Section 236 units and 165,000 units receiving assistance through Rent Supplement, along with 1.15 million public housing units. The first Section 8 units received assistance in 1976—105,000 units received project-based assistance under the New Construction program, and 162,000 received tenant-based assistance under the Existing Housing program.

With the creation of Section 8, the total number of assisted units increased rapidly. It reached two million in 1976, three million in 1981, and four million in 1988. Project-based and tenant-based assistance each accounted for roughly half of the growth between 1977 and 1988; even though Section 8 New Construction was repealed in 1983, about 150,000 units were added to the assisted housing stock over the next several years, as projects that had been approved before the program was terminated were completed and occupied. From 1985 on, vouchers and certificates accounted for more than half of the incremental units in each year.[13] The decline in project-based units after 1995 reflects the demolition of some public housing projects as part of HOPE VI, and the decision of some Section 8 project owners to opt out of the program as their original twenty-year subsidy contracts expired. The total number of assisted units has drifted down from about 4.86 million in 2001 to slightly less than 4.75 million in 2010, as the numbers of both project-based and tenant-based units have declined slightly. The data do not include Section 202 and Section 811 until 2001. Projects are included beginning in 2001 (about 75,000 units, rising by 5,000 to 10,000 in each succeeding year). In 2002, Section 811 "mainstream" vouchers for the disabled are included in existing housing, amounting to about 13,000 in 2002 and 14,000 to 15,000 in each succeeding year.

TABLE 4-5
TOTAL ASSISTED HOUSING UNITS, 1941–2010

	(Number of Assisted Units)			
Year	Existing Housing	New Construction	Total	% Existing
1941	0	23,785	23,785	0
1945	0	141,569	141,569	0
1950	0	146,549	146,549	0
1955	0	304,383	304,383	0
1960	0	425,481	425,481	0
1965	0	577,347	577,347	0
1970	0	866,675	866,675	0
1975	0	1,716,686	1,716,686	0
1976	162,085	1,904,646	2,066,731	8
1977	297,256	2,053,147	2,350,403	13
1978	427,331	2,122,696	2,550,027	17
1979	521,329	2,275,463	2,796,792	19
1980	599,122	2,286,466	2,885,588	21
1981	650,817	2,405,195	3,056,012	21
1982	690,643	2,575,326	3,265,969	21
1983	728,406	2,768,966	3,497,372	21
1984	748,543	2,910,070	3,658,613	20
1985	797,383	2,945,384	3,742,767	21
1986	892,863	3,001,652	3,804,515	23
1987	956,181	3,035,696	3,991,877	24
1988	1,024,689	3,054,755	4,079,444	25
1989	1,089,598	3,085,159	4,174,757	26
1990	1,137,244	3,119,096	4,256,340	27
1991	1,166,257	3,140,990	4,307,247	27
1992	1,326,250	3,136,860	4,463,110	30
1993	1,391,794	3,167,372	4,559,166	31
1994	1,486,533	3,072,515	4,559,048	33
1995	1,413,311	3,234,659	4,647,970	30
1996	1,464,588	3,218,375	4,682,963	31
1997	1,499,329	3,141,406	4,640,735	32
1998	1,605,898	2,997,645	4,603,543	35
1999	1,681,774	2,954,773	4,636,547	36
2000	1,837,528	2,902,098	4,739,626	39
2001	1,906,171	2,953,953	4,860,124	39
2002	2,060,292	2,789,860	4,850,092	42
2003	2,109,774	2,743,155	4,852,929	43
2004	2,101,787	2,741,795	4,843,582	43
2005	2,071,169	2,697,222	4,768,391	43

(continued)

TABLE 4-5
TOTAL ASSISTED HOUSING UNITS, 1941–2010 (*continued*)

	(Number of Assisted Units)			
Year	Existing Housing	New Construction	Total	% Existing
2006	2,099,151	2,689,346	4,788,497	44
2007	2,124,636	2,658,657	4,783,293	44
2008	2,082,733	2,666,263	4,745,366	44
2009	2,112,353	2,643,020	4,755,373	44
2010	2,118,984	2,619,142	4,738,126	45

SOURCES: U.S. Department of Housing and Urban Development, Budget Office of the Office of Housing, unpublished tabulation (for 1941–2001); U.S. Department of Housing and Urban Development, "Office of Housing: Housing Payments," in Congressional Justifications for (year) Estimates (for 1998, 2000–2011).

NOTES: Existing Housing includes Section 811 "mainstream" vouchers beginning in 2002; New Construction includes Section 202 and Section 811 projects beginning in 2001. Existing Housing figure for 2007 includes an estimate for Housing Choice Vouchers; in that year PHAs were given the "flexibility to maximize the number of units they can lease" and HUD estimated the number of vouchers funded based on previous program experience. "Congressional Justifications for 2009 Estimates: Housing: Housing Payments," 130.

The LIHTC. Table 4-5 does not include units funded through the Low-Income Housing Tax Credit, for the same reasons as Table 4-2. Instead, table 4-6 reports the number of LIHTC units placed in service annually from 1987, the first year of the program, through 2009, the latest year for which the HUD database is available. This gives a general sense of the extent to which the LIHTC funds incremental low-income units. The table shows the number of LIHTC units that are designated as qualifying for the tax credit and therefore might be HUD-assisted low-income units. It first excludes units not designated as low-income and therefore not eligible for the credit. Units receiving project-based assistance as well as tax credits from either the Section 515 program or HUD project-based programs are enumerated, and then subtracted. A small number of units (about 12,000) are reported as receiving funding from both the Department of Agriculture and HUD. The column labeled "Neither" shows the number of low-income units that may be incremental—units not otherwise being subsidized through Section 515 or HUD project-based programs. The right-hand column, "None," excludes 576,000 units receiving CDBG (25,000) or HOME funds from HUD (100,000), or state tax-exempt bond financing (530,000). The 959,000 units identified as receiving no project-based subsidy amount

TABLE 4-6

LOW-INCOME HOUSING TAX CREDIT UNITS BY YEAR PLACED IN SERVICE,
INCOME AND RECEIPT OF OTHER SUBSIDIES

(Number of Units Placed in Service)

Low-Income Units by Subsidy

	Number of Units		Project-Based Subsidy			
Year	Total	Low-Income	515	HUD	Neither[a]	None[b]
1987	18,843	16,891	5,254	32	11,669	9,180
1988	39,828	37,045	7,435	495	29,390	25,004
1989	49,140	43,930	9,076	359	34,575	28,151
1990	51,235	44,099	10,230	819	33,579	25,230
1991	51,931	46,837	10,419	1,724	35,370	30,310
1992	52,066	46,692	10,223	1,942	35,403	30,601
1993	64,394	58,208	9,516	1,704	48,210	42,143
1994	69,511	66,384	9,107	2,020	56,147	46,406
1995	89,696	83,591	8,458	1,611	74,187	66,727
1996	91,361	84,561	4,990	1,242	78,825	65,287
1997	90,127	81,897	4,688	1,804	75,678	58,490
1998	95,899	87,386	3,951	1,512	81,923	54,462
1999	119,315	108,583	4,410	1,655	102,755	60,643
2000	105,670	95,625	3,382	3,586	88,714	45,408
2001	107,491	98,376	4,973	2,573	91,010	44,696
2002	108,664	98,179	3,052	2,912	92,215	46,625
2003	127,613	114,787	2,124	5,783	106,974	48,723
2004	126,396	113,058	3,706	5,029	104,323	43,513
2005	130,696	117,986	2,854	8,863	106,936	48,485
2006	121,403	114,523	3,460	21,954	89,890	54,078
2007	112,592	103,743	3,320	26,024	76,205	38,619
2008	71,689	58,521	1,761	6,627	51,106	29,229
2009	41,007	33,643	1,449	3,135	29,691	17,482
TOTAL	1,936,567	1,754,545	127,838	103,405	1,535,707	959,492[c]
Share	100.0%	90.6%	6.6%	5.3%	79.3%	49.5%

SOURCE: Calculations by author from U.S. Department of Housing and Urban Development, Office of Policy Development and Research, "LIHTC Database," available at http://www.huduser.org/portal/datasets/lihtc.html.

NOTES: a = Some projects received both Section 515 and HUD project-based rental assistance; b = Project did not receive HOME or CDBG funds, tax-exempt bond financing from the state, Rural Housing Service Section 515 grants, or project-based funds from HUD; c = Units occupied by households receiving Housing Choice Vouchers are included; estimated at 140,000 to 280,000 households (Carissa Climaco et al., *Updating the Low-Income Housing Tax Credit (LIHTC) Database: Projects Place in Service Through 2006* (Washington, D.C.: U.S. Department of Housing and Urban Development, 2009, section 4.6).

to just under half of all LIHTC units. If 140,000 to 280,000 of these units are occupied by families with vouchers, then the number receiving no subsidy besides the tax credit is about 680,000 to 820,000, about 35 to 42 percent of all LIHTC units.[13]

The data in Table 4-6 measure units placed in service by year. There is no particular reason to report data in terms of annual units allocated. There were more units allocated than were placed in service in the earlier years, particularly through 1995; and fewer units allocated in the later years, particularly since 2005. The total number of units in both categories is about the same.

Conceptual Confusions

Tables 4-1 and 4-2, on the one hand, and tables 4-4 and 4-5, on the other, give very different pictures of housing policy. Budget authority and incremental units indicate a sharp reduction in spending in the early 1980s, which has not been made up in the ensuing quarter century; the modest real growth in budget authority since then, averaging about 1.3 percent per year, still leaves the total at about one-third the level of the late 1970s, in constant dollars. Even with the tax credit, the annual number of incremental units is down about one-third. But there has been steady growth in the money actually spent by the federal government and the total number of households being helped, until the last few years. The rate of growth has varied, but every administration has left its successor with a larger budget than it inherited.

Advocates of low-income housing programs, particularly production programs, often point to the decline in budget authority as an indication of a lessened federal government commitment to housing, and even today consider the late 1970s a kind of golden age of federal housing policy.[14] But judging housing policy by budget authority alone ignores the fact that more than twice as many households are receiving housing assistance today as were receiving it twenty-five or thirty years ago. Those who judge in this way either are guilty of a conceptual confusion or think that the best form of housing subsidy is a particularly expensive kind.

The significance of the distinction between budget authority/incremental assisted units and outlays/total assisted units is also illustrated by a continuing controversy over homelessness. Advocates have often blamed Reagan administration budget cuts in subsidized housing for the apparent emergence of homelessness as a national problem in the early 1980s.[15] But the appropriate indicator of policy for this issue is not budget authority— not, that is, dollars committed for subsidies in the future—but the change in the number of households receiving assistance in the present. The number of assisted households rose from 2.1 million in 1975 to 3.1 million in 1980, and then to 3.9 million in 1985. These are the two largest five-year increases on record. It is hard to believe that homelessness was caused by a housing policy which almost doubled the number of subsidized households within a ten-year period.[16] It is easier to believe that critics who blamed housing policy for the rise in homelessness were interpreting HUD budgets incorrectly.

Appendix to Chapter 4: HUD Funding for Rental Housing Assistance

This appendix lists the sources for and explains the construction of the tables in chapter 4 that show the total funding for low-income rental housing and the number of units and households receiving assistance (that is, all the tables except 4-3).

HUD Budget Authority and Outlays

The basic data source for both budget authority and outlays is the Public Budget Database maintained by the U.S. Office of Management and Budget (OMB).[17] The database lists budget authority and outlays for each federal budget account. The budget authority table contains data back to 1976, the outlays table to 1962. I have started the time series at 1977 for both table 4-1 and table 4-4 because of the "transition quarter" anomaly created when the federal fiscal year was changed from July through June (ending in June 1976) to October through September (starting in October 1976).

From the database, I have identified the appropriate accounts for low-income housing assistance. These are shown in tables 4A-1 and 4A-2. Each table first lists the accounts for housing assistance that have been in use during 1977–2009, and thus have been funding HUD-assisted housing. The tables also include accounts established in the Obama administration's HUD budgets beginning in 2010; these accounts did not exist in 2009, and very little was spent in 2010.

In the case of budget authority, the totals from the accounts have been compared to two widely used secondary sources: a 1994 Congressional Budget Office report,[18] and the biennial Green Book prepared by the House Ways and Means Committee.[19] The Green Book itself relies in part on the CBO report; both ultimately rely on data provided by the budget office of HUD. The accounts included in the budget authority tabulations in chapter 4 are listed in appendix table 4A-1.

TABLE 4A-1
HUD BUDGET AUTHORITY ACCOUNTS FOR SUBSIDIZED HOUSING

Account Name

Public Housing Operating Fund
Annual contributions for assisted housing[a]
Drug Elimination Grants for Low-income Housing
Revitalization of Severely Distressed Public Housing (HOPE VI)
Native Hawaiian Housing Block Grant
Tenant Based Rental Assistance
Project-based Rental Assistance
Public Housing Capital Fund
Preserving existing housing investment
Native American Housing Block Grant[a]
Section 8 reserve preservation account
Housing Certificate Fund[a]
Moving to work
Low-rent Public Housing—Loans and Other Expenses
Rental rehabilitation grants
Home Investment Partnership Program (HOME)
Youthbuild program
Housing Opportunities for Persons with AIDS
Rural housing and economic development
Troubled projects operating subsidy
Congregate services
Section 8 moderate rehabilitation, single room occupancy
Homeownership and Opportunity for People Everywhere Grants (HOPE Grants)
Other Assisted Housing Programs[a]
Housing for Persons with Disabilities
Development of additional new subsidized housing
Capital grants/capital loans preservation account
Housing for the Elderly
Rental Housing Assistance Fund
Flexible Subsidy Fund
Nehemiah Housing Opportunity Fund
Housing for the elderly or handicapped fund liquidating account[a]

Addendum: Accounts Created in FY2010, FY2011, or FY2012 Budgets

Deltas between the Annualized CR Amounts and the FY 2011 Budget Request
Adjustment for Outyear Discretionary Policy
Choice Neighborhoods
Transforming Rental Assistance
Housing Trust Fund
Green Retrofit Program for Multifamily Housing, Recovery Act

SOURCE: Office of Management and Budget, "Budget Authority," in Public Budget Database, Budget of the United States Government, FY2012, http://www.whitehouse.gov/sites/default/files/omb/budget/fy2012/assets/budauth.xls.
NOTE: a = Includes all accounts with this name.

TABLE 4A-2
HUD OUTLAY ACCOUNTS FOR SUBSIDIZED HOUSING

Account Name

Public Housing Operating Fund[a]
Annual contributions for assisted housing[a]
Drug Elimination Grants for Low-income Housing
Revitalization of Severely Distressed Public Housing (HOPE VI)
Native Hawaiian Housing Block Grant[a]
Tenant Based Rental Assistance[a]
Project-based Rental Assistance[a]
Public Housing Capital Fund[a]
Prevention of Resident Displacement[a]
Preserving existing housing investment
Native American Housing Block Grant[a]
Section 8 reserve preservation account
Housing Certificate Fund[a]
Moving to work[a]
Low-rent public housing—loans and other expenses[a]
Rental rehabilitation grants
Home investment partnership program[a]
Youthbuild program
Housing Opportunities for Persons With AIDS
Troubled projects operating subsidy
Congregate services[a]
Section 8 moderate rehabilitation, single room occupancy
Homeownership & Opportunity for People Everywhere Grants (HOPE Grants)[a]
Other Assisted Housing Programs[a]
Housing for Persons with Disabilities
Development of additional new subsidized housing
Housing for the Elderly[a]
Rental Housing Assistance Fund[a]
Nonprofit sponsor assistance liquidating account[a]
Flexible Subsidy Fund
Nehemiah Housing Opportunity Fund
Housing for the Elderly or Handicapped Fund Liquidating Account[a]

Addendum: Accounts Added in FY2010 or 2011 Budgets

Deltas between the Annualized CR Amounts and the FY 2011 Budget Request
Choice Neighborhoods
Transforming Rental Assistance
Housing Trust Fund
Green Retrofit Program for Multifamily Housing, Recovery Act

SOURCE: Office of Management and Budget, "Outlays," in Public Budget Database, Budget of the United States Government, FY2012, http://www.whitehouse.gov/sites/default/files/omb/budget/fy2012/assets/outlays.xls.

NOTE: a = Includes all accounts with this name.

In the case of outlays, I have compared my tabulation with the 2004 Green Book.[20] (The CBO report does not include outlays.) The accounts included in the outlay tabulations in chapter 4 are listed in appendix table 4A-2.

Public Housing Modernization

Although modernization funding began in 1968, it was not a separate budget account prior to 1997 and therefore cannot be taken from the public use database. Instead, it was included within the account titled "annual contributions for assisted housing." Modernization funds were calculated by reopening the original development contract for the project and amortizing the contract's costs over its remaining years. Beginning in 1978, modernization was amortized in a separate contract, over a twenty-year term.[21] The capital cost of repairs financed by these contract amendments or by new contracts is counted as "budget authority" in table 4-1.

In 1987, funds were provided annually for the cost of modernization, as a grant rather than a loan, but still within the budget account for annual contributions for assisted housing. In 1997, a separate account, the "public housing capital fund," was created; data for the years since 1998 are taken from this account for both budget authority and outlays.

Incremental Units

Data on incremental units come from HUD Budget Office documents. For 1977–1996, the data are taken from an unpublished Budget Office table. For 1997–2010, the data are taken from the annual "Congressional Justifications for [Year] Estimates," prepared by the Budget Office for the use of the appropriations subcommittees. The justifications report the number of incremental units by program, with separate sections for vouchers ("Housing Certificate Fund" in the FY2006 budget and previously, "Tenant-Based Rental Assistance" in later budgets), Section 202 ("Housing for Special Populations" in the FY2003 budget and previously, "Housing for the Elderly (Section 202)" in later budgets), Section 811 ("Housing for Special Populations" in the FY2003 budget and previously, "Housing for Persons with Disabilities (Section 811)" in later budgets), and HOPE VI ("Revitalization of Severely

Distressed Public Housing (HOPE VI)"). The budget justifications back to FY1998 are most readily available at http://portal.hud.gov/portal/page/portal/ HUD/program_offices/cfo/reports/cforept. They contain data for 1996–2009 in the budgets for 1998–2011. The justifications for any particular fiscal year report the actual data for the second previous year; for example, the justifications for FY 2011, published in the spring of 2010, report the actual data for FY 2009, the most recently completed year; the projected data for FY 2010, which is about half finished at the time; and the president's proposed budget for FY 2011, for which he is seeking congressional approval.

Data are also available in other published sources, notably the *2004 Green Book*, which has data for 1980–2002.[22] The congressional justifications for FY2001 and FY2002 match with the *2004 Green Book*, so a consistent series can be created from the *Green Book* and the congressional justifications that are available on the web.

In the case of HOPE VI, the budget does not report the incremental units to be built with the funds appropriated in a given year. However, the Office of Public and Indian Housing within HUD maintains a management information system on HOPE VI. The data publicly available from this system identify projects but not the number of proposed units. I have therefore relied on a secondary source, a listing of projects in appendix B of a recent book, *From Despair to Hope: HOPE VI and the New Promise of Public Housing in America's Cities*, edited by former HUD secretary Henry G. Cisneros and Lora Engdahl.[23] This tabulation lists the number of units in each project, and disaggregates by tenure and subsidy status. The numbers I report in table 4-2 are rental units covered by public housing annual contributions contracts, which provide assistance in the same way as that to the units being replaced. I have excluded rental units with income restrictions, which are not necessarily lower-income or subsidized, market-rent units, and units intended to be owner occupied. The data are taken from the plans submitted by public housing authorities at the time of grant application; they are expected new units, not actual.

The Total Stock of Assisted Units

The data on the stock of assisted units are taken from two sources: an unpublished table prepared by the HUD Budget Office, covering

1941–2002; and the "Housing Payments" section of the annual "Congressional Justifications for [Year] Estimates," covering 1997–2010, which are also prepared by the HUD Budget Office. As mentioned in the preceding section, the budget justifications back to FY1998 are available at http://portal.hud.gov/portal/page/portal/HUD/program_offices/cfo/reports/cforept, and contain data for 1996–2009 in the budgets for 1998–2011.

The data for the overlapping years are consistent except for two years: 1999, the year HUD changed its accounting reporting procedures for Section 8 in the congressional justifications, and 2002, the last year in the table and possibly reflecting incomplete data. I have used the table for 1999, because it reports the Housing Choice Voucher separately from the other Section 8 programs; the HUD budget did not begin separate reporting for tenant-based Section 8 and project-based Section 8 until 2001. I have used the congressional justifications for 2002, because they report actual data after the end of the fiscal year. As mentioned in chapter 4, Section 202 and 811 were not included in the "Housing Payments" section until 2002, and indeed were specifically excluded (both units and outlays) in 2001 and prior years.

The Low-Income Housing Tax Credit

I have included the LIHTC in tables 4-1 and 4-4 because it has become a major funding source for assisted housing, but it does not appear in tables 4A-1 and 4A-2 because it is not part of the federal budget. The concepts of "budget authority" and "outlays" do not directly apply to a tax credit. The tax credit is reported in the budget only as a "tax expenditure," but the amount of the tax expenditure does not correspond to either budget authority or outlays. For purposes of comparison to budget authority and outlays for subsidy programs, the LIHTC requires special treatment. The appropriate concepts are as follows: for budget authority, the amount of tax credit available in each budget to be allocated to projects; for outlays, the amount of tax credit actually utilized in a given year.

For budget authority, I have used the tabulations prepared annually by the National Council of State Housing Agencies (NCSHA), whose member agencies are responsible for approving projects and allocating credits within their states.[24] NCSHA reports the total amount authorized for allocation each year. The tax credit can be taken for the first ten years of the life of a project, and it is common to use the ten-year total as the dollar amount of the tax credits available in a given year (e.g., $3 billion over ten years). I have used the ten-year total as the analogous measure to HUD program budget authority. For example, $62.9 million was allocated in 1987; this translates to $629 million that can be claimed as tax credits over the next ten years, until 1996.

Outlays are also calculated from the NCSHA data on LIHTC utilization published by the National Council of State Housing Agencies, reporting the actual amount of the tax credit allocated in each year. The allocation amount reported is that for the first year of each ten-year period. These amounts are cumulated over the ten-year life of the credit. For example, $63 million was allocated in 1987, $210 million in 1988, and $307 million in 1989 (in nominal dollars). Outlays are measured as $63 million for 1987, $273 million for 1988, $580 million for 1989, and so on.

Although LIHTC units are not reported in the HUD budget, it is useful to include them in discussions of low-income housing. The HUD LIHTC database includes the years in which the credits are allocated to a project and the year when the units are placed in service. Allocations occur before projects are put in service, and thus precede the date at which units are placed in service by, on average, about eighteen months.[25] The HUD database was first compiled in 1996 for the years 1987–1994[26] and updated numerous times subsequently; the latest data available are for projects receiving tax credits in 2009.[27] Each update has included information for some projects approved in earlier years that had not previously been included in the database; the 2009 update provides the latest information for projects receiving tax credits from 1995 to 2009. The latest annual data for 1987–1994 are reported in the 2006 update.

As discussed in chapters 3 and 4, some LIHTC units do not qualify as "lower-income" and some are assisted through the Rural Housing Service Section 515 program, rather than by HUD.[28] In addition, some units also receive HUD project-based assistance, and some residents have Housing Choice Vouchers. These are already included in the tabulations of units assisted by HUD; including them in Tables 4-2 and 4-5 would be double counting. Further, some units receive funds from the HOME and CDBG block grants, and some are financed by tax-exempt bonds issued by state governments. Table 4-6 separates these various categories in order to produce a calculation of LIHTC units that approximately corresponds to the tabulation of units receiving project-based assistance from HUD in Table 4-5. This is the category entitled "Neither" in Table 4-6. Finally, a substantial number of units are occupied by households with vouchers; the number is estimated at 140,000 to 280,000. To my knowledge there is no information on year placed in service for these units, and they are therefore excluded from the body of Table 4-6.

5

The Voucher/Production Debate: Program Comparisons

Comparisons of housing programs are essentially comparisons of vouchers and production programs. For over three decades the central focus of housing policy has been a voucher/production debate: should the government make use of the existing privately owned housing stock to house the poor, or should it build new housing specifically for them?

This debate arose in the 1970s in the wake of dissatisfaction with public housing and the other project-based programs. It has been addressed in each of the last four major housing policy studies, from the Kaiser Committee in 1968 to the Millennium Housing Commission in 2002, and it has been at the center of major housing policy reforms proposed in 1974 and 1995. Because housing assistance is not an entitlement, the number of households receiving assistance—in particular, the number of new households to be assisted and the form and cost of that assistance—is a subject for legislation and appropriation every year. Thus the issue is regularly revisited, and the voucher/production debate recurs each time Congress considers major changes in housing policy.

This chapter lays out the evidence available on how well the different programs provide decent and affordable housing to the poor. That is, it provides a factual basis for the perennial debate over vouchers and production programs. It looks first at the programs' effects on the housing of assisted households. It focuses next on program participants and compares the characteristics of households served. In the final section, it discusses the effects of government-subsidized programs on the housing market. The evidence indicates overall that by objective measures, vouchers are about as effective as production programs in improving the housing of the poor, but the subjective assessments of the assisted households

127

themselves show that voucher recipients are generally more satisfied with their housing.

Program comparisons draw primarily on three sources of data: surveys, notably the American Housing Surveys; administrative program records; and information developed in the course of scholarly research and formal program evaluations. They are primarily among public housing, Section 8 New Construction, and tenant-based assistance. These are the programs intended to serve the poorest households, and they provide most of the assistance to low-income households. The comparisons do not include Section 221(d)(3)(BMIR) and Section 236, which were designed to reach people who were too well-off for public housing; although many projects in these programs have subsequently received Section 8 subsidies, the programs themselves were terminated long ago and have received little analytical attention for many years. Nor do they include Section 202 and Section 811, which serve specialized clienteles.

The programs created since 1986—the LIHTC, HOME, and HOPE VI—were not designed to serve poor households to the same extent as the voucher or the earlier production programs, and with the exception of the LIHTC they are not separately tabulated either in the major surveys or in program data, so there is little evidence on the extent to which they result in better housing for the poor. Comparisons involving these programs are also complicated because both HOME and the LIHTC are commonly used in combination with other subsidies (and sometimes with each other) to reach very low-income and extremely low-income households, and because HOPE VI explicitly serves community development purposes as well as providing lower-income housing. Comparisons are further complicated because there is relatively little information available about the characteristics of the households served by the LIHTC and HOME, and the studies of HOPE VI mainly date from 2000–2004, when few projects had been completed.

Limitations of the Literature

Unfortunately, while the literature on the various programs is substantial, it has limitations. There have actually been few comparative evaluations of program outcomes. Moreover, the comparisons are not recent. This is largely because the different types of programs have been dominant at different times—dominant in the sense that they received most of the funds appropriated by Congress to provide additional subsidized housing beyond the units already being subsidized. Public housing was the only subsidy program until about 1960 and the major program until the mid-1960s, while tenant-based assistance has predominated since 1983. Between the mid-1960s and 1974, public housing and privately owned projects were both large programs, and from the mid-1970s to 1983 all three types of programs were active. Thus it happens that nearly all of the most extensive program comparisons date from the years between 1974 and 1983, although the process of analyzing the data results in somewhat later publication dates. Finally, the "debate" in housing policy has tended to be not between actual programs but rather between actual programs and proposals. (There have been more frequent and more recent studies comparing programs' costs, which are discussed in chapter 7.)

The most extensive comparison of vouchers and production programs was a 1981 analysis that covered Section 8 New Construction and the certificate program (Section 8 Existing Housing) in the late 1970s.[1] Thirty years later, a long-term evaluation of the Moving to Opportunity (MTO) demonstration program compared voucher recipients to public housing residents. MTO was the subject of an interim evaluation (four to seven years after households began to participate in the demonstration, published in 2002) and a final impacts evaluation (10 to 15 years after initial participation, published in 2011). As its name suggests, the purpose of MTO was to test whether families living in public housing projects located in high-poverty urban neighborhoods and usually classified as "severely distressed" could improve their lives by using housing vouchers to move to lower-poverty neighborhoods.[2] It therefore compared families continuing to live in public housing with those who were offered vouchers. The 1981 analysis of Section 8 included households in a larger number of metropolitan areas at one point in time, with a focus on housing outcomes; the MTO demonstration covered a much longer period of time, and a broad range of neighborhood outcomes and social and economic outcomes for the participants. Two other comparative studies of programs have been important for policy changes: the 1974 National Housing Policy Review, which compared production programs, particularly public housing and Section 236, with the Section 23 leased housing program, the forerunner of Section 8 existing housing;[3] and a 1990 evaluation that compared certificates and vouchers as of the late 1980s.[4] Other major studies have directly concerned only one program or program category. They include a 1978 evaluation of the early years of Section 8 Existing Housing,[5] and a 2006 analysis of the Housing Choice Voucher in the context of a demonstration program to investigate whether vouchers could reduce welfare dependency (the Welfare to Work Voucher program).[6]

The EHAP analyses remain the best information for some aspects of housing programs, more than thirty years later; the Supply Experiment, in which housing assistance was offered as an entitlement in the Green Bay and South Bend metropolitan areas, is particularly useful. Because the experiment was partly intended to address the possibility of using vouchers or certificates to replace project-based programs, analyses of it compare programs explicitly or implicitly.[7]

"A Decent Home": Housing Quality

Housing quality has historically been the central concern of housing policy, so it is appropriate to begin the comparison of programs by looking at how well they improve the quality of housing for poor people.

Measuring Housing Quality. The discussion must begin with the issue of measurement. For public policy purposes, by far the most common way to measure housing quality is to identify a threshold criterion or set of criteria and categorize housing units as "satisfactory" or "unsatisfactory" according to whether they meet the threshold. The history of housing legislation suggests that policymakers have usually thought of housing quality problems as a failure to meet a certain standard, and that the objective of housing programs has been to raise housing quality to the standard. The 1949 national housing goal of "a decent home in a suitable living environment for every American family" implies a threshold, as does the 1948 report of the Congressional Joint Committee on Housing. The criteria developed by several government agencies using the American Housing Survey establish thresholds, and the AHS reports the number of units with "severe physical problems" and "moderate physical problems" every two years. HUD's reports to Congress on worst-case needs use the same thresholds to measure housing quality. Housing improvement is most often measured in terms of how many households fall below the thresholds, before and after receiving assistance.

Recent Research on Vouchers. The Moving to Opportunity evaluations compared public housing residents who were not offered vouchers (termed the "control" group) with residents who were. Some families were required to move to lower-poverty neighborhoods in order to use their vouchers (the "experimental" group), while others were offered standard vouchers with no such requirement (the "Section 8" group). Thus the comparisons are between families receiving vouchers and families continuing to live in public housing; every family in the demonstration was receiving housing assistance at the beginning of the demonstration and continued to receive it, at least initially. But equally importantly, it should be remembered that the families in all groups experienced many changes during the 10 to 15 years of the demonstration. The demonstration lasted from about 1993 to about 2008, a period of two strong economic expansions with a moderate recession during 2000–2001, and the members of the families were all 10 to 15 years older. Major social welfare policy changes occurred as well, notably the welfare reform in 1996. Most immediately relevant to MTO, the HOPE VI program to raze the most severely distressed public housing projects was enacted in 1992; by 2007, over 150,000 units either had been or were scheduled to be torn down. About 22 percent of the families in the control group were living in these projects when the demonstration began.

It should perhaps therefore not be too surprising that most families who did not receive a voucher nonetheless moved. About 70 percent of the families in the control group had moved by the time of the interim evaluation, four to seven years later; so did over 60 percent of the families in the other two groups who were offered vouchers but did not make use of them. Moreover, among the families who took the vouchers and moved, about two-thirds had moved a second time.[8] By the final evaluation, the families in the control group had moved twice, on average, and the families who received vouchers had moved three times. Among the control group, only 30 percent still lived in public housing, while 25 percent had obtained a voucher at some point, and about 35 percent were no longer receiving any housing assistance at all; at the same time among those who used the vouchers they were offered at the beginning of the demonstration, only 55 to 60 percent still had vouchers. (Almost none had moved back to public housing.)[9]

The MTO evaluations therefore compare families who originally either received vouchers or stayed in public housing, but whose housing situation changed over the next 10 to 15 years; only about half were still receiving housing assistance in the same program. Nonetheless, there were significant differences between the groups in the quality of their housing. Those who used the vouchers were living in housing that was better, for most of the half-dozen attributes included in the evaluation, than those in the control group. The largest improvements came in problems with vermin (an incidence of 52 percent for those in the control group compared to 38 percent in the Section 8 group and 39 percent in the experimental group), and walls with broken plaster or peeling paint (47 percent compared to 27 percent in the Section 8 group and 28 percent in the experimental group). These differences are statistically significant. Smaller but significant improvements occurred for plumbing problems and broken windows; small (in the range of 3 to 6 percentage points) and marginally significant or insignificant improvements occurred for heating system problems and missing or broken door locks.[10]

These results cannot be used to determine the extent to which participants moved from "severely inadequate" housing to "moderately inadequate" or "adequate," because they are not commensurate with the standard definitions of housing quality reported in Exhibit 2-2. Of the six dimensions, only the existence of heating problems is a sufficient criterion to classify a housing unit as severely or moderately inadequate. Plumbing problems can classify a unit as moderately inadequate, but the absence of complete plumbing is the criterion for severely inadequate. Vermin and broken plaster or peeling paint are two of the "Upkeep" problems, but a unit is severely inadequate only if it has five of the six listed problems, and moderately inadequate only if it has three of them. In addition, the MTO evaluation asked if a problem is "big or small," without further elaboration. The standard criteria for inadequacy are more detailed; big or small heating problems as defined by the household may not agree with the definition of severely or moderately inadequate.

The MTO evaluations also collected information on space as well as quality. In both the interim and final evaluations, there were no significant differences in the extent of overcrowding between the groups. There were also no significant differences in the incidence of frequency of homelessness. Families in the Section 8 group in the final evaluation, however, were more likely to be "doubled up" at least once, meaning that they stayed with other family members or friends (19 percent for those not offered vouchers compared to 26 percent). This was not evident in the interim evaluation.

The usefulness of rating housing quality on a pass-fail basis has lessened over time, as inadequate housing has become a small and steadily diminishing share of the housing stock. An alternative is to measure housing quality along a continuum in order to determine how many households have improved their housing, and by how much. There is some rather limited evidence on the extent of quality improvement.

Both the threshold and the continuum measurements for housing quality are objective. A third approach is subjective: measuring housing quality in terms of the satisfaction of the households receiving the subsidy. This has the advantage of considering the question from the standpoint of the household that is intended to benefit from housing assistance, and the further advantage of simplicity—the household makes its own assessment of the benefits it has received. There are also disadvantages. Some households may implicitly take their economic circumstances into account and give a high rating to a unit with major problems, because they consider it the best housing they can afford. In addition, this subjective measure does not necessarily correspond to objective program standards or dollars spent, although that may indicate that the objective standards are not what really matter to the household, or that some households are skilled shoppers in the housing market.

This issue of quality improvement, however measured, is raised most often in connection with tenant-based assistance. Policymakers and housing advocates have been skeptical that assistance programs help the people who live in bad housing. There are concerns that poor people will not use the subsidies to live in better housing; either they will not choose to do so, or they will not be able to do so because landlords will simply raise rents. These questions are seldom raised in connection with any of the new construction programs, since it is commonly assumed that new projects solve housing quality problems. But the issue of quality is certainly relevant, at a minimum in order to compare programs. In fact, the extent to which new construction improves the quality of housing for poor tenants is not obvious. From 1968 through 1987 no housing program stipulated that subsidy recipients had to live in bad housing in order to be eligible for assistance.[11] They did have to fall below the income limits for the various programs, but not all such low-income families lived or live in bad housing.

Program comparisons using each of the three measurement approaches are discussed below.

Achieving Decent Housing. There has been only one systematic comparison of housing quality improvements in new construction and tenant-based assistance, the Section 8 evaluation of the late 1970s mentioned earlier.[12] This study compared improvements for participants in the New Construction program and the certificate program based on the household's original housing quality, using a threshold criterion—that is, counting the number of households that experienced an improvement from substandard to standard quality housing.

The relevant findings of this study are shown in table 5-1. Each program reached households in inadequate housing about in proportion to the incidence of these households in the eligible population.[13] Some 24 percent of participants in Section 8 New Construction originally lived in inadequate housing, compared to 21 percent of the eligible population. In the certificate program, 19 percent of participants originally lived in inadequate housing, compared to 19 percent of the eligible population. (The percentages for the eligible populations differ because two additional metropolitan areas were included in the certificate sample.) The difference in participation rates was on the margin of statistical significance, given the sample sizes. In other words, both programs were about equally effective in reaching the eligible population. Section 8 New Construction did a better job in helping people improve their housing, however. Among households that moved, only 1 percent of those in the newly built units lived in inadequate housing, compared to 6 percent of certificate users. The net effect was that 23 percent of households in the New Construction program moved from inadequate to adequate housing, compared to 13 percent for certificate holders.

This comparison is incomplete, however, because it ignores differences in the willingness to participate in different programs. Any household

TABLE 5-1
EXTENT OF HOUSING QUALITY IMPROVEMENT BY PROGRAM, 1979

Panel A: Percentage of Households Living in Inadequate Housing

Program	Eligible Population	Program Participants: Original Housing	Assisted Housing
Section 8 New Construction	21	24	1
Certificates (all households)	19	19	6
Certificates (movers)	NA	32	7

Panel B: Extent of Housing Improvement

	Dollar Value (1979 dollars)	Percentage Increase
Section 8 New Construction	$44	25
Certificates (movers)	$19	14
Certificates (stayers)	$1	--

SOURCES: James E. Wallace et al., *Participation and Benefits in the Urban Section 8 Program: New Construction and Existing Housing* (Cambridge, MA: Abt Associates), 1981, table 4-9 (for panel A, Section 8 New Construction); table 6-9 (for panel A, certificates); table 4-18 (for panel B, Section 8 New Construction); table 6-22 (for panel B, certificates).
NOTE: NA = not available.

willing to participate in Section 8 New Construction is willing to move, by definition, whereas households in the certificate program did not necessarily have to move; they could use their certificates in their present unit if it met program standards. Given that the certificate program reached a broader universe, a more appropriate basis for comparison would be participation rates by housing quality for those households willing to move. Among certificate holders, this was almost the same as for those who did move: 90 percent of those who moved were willing to move, and 90 percent of those who stayed in the same unit were unwilling to move.[14] Table 5-1 shows the improvement in housing quality for households that moved, as well as for all households. Some 32 percent of movers originally lived in inadequate housing; 7 percent still did so after they moved, so 25 percent of the people who moved went from inadequate to adequate housing. These figures are comparable to those for Section 8 New Construction.[15]

The later comparison of success rates in the certificate and voucher program, the freestanding voucher demonstration study, includes some information on the willingness to move and the quality of the original housing occupied by both program participants able to use their voucher or certificate ("successful") and those unable to use it ("unsuccessful"). About 20 percent of successful participants who were willing to move lived originally in inadequate housing.[16] Success rates varied by the quality of the housing originally occupied by program participants. Around 35–40 percent of those households that lived in inadequate housing were able to find new apartments that met program standards, compared to 60–65 percent of those who lived in adequate or moderately inadequate housing. The study does not report the quality of the housing occupied by successful participants.[17] It is perhaps reasonable to assume that most if not all did move to adequate housing.

The safest conclusion seems to be that both the tenant-based and project-based Section 8 programs did about equally well in helping low income households upgrade from inadequate to adequate housing. The New Construction program may have done marginally better.

The Welfare to Work demonstration also included some limited information on housing quality improvement for voucher recipients, compared to households receiving no assistance. The demonstration evaluation reported changes in the incidence of "housing problems," defined as any two of the seven specific problems that are part of the "severely inadequate" measure. Voucher recipients showed improvement, but the changes were not statistically significant. The analysts noted that most members of the control group (households not receiving assistance) reported good-quality housing, and that only one-eighth reported major housing problems; they concluded that the room for improvement was limited, and also that many respondents were more concerned with their neighborhood than their housing. The evaluation did find that the Welfare to Work demonstration improved housing quality by providing more rooms per unit and less crowding, and also by substantially reducing homelessness. The reduction in crowding appeared to result largely from a drop in multigenerational households; those receiving assistance were able to move out of units they shared with friends or relatives.[18] These results differ from the MTO findings. One reason may be that Welfare to Work participants were not receiving any housing assistance before they participated in the demonstration.

These studies generally indicate that households receiving tenant-based assistance achieved better housing to about the same extent as comparable households living in Section 8 projects, and perhaps to a greater extent than public housing residents.

Improving Housing Quality. The best evidence on quality changes as measured along a continuum comes from the comparative evaluation of Section 8 New Construction and certificates, specifically from data on changes in rent. The market rent of each unit is estimated in this evaluation, based on its characteristics and the value placed on them in the market for unsubsidized units with similar characteristics.

The evaluation found that households in the New Construction program enjoyed a greater improvement in housing. The average improvement was about 25 percent for those who moved into new units, compared to 15 percent for movers in the certificate program. Households that did not move showed very little improvement. The dollar value of the improvement was also larger—more than twice as large for households in the New Construction program than for movers in the certificate program. The estimated value of the average improvements was $44, $19, and $1 per household per month, respectively (measured in 2010 dollars, the amounts would be almost exactly three times as large). These are shown in panel B of table 5-1.

There are several reasons for these differences. The new units were simply of better quality than existing housing; the market rent of the typical certificate unit was estimated at $265, while the typical Section 8 New Construction unit had an estimated market rent of $291 (measured in 1979 dollars).[19] A second reason is that the subsidies for the new units were larger.

There is also some evidence from the EHAP Supply Experiment that is consistent with the evaluation of the certificate program. Assisted households raised the quality of their housing by about 5 to 10 percent. Less than 20 percent of the assistance payments went for better housing; the rest was used in effect to buy other goods and services. However, there was some upgrading in the existing stock—about $425 to $500 worth per unit, in 2010 dollars, for about one third of the units that did not originally meet program standards. Moreover, these modest improvements enabled a substantial number of participants to meet the program quality standards;

about three-quarters of program participants were living in standard housing after two years, compared to less than half originally.[20]

The quality improvements for certificate and voucher holders are smaller than most housing economists anticipated when the certificate program was created in 1974. Academic research generally indicated that households could be expected to devote a fairly large share of any additional income to better housing. The general consensus was that the income elasticity of demand for housing was high, at least unity or higher—in other words, that for every 10 percent increase in income, household expenditures on housing would rise by 10 percent or more. Thus tenant-based assistance would not only raise the overall level of well-being for the poor, it would also raise their housing consumption substantially because households would consider spending a larger share of their income on housing as the best way to improve their standard of living.[21]

Subsequent research has found much lower income elasticities of demand, however. This includes the findings of the housing allowance experiments, which are probably the most immediately relevant for housing policy.[22] It now appears that the earlier estimates were too high, and that poor households with rising incomes would use their new wealth on day care, cars, or health insurance—that is, on things other than better housing. Perhaps the best explanation for the difference between the findings of earlier and later studies is that the earlier studies relied on data that is averaged for groups in the population, while the later research uses observations of individual households.

Choice and Satisfaction. The American Housing Survey has the best evidence available on the third measure of housing quality, household satisfaction. The survey asks households in each of the three major program categories to rate their housing unit on a scale of 1 to 10. Because households' responses about whether their units are subsidized have been inconsistent with the number actually receiving assistance,[23] HUD has in some years performed a systematic reconciliation between the AHS and program data, most recently in 2003. This section reports the 2003 data.[24]

In drawing conclusions from the data, it is important once again to remember that households are offered different opportunities in project-based and tenant-based programs. Under the Housing Choice Voucher, they can select any housing unit renting for the FMR or less, if it meets quality standards and the landlord is willing to rent to them. Under the project-based programs, however, their choice is limited to one subsidized unit: the unit available when they come to the top of the waiting list. If they do not wish to move to that unit, or to the project in which it is located, they receive no subsidy, go to the bottom of the waiting list, and continue to pay the full rent on their present housing unit from their own resources. The household's only choice is to take the unit or leave it.

It is therefore to be expected that households in the voucher program are more satisfied with their housing units than households in public housing or the privately owned projects. Their choice is much less constrained. They can spend the subsidy on whatever housing they like best, within the program constraints. In the project-based programs, if a household does not like some feature of the project or the unit, the household cannot do anything about it, but must decide if that feature justifies rejecting the unit and the subsidy altogether.

The results concerning satisfaction with housing under the different programs are shown in table 5-2, along with ratings for unsubsidized households whose incomes are low enough to make them eligible for assistance. The table reports all unassisted households and also those with worst-case needs; eligible unassisted households have somewhat higher incomes than those in any of the other four categories, and therefore are more likely to have satisfactory housing. The table reports the proportion clearly dissatisfied, that is, households scoring their units at less than 5 on the scale of 10, and also the median rating. The most common ratings are 5 and 10, and the third most common is 8, suggesting that ratings below 5 indicate unsatisfactory housing.

The patterns are quite different for elderly and non-elderly households, and they are therefore shown separately. Panel A shows that elderly households find all subsidized housing to be quite satisfactory, on average. The share of unsatisfactory ratings is extremely low, and the typical subsidy recipient in each program rates his or her unit as higher than 9 on a scale of 10. Indeed, in all three programs the modal score is 10. Somewhat surprisingly, project-based programs score slightly lower than the other two categories, even though they include a substantial number of projects specifically for the elderly, with amenities designed for them, and they serve

TABLE 5-2
SUBJECTIVE RATING OF HOUSING QUALITY
BY ASSISTED HOUSING PROGRAM, 2003

Panel A Elderly Households			
	% Rating <5	Median Rating	Median Income
Vouchers	0.4	9.6	$9,346
Public housing	1.0	9.7	$9,206
Privately owned projects	0.5	9.1	$9,876
Worst-case needs	4.4	8.4	$9,386
Unassisted, eligible	3.3	8.5	$11,047

Panel B Non-Elderly Households			
	% Rating <5	Median Rating	Median Income
Vouchers	3.6	8.0	$11,132
Public housing	10.9	7.7	$10,705
Privately owned projects	6.7	7.8	$11,752
Worst-case needs	9.2	7.6	$9,893
Unassisted, eligible	8.8	7.6	$14,748

Panel C Crowding of Non-Elderly Households			
	% Crowded	Persons/Unit (Median)	% with Children
Vouchers	4.2	2.5	65.0
Public housing	4.2	2.2	54.3
Privately owned projects	4.6	2.0	51.0
Worst-case needs	7.7	2.0	43.3
Unassisted, eligible	8.8	2.2	48.0

SOURCE: U.S. Department of Housing and Urban Development, Office of Policy Development and Research, *Characteristics of HUD-Assisted Renters and Their Units in 2003*, Washington, DC, May 2008. NOTE: Median ratings in panels A and B are on a scale of 1 to 10.

a higher proportion of the elderly than the others. Assisted households in general are more satisfied than unassisted lower-income households, but the overall ratings for unassisted households are also high.

Panel B shows the pattern for non-elderly households. Ratings are consistently lower than for the elderly. The rating for public housing is particularly low; almost 11 percent rate their unit as unsatisfactory, compared to 9 percent of unassisted households with worst-case needs. The ratings of voucher recipients are consistently the highest.

Panel C reports data on crowding for the same households. Crowding is an objective rather than a subjective criterion, but since the data are taken from the same survey, they are reported here. All three programs show lower incidences of crowding than do unassisted households, which is somewhat remarkable given that more of the households receiving assistance include children. The voucher results are particularly noteworthy; despite being larger on average than households in the other programs, they are crowded less often. The pattern reported in the Welfare to Work demonstration—that households receiving vouchers moved to larger units and were less often crowded than those who remained in public housing—is consistent with these program data from the AHS.

There are some limited data on satisfaction with tax credit projects. A study in 1999 of thirty-nine projects placed in service during 1992–1994 found that about two-thirds of residents rated their apartments as "good or excellent," while one-third rated them as "fair or poor." Comparing this to the scale used in the AHS is necessarily problematic; the ratings are not reported separately for elderly and non-elderly households, although since thirty-three of the projects were developed for non-elderly residents, the ratings are probably most comparable to those for the non-elderly households in the HUD programs, reported in table 5-2. The data suggest that satisfaction was no higher in tax credit projects than in the HUD-subsidized programs, which is somewhat surprising, given that about half the properties in the tax credit program were new construction and thus no more than five to seven years old at the time the residents were surveyed, while all those in the HUD programs as of 2000 were at least fifteen years old (although some voucher recipients may have been in newer properties).[25]

The Moving to Opportunity evaluations included a subjective measure—rating the current housing as "excellent" or "good"—as well as the objective criteria of quality mentioned earlier. Families who made use of vouchers generally rated their housing better than families who were not offered vouchers; but surprisingly, the difference was greater in the interim evaluation. At that date 52 percent of households in the control group rated their housing as good or excellent, compared to 64 percent of those using the standard Section 8 voucher and 73 percent of those using the experimental voucher, and both differences were significant. In the final evaluation, satisfaction among the control group had increased, to 57 percent, while satisfaction among the voucher recipients had declined to 62 percent among the Section 8 group and 68 percent among the experimental group, and only the latter was significantly different from the control group.

The Welfare to Work evaluation included the same measure, and it also found that voucher recipients gave their housing higher ratings than public housing residents, but the difference was not statistically significant.[26]

Changes in Housing. Comparisons between assisted and unassisted households perhaps implicitly encourage the inference that the assisted households had been living, before they received assistance, in the sort of housing still occupied by unassisted households. To the extent that such is the case, the difference can be interpreted as representing a change for the assisted household. This is an assumption, however, not a fact.

Some evidence about changes in housing for assisted households comes from the AHS, which asks households that move during the preceding year for a subjective comparison of the present and former units. Households in this category included about 20 to 30 percent of those assisted in each program category. Table 5-3 reports the share of recent movers by program who considered their new unit better than their previous unit. The table is limited to non-elderly households, because the sample sizes for the elderly are quite small; it seems appropriate to exclude the elderly, moreover, because the elderly tend to be so much more satisfied with their housing than the non-elderly. Among the non-elderly, as table 5-3 shows, voucher holders were much the most likely to feel they had moved to better housing, while a startlingly large share of public housing residents felt their housing was now worse.

LIHTC residents were also asked to compare current and previous units; 54 percent rated their current units as better, while 22 percent said they were not as good. The remainder said their new housing was no different from the housing they left.[27]

These data suggest that households in the project-based programs are generally satisfied with their housing, even though they have had a limited choice; public housing residents are least satisfied, but at the same time most

TABLE 5-3
SUBJECTIVE JUDGMENT OF HOUSING IMPROVEMENT FOR NON-ELDERLY
ASSISTED HOUSEHOLDS MOVING DURING PREVIOUS YEAR, 2003

| | Percentage Moving to: | |
	Better Housing	Worse Housing
Vouchers	75	10
Public Housing	65	31
Privately Owned Projects	52	16

SOURCE: U.S. Department of Housing and Urban Development, Office of Policy Development and Research, *Characteristics of HUD-Assisted Renters and Their Units in 2003*, Washington, DC, May 2008. NOTE: Percentages do not add to 100 because some households responded "about the same" and others did not respond.

believe that their current housing represents an improvement. Residents of privately owned projects are generally more satisfied, but conversely are less likely to consider that they have improved their housing. The data also indicate that voucher and certificate holders are generally as well satisfied with their housing as residents of subsidized projects.

HOPE VI: A Special Situation

HOPE VI provides information about housing improvement for a different group of households: those already living in public housing who have to move when the project is rebuilt or rehabilitated. Studies of this group have addressed both objective changes in quality and subjective evaluations. Federal law requires PHAs to provide displaced households with a comparable unit and to pay moving expenses. But in the early years of the program, there was little effort to track the households, and there has been much controversy about their housing as a result.

Objective evidence comes from a HOPE VI panel study of five projects conducted by the Urban Institute beginning in 2001.[28] The original residents reported much lower incidence of four specific housing quality problems after moving, and also much lower incidence of multiple problems. Those who received vouchers saw particular improvement. However, their housing was still lower in quality than that of other poor renters, as reported in the AHS—including both assisted and unassisted renters, mostly the latter. These comparisons cast a vivid light on the quality of the public housing projects: residents who moved were much better housed than they had been, but still worse than other poor renters. Further, public housing residents who had not yet relocated reported that their housing remained in poor condition.[29]

Subjective information comes from two studies. The first is the Urban Institute HOPE VI panel study, which surveyed relocated households twice, in 2003 and 2005. The earlier survey found that two-thirds of those who moved considered their housing "good or excellent," and the same proportion considered their current housing better than their public housing unit. The proportions were highest for those receiving vouchers and lowest for those who relocated to other public housing projects. Interestingly, two-thirds of those who did not receive any assistance at all considered their new housing to be an improvement. The second survey also found that more than two-thirds of voucher holders considered their current housing to be an improvement, but only 40 percent of those who relocated to public housing did so.[30]

The second source of subjective information is a HOPE VI resident tracking study conducted by Abt Associates, which asked original residents of eight projects whether their new housing was better than their public housing unit. The residents were surveyed in 2001, and they might have moved more than once since they were required to move out of the project. Two of the projects had been completed and reoccupied by the time of the survey, and four others were partially reoccupied, so moving back into the HOPE VI project was an option for 20 to 30 percent of the households.[31] Other options included other public housing, a voucher, or a combined category of unsubsidized rental housing or homeownership. Considering that these households lived originally in some of the worst public housing projects in the country, it seems likely that most would find their new housing significantly better than their former unit. Overall, 56 percent did think their new housing was better; 29 percent considered it to be about the same, and 15 percent worse. The 25 percent who were able to move back into the new HOPE VI project were most positive, with 76 percent of these rating it better than the original project; those who received a voucher were least positive, with 46 percent rating it better. Vouchers scored least well among all surveyed households. Follow-up interviews with a small number of households revealed that some voucher recipients had to relocate too quickly to make a good choice; but some recipients said they preferred having a voucher to living in public housing, including even the new HOPE VI project.[32]

Edward G. Goetz surveyed households that had been relocated from a HOPE VI project in Duluth, and compared their subjective views of their new housing and neighborhoods with objective data on households living in the Census tract to which relocatees had moved. He found that the new neighborhoods were objectively better in terms of households' economic well-being, but the relocatees' subjective assessments generally were negative; they considered the new neighborhoods inferior to their original neighborhoods across a number of dimensions, some two years after moving.[33] This conclusion is at variance with the results of the resident tracking study.

Sheila Crowley of the National Low Income Housing Coalition has been sharply critical of HOPE VI relocation efforts and general treatment of the original residents. She points out that 20 percent of displaced residents "are not able to be assessed." Unless they move to public housing or receive a voucher, they often cannot be located by the PHAs that have the responsibility of providing them with vouchers or alternative public housing. Crowley describes the process as "forced relocation" and likens it to urban renewal half a century ago.[34] She also notes that residents claim that they were misled about whether they would be able to move back into the project after redevelopment.

Affordability and Rent Burden

Chapter 2 noted that Congress has given priority for housing assistance to very low-income renters, defined as those having incomes below 50 percent of the area median income and either paying more than 50 percent of income for rent or living in housing with severe physical problems.

Quantitatively, affordability is a much more important policy issue than quality. Far more low-income renters incur high rent burdens than live in seriously inadequate housing—as shown in table 2-2, more than fifteen times as many. Over six million very low-income renters live in housing with no substantial quality problems, but pay more than 50 percent of their income for rent; about 400,000 live in housing with severe physical problems.[35]

Virtually all subsidy programs now bring down the cost of housing for participants. This is so, however, only because programs now condition the subsidies on the income of the household. In both its tenant- and project-based forms, Section 8 has been income conditioned since it was enacted in 1974, and public housing assistance has been income conditioned since passage of the Brooke Amendments and the provision of operating subsidies beginning in the late 1960s. Neither public housing nor Section 221(d) (3)(BMIR) was originally conditioned on income; and Section 236 had a hybrid form of subsidy, under which tenants had to pay at least 25 percent of their income but could be required to pay more if the project mortgage and operating costs exceeded that amount. As discussed in chapter 3, these programs were not expected or designed to serve the lowest-income households. To the extent that the privately owned projects have not received subsequent Section 8 subsidy contracts, they still may not be affordable to very low-income households.

For participants in subsidized housing programs, the standard required share of income to be paid for rent is 30 percent; the dollar amount of assistance is designed to reduce an assisted tenant's rent burden to the 30 percent ratio.[36] In the case of the Housing Choice Voucher (and the earlier voucher program), however, the assisted household has the option of spending more than 30 percent of its income for rent if it chooses. Tenants may choose more expensive housing and pay the amount of rent not covered by the voucher. In fact a substantial number of voucher holders have chosen units that rent for more than the FMR, apparently preferring to devote more than 30 percent of their income to rent.

The data discussed below indicate that, overall, both the voucher and the major production programs make housing somewhat more affordable for lower-income households, while the newer programs, such as HOME and the LIHTC, commonly do not, without additional subsidy.

Combining AHS and Program Data. The reconciliation of AHS and program data on assisted households has the most recent information on rent-income ratios as well as on housing quality, but the data for rent burdens is problematical. Although households in the major project-based programs are intended to have rent-income ratios of exactly 30 percent (or somewhat lower when the statutory exclusions from income are taken into account), almost 40 percent of public housing residents, and over half of those living in subsidized privately owned projects, report rent burdens above 30 percent (table 5-4, panel A). In addition, over 30 percent of public housing residents and almost 20 percent of privately owned project residents report rent burdens below 20 percent. Among households receiving vouchers, two-thirds report rent burdens above 30 percent—a possible but unlikely figure. Almost 40 percent report rent burdens above 50 percent.[37]

Similar patterns occurred in all of the earlier reconciliations (1989, 1991, and 1993). They resulted in systematic efforts by HUD and the Census Bureau to identify and investigate possible explanations for the high reported rent burdens. The analysts concluded that the basic problem appeared to be response error for both income and rent.[38] Support for this hypothesis comes from comparisons of AHS responses to those in other surveys, such as the Current Population Survey. Yet such an explanation is only partly plausible. While it is perhaps not surprising that some assisted households might want to understate their incomes, and might expect or fear that the Census Bureau would report their response to the local public housing authority despite assurances to the contrary, there is no reason for these households to overstate their rent. An alternative or additional explanation has to do with the census procedure used when households fail to report their income—that is, with the allocation of an estimated income from a demographically similar household. Income and rent are not imputed in the relevant HUD program data, so those ratios, while averages, should be more accurate.

More recent HUD program data indicate that all of the major subsidy programs reduce rent burdens. As shown in panel B of table 5-4, the average burden in each program was less than 30 percent as of 2008. It was highest in the housing choice voucher, probably reflecting the ability of voucher residents to choose to spend more than 30 percent of their income for rent.[39]

An alternative indicator of program effectiveness is the income levels of the assisted households. These are also shown in panel B of table 5-4. At least 70 percent of the households in each program had extremely low incomes (less than 30 percent of the local median). Over 95 percent of participants in each program had very low incomes, except public housing.

Disaggregated data from a few years earlier, about the same time period as the AHS data in panel A, give a somewhat different picture for the

TABLE 5-4
MEASURES OF AFFORDABILITY BY PROGRAM

Panel A: American Housing Survey (2003)

Program Category	Mean Rent-Income Ratio	Percentage with Rent Burden of		
		<20%	<30%	>50%
Housing Choice Voucher	40	11	33	39
Public Housing	27	31	62	16
Privately Owned Projects	32	18	45	20

Panel B: Picture of Subsidized Households (2008)

Program	Mean Rent-Income Ratio	Percentage by Income:	
		Extremely Low	Very Low
Housing Choice Voucher	29.7	75	96
Public Housing	22.5	71	89
Section 8 New Construction	26.3	75	96
Section 236	27.2	78	96

SOURCES: U.S. Department of Housing and Urban Development, Office of Policy Development and Research, *Characteristics of HUD-Assisted Renters and Their Units in 2003*, Washington, DC, 33–34 (for panel A); U.S. Department of Housing and Urban Development, Office of Policy Development and Research, A Picture of Subsidized Households—2008, http://www.huduser.org/portal/picture2008/index.html (for panel B).

voucher program. As of FY2000, about 54 percent of voucher recipients paid less than 31 percent of their income in rent; the proportion rose to 62 percent for FY2001 and 2002. About 22 percent of voucher recipients in FY2000, and 16 percent in FY2001 and 2002, had rent burdens above 40 percent of their incomes. About 7 percent had rent burdens above 60 percent. High rent burdens were most common at the very bottom of the income distribution, among households with incomes below 10 percent of the area median (about $6,250 for a family of four in 2002). The median income for households with rent-income ratios above 60 percent was less than $3,500 in FY2002. Households with high rent burdens were disproportionately found in the South and in rural areas.[40]

HOME. There is no similar analysis of rent burdens or income levels for residents of public housing or the privately owned projects, but data are available for households living in HOME-assisted units. Income limits in

HOME are higher than for the older subsidy programs; most units must be affordable to households with incomes below 65 percent of the area median, and only 20 percent must be affordable to very low-income renters. Not surprisingly, rent burdens have been higher in this program. The most extensive analysis provides information as of 2000. At that time, average rent burden was 41 percent, well above the averages for any of the programs listed in Panel B of table 5-4, and the median was 33 percent, well above the voucher median. About 40 percent of occupants had rent-income ratios of 30 percent or less; another 40 percent had ratios of 31 to 50 percent; about 20 percent had rent burdens above 50 percent. About a third of HOME occupants received other housing subsidies, which brought down their rent burden substantially—to, on average, about 35 percent of their incomes. Although the program rules permit rents greater than 30 percent of tenant incomes, HOME serves predominantly low-income renters. About 80 percent had very low incomes, and almost 50 percent had extremely low incomes.[41] This implies that about one-sixth of HOME participants were extremely low-income households not receiving any other income-conditioned subsidy, which is about the same proportion as those who had rent burdens above 50 percent. HOME by itself does not make apartments for extremely low-income renters more affordable, unlike voucher and project-based programs.

HUD collects and publishes a brief summary of HOME program activity each year. This report includes the income level of assisted households, but not their rent burden. The latest data, through 2008, indicate that 57 percent of assisted renters have extremely low incomes, and another 31 percent have incomes below 50 percent of median.[42] These data suggest modestly better targeting than did the data for 1998.

LIHTC. Discussion of affordability in tax credit projects is hampered by the limited data available for resident households. What is available suggests that the effects of LIHTC are much like those of HOME.[43] As with HOME, rents are set as a percentage of median income, and there is no income-related subsidy to make units affordable for extremely low-income renters. The tax credit by itself is not enough to provide housing for extremely low-income renters. The most extensive review of households was conducted by the General Accounting Office (GAO) for projects placed in service between 1992 and 1994. About 75 percent of the residents had very low incomes. Almost the same proportion—71 percent—lived in units receiving additional subsidies; 39 percent received either tenant-based or project-based subsidies, and another 32 percent received concessionary financing from other sources such as state governments. Households receiving rental subsidies had incomes about half of those that did not. The typical voucher or certificate recipient had an income of about 20 to 25 percent of the area median; the typical unassisted household had an income of about 40 to 45 percent.[44] A detailed analysis of a sample of these projects, which was conducted by Abt Associates for HUD, found that some 37 percent of residents were receiving subsidies—31 percent in the form of project-based assistance and 6 percent in the form of tenant-based assistance. Again, households receiving assistance had incomes about half of those that did not. The assisted households generally had extremely low incomes (65 percent of those receiving project-based assistance, 74 percent of those receiving tenant-based assistance) and were nearly all minorities (99 percent and 95 percent, respectively), and predominantly African American (84 percent and 71 percent).[45] The high proportion of project-based assistance in these early years of the tax credit indicates that the credit was being used as part of efforts to preserve subsidized projects, probably built under Section 236 or Section 8.

Using a more extensive sample of projects covering the first ten years of the tax credit (1987–1996), Jean L. Cummings and Denise DiPasquale estimated affordability from program rent data. They estimated that the median rent in an LIHTC project implied a household income at about 48 percent of the national median—in other words, a bit more than half of the units were affordable to very low-income households. Few were affordable to extremely low-income households. The authors found: "While our data suggest that LIHTC projects serve low- and moderate-income households, these projects generally do not serve the poorest households." This conclusion is based on the rent affordability calculation; Cummings and DiPasquale did not have data on tenant incomes or on whether the tenant had a voucher.[46]

The 2006 update of the LIHTC database estimates that 140,000 to 280,000 of LIHTC residents are receiving vouchers, as mentioned in chapter 3.[47] These varied analyses lead to the general conclusion that tax credit projects are not likely to serve extremely low-income households unless those households are receiving other subsidies. Subsidies go either to moderate-income families that might otherwise be ineligible for assistance or to tenants with extremely low incomes.[48]

Subsidy Utilization and Program Participation

Before a household can enjoy whatever benefits it may receive from a housing program, it has to be both willing and able to participate in that program. The importance of a household's willingness to participate has often been overlooked in housing policy debates; a household's ability to participate has received substantial attention, but almost entirely with respect to tenant-based assistance.

Willingness to Participate. As explained in the discussion of housing quality earlier in this chapter, a household seeking to participate in any of the project-based programs must first of all be willing to move. This is not true for a household seeking tenant-based assistance. This difference is usually ignored in program utilization discussions as well as in measuring housing improvement.

Evidence on tenants' willingness to participate comes from two sources: the Experimental Housing Allowance program of the 1970s, and the comparative evaluation of tenant-based assistance programs conducted in the late 1980s, when both the certificate and voucher programs were active.

The EHAP Supply Experiment is the only entitlement housing program ever created, and as such it provides the best basis for estimating overall willingness to participate in a housing assistance program. Somewhat more than half—56 percent—of eligible low-income renters in Green Bay (those with incomes below 140 percent of the poverty line) and South Bend (those with incomes below 130 percent of the poverty line) wanted to participate in the housing allowance program.[49] Whether this rate is high or low is a matter of subjective judgment. It is fairly close to the participation rate in the Food Stamp program a few years later, when that program had a similar income limit; in the early 1980s the income ceiling for food stamps was lowered from 185 percent to 130 percent of the poverty line (except for households with an elderly member), and the participation rate was about 65 percent.[50]

Households in the Supply Experiment did not have to move in order to receive assistance if their current home met the program quality standards. Outreach efforts stressed this feature. Thus the 56 percent figure is probably a good indicator of willingness to participate.

Of those willing to participate, however, not all were willing to move. About 50 percent of those who enrolled in the Supply Experiment lived in units that failed a minimum quality inspection; 20 percent of these households (10 percent of all enrollees) responded by dropping out of the program.[51] This figure is certainly a lower bound; of the half whose home passed inspection, some at least would surely have been unwilling to move.

About 30 percent of the households in the Demand Experiment were satisfied with their living conditions and made no effort to search for better housing. Similarly, about 30 percent of participants in the certificate and voucher programs in the late 1980s were unwilling to move.[52]

All housing programs have quality standards; these are a second factor influencing willingness to participate. The housing standards requirement is unique among low-income benefit programs. Households have to select housing with certain specific attributes in order to participate, whether they value those attributes or not. Food stamps, by contrast, can be used for almost any foodstuff; and while Medicaid does not cover some medical services, it is unlikely that program participation is reduced because low-income households would rather have other medical services than those provided by the program. But assisted households may find themselves facing precisely this type of decision about housing.

Actual participation in the EHAP Supply Experiment, for example, was much lower than 56 percent (the share willing to participate), either because housing had to meet the program's quality standards in order for households to receive the allowance payments, or because the benefit they would receive was too small to bother with (the subsidy was smaller for households with higher incomes). Only about 75 percent of the interested renters were able and willing to meet the standards or felt it worthwhile to participate. The overall participation rate was therefore about 42 percent.[53]

It is important to recognize how the standards requirement affects program participation: the higher the standard, the fewer the households that are willing to participate in existing housing programs. This is clearest in the EHAP Demand Experiment, where some households were required to live in housing that met certain standards and some were not. Participation rates were substantially higher for the latter group. It also seems to be a reasonable inference from comparisons between the experiments. The Supply Experiment had the lowest quality standards, and the highest participation rate.[54] (Indeed, because the Supply Experiment standards were the lowest ever established for any housing program, the participation rate in the Supply Experiment is probably an upper bound on the participation rate in any program of tenant-based assistance.) It is also the case that the higher the standard, the fewer the units that will meet the standard, and the more likely that the standards will include some features that are unimportant to at least some of the households being offered assistance.[55] Quality standards serve the desirable purpose of ensuring that assisted households do in fact live in decent housing, and the program does achieve its public purpose; at the same time, they can be unduly restrictive, and they substitute the judgment of program administrators for the preferences of the people who are actually living in the housing.

Although participation rates have been studied only in existing housing programs, these findings are certainly relevant to the willingness of low-income households to participate in new construction programs. The evidence on participation and mobility in both the Demand Experiment and Supply Experiment suggests that, given the opportunity, a significant number of eligible households would not have chosen to move into a public housing or other subsidized project. They reported that they liked their neighborhood and they liked their present home.[56] The 30 percent of participants in the certificate and voucher programs who were unwilling to move would also be unlikely to participate in project-based programs.

Ability to Participate: Success Rates. The ability of households to participate in existing housing programs (as distinct from their willingness) has been a policy concern ever since the earliest evidence from the certificate program indicated that less than half of all participants were actually able to find satisfactory housing. This immediately raised the question of whether certificates or vouchers could "work." But over time, success rates steadily rose—from 45 percent in 1979 to 73 percent in 1985 and 87 percent in 1993.[57] The most plausible explanation for this improvement is that it takes time for landlords, tenants, and PHAs to become familiar with a new program, especially one as different in concept and detail as the certificate program was from public housing. Gradually, all these individuals and organizations became familiar with the programs, and tenants became more successful in using vouchers and certificates.

Evidence for this explanation comes from the pattern of relative success rates in the certificate and voucher programs. When the voucher program started, success rates were lower for those with vouchers than for those with certificates, even though voucher recipients had a wider range of options (because they could choose units with rents above the FMR). By 1993, after a decade's experience with vouchers, success rates with certificates and vouchers were about the same.

Between 1993 and 2000, however, the overall success rate for certificates and vouchers dropped to 69 percent, close to its level in 1985.[58] There is no obvious explanation for the decline. The analysts who conducted the 2000 study noted that success rates were positively correlated with local vacancy rates on a cross-sectional basis, but this does not explain the trends over time; vacancy rates were rising after 1996. For that matter, the increase in success rates between 1985 and 1993 is not explained by vacancy rates, either; rates in most markets did not rise during that period.[59] One reason for the decline may be the drop in the proportion of voucher holders who chose to remain in the same unit. In 1976, about half remained in place; in 1985–1987 and again in 1993, the proportion was 37 percent; by 2000, the proportion was 21 percent.[60]

Utilization of Available Assistance. "Success rates" measure the experience of individual households, not the record of the programs as a whole. For most of the history of the tenant-based programs, all funds allocated for certificates and vouchers by the federal government were used in those programs. Whenever a household was unable to use a certificate or voucher within a three-month period, it went to the next household on the waiting list, and was successfully used either by that household or by another one on the waiting list in the same market. This pattern changed in the late 1990s, and created concern about systematic underutilization of vouchers. In retrospect, the concern may have been overstated. Utilization rates rose rapidly in 2001 and 2002, apparently as a result of HUD pressure on PHAs.[61]

A study of utilization rates in 2002 among forty-eight PHAs—of which about half had high utilization rates and half had low—found an average utilization rate of 93 to 94 percent. The study also found that utilization rates for individual PHAs fluctuated fairly sharply over short periods of time. The study focused on differences in utilization rates between PHAs. It found that program management practices were largely responsible for these differences. Utilization rates were lower for PHAs that did not have a system for determining how many vouchers to issue in a given month, that had not developed good relationships with landlords, that devoted relatively fewer staff members to the program, and that were judged to have "poor management" policies. Also, rates were lower for a few PHAs that had recently received an additional allocation of vouchers, because some time is required for new voucher recipients to find and lease new units. In addition, there was some evidence of lower utilization rates in tighter markets with lower vacancy rates, but there were quite a few exceptions to the pattern. Utilization rates for vouchers were not related to the quality of housing stock.[62]

Program data in recent years show fluctuation in overall voucher utilization. All voucher funding was used in 2004, but the utilization rate dropped to 90 percent in 2006, before rebounding to 93 percent in 2007.[63]

It is instructive to compare utilization of vouchers with utilization in other programs. HUD data for the year 2008 show that the utilization rate for vouchers and the occupancy rates in the various project-based programs were virtually identical; all were 93 percent or very close to that number. Occupancy rates ranged from 91 percent for tax credit projects to 94 percent for Section 8 New Construction.[64] Despite the overall similarity between programs, policy discussions have focused much more on the ability of households to make use of tenant-based assistance programs than production programs, except perhaps in connection with projects that have become unfit to live in and largely or entirely vacant.

Demographics of Program Participation

Housing policy has long been concerned with the problems of particular groups among the low-income population, such as minorities, the elderly, and large families. This section looks at which of these groups participate in which housing programs, and at how well the different programs serve the needs of these groups. Using the program data shown in table 5-5, it reports on housing outcomes—measured primarily as the percentage of households in each program who are members of a particular group. All data are for the year 2004 except in the case of the LIHTC, where the data refer to projects completed during 1992–1994 and more recent data are not available, and in the case of HOPE VI, where data are for 2000–2002, depending on the completion date of the project. (Data as of 2008 for the voucher, public housing, Section 8, and Section 236 are similar to the data reported in table 5-5.)

Income. Household incomes are much higher in HOPE VI and the LIHTC than incomes for households in any of the other subsidy programs, even though the HOPE VI and LIHTC data are for earlier years.If household incomes rose with inflation, the median LIHTC income in 2004 would have been about $14,700, and the median income in HOPE VI would have been about $16,100.[65]

For both HOPE VI and the LIHTC, the income distributions are bifurcated between those who receive rental subsidies and those who do not. Over three-quarters of HOPE VI projects are explicitly designed as mixed-income housing and are intended to house a substantial share of residents not eligible for conventional public housing. About the same number of projects include owner-occupied housing, also not limited to households eligible for public housing.[66] These higher-income households often have incomes above the national median.[67] In tax-credit projects, incomes of unsubsidized households tend to be about double the incomes of those receiving assistance.

Minority Households. Minority households are the subject of special interest in housing policy because of the concern that their ability to use tenant-based assistance is limited by racial and ethnic discrimination in the private rental market. Production programs are sometimes thought to circumvent the problem of discrimination by directly providing minorities with decent housing.

Program data do not bear out this concern about tenant-based assistance, however. All programs except Section 8 New Construction serve black households disproportionately to their numbers in the eligible population. By contrast, only public housing serves Hispanic households

TABLE 5-5
HOUSEHOLD CHARACTERISTICS BY PROGRAM

	Voucher	Public Housing	Section 8 New Construction	Section 236	HOPE VI	LIHTC
Median Income	$9,100	$8,500	$9,100	$8,600	$15,300	$12,200
Mean Persons/Unit	2.6	2.2	1.5	1.9	NA	2.2
% Elderly	17	32	58	38	19	26
% with Female Head and Children	54	38	19	34	39	NA
% on Welfare[a]	11	9	4	7	14	NA
% White	37	32	61	43	7	53
% Black	43	44	24	38	74	33
% Hispanic	17	21	11	13	12	11

SOURCES: For voucher, public housing, Section 8 New Construction, and Section 236: U.S. Department of Housing and Urban Development, Office of Policy Development and Research, A Picture of Subsidized Households—2004-2007, http://www.huduser.org/portal/picture/query.html (data are for 2004);
For HOPE VI: Mary Jo Holin et al., Interim Assessment of the HOPE VI Program Cross-Site Report (Cambridge, MA: Abt Associates Inc., 2003) (covers 11 projects completed and fully or partially reoccupied as of 2000–2002).
For LIHTC: U.S. General Accounting Office, Tax Credits: Opportunities to Improve Oversight of the Low-Income Housing Program, GAO/GGD/RCED-97-55, Washington, DC, 1997 (covers 423 projects placed in service between 1992 and 1994).
NOTES: NA = not available. a = For voucher/certificate, public housing, Section 8, and Section 236, welfare is principal source of income; for HOPE VI, household receives some welfare.

disproportionately.[68] Minorities are served least well by privately owned subsidized projects. The tenant-based programs serve black households less well than public housing, but much better than Section 8, and better than the other categories of privately owned projects. The same is true, to a lesser extent, for Hispanic households.

This pattern has changed since in the early years of the certificate program. As of 1979, for example, about half of white certificate holders were successful in finding new homes, compared to just over a quarter of minority households.[69] Success rates of both non-Hispanic whites and blacks increased steadily until the early 1990s, while success rates for Hispanic households apparently rose after 1985.[70] By 1993, members of all major racial and ethnic groups were about equally successful in using certificates or vouchers.[71] This pattern held in 2004 as well; success rates in that year did not vary by race or ethnicity, taking account of household size, age of head (elderly or non-elderly), and household composition.[72] Thus, despite widespread concerns that discrimination against minorities in the private market would limit their ability to use tenant-based assistance, in fact the voucher and certificate programs have been more effective in providing housing for minorities than any of the project-based programs except public housing.

The Elderly. The picture is quite different for elderly households. They constitute over half of the residents of Section 8 New Construction, and are also disproportionately served by Section 236, public housing, and the LIHTC.[73] The percentage of elderly is lowest in the tenant-based programs. One reason why the elderly are served so much more in project-based programs is that many projects are designed specifically for them. Another is that while the elderly have apparently become especially successful in using tenant-based assistance in their current housing unit, they are much less successful than other groups in using vouchers or certificates to move to new units.[74] Earlier studies indicated that the elderly were more successful in using tenant-based assistance, partly because their initial housing was better, enabling them to move less often, and partly, apparently, because they were given the benefit of the doubt in PHA enforcement of housing standards, enabling them to qualify more easily for housing subsidies.[75]

Household Size and Composition. The pattern for household size is the reverse of that for the elderly. Despite concern that large families face a shortage of housing in the private market, in fact they are served to the greatest extent in the voucher and certificate programs, judging by the average number of persons per unit, as shown in table 5-5.[76] The privately owned projects serve large families least well. Concomitantly, tenant-based assistance is the most effective program in serving female-headed families with children. As of 2001, 29 percent of very low-income renters were female-headed families with children, indicating that all of the programs except Section 8 New Construction serve these families disproportionately. Finally, tenant-based assistance also has the highest proportion of families whose primary income source is welfare, although when elderly households are excluded, public housing has the highest. Section 8 New Construction has the lowest, even allowing for the high proportion of elderly.

Overall. The data show pronounced differences in participation by program. Section 8 New Construction is very much a program that in practice serves low-income white elderly households. This has been true since its inception; in the early years some 80 percent of project residents were elderly, and 85 percent were white.[77] Efforts to redirect the program had some success by the time it was terminated in 1983, but as table 5-5 shows, it continued to serve predominantly the elderly and white households. Section 8 New Construction stands out from all of the other programs in this respect.

The record of production programs as a whole is certainly mixed, and suggests that they do not automatically provide minorities with decent housing and avoid the problem of discrimination. Ironically, the concerns that tenant-based assistance would fail to serve minorities and large families have turned out to be misplaced. Large families in particular are better served by tenant-based assistance than by any of the project-based programs. Minority households are better served by tenant-based assistance than by any program except public housing.

Housing Market Effects

This section shifts the focus from the effects of housing subsidies on individuals to their effects on the housing market as a whole. The major issues are whether tenant-based assistance drives up rents, either for assisted or unassisted households, and whether tenant-based assistance works in tight markets.

Rent Inflation. Probably the most common concern expressed by critics of tenant-based assistance has been that these programs simply let landlords raise rents without improving housing quality. This concern was raised at the beginning of EHAP and was one of the major topics analyzed in that program.[78] Nearly all the major studies of tenant-based assistance programs have addressed the issue of rent inflation since then.

The general finding, however, is that tenant-based assistance has not resulted in rent inflation:

- The EHAP Supply Experiment sites should have experienced the largest price increases, because the Supply Experiment was an entitlement program. Rent increases in both Green Bay and

South Bend were negligible, however, both for assisted and unassisted households.[79]

- The Demand Experiment showed a similar pattern for assisted households, with the exception of one program variant in which the housing quality standard was simply a high minimum rent; households paid the higher rent without trying to find out if they were getting the best value for the dollar.[80]

- The large-scale evaluation of the certificate program in the late 1970s found rents for subsidized units to be about 4 to 5 percent above the expected market rent, based on the characteristics of the units, but attributed the higher rents to "the fact that recipients paid the normal market rate when they were related to the landlord, as opposed to receiving the discounts usually obtained in such situations."[81]

- The freestanding voucher demonstration study in the mid-1980s found that rents rose by about 10 percent for households that remained in the same unit, but this is not adjusted for quality increases. Repairs were made in the housing of about 40 percent of those who used their voucher in their current residence, and the rent increases for these households were about twice as much as for those whose units were not repaired.[82] The "pure" rent increase was therefore something less than 10 percent. The demonstration study did not take account of family relationships between tenant and landlord, which might result in below-market rent. In addition, households that successfully participated in the program apparently did not experience rent inflation. The demonstration study found that, after a year, rents rose by about 4–5 percent, in line with the housing market.[83]

There is some research that finds rent increases resulting from tenant-based assistance, but it is less reliable than the studies mentioned above. The largest reported rent increases were found in the earliest and least extensive evaluation, reporting information on rent changes for participating households as of late 1976, about two years after the Section 8 program was enacted. This evaluation reported changes in rents for participating households, separated on the basis of whether the household did or did not move after receiving subsidies, and further separating the latter into those whose units did or did not require repairs. The rent changes for the category of "stayers whose units required no initial repairs" perhaps comes reasonably close to measuring rent inflation induced by the program, and here the data did show sharp differences based on preprogram rents. Among households with extraordinarily low preprogram rents (under $50 a month), rents more than tripled, rising by an average of $100 per month. (These very low rents are probably explained by a family relationship between tenant and landlord. Few decent units could be rented on the open market for less than $50 per month in the late 1970s, but more than three-quarters of the units in this rent range that were successfully occupied by program participants—meaning that they met program quality standards—did not require repairs. These units probably were being rented for well below their market value.) Among stayers whose units rented for $50 to $150 and did not require repairs, rents increased by 33 percent on average; among those whose units rented for more than $150, the increase was 4 percent.[84]

Except for the Supply Experiment, all of these studies analyzed only the effect of housing subsidies on the rents of assisted households. There was no further research for about a decade or more after the freestanding voucher study referred to above completed its data collection in 1988. Then two studies around the year 2000 addressed the question of whether vouchers raised rents for unassisted tenants in the local market. The first, by Scott Susin, looked at changes in rents over the first twenty years of tenant-based assistance across ninety metropolitan areas, and found that as of 1993 vouchers had raised rents by 16 percent, on average, for unassisted low-income households; higher-income renters were not affected. This is a much larger increase for unassisted renters than any of the program evaluations had found for assisted renters. Susin calculated that tenant-based assistance had raised rents for unassisted renters by substantially more than it benefited those who were assisted, resulting in a net reduction of economic well-being for lower-income renters.[85]

Susin's analysis is the only study reporting significant rent inflation, and the only analysis using the AHS rather than program data. He calculated what rents would be—that is, he determined hedonic estimates of rents—in each of the ninety metropolitan areas, using units that were identified in the 1993 AHS as being unsubsidized. But the AHS data on subsidy status have long-recognized problems; as discussed earlier, AHS respondents have not been very accurate in answering questions about whether they are receiving housing subsidies. In particular, unsubsidized households are prone to say that they do receive assistance, and some subsidized households say they do not. In 2003, for example, the sample for the bottom trecile of the rent distribution included about 5,200 individual occupied units.[86] About one-third of these units—1,734—were described as assisted by the person interviewed. Subsequent matching of households in the sample with households receiving assistance according to HUD administrative records, however, found that 738 units were reported as assisted by the interviewee, but were not assisted according to HUD records; and conversely 477 units were assisted according to HUD records, but reported as unassisted by the interviewee.[87] The sample of unassisted units in the bottom trecile would consist of about 4,462 units, of which 477 or 10.7 percent were actually assisted; and it would exclude 738 units that were actually unassisted.[88] A related complication is that the sample sizes drawn from the national AHS are generally small (the median sample size is thirty-three)—too small for estimating a hedonic equation that attempts to take account of the various factors that affect rents.

At about the same time, a group of HUD analysts studied the location patterns of voucher recipients as of 1998 in the fifty largest metropolitan areas.[89] While this study does not directly address rent levels, it does provide evidence bearing on how housing vouchers affect rents. The study found that vouchers were used widely across neighborhoods. Voucher holders lived in 83 percent of the census tracts in these metropolitan areas. Typically the concentrations were low; in over half of the census tracts surveyed, fewer than 2 percent of residents had housing vouchers. A very small number of tracts—0.2 percent—had concentrations of 25 percent of residents receiving vouchers, and less than 1 percent of voucher holders lived in these tracts. Fewer than 15 percent lived in tracts with a concentration of 10 percent or more. (The distribution is shown in table 5-6.)

In central cities as a whole, rents were higher in tracts where the concentration of voucher holders was above 8 percent of the occupied housing stock, suggesting that a large number of voucher holders indirectly resulted

TABLE 5-6
CONCENTRATION OF VOUCHER HOLDERS BY CENSUS TRACT, 1998

Percentage of Residents within Tract Holding Vouchers	Percentage of All Tracts	Percentage of All Voucher Holders[a]
<2	50.5	22.6
2–5	20.6	34.4
5–8	6.7	20.4
8–10	2.1	8.4
10–25	2.4	13.4
≥25	0.2	0.8

SOURCES: Deborah J. Devine et al., *Housing Choice Voucher Location Patterns: Implications for Participants and Neighborhood Welfare* (Washington, DC: U.S. Department of Housing and Urban Development, Office of Policy Development and Research, 2003), tables II-3, V-1.
NOTE: a = Estimated by author from Devine et al., *Housing Choice Voucher Location Patterns*, table V-1.

in moderate rent increases for everyone. Looking at individual cities, however, the more common pattern was that rents were negatively correlated with the degree of concentration. That would be expected, in general; higher-quality housing results in higher rents, and units that voucher holders can afford are generally lower-quality ones. The study simply reports the general relationship between voucher concentration and median rent, and does not attempt to estimate a statistical relationship that takes account of other factors that would influence rents (such as the quality and size of housing units). Thus the evidence does not suggest that voucher holders are bidding up rents in neighborhoods where they are concentrated, and the data show clearly that most tenants with vouchers live in neighborhoods without many other voucher holders; they do not tend to be very concentrated at all. It is difficult to reconcile this dispersed pattern with Susin's results.

The bulk of the evidence, then, should allay the concern that tenant-based assistance drives up rent.[90] But that concern—widespread long before Susin's research, and indeed before any program experience or analysis—continues in spite of evidence to the contrary. In conversations with policymakers and local housing officials, I have found that the likelihood of rent inflation is usually the first objection raised to tenant-based assistance.

Tight Markets. The effectiveness of tenant-based assistance in tight housing markets is another long-standing policy concern. The term "tight market" is actually shorthand for several possibly interrelated problems: lower successful participation rates for voucher recipients, less quality improvement, and rising rents—not just for participants, but for all low income households in the metropolitan area. Tight markets are usually thought of in terms of vacancy rates, but housing quality and the ability of housing producers to respond to increases in demand are arguably more important factors.

Here again the best evidence comes from the EHAP Supply Experiment, and again because it was an entitlement program. The data show that the allowance actually worked better in the tighter market, Green Bay. The participation rate was higher there, and the effect on rents throughout both markets was negligible. Green Bay's housing stock was generally better than South Bend's.[91]

The voucher demonstration evaluation provides later evidence on participation rates in different market conditions. Both certificates and vouchers worked well in a variety of market types, but there were exceptions. New York and Boston, both classified as tight markets by HUD area offices, had much lower success rates than other markets: 33 percent of vouchers were used in New York and 47 percent in Boston. But success rates in two other tight markets, New Haven and Montgomery County, Maryland, were much higher, around 65 percent. Their rates were comparable to those in much looser markets.[92]

New York subsequently continued to show relatively low, though rising, success rates; HUD's utilization study reported that New York's utilization rate was 62 percent in 1993, compared to 42 percent in 1985–1987 (reweighting the earlier data to reflect the utilization study racial and demographic composition). Of course New York is unique in many ways; these figures need to be understood in the context of a long history of rent control and relatively low-quality rental housing stock. The 1993 national success rate was 87 percent.[93] Cross-sectionally, however, success rates were lower in tight markets and higher in loose markets, though the correlation varied by the measure of the vacancy rate.[94]

It is important to put these figures in perspective. There are no similar data for project-based housing programs; the question is simply not raised. But as a policy matter, there is some basis for comparison. The tight market issue is usually a short-run concern—what can be done here and now? In the short run, unfortunately, no program "works" in a tight market. Sudden changes will drive rents up or down until the market or the government can begin to respond, and neither the private sector nor the government will respond fast enough for those facing large rent increases. The best evidence is that private builders will take perhaps five years to produce enough new housing to loosen an unexpectedly tight market.[95] The government is likely to take about as long. Indeed, the slow pace of production has been a constant complaint about subsidized housing programs from at least the Douglas Commission in the late 1960s; this complaint is still heard today in connection with HOPE VI. In the late 1970s both public housing and Section 8 New Construction projects typically took about three years from HUD approval to completion.[96] HOPE VI projects have averaged about five and a half years.[97] And in fact these response times are understated, because they leave out the period of time before HUD approves a project.

The reality is that before the government can respond effectively to tight housing markets, these markets will probably begin to loosen. Today's tight markets are not tomorrow's. In the early 1980s, the tight housing markets in the United States were in oil-producing areas, such as Houston and Denver. Five years later, the markets in these cities were depressed, and the tight markets were in the Northeast. Any public housing projects in Houston and Denver begun by the government when those markets were tight would not have been finished until they were unnecessary and even redundant.

Conclusion

The original rationale for housing assistance, providing decent housing for poor households, has become less important as the housing stock has improved over the decades; the evidence is that vouchers and production programs result in better housing about equally well. Production programs may enable slightly more households to move from substandard to standard housing, but voucher holders are more satisfied with their housing. Affordability, which has become the most important problem, is directly addressed by all of the older programs. However, program data indicate that a surprisingly large number of assisted households continue to incur high rent burdens—not just in the voucher program, where rents in excess of 30 percent of income are permitted, but in the production programs, where the rent is required by statute to be no more than 30 percent of income. (Substantially more voucher holders report a high rent burden, as is to be expected.) The newer programs—the LIHTC and HOME—do not serve the poor without additional tenant-based or project-based assistance.

Minority households are much better served in the voucher and public housing programs than in Section 8 New Construction and other privately owned projects; the converse is true for the elderly. Large families are best served by vouchers.

The best evidence is that vouchers do not drive up rents for either assisted or unassisted households, despite widespread opinion to the contrary. One good reason is that voucher holders are widely spread across urban neighborhoods, rather than being concentrated in a few areas.

6

The Voucher/Production Debate: Neighborhood Issues

This chapter looks at the location of subsidized housing, and considers the impact of subsidized housing on the neighborhoods in which it is located. Specifically, it looks at whether the neighborhoods where voucher recipients live differ from neighborhoods having subsidized projects, and how voucher and production programs affect neighborhoods.

Locational issues have often loomed large in policy debates, because they involve the well-being of households not receiving assistance but living in the same neighborhood as those that are. Long-time residents worry that construction of subsidized housing in their neighborhood or an influx of voucher holders might lower property values, increase crime, or substantially change the economic and demographic composition of the neighborhood. A close look at available data and analyses makes it possible to address these concerns with facts.

The chapter starts by reporting the characteristics of neighborhoods where subsidized housing is located, along with resident satisfaction by neighborhood. It draws on the same data sources that were used in looking at housing quality in chapter 5. It then reviews program research and evaluations that analyze specific policy issues, including the effect of subsidized housing on neighborhood revitalization, on racial segregation and integration, and on economic integration and opportunity.

"A Suitable Living Environment": Where Assisted Households Live

There are several types of information on the neighborhoods in which assisted households live: objective data on neighborhood characteristics and location; subjective assessments of the neighborhood by households receiving assistance; and comparisons of the neighborhood where the household lived before it received assistance to the neighborhood where it lives with housing assistance.

Objective Measures. The basic sources of objective information are HUD program data on housing and decennial census data on neighborhoods. HUD's Picture of Subsidized Households database provides a convenient combination of these data: the characteristics of assisted households, attributes of their housing, and aspects of the census tracts where they live. Tracts are not necessarily neighborhoods, but each tract is intended to have similar demographic and economic characteristics, and each is typically delineated by natural or manmade features, such as major streets or highways.[1] The tracts also provide a uniform national basis for describing a household's or housing unit's locale. Table 6-1 reports three neighborhood characteristics, by program, for assisted households, on the same basis as table 5-5. Locational data for tax credit projects are routinely available (although household information is not), so the information for tax credit projects in table 6-1 is directly comparable to the information for the HUD programs.

Public housing stands out as being located in tracts with the highest poverty rate, close to 30 percent on average (the average is calculated by resident, not by project); in all the other programs, as table 6-1 shows, the average poverty rate in a tract is close to 20 percent. A 20 percent poverty rate is also the threshold for officially designating a tract a "poverty area." Data on the poverty rate of assisted households is not available, but given the fact that at least 60 percent in each program have extremely low incomes, it seems clear that assisted households generally live in tracts where their unassisted neighbors have somewhat higher incomes than they do.

With respect to homeownership, voucher holders, residents of tax credit projects, and residents in Section 8 New Construction projects all live in tracts with a homeownership rate around 35 percent; residents of public housing and Section 236 live in tracts where the rate is less than 30 percent.

Differences in the concentration of minorities in a neighborhood are more marked. Minority concentration ranges from a high of about 55 percent for public housing to a low near 40 percent for Section 8 New Construction. Table 6-1 also reports for each program the share of assisted

TABLE 6-1
NEIGHBORHOOD CHARACTERISTICS OF
ASSISTED HOUSEHOLDS BY PROGRAM, 2008

(Percentage of Population in Tract Where Assisted Household Lives)

Program	Poverty Rate	Homeowner (Single-Family)	Minority in Tract	Minority in Program
Voucher	18	37	45	62
Public Housing	29	27	56	69
Section 8 NC/SR	21	35	42	45
Section 236	23	29	49	59
LIHTC	19	36	44	NA

SOURCE: U.S. Department of Housing and Urban Development, Office of Policy Development and Research, A Picture of Subsidized Households—2008, http://www.huduser.org/portal/picture2008/index.html.
NOTES: NC/SR = New Construction/Substantial Rehabilitation. NA = not available.

households whose members are minorities (except for the LIHTC, where data are not available). In each case other than Section 8 New Construction, the share of minority assisted households in the program is higher than the share of minority households in the neighborhood. The typical tract has more assisted than unassisted households belonging to minority groups, and the difference is about the same in each program.

Data on HOPE VI are much more limited and are not shown in table 6-1. Few HOPE VI projects have been completed, so the only available data on the current characteristics of neighborhoods for completed projects come from just four projects from the 2003 interim assessment of the program. Three of the four projects were redeveloped as public housing; in those neighborhoods the population consisted almost entirely of minority renters both before and after the HOPE VI redevelopment, and the post-redevelopment poverty concentration ranged from 56 to 68 percent in 2000. The fourth project was redeveloped as a mixed-income community; in this instance the minority population declined from 84 percent to 65 percent, and the post-redevelopment poverty rate was 38 percent, still high enough to classify the neighborhood officially as "poor."[2] For all three characteristics shown in table 6-1—concentration of poverty, of minorities, and of homeowners— these neighborhoods had higher concentrations than public housing tracts in general. This of course is a small sample and possibly unrepresentative.

TABLE 6-2

LOCATION OF ASSISTED HOUSING BY TRACT CHARACTERISTICS

(Proportion of Units in Census Tracts with Attribute)

Program	Median Income < $10,000	40% of Households on Welfare	40% of Households with Minority Head	40% of Households in Poverty	Underclass Tract
Tenant-based	2.3	0.9	26.4	5.3	2.4
Public housing	25.4	18.6	55.9	36.3	16.4
Elderly	17.1	4.4	27.7	17.2	5.2
Family	29.2	23.6	65.3	43.4	20.3
HUD-assisted projects	8.4	4.3	34.5	12.6	5.2
LIHTC	7.5	2.8	31.4	10.3	4.0
Welfare	6.0	NA	33.2[a]	11.6	5.7

SOURCE: Sandra J. Newman and Ann B. Schnare, "'And a Suitable Living Environment': The Failure of Housing Programs to Deliver on Neighborhood Quality," *Housing Policy Debate*, 8, no. 4 (1997), table 12.
NOTES: Underclass tract is at least one standard deviation above the national average on all of the following: (1) high school dropouts; (2) working age males not regularly attached to the labor force; (3) welfare recipients; (4) households headed by women with children. NA = not available; a = interpolated by author.

A study by Sandra J. Newman and Ann B. Schnare made use of program data from HUD and other sources to look at the share of subsidized units located in neighborhoods at an extreme of the distribution of various attributes. Their results, shown in table 6-2, indicate that public housing is typically located in tracts with low median incomes, with high concentrations of households on welfare or in poverty, or qualifying as "underclass tracts." In addition, more than half of public housing units are located in tracts where at least 40 percent of the population is minority. On each of these dimensions, public housing stands out from all the other program categories. As the table shows, public housing projects for families are in much lower-income neighborhoods, with much higher minority concentrations, than are projects for the elderly or handicapped.[3]

Newman and Schnare also compared assisted households to all households receiving welfare, and found that HUD-assisted privately owned projects and tax credit projects were about as concentrated in tracts with

TABLE 6-3
NEIGHBORHOOD POVERTY RATES BY PROGRAM, 1998

(Percentage of Households with Incomes Below Poverty Threshold within Census Tract)

Program	0–10%	10–20%	20–30%	30–40%	Above 40%	Poverty Area (above 20%)
Voucher	28.4	30.2	19.2	12.7	9.5	41.4
Movers	31.9	30.7	17.7	10.9	8.7	37.4
Remaining in Place	26.4	29.4	19.1	14.6	10.4	44.2
Public Housing	7.0	15.4	11.5	17.5	48.6	77.6
Section 8 Project	18.2	22.1	15.2	17.3	27.1	59.7

SOURCE: Deborah J. Devine et al., *Housing Choice Voucher Location Patterns: Implications for Participants and Neighborhood Welfare* (U.S. Department of Housing and Urban Development, Office of Policy Development and Research, 2003), tables III-6, III-8.
NOTE: Data are limited to households with children.

high concentrations of poverty and other problems as were welfare recipients as a whole.[4] Only voucher and certificate holders were consistently and substantially less concentrated in high-poverty and underclass areas than welfare recipients as a whole. The same pattern occurred for tracts with high concentrations of minority households.

Table 6-3 reports information from the HUD study of voucher recipient location to describe the distribution of the poverty concentration for households with children as of 1998, for voucher holders, residents of public housing (including the few completed HOPE VI projects), and residents of Section 8 projects (including Moderate Rehabilitation as well as New Construction/Substantial Rehabilitation). More than half—almost 60 percent—of all voucher holders lived in tracts with a poverty rate below 20 percent (i.e., tracts not designated officially as "poverty areas"); more than a quarter lived in tracts with a poverty rate below 10 percent. By comparison, only about 40 percent of Section 8 project residents, and only about 20 percent of public housing residents, lived in tracts that were not poverty areas. Indeed, almost half of public housing residents lived in tracts where the poverty rate was more than 40 percent. Such tracts verge on the completely dysfunctional, with high rates of single-parent households and low rates of labor force participation. Less than 10 percent of voucher holders lived in tracts with so high a poverty rate.

Within the voucher program, data are available separately for those moving from and those staying in their original unit; these are also reported in table 6-3. Movers live in neighborhoods with a modestly lower poverty rate; the median poverty rate is 15.9 percent for movers, and 18.0 percent for nonmovers. About 37 percent of those who move end up in tracts which are poverty areas, compared to about 44 percent of those who do not move. The biggest difference is in the lowest poverty category; at the other end, slightly more of those who do not move live in tracts with poverty rates above 40 percent.

Similar data for projects with children are not available for the newer programs, so these are not included in table 6-3; but among all tax credit projects placed in service between 1995 and 2006, about 38 percent were located in poverty areas. It is not clear whether the difference between tax credit projects and HUD-subsidized housing arises because a large share (about 40 percent) of the tax credit projects are not intended for families, or because tax credit projects are generally located in tracts with fewer poor people than projects funded through the older programs.[5]

Subjective Assessments. The opinions of assisted households about their neighborhoods are available from the AHS. Table 6-4 (which parallels table 5-2) reports ratings for neighborhood, disaggregated between elderly and non-elderly households, as of 2003. In both groups, public housing stands out: more residents of public housing are seriously dissatisfied with their neighborhood than recipients of other types of housing assistance. The dissatisfaction figure for the elderly living in public housing—6.3 percent—is more than twice as high as that for residents of privately owned projects and for unassisted households with worst-case needs. There are literally no seriously dissatisfied elderly voucher holders. The fact that the medians are close indicates that the dissatisfaction with public housing is fairly concentrated; about the same proportion in all three program categories give high ratings to their neighborhood. Among the non-elderly, dissatisfaction is much higher across the board, and very strong in public housing. Indeed, 11 percent of non-elderly public housing residents give their neighborhood the lowest possible rating—1 on a scale of 1 to 10. The median rating is 6.8, lower than the ratings for the other programs, and for unassisted households as well.

TABLE 6-4
SUBJECTIVE RATING OF NEIGHBORHOOD BY ASSISTED HOUSING PROGRAM, 2003

	% Rating <5	Median Rating	Median Income
Panel A: Elderly Households			
Tenant-Based Assistance	0.0	9.3	$7,949
Public Housing	6.3	9.1	$7,709
Privately Owned Projects	2.9	8.6	$7,957
Worst-Case Needs	2.7	8.5	$7,845
Unassisted, Eligible	2.7	8.5	$8,420
Panel B: Non-Elderly Households			
Tenant-Based Assistance	7.8	7.8	$8,189
Public Housing	24.9	6.8	$8,191
Privately Owned Projects	17.2	7.3	$9,038
Worst-Case Needs	10.1	7.5	$7,701
Unassisted, Eligible	9.7	7.6	$9,534

SOURCE: U.S. Department of Housing and Urban Development, Office of Policy Development and Research, *Characteristics of HUD-Assisted Renters and Their Units in 2003*, Washington, DC: U.S. Department of Housing and Urban Development, May 2008.
NOTE: Median ratings are on a scale of 1 to 10.

Comparison of table 6-4 with table 5-2 suggests that elderly voucher recipients are making a trade-off between their housing and their neighborhood, using their voucher to live in somewhat less satisfactory housing than unassisted elderly with worst-case needs, but moving to a better neighborhood. Non-elderly households may be making the opposite choice—moving to better housing in a slightly worse neighborhood.

The study of thirty-nine LIHTC projects mentioned in the previous chapter—the only relevant study of any of the newer programs—finds a similar pattern. While two-thirds of the residents rated their housing as "excellent or good," fewer than half (46 percent) gave this rating to their neighborhood.[6]

The Moving to Opportunity demonstration has the opposite pattern. In both the interim and final evaluations, households that were required to move to low-poverty neighborhoods in order to receive a voucher liked their neighborhood slightly better than their housing. In the final evaluation, 68 percent considered their housing unit good or excellent, compared to 71 percent giving those ratings to their neighborhood. Households receiving a voucher but not being required to move had a similar pattern; 62 percent liked their housing compared to 65 percent liking their neighborhood. Neither of these differences appears to be statistically significant. These households were all families; none were elderly. They are thus comparable to the households in panel B of table 6-4.[7]

Mobility and Neighborhood Change. As in the case of housing conditions, comparisons between assisted housing programs and unassisted households or welfare recipients perhaps implicitly encourage the inference that before receiving assistance, the assisted households had lived in the same sort of neighborhoods as unassisted households or welfare recipients (or in the case of vouchers, that movers originally lived in the same sort of neighborhoods as nonmovers). The difference has sometimes been interpreted as a change in the neighborhood for those who receive assistance (or who move).[8] But—again as in the case of housing quality—this is an assumption rather than a fact.

Some research has been conducted on the change actually experienced by households receiving vouchers. Two studies have analyzed the mobility of voucher holders over several years. Judith D. Feins and Rhiannon Patterson tracked all families with children who entered the program between 1995–2002—some 628,000 households, as long as they remained in the program, and including all moves during the period. About a quarter of recipients originally chose to remain in place when they first received the voucher; but after the initial decision, both those who moved and those who did not were almost equally likely to move at a later time, fewer than 20 percent in each category.[9]

The study measured the change between the original and new neighborhoods across eight indicators of neighborhood poverty, six indicators of economic opportunity, and three categories of neighborhood race and ethnicity. Of these 17 attributes, the difference between the neighborhoods was 1 percentage point or less for nine (including the Hispanic share of the population), and 1 to 3 percentage points for five others (including the poverty rate, the African American share of the population, and the total minority share). Ten of the 14 of the poverty and economic measures indicated that the new neighborhood had more poverty and less opportunity.

The new neighborhoods also had more members of minority groups, in all three categories. The homeownership rate in the new neighborhood was lower by 5 percentage points. The pattern was the opposite, however, for the 19 percent who moved again, or who moved after their initial decision to remain in their original unit: 13 of the 14 poverty and opportunity indicators showed improvement, and the other was the same in both neighborhoods. The changes were even smaller than for the initial moves: 11 improved by less than 1 percentage point, and the other two by between 1 and 2 percentage points. The proportion of Hispanic residents increased, while the proportions of African Americans and all minorities decreased, in each case differing by less than 1 percentage point.[10]

As Reins and Patterson make clear, their study is limited by the fact that more than half of these households participated in the voucher program for no more than two years, for two reasons: (1) almost half entered the program in 2000 or later, and since the study ends with 2002 data, there is no record of their participation after that year; and (2) over half the households had dropped out of the program by 2001. The Moving to Opportunity demonstration tracked a much smaller number of households for a much longer period—4,600 households over 15 years. Over that time, changes in neighborhood composition were much larger. At the beginning of the demonstration, the poverty rate was about 42 percent in all three groups. For the control group, the poverty rate in their neighborhood declined to 39 percent at the interim evaluation and 31 percent at the final. For the group receiving standard Section 8 vouchers, the neighborhood poverty rate was 29 percent at the interim and 27 percent at the final; for those receiving the experimental vouchers requiring them to move to low-poverty areas, the rates were 20 percent at the interim and 23 percent at the final. These differences were statistically significant; voucher recipients moved to neighborhoods with lower poverty rates.

The racial and ethnic composition of the neighborhood was less affected by having a voucher. At the beginning, minority households constituted between 91 and 92 percent of the neighborhood residents in all three groups. For the control group, the minority share declined to 88 percent in the interim evaluation and 84 percent in the final. For the group receiving standard Section 8 vouchers, the changes were virtually identical: 86 percent of residents in their neighborhoods were members of minority groups

TABLE 6-5

SUBJECTIVE JUDGMENT OF NEIGHBORHOOD CHANGE FOR NON-ELDERLY
ASSISTED HOUSEHOLDS MOVING DURING PREVIOUS YEAR, 2003

	Percentage Moving to:	
	Better Neighborhood	Worse Neighborhood
Tenant-Based Assistance	55	7
Public Housing	32	18
Privately Owned Projects	42	18

SOURCE: U.S. Department of Housing and Urban Development, Office of Policy Development and
Research, *Characteristics of HUD-Assisted Households and Their Units in 2003*, Washington, DC, May 2008.
NOTE: Percentages do not add to 100 because some households responded "about the same" and
others did not respond.

at the interim evaluation and 84 percent at the final. For the group required
to move to low-poverty neighborhoods, minorities constituted 77 percent
of their neighborhoods at the interim, and 75 percent at the final. For this
experimental group, the difference was statistically significant, but clearly
much smaller than the change in the poverty rate.[11]

Subjective assessments of neighborhood change for assisted households
are generally positive. Table 6-5 reports the opinions concerning the change
in the neighborhood for those non-elderly assisted households that moved
within the previous year. (This table parallels table 5-3 for changes in housing quality.) Households in all three programs generally believed that they
had moved to a better neighborhood rather than a worse one. Voucher
holders were especially positive: a majority (55 percent) believed the new
neighborhood was better; a very small minority (7 percent) believed it was
worse. Smaller but still substantial pluralities in the other programs considered their new neighborhood better: 42 percent to 18 percent among
residents of privately owned subsidized projects, 32 percent to 18 percent
in public housing.

The Moving to Opportunity demonstration was designed to measure
the effects of changing neighborhoods on families receiving vouchers. As
mentioned previously, one set of households received vouchers which
they could only use to move to low-poverty neighborhoods; another set
received vouchers to be used as they chose; a third group received no
vouchers at all. The evaluations asked families whether they thought their

new neighborhood was a good place to live, not whether they liked their new neighborhood better than their old one. Among those who were not offered vouchers as part of the demonstration, 48 percent considered their neighborhood "excellent" or "good" at the time of the interim evaluation (four to seven years after the demonstration began), and 52 percent at the final evaluation (10 to 15 years after the beginning). Those who were offered vouchers with no constraints and used them to move had more positive ratings: 66 percent at the interim evaluation and 62 percent at the final. Those who were required to move to low-poverty neighborhoods were still more positive: 77 percent at the interim evaluation and 68 percent at the final.[12]

When asked if their new neighborhood was better than their old one, households in tax credit projects were split: one-third thought their new neighborhood was better, one-third not as good, and one-third about the same.[13]

There are several possible explanations for the difference between the objective and subjective ratings. Unlike the objective ratings, the subjective ratings do not specify whether the moves are first moves or subsequent ones, and while subjective ratings are ordinal rankings—is the new neighborhood better than the previous one?—the objective measures are cardinal—is the new neighborhood good? It seems problematic to assume, moreover, that slight differences in such neighborhood characteristics as the poverty rate or even the homeownership rate are enough to cause assisted households to rank neighborhoods as clearly preferable; without any direct data, it is unclear that such differences are even visible.

Perhaps the best explanation for the difference between the objective and subjective ratings has to do with the freedom to choose. This freedom certainly seems to account for much of the difference between ratings of vouchers and other programs. Voucher holders have been able to make their own choices; those in projects have been able to choose only whether to accept the unit offered to them, wherever it may be, or to continue living without housing assistance, and probably pay a high share of their income for rent. Households in the three major programs have moved to better housing, in their own judgment. But in the minds of those assisted, tenant-based assistance is clearly better than project-based assistance in helping tenants move to a better neighborhood.

Neighborhood Revitalization and Preservation

Recipients of housing subsidies, particularly voucher holders, are generally able to move to better neighborhoods. What happens to the neighborhood when they move in? This section addresses both objective and subjective evidence about how the presence of households receiving assistance affects the neighborhood.

Vouchers and Neighborhoods. Local concerns that housing vouchers will damage neighborhoods date back to EHAP in the 1970s and have been raised in a number of places since then. In 1994, for example, the Moving to Opportunity demonstration was strongly opposed by neighborhood groups, most notably in Baltimore County, Maryland, who did not want public housing residents using vouchers to move into their suburban neighborhoods. Congress responded by terminating funding for an expansion of the demonstration, even though it had been supported by HUD Secretary Henry Cisneros.[14]

The concerns have been frequent enough that in 1999 HUD funded a study of community controversies about tenant-based assistance; the researchers identified more than forty potential locations for study, and eventually conducted in-depth analyses in eight.[15] The potential sites on the larger list were geographically concentrated: "repeated instances of Section 8 community conflict were abundant in the Northeast, less frequent in the Midwest, and quite rare in the South and West."[16] The analysts also found that neighborhoods with conflict were all places that had experienced economic decline. They were not necessarily poor, or even the poorest sections of their cities or metropolitan areas. Indeed, several of the eight that were studied in detail had poverty rates below 10 percent.[17] This figure should be treated with caution, since it comes from the 1990 census, and the community conflicts occurred later—though some communities had experienced controversy as far back as the 1970s. Whatever they were like in 1990, the neighborhoods were changing by 2000, for a variety of reasons ranging from immigration to loss of major employers. Some of the controversies were extremely local, as small as a few families on a single block. But in each case the controversy occurred in a declining neighborhood, and local residents blamed the housing vouchers for the decline, or felt that the program was exacerbating it.

The HUD study reviewed the practices of the local program administrators and noted several common features that contributed to the controversy, including failure to respond to neighborhood complaints and failure to help families find housing in a broad range of neighborhoods; in general, program administrators did not see themselves as having any responsibility for neighborhood effects.[18]

These controversies about small numbers of vouchers can be contrasted with the results of the EHAP Supply Experiment, the only entitlement housing program ever created. Neighborhood effects were systematically studied in the two Supply Experiment metropolitan areas, with inconclusive but still suggestive results. Modest repairs were made to a large number of housing units in which voucher recipients lived; disproportionately more units were repaired in the neighborhoods with the worst housing. This pattern probably minimizes the neighborhood impact; the worst neighborhoods are not the best candidates for revival, even if a large number of housing units are modestly upgraded. It appears that repairs were not widespread enough to reach a critical mass and start any neighborhood on a clear path to revitalization, at least through the end of the experiment. However, many households thought that the neighborhood had improved, particularly in neighborhoods with high participation rates.[19] Thus in communities with large numbers of voucher recipients, the neighborhood improved, in the judgment of residents, while in communities with small numbers, the neighborhood was at least sometimes thought to have deteriorated. The differences between the EHAP results and the more recent local controversies have not been studied; they would appear to be a fertile subject for future research.

Project-Based HUD Programs. Most of the recent controversies over the possible harmful effects of housing subsidies on neighborhoods have concerned tenant-based assistance, partly because the voucher has for many years been the only active program providing much in the way of incremental assistance to lower-income households. But there have been serious local issues in project-based programs as well. Since the late 1980s federal policy has sought to preserve Section 8 projects as low-income housing, culminating in 1998 with the Mark-to-Market program, which writes down the project mortgage and lowers the rental subsidy in an effort to reduce program costs without greatly reducing the number of assisted projects. Some local governments have been strongly opposed to preserving particular projects, on the grounds that the projects interfere with plans to revitalize the neighborhood; examples include Baltimore County, Pittsburgh, Indianapolis, and Joliet, Illinois—again a concentration in the Northeast and Midwest. In these situations, there is a sharp conflict between the HUD program, designed to preserve the project if at all economically feasible, and the local plan.

Similar problems have arisen in neighborhoods with public housing projects, built decades ago, that turn out to be in the path of neighborhood revitalization or gentrification; examples are Chicago's Near North Side, where Cabrini-Green was located, and the area north of the Walter E. Washington Convention Center in Washington, DC, which has a concentration of public and other subsidized housing. These issues arise because of a widely held belief that subsidized housing thwarts neighborhood preservation or revitalization. In the words of a review of HOPE VI, "In many cities, severely distressed public housing projects have been regarded as major causes of social and economic deterioration in the neighborhoods that surround them."[20]

A number of studies have attempted to determine if public housing projects do in fact make things worse in their neighborhoods, with particular focus on the concentration of the poor. They typically show that poverty rates are higher in census tracts where projects are located, and that poverty rates rise in neighborhoods after projects are built there. Some studies also show that the poverty rate declines with distance from the project.[21] They do not generally address the question of causality, however; some analysts argue that projects are located in neighborhoods that are deteriorating and likely to experience increases in poverty whether public housing is built there or not.[22] This is the same point made in the HUD review of local controversies over housing vouchers: the program is being blamed for neighborhood changes that may well have occurred anyway. But the research issue here seems to have been narrowed: the projects are not contributing to neighborhood revitalization, whether or not they are contributing to neighborhood decline.

An in-depth study of several neighborhood housing markets for Chicago, which addressed the relationship between federal housing programs and neighborhood conditions in the early 1980s (when both project-based and tenant-based Section 8 programs were quite active), concluded that older big city neighborhoods were better served by existing housing programs; the programs encouraged the occupancy and maintenance of the better older housing in the neighborhood. New construction programs, by contrast, weakened the neighborhood by reducing the demand for existing housing, particularly in neighborhoods with declining population.[23] Later research supports this conclusion.[24]

LIHTC. The newer project-based programs such as HOPE VI and the LIHTC are targeted at somewhat higher-income households, and HOPE VI is to some extent explicitly designed as a neighborhood revitalization program. The record of these programs in generating neighborhood improvement is mixed, however, at best.

In their analysis of LIHTC projects during the first ten years, Cummings and DiPasquale found that in many of the neighborhoods studied, "LIHTC projects represent[ed] the only new residential construction in recent years."[25] This was particularly true for central city neighborhoods. A tenth of LIHTC city projects were in tracts with no new housing construction during the previous five years; a quarter were in tracts with no new rental housing. They also found that virtually all projects were built in low-income and moderate-income neighborhoods; in five large cities, between 60 and 90 percent of these projects were located in tracts where the median income was less than 60 percent of the area median.[26] This finding could be interpreted to mean that the LIHTC contributes to neighborhood revitalization in the sense that new housing is being built in these areas; but it is also true that the new housing is serving the same population rather than attracting higher-income residents. "Revitalization" in this sense consists merely of adding more lower-income housing to a neighborhood that already consists predominantly of lower-income housing—possibly improving the housing quality and certainly adding new housing, but not otherwise changing the neighborhood.

Other evidence is generally consistent with this finding. GAO developed a sample of projects as of 1997 and found that over half were located in tracts where the median income was less than 40 percent of the area median, and that 85 to 90 percent were in tracts where the median income was less than 50 percent of the area median; in other words, more than half the residents of the tract had very low incomes.[27] Looking at a somewhat earlier period, Newman and Schnare found that the geographic distributions of tax credit projects and other privately owned assisted projects were similar, and both closely resembled the distribution of welfare recipients, "suggesting that the location of these developments does little to alter existing residential patterns."[28] The Abt Associates analysis of thirty-nine properties placed in service between 1992 and 1994 found that half were located in very low-income neighborhoods, a lower share than that found in other studies.[29] The most recent data indicates that about 38 percent of tax credit units placed in service between 1995 and 2006 were located in poverty areas (defined as census tracts with at least 20 percent of households with incomes below the poverty line), compared to 28 percent of all rental housing.[30] None of these studies suggests that tax credit projects have contributed to neighborhood revitalization.

HOPE VI. HOPE VI started as a program to replace the worst public housing, but by 1997 the focus had shifted toward providing mixed-income housing, explicitly for the purpose of strengthening the neighborhood as well as improving housing in the existing project. Evaluating the program's impact on a neighborhood is complicated for several reasons. First, a HOPE VI project is itself part of the neighborhood being looked at, although this problem is mitigated somewhat in that some of the evaluations define and measure the neighborhood more broadly than as just a census tract. Second, neighborhood data are generally available only from the decennial census, which does not necessarily coincide with the completion date of a project. A third problem is that projects take so long to complete, and research takes additional time; although the program was enacted in 1992, and as of 2008 about 40 percent of projects had been completed,[31] there are still relatively few cases where a before-and-after comparison is feasible. Some studies have been forced to make before-and-partially-after comparisons, and also to drop some projects from their samples because the project had not completed—or in some cases even begun—reconstruction. The result is that studies of HOPE VI have generally concentrated on a limited number of projects, and the samples have overlapped; thus generalizations to the overall program are problematic, and it is hard to be sure just what the program outcomes have been. The four most extensive studies between them have covered twenty-five projects, of which a substantial share, perhaps more than half, were only partially completed at the time of the study.[32]

The interim assessment conducted by Abt Associates researchers includes seven completed projects and six partially reoccupied projects, and contains the most extensive data.[33] Overall, three of the completed project neighborhoods and one of the partially reoccupied projects were classified as "appreciably improved," two of the completed projects and three of the partially reoccupied as "moderately improved," and two in each category as "slightly improved."[34] The ratings, based on about a dozen economic and demographic characteristics, compare the neighborhood at completion (or shortly before, for projects completed after the 2000 census) to the neighborhoods before the project was redeveloped (using 1990 census data); they also compare the changes in the project neighborhood to the changes in the city as a whole during the same period. The interim assessment includes both projects redeveloped as mixed-income communities and those redeveloped exclusively as public housing; ratings from tenants were generally higher for the mixed-income projects. Two additional projects, included in a 2005 Brookings Institution study, show strong gains in income, employment, education, and safety, although it should be noted that this study was at least partly intended to counteract Bush administration proposals to terminate HOPE VI, and looked at "probably the most seasoned mixed-income developments" and those "widely regarded as having positive neighborhood impacts."[35] A 2003 study by GAO comparing four mostly completed projects to similar neighborhoods in the same cities was inconclusive; it found that "some variables indicated greater improvements in the HOPE VI neighborhoods than their comparable neighborhoods, such as in mortgage lending activity, but other variables indicated inconsistent results among the sites."[36]

Evaluation of partially rebuilt or reoccupied sites is limited by the fact that the demolition or rehabilitation of the project necessarily causes the residents to move out of the project and usually the neighborhood. Since they are often the poorest of the poor in their neighborhood, their displacement by itself generates an improvement in statistical measures of neighborhood resident well-being. Thus GAO "found that the demolition of old public housing alone may influence changes in neighborhoods," based on six neighborhoods where the projects had been demolished but no new construction had yet been completed.[37] Whatever a final assessment of these projects may eventually indicate, it is important to remember that while demolition of a public housing project will make a project neighborhood "look better," it is only the first stage of the process.

The limited literature generally makes the point that the comparisons over time or between neighborhoods do not necessarily show that the HOPE VI project itself is responsible for the neighborhood improvement.[38] This general methodological point is important; no two neighborhoods are alike, some projects are located in booming cities and others in stagnating ones, and comparisons over time suffer from the infrequent availability of neighborhood data. In addition, some projects may be located in neighborhoods that were already in the process of gentrification or redevelopment, and the elimination of a housing project may contribute to neighborhood redevelopment but deny the public housing residents the chance to live in the redeveloped neighborhood.[39]

Another type of evidence suggests that neighborhood improvements under HOPE VI may be less extensive than had been previously thought. A study of original residents of eight HOPE VI projects included some questions on neighborhood conditions at the new location. Those who moved back into the new project consistently reported more "big problems" with crime and drugs in the neighborhood, compared to those who were using vouchers or who had moved into other public housing projects. Residents of the HOPE VI projects, however, had better opinions about their neighbors and more interaction with them.[40] These findings may or may not match with the neighborhood assessments, since only two of the eight neighborhoods are also in the sample of twenty-five covered by the four studies, but they suggest further caution in concluding that HOPE VI projects have generally resulted in neighborhood revitalization.

Finally, it is important to note that HOPE VI often has involved more than new or rehabilitated housing. Residents of the new project have been offered supportive services, such as child care, after-school programs, and adult education; such services have been provided in some but not all of the original projects. These services have apparently contributed to the residents' satisfaction with the new project and the new neighborhood.[41] The inclusion of these services as part of the redevelopment suggests at least an implicit recognition that new subsidized housing by itself is not enough to revitalize a poor neighborhood.

House Prices

To an economist, the best indicator of neighborhood conditions is the price of housing. If prices are rising, the neighborhood is becoming more attractive; if they are falling, the neighborhood is deteriorating. In theory, then, analysis of the relationship between subsidized housing and house prices should show clearly whether subsidized housing makes a neighborhood better or worse. In reality, such analyses face several limitations.

(1) Subsidized housing is not likely to be located in neighborhoods where a large share of the private housing is owner-occupied. (The same analyses could conceptually be conducted with rents, but rent data are not public information, while the sale price of a house is recorded for each transaction by the local government.)

(2) The analysis itself is difficult. The standard technique is to create a sample of transactions, including the price of the house, its characteristics (size of house, size of yard, age of house, number of rooms, number of bathrooms, etc.), and the characteristics of the local neighborhood (distance to the center of the city, distance to the nearest park, quality of the local schools, crime rate, etc.). The statistical relationship between the price and each characteristic is estimated by multiple regression analysis; the estimated coefficient of each characteristic is its implicit "hedonic" price. For purposes of estimating the impact of subsidized housing, one neighborhood characteristic is "distance from assisted housing." This characteristic may be related to other neighborhood attributes—school quality, crime rate, location relative to other amenities or to undesirable land uses. Separating the effect of the subsidized housing from these other characteristics may be imprecise, if not nearly impossible.

(3) An alternative is to analyze trends in the prices of the same houses over time, but repeat sales are likely to be infrequent in any given neighborhood, and small samples typically produce inconclusive results.

(4) The causal relationship may be indeterminate. Did a new public housing project cause the neighborhood to deteriorate or revive, or conversely was the project located in a neighborhood that was already deteriorating or reviving?

Perhaps not surprisingly, the research yields varied conclusions. Studies from the 1960s through the 1980s typically found no effect of subsidized housing projects on local house prices, though a few found that house prices rose, suggesting some revitalization. Research during the 1990s, however, produced more mixed results; both positive and negative impacts on house prices were found, often in the same study of the same metropolitan area.[42]

Within the last few years several analysts have employed a more sophisticated method that attempts to isolate the effect of subsidized housing on local prices by constructing before-and-after comparisons of both the level of and the trend in prices in the neighborhood, and comparing these price changes with those in similar neighborhoods or the entire metropolitan market. In the earliest of these studies, George Galster and several coauthors found a variety of results from certificates in Baltimore County in the early 1990s, depending on the number of certificate holders living in the neighborhood, the distance of the house from the location of the certificate holders, and the overall quality of the neighborhood. A small number of certificates in a neighborhood resulted in a small increase in house prices (less than 5 percent), but a larger number—more than five buildings in the neighborhood with certificate holders—resulted in a decrease, and the greater the number, the larger the decline; with forty buildings or eighty certificates, property values fell by more than 20 percent. These effects were concentrated; they applied to houses within 500 feet of buildings with certificate holders. For houses located 500 to 1,500 feet away, the declines were less than 8 percent. House prices fell in less attractive, "vulnerable" neighborhoods, while they rose in strong neighborhoods.[43]

A subsequent analysis of scattered-site public housing in Denver using the same methodology found roughly similar results: small rises in housing prices with a small number of nearby sites, drops in housing prices with more than four sites in vulnerable neighborhoods; and the same pattern, with larger effects, in stronger neighborhoods (with the breakpoint at more than five sites).[44]

A more extensive study of four subsidized housing project categories in New York City over two decades (1977–2000) also found mixed results: housing prices fell near Section 8 projects, stayed the same near family public housing projects or Section 202, and rose for homes near tax credit projects and public housing for the elderly. These results are somewhat unexpected; Section 8 generally has higher-income tenants and more elderly occupants than public housing, and there is no explanation of the divergent results for elderly public housing and Section 202, which serve the same population. The largest rise in housing prices was about 12 percent for elderly public housing; all others were less than 5 percent.[45] Neither tenant-based assistance nor scattered-site public housing is intended as a neighborhood revitalization program, so it is perhaps not surprising that outcomes were so mixed. A study of tax credit projects in Cleveland, Portland (Oregon), and Seattle found similar results to the New York study: house prices rose within 300 meters of the projects, although the effect diminished as the size of the project increased in vulnerable neighborhoods (all in Cleveland), and house prices dropped within 300 to 600 meters of a project.[46]

HOPE VI projects are intended to revitalize neighborhoods. It seems fair to say that their success has been mixed. The interim assessment of HOPE VI was able to analyze home prices around two of the eight projects (in New Haven and San Francisco) and found no effect near either project; in fact, prices in project neighborhoods were generally flat in the late 1990s as prices in the overall metropolitan area were rising. More recent studies of Baltimore, Boston, and Washington found rising property values around four of the seven projects analyzed, but these projects were located in neighborhoods that were generally better and in the process of revitalization to begin with.[47]

This limited recent literature—which looks at a few scattered metropolitan areas, with only one or two studies of each program—does not invite generalization. What does seem clear is that subsidized housing at best only occasionally promotes neighborhood revitalization. To quote a recent paper by two experienced housing analysts, "The case for using production of subsidized rental housing as a revitalization tool remains weak."[48]

Racial Integration

Related to the question of whether subsidized housing promotes neighborhood revitalization is whether it promotes racial integration. Facilitating residential racial and ethnic integration has certainly been a federal housing policy goal since the 1960s. This goal, however, is not universally shared, and some local groups and neighborhood residents explicitly or implicitly oppose the policy. Given that African American, Hispanic, and Native American households in general have lower incomes than whites, concern that subsidized housing brings lower-income households to a neighborhood easily becomes a concern that it brings minority households.

Integration is a different process in project-based and tenant-based programs. In the former, the question is, "Where are projects to be located?" In the latter, it is, "Where will assisted households choose to move?" This distinction can be overdrawn; households can refuse the offer of a unit in a project (and some projects have become nearly or completely vacant as a result), and local housing authorities can steer voucher holders into particular neighborhoods. But the distinction between the two questions is useful, and suggests that the two categories of programs should be considered separately.

Tenant-Based Assistance. Local newspapers often write about the reaction of white residents when subsidized minority households move into their neighborhoods in significant numbers. Most of the local voucher controversies described in the HUD-funded study discussed earlier involved neighborhoods where the minority population was growing, and in some communities, concerns about this growth were explicitly raised by residents; as the study noted, "many of the communities . . . were undergoing racial as well as economic transition."[49] This concern on the part of white residents is sometimes alleged to be a "problem" with tenant-based assistance.[50]

The question of whether a housing allowance would promote integration was raised when EHAP was begun in the early 1970s. Some housing advocates were concerned that the allowance would not promote integration, but some local groups and citizens were afraid that it would; the ability of low-income minority families to move where they wanted was seen as a threat to the neighborhood. The two entitlement sites were to be selected on the basis of population growth and minority composition: "fast-growth/ low-black" and "slow-growth/high-black." Suburban officials in two high minority metropolitan areas who felt that the allowance would help blacks and other minorities move from the central city into their predominantly white jurisdictions rejected the Supply Experiment.[51] In South Bend, the area finally selected, the suburban jurisdictions also refused to participate until the experiment had been in operation for more than a year, and the last small town in the South Bend metropolitan area did not join for almost three years.[52]

In the event, neither the hopes nor the fears were justified. Both minority and nonminority households moved less than expected, and most moves occurred within the neighborhood. There was some tendency for minority households to move out of the worst neighborhood in South Bend, but this tendency had begun before the experiment started.

In the Demand Experiment, assisted black households in Pittsburgh did not move to more integrated neighborhoods, but assisted Hispanic households in Phoenix did, to a modest extent. Most analysts have concluded that the allowance had little if any effect on neighborhood racial composition.[53] At most, it might have slightly accelerated racial mobility patterns—between central cities and suburbs, or from one part of a city to another—that were already established.

Subsequent experience with the certificate, voucher, and Housing Choice Voucher programs is generally similar. The data in table 6-1 on minority participation and location data for the Housing Choice Voucher as of 2008 appear to be consistent with the EHAP pattern. About 60 percent of voucher holders are minority households; they live in neighborhoods that are on average less than 50 percent minority. Actual mobility data from the program evaluations have also been consistent with this pattern. In the certificate program during the early 1980s, African American households were able to move to neighborhoods with a slightly lower minority concentration, on average.[54] Thus the program probably does generate some degree of integration.

Further evidence on how tenant-based assistance influences the racial makeup of neighborhoods comes from the two recent demonstrations. As already mentioned, there were no significant differences between families receiving standard Section 8 vouchers and those receiving no vouchers at all. For those receiving the experimental vouchers requiring them to move to low-poverty areas, the minority share of population in their neighborhood was 7 percent lower than for the other two groups—statistically significant, but not particularly large over a period of 10 to 15 years.[55] The evaluation of the Welfare to Work voucher demonstration during 1999–2004 found that when households moved, their new and old neighborhoods had roughly similar percentages of minorities; the difference was less than five percentage points on average from an initial 70 percent proportion. The small changes for African Americans were statistically significant; those for Hispanics were not.[56]

Finally, the analysis of mobility for all new voucher recipients during 1995–2002 showed slight changes in neighborhood minority concentration among voucher recipients who moved ranging from less than 1 percent to 3 percent.[57]

The general pattern over a long period of time is that minority households move on average to neighborhoods with a slightly lower minority concentration than their original neighborhood, contradicting the fears of some white households that neighborhood racial changes will be dramatic.

All of these analyses were limited to families with children. At the time they were conducted (the mid-1990s to the early 2000s), members of all major racial and ethnic groups were about equally successful in using certificates or vouchers.[58]

Public Housing and Privately Owned Projects. Promoting residential racial and ethnic integration has been a federal housing policy goal since the 1960s. Before that time, however, the goal was often to preserve the racial composition of a neighborhood. Project residents were generally of the same race as the other residents of the neighborhood; projects for minority families were located in minority neighborhoods. This placement reflected public attitudes of the time. Indeed, when the Trumbull Park public housing project, located in a completely white neighborhood on the far South Side of Chicago, inadvertently admitted a light-skinned black family in 1953, there were riots, and for many years a large police presence was required in the project neighborhood.[59]

When public policy changed in the 1960s, the federal goal sometimes met local resistance, or at least concern. As the Regency House public housing project (to be occupied predominantly by lower-income minority elderly individuals) was being built in the mid-1960s in a predominantly white upper-income area in northwest Washington, DC, residents worried about declines in property values, but did not actively protest.

The concern that public housing in particular has been sited in minority communities, and that its location there has reduced the ability of minority households to move to more integrated communities, has led to lawsuits. In response to court rulings, HUD has implemented programs that allow minority households to use their housing subsidies to move to higher-income, predominantly white neighborhoods in the suburbs. The most famous case is *Gautreaux v. the Chicago Housing Authority*, a class-action suit filed in 1966 and settled in 1976; the ruling required HUD and the housing authority to locate new public housing in the suburbs, or provide vouchers for minority families to move to predominantly white or mixed neighborhoods. Probably the longest case, and perhaps the largest, involved thirty-six counties in east Texas and lasted twenty-four years; it started as *Young v. Landrieu* and ended six HUD secretaries later as *Young v. Jackson*. The suit concerned segregation of all 219 public housing projects in the region, including a pattern of assigning black households to older projects and white households to new projects.

Table 6-1 reports minority participation and location data for the project-based HUD subsidy programs as of 2000 as well as for housing vouchers, and these minority participation rates appear to be similar across programs and for that matter consistent with the EHAP pattern. With the exception of Section 8 New Construction, the proportion of minority households served in each program is higher than the proportion of minority households in the census tracts where they live, by 10 or more percentage points. This suggests that, on average, assisted minority households have moved to modestly more integrated neighborhoods; but except for the voucher program, "on average" can be very misleading in individual instances—if, for example, a largely minority project is located in a largely white tract (such as Regency House). Data for individual projects, however, indicate that such disparities are not common.

In Section 8, the proportion of minority households served is close to the same as the proportion of minority households in the census tract (45 percent in the program compared to 42 percent in the tract). As discussed earlier, Section 8 was an unusual subsidy program. Most new Section 8 projects were built in reasonably good city or suburban neighborhoods and have served mainly white elderly households.[60] A disproportionately small number of minority households, mainly elderly, have been served. Some of them have been able to move from predominantly minority neighborhoods into predominantly white ones in the process. But the Section 8 New Construction program appears to be the least effective of all HUD programs in promoting integration.

The Newer Programs. The LIHTC and HOPE VI were both developed after racial integration became an explicit goal of housing policy. Neither one, however, appears to have done much toward achieving this goal.

Table 6-1 shows that tax credit projects are located in census tracts with similar or somewhat lower minority concentrations than the older subsidized programs. A substantial share is located in tracts that are overwhelmingly white or minority. Cummings and DiPasquale found an average of 41 percent minority population in the neighborhood for their sample of 1987–1996 projects, very close to the proportion in table 6-1, but this masked the fact that almost half the projects (48 percent) were located in either overwhelmingly white (30 percent) or minority (18 percent) neighborhoods, with concentrations of 90 percent or more in one group or the other; only 10 percent of projects were "integrated." In central cities, the pattern was more extreme: 90 percent of projects were in overwhelmingly white (39 percent) or minority (51 percent) neighborhoods.[61]

The analysis of thirty-nine tax credit projects from 1992–1994 reports the minority concentration of both the projects and the neighborhood. About half of all projects were either largely white (36 percent) or minority (14 percent), having at least 80 percent concentrations. About half of all projects had a higher percentage of minorities than the surrounding neighborhood, indicating some degree of integration; only 5 percent had higher concentrations of white residents.[62] The tax credit database indicates that about half of projects placed in service between 1995 and 2006 were in largely white (29 percent) or minority (23 percent) tracts.[63] In comparing these results to the earlier programs, it should be remembered that income limits are higher for tax credit projects, meaning that integration should be somewhat easier to achieve.

Research on HOPE VI projects is limited, but to date it indicates that there is little change in the racial and ethnic composition of either the projects or the project neighborhoods, and that both remain overwhelmingly minority. For the thirteen projects in the interim assessment, the overall composition changed from 84 to 74 percent African American, from 11 to 12 percent Hispanic, and from less than 5 to 7 percent white.[64] The tracking study of former HOPE VI residents in eight projects, comparing those who originally lived in the project to those who returned after redevelopment, shows a similar pattern; the original composition of the project was 69 percent African American, 24 percent Hispanic, and 3 percent white, while among returnees it was 58 percent African American, 37 percent Hispanic, and 3 percent white.[65] It should be noted that the eight projects studied were in various stages of redevelopment and reoccupancy, and that data for each individual project are not available.

The tracking study also reports that none of the eight HOPE VI projects studied changed the racial and ethnic composition of the neighborhood in a substantial way.[66] This is consistent with Zielenbach's study of eight projects, which reports a pre-redevelopment composition in 1990 of 40 percent African American, 36 percent Hispanic, and 9 percent white, compared to 32 percent, 40 percent, and 10 percent, respectively, a decade later.[67] Since most of these projects had not been completed and fully reoccupied by 2000, the post-redevelopment composition is likely to change.

Despite the limitations of the data, it appears fairly clear that HOPE VI does little to promote racial integration in either the project or the neighborhood. It is also clear that project-based assistance can be, but is not often, used as a tool for racial integration. Tenant-based assistance is harder to use for desegregation, because policymakers have little control over where tenants use their vouchers. But because in practice tenants tend to use their vouchers to move to more racially mixed neighborhoods, vouchers seem more often to result in mixed neighborhoods than projects. Thus neither the hopes of federal policymakers nor the fears of some local residents that vouchers would substantially change the racial balance of neighborhoods seem to have been realized.

Economic Opportunity

Interest in promoting economic integration through housing programs has developed concomitantly with interest in promoting racial integration, and several relatively recent programs and demonstrations have attempted to see if low-income households can increase their earnings as a result of moving into a better neighborhood. These programs have been developed more or less in response to the same public policy concerns that led to the federal and state efforts at welfare reform beginning in the early 1980s and culminating in the Temporary Assistance to Needy Families (TANF) reform of 1996.

The Gautreaux program, one of the outcomes of the *Gautreaux* lawsuit in Chicago, gave certificates to public housing residents in the city who agreed to use them to move to predominantly white or mixed neighborhoods. The program began in the late 1970s. Early research suggested that relocation was having little effect on the lives of the participants, but by the late 1980s, more positive results began to appear, at least for families who had moved to the suburbs. Adults were more likely to be employed, and children were more likely to complete school and go to college or find employment, than participants who had moved to other central-city neighborhoods.[68] These improvements took seven to ten years to materialize.

In 1984, a demonstration known as Project Self-Sufficiency provided Section 8 certificates to PHAs that provided a coordinated program of job training and placement, education, child care, transportation, and other services to the certificate holders. Eligibility was limited to single-parent households on local waiting lists for tenant-based assistance. In 1989, after Project Self-Sufficiency had concluded, HUD established Operation Bootstrap, a demonstration including two-parent families on local waiting lists. A full-fledged program, Family Self-Sufficiency, was enacted in 1990 and included residents of public housing as well as certificate holders. The program began in FY1991 on a voluntary basis; in 1991 and 1992, there were 26,000 participating families who received vouchers, and 3,000 who remained in public housing. A package of services was tailored to each participating individual adult, and embodied in a contract. The services provided most often were job training and education to help individuals become self-sufficient, as well as child care and transportation to enable them to take advantage of the job training and education. Families were given incentives to participate: the family's rental payment did not rise with its earned income until its income went above 50 percent of the local median income, and the additional rent that the family would have paid went into an interest-bearing escrow account. When the family fulfilled the requirements of the contract, such as completing the education or training program, it received the money in the escrow account.

The Moving to Work (MTW) demonstration was enacted in 1996, more or less contemporaneously with TANF, and motivated in part by it. The main purpose of this demonstration was to allow PHAs to relax program regulations in both the public housing and voucher programs, with the purpose of enabling assisted households to participate more effectively in the labor market. Some participating agencies sought to promote work effort by modifying program requirements, but none required households to move. Inducements to work included both "carrots," notably weakening the requirement that 30 percent of household income be paid as rent and allowing households to keep all or most of an increase in their earned income, and "sticks," such as minimum rents that were not reduced if household members left their jobs or reduced their hours of work. Some authorities also provided supportive services to participants, while others did not.[69]

Studies of these programs suggest some improvement in the economic status of participants, but except for Gautreaux, none was designed to facilitate rigorous assessment. HUD did not formally evaluate Project Self-Sufficiency, but an assessment it conducted of program data from forty communities found an increase in labor force participation. Some 25 percent were employed at the time they applied for the program; two years later, 48 percent were employed. Wage rates for employed workers were 20 percent higher at the later date. The typical employed participant was earning income above the eligibility limit for Aid to Families with Dependent Children (AFDC) and Medicaid, though not for housing assistance. It should be noted that Project Self-Sufficiency participants were selected based on the likelihood of their success; they were not a random sample of AFDC recipients or households eligible for housing assistance.[70]

A formal evaluation of Project Bootstrap, begun in 1991 and completed in 1994, found that participants improved their economic position but did not achieve self-sufficiency. The proportion with jobs increased from

40 to 49 percent, and the number of unemployed participants looking for work increased by 8 percent. Fewer than half were earning $4.25 an hour or more. About 10 percent surrendered their certificates rather than participate in the program, which is almost the same as the proportion who became employed. The proportion on welfare declined by only two percentage points.[71]

By 2000, there were 52,000 Family Self-Sufficiency participants in 1,400 local programs. An evaluation in that year found larger increases in income for participants enrolled between 1996 and 2000 than for non-participants—about 19 percent higher, taking account of demographic characteristics. But the evaluation also found that Family Self-Sufficiency participants were generally better educated than nonparticipants, which could be at least partly responsible for the higher incomes. The evaluation did not measure earnings from work.[72]

Nearly all PHAs in the MTW demonstration reported increased employment, hours of work, and earnings among program participants, but the changes were not related to specific reforms, either carrots or sticks. Nor was it possible to separate the effects of the program changes from other factors, such as the imposition of more stringent work requirements in TANF, or the overall strength of the economy between 1997 and 2004. The demonstration also did not distinguish between public housing residents and voucher recipients.[73]

Findings from later demonstrations with more rigorous evaluations have been less positive. The most rigorous demonstration was certainly Moving to Opportunity. Neither the interim nor the final evaluation showed evidence that moving to lower poverty neighborhoods, or using regular Housing Choice Vouchers, resulted in better economic outcomes than remaining in public housing. There were no effects on adults' employment or earnings, or changes in receipt of welfare.

The only notable difference in employment was that families who moved with a voucher experienced a temporary decline in employment during the first two years compared to those who did not move, perhaps because of difficulties in finding a job or child care in the new neighborhood. This difference disappeared in subsequent years. Families who were required to move to low-poverty neighborhoods made more use of food stamps by the time of the final evaluation, receiving about 20 percent more than the group that were not offered vouchers, over the last two years of the demonstration. There had been no difference at the time of the interim evaluation. The analysts of the final evaluation concluded that:

> For adults, it appears that training, education, and employment services that directly enhance marketable skills and changes in work incentives more directly affect labor market and economic outcomes of low-income adults than do the indirect effects of changes in neighborhood environments, at least in the range observed in the MTO demonstration.[74]

In the interim evaluation, there were a few significant differences in children's educational attainment. Young women who participated were more likely to remain in school, and make plans to attend college and participate in the labor force. These differences, however, disappeared by the time of the final evaluation.

The Welfare to Work Voucher program offered vouchers to current or former welfare recipients, with no requirement that they be living in subsidized projects to begin with. The program began in 2000–2001; participants were interviewed in 2004–2005. The findings thus represent a shorter period of participation than findings either for Moving to Opportunity or Gautreaux. The results were modest and, initially, negative. Participants were less likely to work during the first year, with no difference subsequently. Over three years, the control group of families that did not receive a voucher averaged 6.1 quarters of employment—that is, they were employed just over half the time. Voucher recipients worked about 1 percent less—a matter of four days less in three years. This difference is not statistically significant. There was also little effect on education and training activities for adults, or on children's school performance.[75]

There have also been statistical studies using program data. A study by Edgar Olsen, which looked at the employment experience of participants in both project-based and tenant-based programs between 1995 and 2002, found that recipients of housing assistance worked and earned less than comparable unassisted households selected from the Panel Study of Income Dynamics (a long-term survey conducted by the University of Michigan for the U.S. Department of Labor). Those receiving tenant-based assistance incurred about a 30 percent reduction in earnings; those receiving either type of project-based assistance incurred about a 35 percent reduction. Voucher recipients were also slightly more likely to be employed. The explanation is the reduction of assistance as income rises; with rent set at 30 percent of income, each additional dollar earned reduces the tenant's rent subsidy by 30 cents. Such high marginal tax rates are a standard feature of most low-income assistance programs. By contrast, participants in Family Self-Sufficiency, whose subsidies were not reduced, had significantly higher earnings.[76]

A similar study by Scott Susin, using program data for 1996–1999, found smaller reductions in earnings of recipients of housing assistance: 10 percent for voucher users (not a statistically significant reduction), and close to 20 percent for residents of both public housing and privately owned projects. This study used the Census Bureau's Survey of Income and Program Participation to identify comparable unassisted households. It did not include Family Self-Sufficiency.[77]

The fundamental problem confronting all income-conditioned housing assistance programs is their work disincentive. The requirement that tenants contribute 30 percent of their income toward their rent imposes a marginal tax rate of 30 percent on each additional dollar earned, in addition to payments into Social Security and Medicare (totaling 7.65 percent) and any federal, state, or local income tax. The 30 percent tax/additional rent is by itself higher than the marginal tax rate faced by single parents with taxable incomes below $190,200 or married couples with taxable incomes below $208,850 (as of 2009). This problem is widely recognized, and there are a number of policies in place to minimize its impact. The Earned Income Tax Credit is intended to offset the impact of Social Security and Medicare taxes; the various exclusions from income for purposes of determining rent are intended in part to mitigate the work disincentive for families receiving housing assistance. All of the demonstrations and programs to encourage work by assisted households have attempted either to waive or defer the higher rent burden (Operation Bootstrap and Family Self-Sufficiency), or to use housing assistance to address other factors that discourage low-income households from working, such as transportation costs, child care, and lack of education or training.

The literature on the economic effects of housing assistance has been almost entirely focused on the voucher, although a few studies have analyzed the educational and economic outcomes for children who live or grew up in public housing. Janet Currie and Aaron Yelowitz found that children in public housing were less likely to be held back a grade than children from unassisted families, taking account of socioeconomic status. Their analysis is limited to children from families with incomes below $50,000, but they did not include income as a separate independent variable. The authors point out that their results contradict the popular view that public housing projects are particularly undesirable environments for children.[78] This result is the more remarkable because during the period covered by the study (1992–1993), families living in public housing gave their neighborhoods a much lower rating than low-income families living in unassisted housing (5 out of 10 for public housing families, 8 out of 10 for low-income families not receiving housing assistance); presumably these families would consider their children's schools as an important aspect of their neighborhood.[79]

Sandra J. Newman and Joseph M. Harkness analyzed the economic circumstances of young adults who lived in public housing at some point between the ages of ten and sixteen. They found that the former public housing residents were less likely to be on welfare and more likely to be working, with higher earnings, the longer they had lived in public housing. They caution that their data, for public housing residence between 1968 and 1982, precede the concentration of poor and dysfunctional households in public housing, but that caveat does not apply to Currie and Yelowitz's results.[80] (Neither of these studies compares public housing to other assistance programs, a limitation recognized by their authors.)

Health

Changes in physical and mental health, for both adults and children, were a particular focus of MTO. Both the interim and the final evaluation asked respondents about their general physical health and several specific problems, and both asked about general psychological distress; the final evaluation included more specific mental health concerns than the interim.

The interim evaluation found a reduction in obesity among adults in both groups of households receiving vouchers, compared to the control group that was not offered vouchers, but no other significant differences.

The final evaluation did not find the same result for obesity, but did find significant differences for diabetes (not addressed in the interim evaluation) and for limits on the adult's ability to climb stairs or carry groceries (the latter only for families required to move to low-poverty neighborhoods). Neither found significant differences in hypertension or asthma, or in general health, as reported by the respondent. Neither found any health differences among youth.[81]

With respect to mental health, both evaluations found significant differences in general psychological distress between adults who utilized the vouchers they were offered and those who were not offered vouchers. In addition, major depression was less common among those who were offered vouchers, as of the final evaluation. There were few other significant differences in either evaluation. In general, those with vouchers reported lower incidences of most problems, which were not statistically significant, in the final evaluation; the exception was a higher incidence of drug or alcohol dependence among households required to move to low-poverty neighborhoods.

The results were different for youth, and different by gender and by type of housing assistance. Among girls, mental health was consistently better for those in families with vouchers, at the time of the interim evaluation, and better on about half of the mental health measures at the time of the final evaluation for those in families with the experimental vouchers requiring them to move to low-poverty areas. Among boys, there were no significant differences for any measure for any type of assistance, except for a higher incidence of post-traumatic stress disorder and a marginally higher incidence of mood disorders, for boys in families offered a standard voucher, in the final evaluation.[82]

Again, it is worth remembering that the differences are between families receiving different forms of housing assistance: vouchers on the one hand, public housing or project-based assistance on the other. The comparison is not between those receiving assistance and those not, or between those living in good housing and those not. In this very important respect, MTO differs from the older studies referenced in chapter 1, such as the analysis of public housing residents in Baltimore by Wilner et al. and most of the research cited by Kasl.[83] Keeping these differences in mind, the MTO results certainly invite further research on the relationships between housing assistance and health.

Crime

The Moving to Opportunity demonstration evaluations addressed the relationship between housing assistance, neighborhood and crime, and there is some other recent research on housing programs as well.

The MTO evaluations studied both the extent to which young people were arrested for crime and also engaged in "risky" behavior; they also asked adults (presumably not criminals) whether they felt safe in their neighborhood. In the final evaluation, most households reported that they felt safe during the day and at night, but a higher proportion of the families with vouchers said they felt safe. For those not offered vouchers, 80 percent felt safe during the day and 60 percent at night; among those with vouchers, 84 to 88 percent felt safe during the day and 64 to 71 percent felt safe at night. These differences were statistically significant.

The evaluation also asked teenagers (ages 13–20) several questions about behavior, and asked everyone whether they had ever been arrested for five categories of crimes. The most general finding was that both adults and youth in families with vouchers were less likely to be arrested for drug distribution. In addition, young males whose families utilized the standard voucher were marginally more likely to have behavioral problems, and young individuals of both genders in families with vouchers that could only be used in low-poverty areas were more likely to be arrested for property crimes.[84]

The effects were stronger at the time of the interim evaluation than at the final evaluation several years later. For instance, the interim evaluation found that arrests for violent crime were less frequent among the children of families with vouchers, particularly among girls.[85] These differences were no longer evident in the final evaluation.

Another comparison of crime rates among voucher holders and other assisted households focused on changes in neighborhoods rather than changes for individuals and families over time. Bringing together crime data and the number of assisted households for census tracts in 91 cities as of the year 2000, this study found that voucher holders on average lived in areas with significantly lower crime rates than did public housing residents, households in LIHTC projects, and poor renters generally. This pattern held both for violent crimes and for all crimes (which are predominantly crimes against property). The lower crime rates were most pronounced for black voucher holders. This study also separately analyzed changes in crime rates experienced by voucher holders in seven cities over the decade from 1998 to 2008 found that voucher holders lived in safer neighborhoods, largely because crime rates went down disproportionately in neighborhoods where voucher holders lived, but to some extent also because voucher holders moved to safer neighborhoods.[86]

HOPE VI is both a housing program and a neighborhood improvement program, and a safer neighborhood is one aspect of its improvement. A close study of several HOPE VI projects in Milwaukee and Washington, DC traced changes in crime in and near the projects, beginning with a baseline before the project got underway, continuing through relocation of the residents, construction, and occupancy of the new project, and concluding with a period of expected stability after completion. In Milwaukee, the effect on crime both in and around the new project was minimal. In Washington, crime rates were generally lower in both the project area and the surrounding communities as and after the project was built. The difference between Milwaukee and Washington may occur because the Washington projects had a much longer timeline, and perhaps because in Washington few of the residents of the original public housing project were able to move into the new HOPE VI project.[87]

Neither of these studies contained information on the propensity of voucher holders or public housing residents to commit crimes, or the degree of safety experienced by individual households who received assistance.

Conclusion

Low-income households that receive housing assistance, particularly vouchers and other tenant-based assistance, generally live in better neighborhoods than those that do not. Public housing neighborhoods are less desirable on average than the neighborhoods of other assisted households; a substantial minority of public housing residents—about a quarter—are very dissatisfied with their neighborhood.

Unassisted renters living in these neighborhoods are sometimes concerned about the consequences of having assisted households move in.

Controversies have occurred mainly in Northeastern cities, rarely in the South or West. In fact most neighborhoods, including most neighborhoods with high poverty rates, have small concentrations of voucher holders. Research suggests, moreover, that established residents sometimes blame housing programs for neighborhood changes that were already underway and that might have occurred anyway.

Public housing projects, commonly located in lower-income neighborhoods to begin with, have not contributed to neighborhood preservation and redevelopment, as their original advocates hoped they would. The same appears to be true of LIHTC projects and of HOPE VI, even though HOPE VI is intended specifically to promote more desirable, mixed-income neighborhoods. So few HOPE VI projects have been completed, however, that any conclusion is tentative if not premature. Overall, there is little evidence that subsidized rental housing is an effective strategy for neighborhood revitalization. Most programs result in modest increases in racial integration. The effect of housing on neighborhood racial composition—a vexed and controversial subject for decades—is actually much less dramatic than the discussions of it have been. Programs do not have much effect on neighborhood economic integration or the ability of assisted households to improve their economic situation; assisted households face a high marginal tax rate as they attempt to work their way out of poverty or dependency.

In a sense, the objectives of housing assistance have come full circle: the latest demonstrations are attempting to find out if housing programs are effective antipoverty programs, as the housing reformers of the New Deal era believed. But there is a fundamental difference between the 1930s and today. The early reformers expected that better housing by itself would reduce poverty; they favored tearing down the slums and building public housing, often on the lots where the slums had stood. The demonstrations of the past two decades are based on the hypothesis that better neighborhoods rather than better housing per se are the driving force behind poverty reduction. Today's reformers emphasize improvements in housing less than higher employment rates and gains in educational attainment, and they focus on neighborhood characteristics such as crime rates. The latest and most rigorous evaluations suggest that better neighborhoods for recipients of housing subsidies do not necessarily lower poverty rates, though the Gautreaux results suggest that subsidy recipients may eventually enjoy higher incomes. The recent demonstrations involve tenant-based assistance rather than project-based, but the program data analyses involve both, and suggest that tenant-based assistance generates better economic outcomes (or more precisely, tenant-based assistance has less of a work disincentive than project-based assistance).

7

The Voucher/Production Debate: Program Costs

The final component of program comparisons is the cost of providing a unit of decent housing. The discussion of budget authority and outlays in chapter 4 should make clear that comparing costs between programs requires care. This is especially true because the relationship between budget authority and outlays is different for different programs; budget authority is spent over a longer period for public housing and other production programs than it is for vouchers. Nonetheless, it is possible to construct measures of cost that have the same time dimension, and to draw some important conclusions about the relative cost of assistance in different programs. Although the programs differ in their budget treatments and in the nature of their expenditures, it is clear that vouchers are much cheaper per unit than any current or former program of project-based assistance.

The remainder of this chapter compares the costs per unit across the housing subsidy programs. There are two existing sets of program comparisons relevant here. The first, and the only recent analysis of program costs, was conducted by GAO in response to a congressional mandate.[1] GAO limited its comparison to programs active in 2000: the Housing Choice Voucher, the LIHTC, HOPE VI, Section 202, Section 811, and the Section 515 program of the Department of Agriculture's Rural Housing Service. Of these, only the voucher and the tax credit are large programs serving a broad range of lower-income households. Sections 202 and 811 have distinctive constituencies who desire special features in their housing, and Section 515 serves only rural areas; HOPE VI has community development as well as housing objectives and is therefore harder to evaluate purely as an assistance program.[2] The GAO report has the advantage of using more up-to-date information, and the disadvantage of making comparisons largely among specialized programs that do not serve the same groups of people.

The second set of program comparisons includes the older programs which are no longer being used to produce incremental units but continue to provide far more assisted housing than most of the programs analyzed by GAO. The comparisons also include tenant-based assistance. They date from the early 1970s to the early 1980s, when (as discussed in chapter 5) all of these programs were active, and there were ongoing debates about the appropriate form of housing assistance. The comparisons are still relevant, however, because of the possibility that old programs may be reactivated or revived in some form. The Millennial Housing Commission, for example, recommended a program of capital grants to build new housing for extremely low-income renters, generically similar to Section 8 New Construction, and it also less explicitly called for funds to replace some existing public housing projects.[3] Cost comparisons among the older programs are also relevant to policy discussions about alternatives for households and projects already being subsidized—how to serve the residents of public housing projects being demolished in HOPE VI, for example, or those living in Section 8 projects whose owners may choose to opt out of the program.

The GAO Cost Comparisons

It is important to note that different households and different units are being subsidized in the various programs, and these differences affect any cost comparisons. The GAO comparisons included very different programs intended for very different constituencies. Section 202 and Section 811 provide small housing units for single elderly and disabled individuals with extremely low and very low incomes. The LIHTC funds housing partly for extremely low-income households that typically receive additional subsidies, and partly for households whose incomes are much higher, at or just above the upper bound of the very low-income category. HOPE VI also serves different groups; according to the development plans for the individual projects, about half the units replace the public housing units demolished to make room for the new project, while the other half are for middle-income households. The Housing Choice Voucher serves a broad

TABLE 7-1
HOUSEHOLD INCOME AND UNIT CHARACTERISTICS BY PROGRAM

	Voucher	LIHTC	HOPE VI	Section 202	Section 811
Average Household Income (1999)	$9,800	$14,200	$9,000	$9,200	$8,000
Median Number of Bedrooms	2.2	1.9	2.4	1	1
Bedroom Size Distribution					
Efficiency	<5%	5%	0%	5%	10%
One-Bedroom	25%	40%	15%	95%	80%
Two-Bedroom	40%	40%	40%	0%	10%
Three or More	35%	15%	45%	0%	0%
Local Distribution					
Metropolitan-Central City	50%	50%	90%	50%	40%
Metropolitan-Suburban	30%	45%	10%	30%	40%
Nonmetropolitan	20%	5%	0%	20%	20%

SOURCE: U.S. General Accounting Office, *Federal Housing Assistance: Comparing the Characteristics and Costs of Federal Housing Programs,* GAO-02-76, Washington, DC, January 2002, 28 (for income), 12–13 (for bedroom size), 14–15 (for location).
NOTE: HOPE VI household income is the average for all public housing projects, not specifically HOPE VI projects.

range of extremely low-income and very low-income households; it is the only one of these five programs with such a broad purpose.

Table 7-1 presents some characteristics of the households and units in the various programs, since it is important to have a sense of what the programs provide, and to whom, before considering their relative cost. Income is perhaps the most important household characteristic for program comparisons. The LIHTC has a much higher average household income for its recipients than any of the other programs, but it should be noted that the income data reported by GAO for HOPE VI actually are for residents of all public housing projects, not specifically HOPE VI projects; GAO assumed that the residents of the new public housing units in HOPE VI projects would have the same incomes as other public housing residents. Given that the HOPE VI program explicitly seeks to redevelop neighborhoods and create mixed-income communities, the actual incomes of HOPE VI residents are likely to be at least as high as the incomes of residents in tax credit projects, once they are finally completed.

Average incomes in the other three programs fall in the extremely low-income category. Unfortunately, GAO reports averages rather than medians or other distributional measures, so it is not certain if most households served by these programs have extremely low incomes, though they probably do. The national extremely low-income upper bound for one-person households was about $10,000 in 1999, which suggests that most Section 202 and Section 811 residents probably had extremely low incomes; the upper bound for three-person households was about $13,000, indicating more strongly that most voucher recipients also had extremely low incomes.

Table 7-1 also reports the size and location of subsidized units. Again, there are clear differences between the programs. Nearly all the units in Section 202 and Section 811 have one bedroom. Units in the other programs typically have two or more, with a much broader size range. Almost half the units in HOPE VI projects have three bedrooms, but it is unclear if these data refer to the units intended as public housing or to all units. A substantial majority of units in all programs are located in metropolitan areas; with the exception of Section 811, half or more are located in central cities. In the case of HOPE VI, over 90 percent are in central cities, and the remainder in suburbs, reflecting the geographic distribution of the worst public housing projects.

Given these differences, it is difficult to compare average per-unit costs across programs. The GAO report makes comparisons by number of bedrooms and location, with adjustments so that households in all programs have the same incomes. Table 7-2 shows the comparative costs by number of bedrooms for units in metropolitan areas, which comprise at least 80 percent of the units in each program; GAO does not separately report central city and suburban averages. The table reports both the first-year cost of the unit, and also the present value of the cost over thirty years, which is approximately the life expectancy of the housing. In general, the latter is a better way to measure housing costs, but it is unfortunately less precise than the first-year cost, since future costs such as rent and maintenance must be estimated.

GAO based its methodology on a comprehensive analysis by Edgar Olsen. Olsen argued that the "life-cycle" approach is conceptually preferable to single-year estimates for measuring housing costs, and further that the bias from comparing only first-year costs is theoretically indeterminate

TABLE 7-2
PER-UNIT COSTS BY PROGRAM

(Metropolitan Area Units, in 1999 Dollars)				
	Voucher	LIHTC	Section 202	Section 811	HOPE VI
One-Bedroom Unit					
One-Year Cost	$6,480	$9,280	$9,480	$9,140	--
Percent over Voucher	--	36%	39%	34%	--
30-Year Cost	$139,520	$166,610	$157,410	$151,280	
Percent over Voucher	--	20%	19%	15%	--
Two-Bedroom Unit					
One-Year Cost	$7,920	$10,240	NA	$10,350	--
Percent over Voucher	--	29%	NA	31%	--
30-Year Cost	$152,170	$182,150	NA	$160,370	--
Percent over Voucher	--	20%	NA	5%	--
2.4-Bedroom Unit—Housing Cost					
One-Year Cost	$8,610	--	--	--	$13,730
Percent over Voucher	--	--	--	--	59%
30-Year Cost	$175,580	--	--	--	$223,190
Percent over Voucher	--	--	--	--	27%
2.4-Bedroom Unit—"All Costs"					
One-Year Cost	$8,610	--	--	--	$15,580
Percent over Voucher	--	--	--	--	81%
30-Year Cost	$175,580	--	--	--	$248,720
Percent over Voucher	--	--	--	--	42%

SOURCE: U.S. General Accounting Office, *Federal Housing Assistance: Comparing the Characteristics and Costs of Housing Programs*, GAO-02-76, Washington, DC, January 2002, 54, table 6.
NOTE: NA = not applicable (no two-bedroom units built in Section 202).

(depending on the relative growth rates of market rents and operating costs for subsidized projects). He presented data to suggest that in practice the first-year cost bias leads to an underestimate of the cost of subsidized projects relative to tenant-based assistance.[4]

Whether measured in terms of first-year or life-cycle costs, the voucher is consistently the least expensive program. For both one-bedroom and two-bedroom units, the voucher is markedly less expensive than the LIHTC. For one-bedroom units, it is less expensive than either Section 202 or Section 811. There are no two-bedroom units in Section 202, and few in Section 811, so the relatively small difference in life-cycle cost for this category between the voucher and Section 811 should not be given too much weight. GAO did not have data for HOPE VI by number of bed-rooms, and therefore compared the cost of the average HOPE VI unit, at 2.4 bedrooms, with an interpolated average cost of a voucher for two-bedroom and three-bedroom units. The cost differences were larger than for any of the other programs; HOPE VI is clearly the most expensive program. Table 7-2 shows two cost figures for HOPE VI: "housing cost," the cost of building the housing; and "all costs," also including tenant relocation, demolition of the original project, construction of community facilities as well as housing, and community-based planning and participation.

These cost estimates—including the "all costs" figure for HOPE VI—do not include all the costs of providing housing under any of the programs. In all programs, there are federal government personnel and management costs that are part of the "Salaries and Expenses" line in the agency budget. Because many HUD personnel do not spend their time exclusively on one program, overhead costs cannot be calculated with precision. This omission probably biases the comparison against the voucher, which is administered with a smaller staff than production programs.[5]

In all project-based programs, there have historically been additional costs for repairs and modernization as projects have aged (described in chapters 3 and 4), and these typically go well beyond the amounts budgeted or expected when the project was approved. The GAO report, following the suggestion of industry officials, estimated the unfunded capital reserves for repairs and modernization for HOPE VI at $300 per unit per year. This measure would add slightly less than 5 percent to the thirty-year cost of HOPE VI. Calculating the unfunded capital reserves at $1,000 per unit per year (the figure suggested by HUD) would add almost 10 percent to the thirty-year cost.[6]

Two other large omitted costs are relevant for HOPE VI. Since public housing projects are owned by local government agencies, they do not pay property taxes, but instead make a much smaller payment in lieu of taxes (PILOT). The GAO report estimated that full property tax payments would add about 10 percent to the cost of HOPE VI. Property taxes and full funding of capital reserves together add 14 to 18 percent to GAO's thirty-year cost estimate (depending on whether $300 or $1,000 is assumed for annual reserves).

A larger omission is the value of the land. HOPE VI projects replace older public housing on the same site. The market value of the land is an economic cost of the project; it could be sold and used for other purposes. Indeed, HOPE VI is perhaps the only subsidized housing program, past or current, which enjoys the privilege of not having to pay for the land on which it is located. The cost of the land is part of the rent charged by private landlords in the voucher program; and private owners of tax credit projects, Section 202, and Section 811 must also buy the land on which they build, or buy both the land and structures if they are rehabilitating a project. To my knowledge, there are no valuations of the land under HOPE VI projects. The traditional rule of thumb in housing construction has been that land is about 25 percent of the cost of the finished product. If these land costs are appropriate for HOPE VI, they would make it more expensive than any other program.

Section 202 and Section 811 projects incur costs of project administration and services that are not covered by the capital grants authorizing project construction. These costs may come from the budgets of health and welfare agencies that serve the poor and disabled. They arise from the specialized nature of the programs—that is, from the type of residents they serve, and how they serve them.[7]

Finally, it should be noted that there are differences in data coverage for the different programs. The voucher data cover 1.4 million households receiving assistance in 2000, about 80 percent of all such households. HOPE VI data include most projects funded by 2000, but fewer than 10 percent of the projects had been completed at that time. The LIHTC data are taken from the Cummings and DiPasquale study covering about 25 percent of all projects funded between 1987 and 1996.[8] By contrast, the Section 202 and Section 811 projects in the study are those placed in service in fiscal year 1998. This suggests that the estimates for the latter two programs are less precise because of the more limited sample, and that the estimates for HOPE VI are more uncertain because so few of the projects had actually been completed at the time the data were collected.

Some independent evidence on the cost of HOPE VI comes from the interim assessment discussed in the previous two chapters.[9] Both the interim assessment and the GAO report calculated total development costs (which GAO then used in calculating the annual and thirty-year costs reported in table 7-2). The interim assessment reported total project costs (excluding community and support services, and demolition costs for units that were not replaced) for thirteen projects in eleven metropolitan areas, calculated in terms of 1998 dollars. This concept of "total project costs" appears to correspond to "all costs" as reported by GAO. GAO calculated a national average of $143,450 per unit; the interim assessment average is $176,500.[10]

Cost Comparisons between Vouchers and the Older Project-Based Programs

The programs covered by the GAO report represent less than half of all housing units currently subsidized by HUD. In particular, they exclude two very large programs: public housing (over 1.1 million units as of 2009) and Section 8 project-based assistance (almost 1.3 million). Neither of these programs is currently active, in the sense that no additional projects are being built and subsidized; but older projects still exist and are still being funded. In addition, from an analytical perspective, the cost analyses of these older programs are generally more detailed and precise than the GAO analyses; as the GAO report states, "Some of the most detailed analyses are based on the housing experiments of the 1970s, and we have not had anything close to the quality and depth of those data."[11]

Probably the most thorough and sophisticated comparative analysis of project-based and tenant-based assistance is the Abt Associates evaluation of Section 8 New Construction and the certificate program as of the late 1970s.[12] This is also the most recent such study because of the change in policy that terminated Section 8 New Construction in the early 1980s; and although it is old and covers one program that has been terminated and another that has been modified in several respects, its detailed methodology identifies and particularizes many of the factors that contribute to

TABLE 7-3

MONTHLY COSTS OF PROJECT-BASED AND TENANT-BASED ASSISTANCE

(1979 Dollars)

	Section 8 New Construction	Certificates
Gross Rent/Unit Cost	$362	$240
Tenant Rental Payments	$112	$110
Federal Government Subsidy	$250	$130
– as % of Unit Cost	69%	54%
Market Rental Value	$291	$265
– Including Long-Term Tenancy Discount		$231
Indirect and Administrative Costs	$91	$36
Total Cost	$453	$276
Total Federal Cost	$341	$166
Federal Cost as a Percentage of Total Cost	75%	60%

SOURCES: James E. Wallace et al., *Participation and Benefits in the Urban Section 8 Program: New Construction, Existing Housing* (Cambridge, MA: Abt Associates, 1981), S-9—S-14; 1:226; Stephen D. Kennedy, "What Do We Know About Housing Assistance?" (paper presented at the American Evaluation Society, Kansas City, MO, October 1986, rev., June 1987), 20–21.

cost differences between project-based and tenant-based assistance. Thus, despite its age, the analysis is still relevant.

Table 7-3 summarizes this study's findings about the comparative costs of project-based and tenant-based assistance on a monthly basis. The gross rent, which is also the unit cost, is divided into the payments made by the tenant and the government. The basic conclusion is that the project-based program was about 50 percent more expensive per unit per month than the tenant-based program, and the cost to the federal government was about twice as high. Simply put, it is expensive to build housing projects for the poor.

Part of the cost difference between project-based and tenant-based subsidies arose because of differences in the quality of the housing units. The market rental value of the unit in the Section 8 New Construction project was about 10 percent higher than that of the tenant-based unit. (The process of calculating market rental value will be discussed in the next chapter.) However, most of the difference occurred because the federal government paid more for the new units, and less for the tenant-based units, than they were worth on the open market. The apparently odd result for tenant-based assistance occurred because some of the certificate holders chose to stay in their current units, and sitting tenants who have rented the same unit for a number of years often pay less than the owner would demand from a new tenant. The Abt Associates analysis summarized in table 7-3 assumed that all tenants had just moved into their unit. When the actual length of tenure was taken into account, the monthly market rent for units occupied by certificate holders was calculated at $231.

These figures are incomplete measures of cost, because they omit both the indirect costs to the government and the program administration costs. The Abt study does not attempt to calculate these costs, but relies on earlier Abt research on the housing allowance and the Section 236 program to suggest that indirect subsidies alone may have added 20 to 30 percent ($72 to $109) to the cost of Section 8 New Construction.[13] The earlier Abt study also concluded that administrative costs added about 15 percent to the cost of the housing allowance.[14] These percentages are used in table 7-3 to create the measure of total cost. Based on this more inclusive figure, the cost difference between the programs remains about the same: the Section 8 New Construction program cost the federal government slightly more than twice as much per unit or per household as the certificate program.

The figures in the table also omit the losses that the federal government incurs on privately owned projects insured by FHA. Expected and actual losses were not calculated until the Credit Reform Act of 1990, and then were calculated only for ongoing programs. Section 8 was terminated in 1983. Perhaps the most relevant information on expected project defaults is in studies of the FHA-insured multifamily housing portfolio as of 1989 and 1995; at those dates, 12 percent and 13 percent, respectively, of Section 8 projects had negative cash flow.[15] Cash flow is not a precise indicator of future defaults, but it certainly indicates problems that may turn into defaults in the absence of additional federal support. FHA typically resells defaulted projects, so the loss relative to the initial mortgage amount would be much smaller than 12 or 13 percent.

Current Cost Estimates and Comparisons

The analyses by the GAO and by Abt are both useful, but neither is directly relevant to current policy issues. The GAO analysis primarily estimates costs

TABLE 7-4
MEDIAN HOUSEHOLD INCOME BY PROGRAM, 1996–2008

(in Thousands of Current Dollars)

	Voucher	Public Housing	Section 8 New Construction	Section 236
2008	10.8	9.6	9.9	9.5
2004	9.1	8.5	9.1	8.6
2000	9.0	8.2	8.8	9.4
1996	8.7	7.6	8.2	8.7

SOURCE: U.S. Department of Housing and Urban Development, Office of Policy Development and Research, *A Picture of Subsidized Households—2008*, http://www.huduser.org/portal/picture2008/index.html, and similarly for earlier years.

for small programs which serve special populations or for programs that are not targeted at extremely low-income households, while the Abt Associates analysis is three decades old. This section compares the costs of the major HUD subsidy programs operating today—public housing, privately owned projects, and the Housing Choice Voucher—and thus bears more directly on current policy concerns.

These programs, like the programs compared in the GAO report, subsidize different households and different units, and here, too, income is the most important household characteristic for program comparisons. Table 7-4 presents median household incomes in the major programs between 1996 and 2008. As of 2008, the median income for voucher recipients was about 10 percent higher than in the three project-based programs. This is important because all of these programs condition the subsidy on household income. The higher income of voucher holders in 2008 may reflect the recent policy change, discussed in chapter 3, that encourages public housing agencies to provide assistance to relatively higher-income households, but the median income increased in all of the programs between 2004 and 2008, noticeably more than during the previous four or eight years.

Nor are household characteristics similar. In 2008, the average voucher household consisted of 2.5 persons, compared to 2.2 for public housing and 1.6 for Section 8 projects. The relationship was similar in 2000. Correspondingly, units are largest in the voucher program (over two bedrooms on average) and smallest in Section 8 (less than 1.5 bedrooms). Household and unit size are important because assistance is conditioned on them as well as on income; larger households, and larger units, receive larger subsidies. The differences should be kept in mind in comparing actual outlays across programs.

Comparisons of costs across the three programs are shown in table 7-5. Some of the cost data are current as of 2010 (the latest completed fiscal year); other data, such as modernization costs, are based on earlier analyses and inflated to 2010 dollars. Older data are especially a problem for Section 236, which is therefore omitted.

Vouchers. Costs are least complex for the Housing Choice Voucher. The HUD budget for FY2012 reports an average expenditure of $7,692 for voucher contract renewals in 2010.[16] This includes a 7.5 percent administrative fee to the PHA for managing the program, calculated on the basis of the FMR rather than the contract amount. The national average FMR in 2010 was $919 ($11,028 annually), so the administrative fee was a little more than $825 per unit. In addition, the tenant's rent contribution was about $324 per month in 2005–2006, or about $3,900 per year.

Public Housing. Measuring public housing costs is more complicated. These costs have three major components: development costs, operating subsidies, and funding for modernization. There have been no appropriations to build conventional public housing projects since 1994, so HUD's calculations of development costs are necessarily somewhat problematic. The official national average total development cost for a two-bedroom apartment was $184,654 for 2011, which translates into an annualized cost of $10,900 at a 4.17 percent interest rate, the thirty-year Treasury bond rate in the spring of 2011.[17] Operating subsidies were funded at $4.8 billion in 2010, or about $4,000 per unit per year. They are calculated by formula, and are based on what it costs a well-managed authority to operate public housing, taking account of the structural characteristics of the housing and the local climate. This figure does not include the household's contribution toward the rent. The average rent contribution by a household living in public housing was $315 per month in 2010 (very close to the figure for a voucher recipient), or about $3,800 per year.[18]

TABLE 7-5
ANNUAL FEDERAL PER-UNIT COST OF SUBSIDY PROGRAMS, 2010

Housing Choice Voucher		
Rental Subsidy	$7,700	
PHA Administrative Fee	800	
Total		$8,500
Public Housing		
Annualized Development Cost	10,900	
Operating Subsidies	4,000	
Modernization:		
Annualized Backlog	1,800	
Annual Accrual	3,150	
Total		$19,800
Section 8 Projects		
Federal Subsidy	11,500	
Annualized Deferred Maintenance	200	
Annualized Backlog	500	
Total		$12,200

SOURCES: U.S. Department of Housing and Urban Development, Chief Financial Officer, "Public and Indian Housing: Tenant-based Rental Assistance," Congressional Justifications for 2012 Estimates, p. H-1, http://www.hud.gov/about/budget/fy05/cjs/part1/pih/housecertiffund.pdf (for housing choice voucher); U.S. Department of Housing and Urban Development, Office of Public and Indian Housing, "2011 Unit Total Development Cost (TDC) Limits," http://portal.hud.gov/hudportal/documents/huddoc?id=DOC_8094.pdf, an attachment to PIH notice 2010-20 (HA), issued May 24, 2010 (for public housing development cost); Abt Associates, *Capital Needs in the Public Housing Program: Revised Final Report* (Cambridge, MA: Abt Associates, 2010) (for public housing modernization); Meryl Finkel et al., *Status of HUD-Insured (or Held) Multifamily Rental Housing in 1995: Final Report* (Washington, DC: U.S. Department of Housing and Urban Development, Office of Policy Development and Research, 1999) (for Section 8 project costs, maintenance and repairs).
NOTE: Cost data for earlier years have been converted to 2010 dollars, using the CPI rent index for the voucher program and public housing operating costs, and the GDP deflator for residential investment for construction and rehabilitation of project-based housing.

Modernization funding fluctuates somewhat from year to year, depending on the outcome of the federal budgeting process. Because it is discretionary, the amount budgeted in any year, or even over a period of years, is not necessarily the best measure of the cost of renovating public housing. Actual expenditures may not correspond to expenditures deemed necessary to renovate and maintain the public housing stock. Since 1985 HUD has funded four studies of public housing modernization "needs." The most recent is an Abt Associates analysis from 2010, using data from 2008.[19] Abt estimated that modernization needs were accruing by about $3.4 billion per year, about $3,150 per unit.[20]

In addition, Abt estimated the backlog of repairs and replacements needed to meet local housing codes or HUD modernization needs at about $20.9 billion, about $15,400 per unit.[21] At the 2010 interest rate on Treasury notes with ten-year maturities (the period over which modernization was funded prior to 1985), the annual cost of this backlog would have been a little less than $1,850 per unit per year.[22]

Thus the total annual cost for building and operating a new unit is perhaps about $14,900, omitting modernization on the assumption that a new unit will not require major rehabilitation for some years, or alternatively about $19,900 on the assumption that the average cost of modernization should be included over the life of the project. Given that the federal government has not actually funded construction of any conventional public housing in recent years, it should be clear that there is a good deal of uncertainty surrounding these estimates.

Privately Owned Projects: Section 8. Like public housing, the Section 8 New Construction program is currently inactive, in the sense that no new projects are being built. Unlike public housing, however, the New Construction program has had no estimates of development cost for over twenty-five years. Perhaps the best available information for the annual cost of building a new project is the annual subsidy for the projects that have been built under the program. This cost has not traditionally been reported in the HUD budget, however. Beginning in 1997, contract renewals have ranged from one to five years, and thus the budget authority for renewals overstates the amount required to pay the cost of a unit for one year. Outlays would be a preferable measure, but prior to 2005, HUD funded both Section 8 New Construction and the Housing Choice Voucher in a single account, the Housing Certificate Fund. In 2005, HUD began to create two separate accounts, Project-Based Rental Assistance and Tenant-Based Rental Assistance; this process was completed partway through FY 2006.[23] By that date, projects containing about 225,000 units (about one-quarter of the units in the program) had completed the Mark-to-Market process, described in chapter 3, that reduced the annual subsidy cost by forgiving part of the mortgage debt on the project, prepaying the original mortgage, replacing it with a smaller mortgage that could be supported based on the FMRs for the voucher, and using second and perhaps third mortgages to pay for the difference between the original mortgage and the new restructured mortgage. Outlays for these projects no longer reflect the full cost of building and operating them. A further, recurring complication is that the cost of contract renewals has sometimes been underestimated. In late FY2007, for example, HUD found itself unable to fund all contracts for twelve months, partly due to a general budget rescission enacted by Congress.[24] Program advocates and project owners stated that the full cost of renewals was about 20 percent higher than the budgeted amount.[25]

Fortunately, there are some earlier studies that provide conceptually appropriate ways of measuring Section 8 costs. In the 1990s, two extensive studies of the Section 8 project inventory were conducted for HUD by Abt Associates. The more recent study describes the program's financial status as of 1995.[26] Updating the figures to 2010 dollars, the mean revenue per unit (approximately the same as the mean rent) was $15,600, of which $11,500 consisted of federal subsidies and $4,100 of tenant rental payments.[27]

An alternative approach makes use of Fair Market Rents. As explained in chapter 3, Section 8 projects are subsidized in terms of FMRs in a way similar to tenant-based assistance, but the FMRs have been calculated on a different basis from other programs. For Section 8 New Construction and Substantial Rehabilitation, the FMRs were originally established by comparison to unsubsidized projects being built by private developers at the same time. They were thus based on the cost of construction, rather than the market rental value of the apartments. The FMRs for Section 8 New Construction were originally set at higher levels than for certificates, and the differential remained in place for over twenty years. A 1993 HUD analysis compared the rents paid in Section 8 projects with the FMRs for housing of the same size and location. The data from that analysis indicate that the mean rent was 24 percent above the FMRs for tenant-based assistance.[28] That would imply a mean rent of $12,900 in 2010 dollars.

The Abt Associates analyses during the 1990s also found that Section 8 projects on average had some deferred maintenance and needed major repairs, even though at that time they were all no more than twenty years old and had been receiving generous annual subsidies based on the New Construction FMRs. The later survey estimated that the typical unit had a backlog of about $5,900; in addition, repair needs were accruing at an annual rate of $2,000 (both measured in 2010 dollars). The survey also calculated that about one-quarter of the backlog and 90 percent of the annual accrual could be met from the financial resources of the project.[29] A 1995 survey by the Ernst & Young Kenneth Leventhal Real Estate Group produced similar results; it estimated these needs at about $4,500 per unit for "immediate deferred maintenance" (to bring the property up to market conditions and underwriting standards), and it calculated that an additional $4,600 would be needed for capital improvements over the next five years.[30]

These costs probably should be included in a measure of the cost of new privately owned projects. HUD was not and is not obligated to pay these repair and renovation costs, but either HUD must do so or the project owner must do so (reducing the return on his investment in the property); otherwise the project will deteriorate over time. If the federal government were to finance the accumulated backlog of repairs and renovations, the upper bound of the annual per-unit cost at 2010 Treasury borrowing rates would be about $500 per year for both the Abt and Ernst & Young estimates.

The Abt calculations using 1995 data suggest an overall annual cost of about $12,200 in 2010 dollars: $11,500 in federal subsidies to cover mortgage and operating costs, plus about $500 annually for deferred maintenance and about $200 for annual needed repairs going forward, taking account of available project financial reserves to pay part of repairs and maintenance. This figure reflects the actual costs incurred in building the projects during the 1970s and 1980s and detailed estimates of repair costs as of the 1990s; adjusted for inflation, it arguably represents the cost of building privately owned projects today.

Expenditures and Market Rents. As mentioned at the beginning of this section, these figures for per-unit expenditures in different programs do not take account of how typical units in the different programs differ in size, quality, and location. One way to take these differences into account is to estimate the average market rent of units in each program—what the unit would rent for in the private market if it were built privately without subsidy. David Vandenbroucke of HUD developed the most recent set of such estimates in 2005. He estimated the statistical relationship between market rent and the attributes of unsubsidized units in eleven markets, deriving imputed values for each attribute—calculating, for example, what a second bedroom or a second bathroom is worth. He then used the estimated value of each attribute to estimate the market rents of units in each program category.[31] Vandenbroucke's estimates for each metropolitan area are shown in table 7-6. Following the GAO report comparisons, the market rents are expressed both in current dollars and relative to the market rent of the typical voucher/certificate unit. As the table shows, market rents for public housing units were below the market rents for voucher/certificate units in all nine metropolitan areas for which comparisons were made, and market rents for units in privately owned projects were below the voucher/certificate market rents in eight of the eleven areas.[32]

These market rent estimates help to provide a context for the outlay differences reported in table 7-5. That table shows that the federal government spends more than twice as much for a public housing unit as for a voucher, on average. Table 7-6 indicates that the market rent of a typical public housing unit is about 87 percent that of a typical unit in the voucher or certificate programs, on average. (Atlanta seems to have unusually low costs both for public housing and for privately built subsidized units, but omitting Atlanta, or taking the median rather than the mean as the basis of comparison, does not have much effect on the numbers.) Assuming that the 1991 market rent estimates can be appropriately combined with the 2010 outlays (and this is admittedly a somewhat heroic assumption), vouchers cost less than half as much as public housing and provide better housing to their residents. Also, the market rent of a unit in a privately owned project is almost 50 percent more than the rent for a typical unit in the voucher or certificate program.

It should be obvious that these comparisons are necessarily imprecise, pulling together data from different periods and attempting to estimate the current cost of producing subsidized housing in programs that are no longer active. The basic point, however, seems clear: the voucher has been much less expensive than any of the production programs. The recent budgetary complications in measuring voucher outlays do not change that result.

TABLE 7-6
ESTIMATED MEDIAN MONTHLY RENTS OF
SUBSIDIZED UNITS BY PROGRAM, 1991

Metropolitan Area	Voucher/ Certificate	Privately Owned Project	Ratio: Project/ Voucher	Public Housing	Ratio: Public Housing/ Voucher
Atlanta	505	400	.79	328	.65
Baltimore	460	458	1.00	373	.81
Chicago	475	550	1.16	440	.93
Columbus	375	395	1.05	340	.91
Hartford	593	570	.96	543	.92
Houston	365	325	.89	NA	--
New York	605	578	.96	520	.86
Newark	568	570	1.00	500	.88
San Diego	480	410	.85	NA	--
Seattle	475	455	.96	445	.94
St. Louis	403	378	.94	380	.94
Mean Ratio	--	--	.96	--	.87
Median Ratio	--	--	.96	--	.91

SOURCE: Unpublished tabulations by David A. Vandenbroucke, reported in Edgar O. Olsen, "Fundamental Housing Policy Reform," unpublished paper, University of Virginia, January 2006, available at http://papers.ssm.com/sol3/papers.cfm?abstract_id=475164.
NOTE: NA = not available

The Ongoing Cost of Providing Housing Assistance

The comparative costs in table 7-5 are relevant to a policy issue which has been raised from time to time over the last quarter of a century: does it make sense to "voucher out" assisted housing projects? That is, should project residents be given vouchers allowing them to choose their own housing in the market, including the assisted projects as an option? While it is clear that vouchers are less expensive than either public housing or Section 8 projects as a means of providing assistance to households that are not now being served (such as households with worst-case needs), this is not quite the right comparison for households already living in public housing or other subsidized projects. The cost of building those projects has already been incurred, and if the project was financed with long-term bonds or mortgages, those payments would necessarily continue whether the projects were occupied or not. For the question of "vouchering out," the appropriate comparison is between the cost of the voucher and the ongoing cost of a subsidized project—operating costs and modernization in the case of public housing, for example.

Table 7-5 shows the average cost of a voucher in 2010 as about $8,500, and the average cost of operating and maintaining public housing (including the cost of needed modernization rather than actual expenditures) as about $8,900. The cost of operating the public housing unit was thus nearly the same or less than the cost of the voucher. Given Vandenbroucke's estimate that the market rent of a typical public housing unit was about 87 percent of a unit in the voucher or certificate program, it appears that the ongoing cost for similar units would be higher for public housing projects.

The costs are comparable despite a recent rapid increase in voucher costs. Actual per-unit outlays for the voucher increased sharply between 1998 and 2004. The most detailed analysis of the increase, conducted by GAO in 2006, reported an increase in the annual subsidy per assisted household from about $4,400 in 1998 to $6,200 in 2004, a 42 percent increase, or 22 percent after adjusting for inflation. GAO attributed most of the increase to three factors:

(1) an increase in FMRs relative to the overall cost of living, accounting for about half of the real increase;

(2) a policy change enacted in the Quality Housing and Work Responsibility Act of 1998, allowing PHAs to set local payment standards at anywhere between 90 and 110 percent of the local FMR without prior HUD approval, accounting for about a quarter of the increase;

(3) relatively slow growth in incomes for voucher recipients, accounting for about one-sixth of the increase.[33]

The first two of these factors are policy variables. An additional reason is a change in the basis for calculating the FMR made in 2001. Prior to that year, the FMR was set at the 40th percentile of the distribution of rents for recent movers, but in 2001, the FMR was split: it was set at the 50th percentile in thirty-nine larger metropolitan areas where low-cost

TABLE 7-7

COST OF TENANT-BASED ASSISTANCE AND ONGOING OPERATION
OF PUBLIC HOUSING, 1980–2010

(in Current Dollars per Unit)

Year	Tenant-Based Assistance	Public Housing (Full Modernization Funding)
1980	$3,000	$ 900
1995	5,200	4,900
2010	8,500	9,000

SOURCES: President's Commission on Housing, *The Report of the President's Commission on Housing*, Washington, DC, April 1982, chap. 3 (for 1980); John C. Weicher, *Privatizing Subsidized Housing* (Washington, DC: AEI Press, 1997), 16 (for 1995); U.S. Department of Housing and Urban Development, Chief Financial Officer, "Public and Indian Housing: Tenant-Based Rental Assistance," Congressional Justifications for 2012 Estimates, p. H-1 http://www.hud.gov/about/budget/fy05/cjs/part1/pih/housecertiffund.pdf; Abt Associates, *Capital Needs in the Public Housing Program: Revised Final Report* (Cambridge, MA: Abt Associates, 2010) (for 2010).

housing and voucher recipients were geographically concentrated in a relatively small number of census tracts, "to provide a broad range of housing opportunities throughout a metropolitan area";[34] elsewhere it remained at the 40th percentile. As a result of these changes, the average FMR increased by 27 percent over this period, compared to 23 percent for the overall CPI and 16 percent for the rent component of the CPI.

Since 2004, FMRs have increased much more slowly, at an annual average rate of 3.4 percent through 2010.[35] The average payment standard increased from 96 to 103 percent of the FMR between 1999 and 2004; over the same period, there was a parallel increase in the average voucher rent, from 94 to 97 percent of the FMR.[36]

The recent increase in voucher costs does not affect the long-term trend that has gradually made "vouchering out" a more feasible policy option. The trend is clear in table 7-7, which compares the cost of tenant-based assistance with the cost of operating public housing. In the early years of the certificate program, for example 1980, annual per-unit public housing operating costs and modernization were about one-third the cost of the voucher. The substantially higher ongoing cost of the certificate, given that the capital costs for public housing had already been incurred, was a major reason why the President's Commission on Housing established by

President Reagan did not in 1982 recommend converting public housing to tenant-based assistance as a general policy.[37] By 1995, the difference had narrowed sharply; voucher per-unit costs were about 8 percent higher than costs for public housing.[38] By 2010, vouchers were less expensive. And of course the cost of the voucher includes the capital costs incurred by the private property owner, and the ongoing cost of public housing omits the capital cost.

Conclusion

Vouchers are much less expensive than public housing or privately owned subsidized projects as a way of providing assistance to households that are not currently being served—of providing the "incremental units" that have been especially relevant for budget authority calculations, as discussed in chapter 4. This is true for any variant of tenant-based assistance and any program of project-based assistance. The difficulties of making precise comparisons complicate the discussion but do not change the conclusion. And for those households that are now receiving assistance—the five million households for whom the cost is measured by outlays—vouchers are at worst only a little more expensive, and at best no more expensive at all.

8

The Voucher/Production Debate: Program Efficiency

Economists have a different measure of program cost from the measures discussed in chapter 7: the market value of the resources used to produce something relative to the market value of what's produced. This measure is related to the standard economic concept of opportunity cost, which recognizes that resources have alternative uses, and that the market price of those resources measures what they can produce in their best alternative. It is not a budgetary concept; nor is it affected by differing budgetary treatments of costs, except insofar as different budgetary treatments affect the resources used in the program. But this measure of cost is useful for understanding one important issue in the voucher/production debate: which approach to housing assistance is more cost-effective or efficient?

The Concept of Program Efficiency

Cost-effectiveness or program efficiency is defined as the extent to which a dollar spent to subsidize housing increases the well-being of the household receiving the subsidy. Program efficiency has three components:

(1) production efficiency: the resource costs, direct and indirect, of providing housing in a particular program.

(2) consumption efficiency: the value of the housing to the subsidized household, relative to its market value; as discussed in chapter 1, a household is better off from its own standpoint if it is given $1,000 in cash every month than an in-kind monthly housing subsidy worth $1,000.

(3) administrative efficiency: the relative cost of managing different housing programs, as opposed to the cost of providing
the housing.

Stated alternatively, production efficiency measures the ability of a program
to increase housing consumption, which many policymakers and housing
advocates consider the purpose of an in-kind housing subsidy, and consumption efficiency measures the extent to which the program increases
the economic well-being of the recipient, in the recipient's own opinion,
which many economists consider at least equally important. Production
efficiency is sometimes combined with administrative efficiency in actual
program analyses.[1]

A variety of factors can affect program efficiency and reduce the
amount of housing produced per dollar of expenditure. Richard K. Green
and Stephen Malpezzi have provided a convenient list: "inappropriate
locations, wages that exceed labor's marginal productivity, incorrect factor proportions, . . . off-budget financing costs, tax breaks, and higher
maintenance costs."[2]

As this list suggests, a key issue in measuring program efficiency is the
ability to identify housing in the private market that is the same in quality,
size, and location as subsidized housing, or, for comparisons across programs, housing that is the same in each program. There are essentially two
ways of doing this. First and conceptually simplest is actually identifying
similar units; unfortunately, given the number of attributes that matter from
the household's standpoint, this is likely to be quite difficult in practice.
Second is to analyze the attributes of a large sample of housing units in
relation to the rents; using hedonic analysis, it is possible to infer the value
of a given attribute (for example, what a second bedroom is worth), and
then calculate the value of a unit with a given set of attributes, comparing
the cost of such units in a program with the rent of the same unit in the
private market.

Since all housing markets are local, studies of program efficiency are
also local, although some have included more than one market in the analysis. It is therefore true that the results of any given study may not reflect the
results in another local market, or nationally. One would expect the results
to be different, at least to some extent, in different places and at different

times. The preferences of households may vary from place to place and may change over time, and the same is true of production costs.

All the studies of program efficiency looked at in this chapter were conducted at least twenty-five years ago; the oldest date back over thirty-five years. This is because the program efficiency comparisons were a more important issue when there were several active programs, both project-based and tenant-based, and policymakers regularly had to determine which programs were to be funded. When tenant-based assistance became prevalent, there was less interest in such studies. The recent legislation establishing the Housing Trust Fund, however, may make them relevant to public policy once again.

Production Efficiency

An analysis of public housing in New York City by Edgar O. Olsen and David H. Barton is a good illustration of how production efficiency has been studied.[3] Olsen and Barton had samples of 35,000 rental housing units in both 1965 and 1968 from the New York City Housing and Vacancy Surveys, which are conducted for New York by the U.S. Census Bureau. These surveys are unique to New York, occasioned by the city's need for information to administer its rent control program.[4] For privately owned units not subject to rent control, Olsen and Barton compared the rent of each unit to measures of unit size (number of rooms and number of bedrooms), quality (overall condition, type of heating system), location (by borough), the age of the structure, whether the unit was on a high or low floor, and whether the building had an elevator. They used the results of this analysis to estimate the market rent of public housing units. They then calculated the annual cost incurred by the New York City Housing Authority to build and operate public housing, measuring the cost of building as the annual interest on the bonds used to finance the per-unit development cost (the direct resource cost), plus two indirect costs not reflected in the PHA or HUD budgets—the reduction in the interest rate from the tax-exempt status of the bonds, and the difference between the full property tax paid by private rental property owners and the payment in lieu of taxes made by the PHA. Comparing the estimate of market rent and the full development cost, they concluded that public housing cost 14 percent more than equivalent private housing in 1965, and 10 percent more in 1968. Stated in terms of production efficiency, public housing was 88 percent as efficient as private housing in 1965, and 91 percent as efficient in 1968.

As Olsen and Barton noted, this was the smallest estimate of inefficiency in the economic literature to that time; and it remains the smallest. Other estimates of the inefficiency of public housing have run as low as 48 percent, which means that public housing is more than twice as expensive as private housing of the same quality; and estimates for other subsidy programs have run between 50 percent and 89 percent. Table 8-1 reports the results of several analyses, by program, date, and market. The earliest analyses were undertaken as part of the National Housing Policy Review (NHPR) in 1973, and they contributed to the policy decision to create the Section 8 Existing Housing (certificate) program. These analyses include estimates for public housing expenses derived from cost data on projects in six cities combined with previous statistical analyses of the relationship between market rent and housing attributes in the same cities.[5] For the other programs, the NHPR analysis relied on national program data for program costs, and it collected the data to calculate efficiency, such as the cost of constructing subsidized and unsubsidized housing, from selected cities or HUD regions. (In the case of Section 23 leased public housing—the forerunner of the certificate and voucher programs—the cost data were taken from a previous study by Frank De Leeuw and Sam Leaman, combined with market rent data collected by NHPR.[6]) A few years later, Stephen Mayo and several colleagues analyzed the cost of various housing programs in Phoenix and Pittsburgh as of 1975, comparing public housing and Section 236 to Section 23 and the housing allowance.[7] They estimated the market rents of subsidized units from analyzing a random sample of about 1,600 unsubsidized rental units in each market.

As table 8-1 indicates, the analyses by Mayo et al. estimated substantially greater production inefficiencies than any of the others, for both public housing and Section 236. In addition, inefficiencies were consistently larger in Pittsburgh than in Phoenix, for Section 23 as well as the production programs. Mayo et al. suggest two reasons for the differences. First, Pittsburgh experienced a sharp decline in its lower-income population during the 1960s, resulting in weak demand for low-rent housing and making new construction especially inefficient; this might explain the difference between the results for Pittsburgh and for the other two studies of Section

TABLE 8-1

ESTIMATES OF PRODUCTION EFFICIENCY IN SUBSIDIZED HOUSING PROGRAMS

Author and Date of Study	Program	Year	City	Estimated Production Efficiency
NHPR (1974)	Public Housing	1972	6 Cities[a]	.71
Olsen & Barton (1983)	Public Housing	1965	New York	.88
Olsen & Barton (1983)	Public Housing	1968	New York	.91
Mayo et al (1980)	Public Housing	1975	Pittsburgh	.45
Mayo et al. (1980)	Public Housing	1975	Phoenix	.56
NHPR (1974)	Section 236[b]	1972	21 Cities[c]	.70
Mayo et al. (1980)	Section 236	1975	Pittsburgh	.50
Mayo et al. (1980)	Section 236	1975	Phoenix	.68
NHPR (1974)	Rent Supplement[d]	1972	4 Cities[e]	.76
NHPR (1974)	Section 236 with Rent Supplement	1972	21 Cities[c]	.84
Wallace et al. (1981)	Section 8 NC	1975–79	16 SMSAs[f]	.80
NHPR (1974)[g]	Section 23 Leased Public Housing	1971–72	Not Stated	.97
Mayo (1986)	Section 23	1975	Pittsburgh	.60
Mayo (1986)	Section 23	1975	Phoenix	.70
Mayo et al. (1980)	Housing Allowance	1975	Pittsburgh	.87
Mayo et al. (1980)	Housing Allowance	1975	Phoenix	.92
Wallace et al. (1981)	Section 8 Certificate	1975–79	15 SMSAs[h]	.96

SOURCES: NHPR = U.S. Department of Housing and Urban Development, *Housing in the Seventies: A Report of the National Housing Policy Review* (Washington, DC: U.S. Government Printing Office, 1974), chap. 4; Olsen & Barton = Edgar O. Olsen and David H. Barton, "The Benefits and Costs of Public Housing in New York City," *Journal of Public Economics* 20 (April 1983): 299–332; Mayo et al. = Stephen K. Mayo et al., *Housing Allowances and Other Rental Assistance Programs—A Comparison Based on the Housing Allowance Demand Experiment, part 2, Costs and Efficiency* (Cambridge, MA: Abt Associates, 1980), chap. 5; Mayo = Stephen K. Mayo, "Sources of Inefficiency in Subsidized Housing Programs: A Comparison of U.S. and German Experience," *Journal of Urban Economics* 20, no. 2 (September 1986): 229–49; Wallace et al. = James E. Wallace et al., *Participation and Benefits in the Urban Section 8 Program: New Construction and Existing Housing* (Cambridge, MA: Abt Associates, 1981).

NOTES: a = Baltimore, Boston, Los Angeles, St. Louis, San Francisco, Washington; b = Excludes projects with rent supplement; c = Cities not named; construction cost data taken from 3 HUD regions (not named); d = Limited to rent supplement projects insured by FHA under Section 221(d)(3), not including Section 236 interest rate subsidy; e = Boston, Pittsburgh, St. Louis, Washington; f = 16 Standard Metropolitan Statistical Areas: Appleton-Oshkosh, Atlanta, Baltimore, Chicago, Cleveland, Houston, Los Angeles–Long Beach, Milwaukee, New York, Philadelphia, Providence-Pawtucket-Warwick, Raleigh, Rochester, St. Louis, San Diego, Seattle-Everett; g = NHPR combined two of its own samples with data from Frank De Leeuw and Sam H. Leaman, "The Section 23 Leasing Program," in U.S Congress, Joint Economic Committee, *The Economics of Federal Subsidy Programs, part 5, Housing Subsidies* (Washington, DC: U.S. Government Printing Office, 1972), 642–59. De Leeuw and Leaman looked at 25 metropolitan areas; h = Same as the SMSAs listed in note f, excluding Appleton-Oshkosh.

236, and the consistent differences between Pittsburgh and Phoenix. Second, construction costs rose very rapidly compared to rents between 1965 and 1975, and Mayo et al. is the latest of the studies. This could help to explain the difference between the findings of Mayo et al. and those of the two studies of New York public housing in the late 1960s, but it probably does not explain the difference between Mayo et al. and the NHPR analysis, which used data that were only three years older.[8]

All these analyses antedated Section 8. Once Section 8 was enacted and began providing both project-based and tenant-based assistance, cost-effectiveness comparisons of these two programs became relevant. The most extensive analysis, the Abt Associates comparative analysis of Section 8 New Construction and the certificate program, compared the programs in sixteen cities, using data on certificate holders in 1978–1979 and on projects built between 1975 and 1979, the first five years of the program.[9]

The results are shown in table 8-1. Production efficiency is defined in the Section 8 New Construction program as the ratio of the market value of the assisted housing unit to the cost of producing a unit ($291/$362, a ratio of .80), and in the certificate program as the ratio of the market value to the gross rent ($231/$240, a ratio of .96). These data indicate that the rent for the new subsidized unit was 20 percent more than for a unit of the same quality in the private market ($291 vs. $231).[10] The Abt analysts suggested that this difference arose to a significant extent because of project location: many of the projects were built in areas where private housing would not be built, because few households would choose to live in those areas.[11]

All the analyses of tenant-based assistance in table 8-1 antedate the voucher. Shortly after the voucher program was created in 1983, a study by Abt Associates compared certificates and vouchers.[12] The study found that vouchers cost the federal government 6 percent more than certificates in the first year of use, but the difference declined to 2 percent in the second year. Differences in later years were not studied. The first-year cost difference is statistically significant; the second-year difference is not. The main reason for the higher initial cost was the "shopping incentive" in the voucher program that let the recipient keep any difference between the FMR and the actual rent. The main reason for the later convergence of costs is that annual rent increases for tenants were automatic in the certificate program and optional for the PHA in the voucher program. The Housing Choice Voucher follows the certificate program in not having a shopping incentive and the voucher program in having optional rent increases; its cost is likely to be similar to the certificate.

During the years after the voucher was created as a demonstration program, and even after it became a permanent program in 1987, there was substantial political controversy over the differences between vouchers and certificates, particularly perceived cost differences. This is rather ironic. Any cost difference between them is quite small compared to the average difference between any of the production programs and either tenant-based program.[13]

All of these analyses also precede the Low-Income Housing Tax Credit. The broad studies of the LIHTC generally indicate that the program is not likely to be a very efficient way to assist households with very low or extremely low incomes, which should not be surprising given the relatively high income limit, 60 percent of area median, for LIHTC residents, and also given the fact that tax credits have generally sold to investors at a discount, as described in chapter 3. It is therefore to be expected that some part of the credit does not result in cost reductions for the project and rent reductions for the occupants. A recent systematic analysis provides evidence to support this view. Gregory S. Burge studied tax credit projects in Tallahassee as of 2002, comparing the rent savings of LIHTC project residents to the foregone tax revenue from the credits. He concluded that the savings amounted to about 35 percent of the foregone taxes. The projects were built between 1995 and 1999, when tax credits sold for between fifty-five and seventy-five cents on the dollar. Burge also concluded that the rent savings to the residents are higher in the early years after the project is completed, because the market rent for the unit declines from year to year as the project ages. The study is limited to the Tallahassee housing market, but Burge also presents data on rents and incomes in other market areas, which suggest that savings would probably be higher in the largest housing markets, on average. Savings would be particularly high in New York, Boston, Miami and Los Angeles, but there is substantial variation among the individual markets.[14]

While the estimates of production efficiency in table 8-1 have a wide variation, it is clear that tenant-based assistance is more efficient than either public or private projects. The twelve estimates of project-based assistance programs range from .45 to .91, with a mean of .70. The seven estimates of tenant-based assistance range from .60 to .97, with a mean of .87.

Consumption Efficiency

Government assistance in the form of subsidized housing, or any other specific commodity, is less desirable for the recipients than the same dollar amount in cash. From a low-income household's point of view, the value of in-kind benefits costing $100 in the market is less than the value of a direct cash transfer of $100. Consumption efficiency measures the recipient's valuation of the in-kind benefit, relative to cash. It is calculated based on the market valuation of the housing subsidy, ignoring the production inefficiencies dealt with in the previous section.

The first published estimates of consumption efficiency, like the first estimates of production efficiency, were produced as part of the NHPR at HUD in 1973–1974. Over the next decade, other analysts produced estimates, first for the older subsidy programs, and then for Section 8 New Construction and the Section 8 Existing Housing certificate program. There have been no consumption efficiency estimates for Section 202 or the newer programs included in the 2002 GAO report on comparative costs discussed in the previous chapter.

In calculating consumption efficiency, it is necessary to estimate the preferences of households for housing relative to all other goods and services. The information used in estimating preferences typically comes from housing program data, such as the applications filled out by households that want to participate in the program, or from survey data on low-income renters.[15] From these data, it is possible to estimate how much a household's expenditures on housing would increase as its income increases, and how its expenditures would change in response to the subsidy. The fact that housing assistance is not an entitlement (unlike Medicaid or food stamps) means that there are many lower-income households that do not receive assistance, as well as many that do, and the differences in the consumption patterns of subsidized and unsubsidized households can be used to measure consumption efficiency.

Table 8-2 reports the results of several analyses of consumption efficiency by program, date, and market, parallel to table 8-1.[16] There are more results for public housing than for any of the other programs, partly because of the rapid succession of privately owned project programs; policymakers are seldom interested in information about defunct programs.

TABLE 8-2

ESTIMATES OF CONSUMPTION EFFICIENCY IN SUBSIDIZED HOUSING PROGRAMS

Author and Date of Study	Program	Year	City	Estimated Consumption Efficiency
NHPR (1974)	Public Housing	1972	6 Cities[a]	.75
Murray (1977)	Public Housing	1971	7 Cities (not named)	.84
Kraft & Olsen (1977)	Public Housing	1972	5 Cities[b]	.73
Olsen & Barton (1983)	Public Housing	1965	New York	.77
Olsen & Barton (1983)	Public Housing	1968	New York	.73
Clemmer (1984)	Public Housing	1977	33 Cities[c]	.67
Mayo (1986)	Public Housing	1975	Pittsburgh/ Phoenix[d]	.86
NHPR (1974)	Section 236[e]	1972	21 Cities[f]	.71
NHPR (1974)	Section 236 with Rent Supplement	1972	21 Cities[e]	.64
Mayo (1986)	Section 236[e]	1975	Pittsburgh/ Phoenix[d]	.74
Wallace et al. (1981)	Section 8 NC	1975–79	16 SMSAs[g]	.72
Sa-Aadu (1984)	Section 8 NC	1979	Wisconsin Cities[h]	.67
Schwab (1985)	Section 8 NC	1979	13 SMSAs[i]	.63
Mayo (1986)	Section 8 NC	1975	16 SMSAs[g]	.63
Mayo (1986)	Housing Allowance	1975	Pittsburgh/ Phoenix[d]	.93
Mayo (1986)	Section 23	1975	Pittsburgh/ Phoenix[d]	.88
Wallace et al. (1981)	Certificate[j]	1975–79	16 SMSAs[g]	.93
Reeder (1985)	Certificate	1976	National	.83
Mayo (1986)	Certificate	1975	16 SMSAs[k]	.82

SOURCES: NHPR = U.S. Department of Housing and Urban Development, *Housing in the Seventies: A Report of the National Housing Policy Review* (Washington, DC: U.S. Government Printing Office, 1974) chap. 4; Murray = Michael P. Murray, "The Distribution of Tenant Benefits in Public Housing," *Econometrica* 43, no. 4 (July 1975): 771–88; Kraft & Olsen = John Kraft and E. O. Olsen, "The Distribution of Benefits from Public Housing," in *The Distribution of Economic Well-Being*, ed. F. Thomas Juster (New York: National Bureau of Economic Research, 1977), 51–69; Olsen & Barton = Edgar O. Olsen and David H. Barton, "The Benefits and Costs of Public Housing in New York City," *Journal of Public Economics* 20 (April 1983): 299–332; Clemmer = Richard B. Clemmer, "Measuring Welfare Effects of In-Kind Transfers," *Journal of Urban Economics* 15, no. 1 (January 1984): 46–65; Mayo = Stephen K.

(continued)

TABLE 8-2
ESTIMATES OF CONSUMPTION EFFICIENCY IN SUBSIDIZED HOUSING PROGRAMS
(*continued*)

Mayo, "Sources of Inefficiency in Subsidized Housing Programs: A Comparison of U.S. and German Experience," *Journal of Urban Economics* 20, no. 2 (September 1986): 229–49; Wallace et al. = James E. Wallace et al., *Participation and Benefits in the Urban Section 8 Program: New Construction and Existing Housing* (Cambridge, MA: Abt Associates, 1981); Sa-Aadu = Jarjisu Sa-Aadu, "Alternative Estimates of Direct Tenant Benefit and Consumption Inefficiencies from the Section 8 New Construction Program," *Land Economics* 60, no. 2 (May 1984): 189–201; Schwab = Robert M. Schwab, "The Benefits of In-Kind Government Programs," *Journal of Public Economics* 27, no. 2 (1985), 195–210; Reeder = William J. Reeder, "The Benefits and Costs of the Section 8 Existing Housing Program," *Journal of Public Economics,* 26 (1985): 349–77.

NOTES: a = Baltimore, Boston, Los Angeles, St. Louis, San Francisco, Washington; b = Boston, Pittsburgh, St. Louis, San Francisco, Washington; c = 33 metropolitan areas surveyed in American Housing Survey during 1974 and 1975 (metropolitan areas not named); d = Averaged across the two cities; e = Excludes projects with rent supplement; f = Cities not named; construction cost data taken from 3 HUD regions (not named); g = 16 Standard Metropolitan Statistical Areas: Appleton-Oshkosh, Atlanta, Baltimore, Chicago, Cleveland, Houston, Los Angeles–Long Beach, Milwaukee, New York, Philadelphia, Providence-Pawtucket-Warwick, Raleigh, Rochester, St. Louis, San Diego, Seattle-Everett; h = All cities in Wisconsin with public housing applicants; i = 13 Standard Metropolitan Statistical Areas: Atlanta, Baltimore, Chicago, Cleveland, Houston, Milwaukee, New York, Philadelphia, Providence-Pawtucket-Warwick, Rochester, St. Louis, San Diego, Seattle-Everett. Limited to elderly households only; j = Based on market rent with tenure discount; k = Same as the SMSAs listed in note g, excluding Appleton-Oshkosh.

The general conclusion is clear: project-based programs to produce new subsidized housing are less desirable than tenant-based assistance. The range of efficiency estimates is .63 to .86 for the various production programs, with a mean of .72; and .82 to .93 for tenant-based assistance, with a mean of .86. Two of the public housing estimates, by Murray and Mayo, are above .82; otherwise there is no overlap between the distributions of efficiency for project-based and tenant-based assistance programs. Low-income households clearly see themselves as deriving more benefit per dollar spent from renting housing that they choose in the private market than from living in public housing or other subsidized projects built for them.

Some of these studies have reported estimates of subjective benefits on a demographic basis. They have typically found that larger households receive greater benefits and have therefore a higher consumption efficiency ratio, and that elderly households tend to receive smaller benefits and have a lower ratio.[17]

There have been no analyses of Section 202, and the program is different enough from public housing and Section 8 New Construction that the results for these programs should not be assumed to apply to Section 202.

Overall Program Efficiency

Program efficiency comprises production efficiency, consumption efficiency, and (where it is not included with production efficiency) administrative efficiency. It reflects both the excess cost of providing housing through government programs rather than through the private market, and the degree to which in-kind housing assistance is viewed as inferior to cash by the recipients.

Program efficiency can be calculated from the ratios in tables 8-1 and 8-2, though only for a few studies. There have been so few because estimating program efficiency requires estimating both production efficiency and consumption efficiency for the same program; different data sets are required to analyze the two types of efficiency, and collecting the data is expensive. To some extent program data can be used, but this is more readily available to analysts within the government than to those outside it, which explains why most of the studies in tables 8-1 to 8-3 have been conducted or funded by HUD.

Another reason is that several studies have measured the production and consumption aspects of the program in different ways, either because of data limitations or because the policy questions being studied were not matters of program efficiency. The 1981 Abt Associates evaluation of Section 8 New Construction and the certificate program, for example, measured the benefits to households in a somewhat different manner from consumption efficiency. Instead of measuring the benefit from the household's point of view of living in a particular subsidized housing unit, the evaluation estimated what the "normal housing expenditure" of the household would be if it did not receive any subsidy. This normal expenditure was then compared to the market rental value of the unit occupied by the assisted household, and the household's payment toward the rent. This approach yielded interesting and important results for housing policy.

Table 8-4 reports the results of this evaluation. For convenience, it restates the results for production efficiency from table 8-1. In addition, it repeats some data from table 7-3, but uses the data for different analytical purposes.

As discussed earlier in this chapter, production efficiency is measured as the ratio of the market value of the assisted housing unit to the cost of

TABLE 8-3
ESTIMATES OF PROGRAM EFFICIENCY IN SUBSIDIZED HOUSING PROGRAMS

Author and Date of Study	Program	Year	City[a]	Estimated Program Efficiency
Olsen & Barton (1983)	Public Housing	1965	New York	.74
Olsen & Barton (1983)	Public Housing	1968	New York	.66
Mayo (1986)	Public Housing	1975	2 Cities	.43
NHPR (1974)	Section 236[b]	1972	21 Cities	.50
Mayo (1986)	Section 236	1975	2 Cities	.40
NHPR (1974)	Section 236 with Rent Supplement	1972	4 Cities	.54
Mayo (1986)	Section 8 NC	1975–79	16 SMSAs	.45
Mayo (1986)	Section 23	1975	2 Cities	.65
Mayo (1986)	Certificate	1975–79	15 SMSAs	.72

SOURCES: Olsen & Barton = Edgar O. Olsen and David H. Barton, "The Benefits and Costs of Public Housing in New York City," *Journal of Public Economics* 20 (April 1983): 299–332; NHPR = U.S. Department of Housing and Urban Development, *Housing in the Seventies: A Report of the National Housing Policy Review* (Washington, DC: U.S. Government Printing Office, 1974) chap. 4; Mayo = Stephen K. Mayo, "Sources of Inefficiency in Subsidized Housing Programs: A Comparison of U.S. and German Experience," *Journal of Urban Economics* 20, no. 2 (September 1986): 229–49.
NOTES: a = Cities listed in tables 8-1 and 8-2; b = Excludes projects with rent supplement.

producing a unit in the Section 8 New Construction program ($291/$362, a ratio of .80), and the ratio of the market value to the gross rent in the certificate program ($231/$240, a ratio of .96). The market value and gross rent for the certificate program take account of the fact that a substantial number of participants continued to live in the same unit; they paid rents that were lower than the market rental value because they were valued by the property owner and received a "tenure discount." When administrative costs are included, the production efficiency of both programs is reduced, to a greater extent in Section 8 New Construction.

Panel B reports the effect of the housing subsidy on the consumption patterns of the assisted household. As mentioned in chapter 7, the market rental value of the unit in the Section 8 New Construction project was about 10 percent higher than that of the tenant-based unit ($291 vs. $265). The tenant-based unit was worth more on the market than its cost to the

TABLE 8-4

COSTS AND BENEFITS OF PROJECT-BASED AND TENANT-BASED ASSISTANCE

(per Month, in 1979 Dollars)

	Section 8 New Construction	Certificates
Panel A: Cost of Producing Housing		
Market Rental Value of Unit	$291	$265[a]
Unit Cost of Producing or Renting	$362	$240[b]
Rental Value to Tenant	NA	$231[b]
Administrative Costs	$ 91	$ 36
Total Costs	$453	$276
Panel B: Consumption Effects		
Market Rental Value of Unit	$291	$265[a]
Tenant Rental Payment	$112	$155
Subsidy to Tenant	$179	$121
Normal Housing Expenditure without Subsidy	$190	$205
Housing Benefit to Tenant – Better Housing	$101	$ 60
Income Benefit to Tenant – Other Goods/Services	$ 78	$ 95
Panel C: Effective Provision of Housing Assistance		
Housing Benefit	$101	$ 60
Federal Cost for Housing (Excluding Administration)	$250	$130
Housing Benefit/Federal Cost	40%	46%
Total Federal Cost (Including Administration)	$341	$166
Housing Benefit/Total Federal Cost	30%	36%

SOURCES: James E. Wallace et al., *Participation and Benefits in the Urban Section 8 Program: New Construction and Existing Housing* (Cambridge, MA: Abt Associates, 1981), S-9–S-14; Stephen K. Mayo, "Sources of Inefficiency in Subsidized Housing Programs: A Comparison of U.S. and German Experience," *Journal of Urban Economics* 20, no. 2 (September 1986): 229–49 (administrative costs).
NOTE: a = rent ignoring "tenure discount," assuming household is moving into the apartment. b = Rent taking account of "tenure discount." NA = not applicable.

assisted tenant ($231) because satisfactory tenants tend to receive "tenure discounts" to persuade them to stay.

Tenant benefits were about 15 percent greater in the project-based program ($179 vs. $155), again reflecting the higher quality of the housing units, since tenant rent payments, based in both programs on their incomes, were similar.

The table also separates the tenant benefit into two components: the improvement in housing resulting from the subsidy, and the extent to which the tenant is able to buy other goods and services—the "housing benefit" and the "income benefit," respectively. This decomposition is calculated from the data in the table, and the amount the household would be likely to spend on rent if it did not receive assistance—its "normal housing expenditure," as described above.[18] For tenants in the new construction program, the normal housing expenditure was $190 per month; for those receiving certificates, the normal expenditure was $205.

The housing benefit is the difference between the market rental value of the unit that the assisted household occupies, and the amount it would spend on rent in the absence of the subsidy; the income benefit is the difference between the amount the household would spend on rent without the subsidy, and the amount it actually has to spend in the subsidized unit. Thus for households living in Section 8 projects, the housing benefit was $101 and the income benefit was $78; for households receiving certificates, the housing benefit was $60 and the income benefit was $95. More of the benefit for each household in the project-based program took the form of better housing, while more of the benefit in the tenant-based program took the form of disposable income to spend on goods and services generally. Residents of subsidized projects received a larger housing benefit ($101 vs. $60), while certificate holders received a larger income benefit ($95 vs. $78); they were able to spend more on other goods and services besides housing.

There is, however, another way to analyze the benefits of the programs, which yields a different conclusion. This is shown in Panel C. If housing benefits are compared to the federal government's expenditure, then the certificate provided more housing benefit per dollar—more of the government expenditures went toward improved housing in the tenant-based program—46 percent ($60/$130) compared to 40 percent ($101/$250) in Section 8 New Construction. This appears in table 8-4 as "Housing Benefit/ Federal Cost"—the tenant housing benefit as a percentage of the federal government subsidy. This result occurs because a substantial share, 28 percent, of the federal subsidy in the Section 8 New Construction program was a payment to the developer or owner that, for whatever reason, did not result in better-quality housing. Payments to project or unit owners that were in excess of the value of the housing were far larger in the project-based program—$71 per month compared to $9 (using the rent measure that takes account of tenure). This can be interpreted as "waste," or as differences in the quality or location of units not captured in the analysis, or a mixture of both.

When administrative costs and indirect government costs are included, the housing benefit is reduced from 40 percent to about 30 percent of per-unit new construction outlays ($101/341), and from 46 percent to about 36 percent of expenditures in the certificate program ($60/$166). This is shown as "Housing Benefit/Total Federal Cost."

In addition, because administrative and indirect costs are so much lower in the tenant-based program, nearly all of the federal government's expenditures actually benefit tenants, in the form of better housing or the ability to buy other goods and services ($155/$166). Only about half of federal expenditures in the new construction program benefit the tenants ($179/$341). The remainder is spent in payments for housing that are in excess of the value of the housing, or on indirect and administrative costs that do not benefit tenants directly.

This comparison captures the essence of the debate between advocates of the two types of programs. Those who prefer project-based assistance believe that improving the housing of the poor is particularly important, and would spend more to achieve that objective. Those who prefer tenant-based assistance believe that the poor can make their own choice between housing and other goods, and would allow them to maximize their welfare according to their own preferences; this group can also point out that tenant-based assistance is so much more efficient that more of the government's expenditures result in improved housing.

Conclusion

The ranges of efficiency estimates from the different analyses are a useful reminder of the imprecision in all of the studies. But although it may not be possible to determine exactly how cost-effective a given program is, it is clear that tenant-based assistance is a less expensive and more efficient way of helping low-income households live in decent, affordable housing than is project-based assistance.

9

Is There Enough Housing?

The previous chapters have shown that tenant-based assistance is clearly less expensive than project-based programs, and that it provides about the same improvement in housing quality. For these reasons, and especially for the former, tenant-based assistance has become the basic housing policy of the United States. But a question remains: Is there enough decent housing available to serve those who, in the view of policymakers, need housing assistance, or is it necessary to build more subsidized housing directly for the poor in order to achieve the national housing goal?

This obviously important question is sometimes explicitly addressed in housing policy debates, as in the worst-case needs reports by HUD discussed in chapter 2, although it is not the central focus of these reports. More often, however, it lies in the background of housing policy discussions, with the answer assumed but never openly stated. Both policymakers and the press typically start from the premise that there is a shortage of adequate housing. This presumption affects their reaction to a wide variety of reform proposals.

This chapter addresses the question directly. It combines the data on housing quality reviewed in chapter 2 with information about the utilization of the existing housing stock in order to determine whether the housing stock is in fact adequate to serve the low-income population in need of housing assistance. Stated differently, the chapter asks whether an entitlement program of tenant-based assistance would be able to serve all eligible households. For the nation as a whole, the analysis concludes that the answer is "yes." But this is only part of the answer, because all housing markets are local. The only systematic study of local markets is twenty years old, but that study in combination with recent available data suggests that tenant-based assistance could serve the eligible population in nearly all of the largest metropolitan areas.

"Enough Housing" for What?

It is important to define the concept of "serving all eligible households." What does it mean to serve a household, and which are the households that should be served?

The "worst-case needs" definition gives priority for housing assistance to households that have incomes below 50 percent of the local median income, and that live in severely inadequate housing or have a rent burden in excess of 50 percent of their income. This priority, established in the early 1980s, has never been met, as the data in chapter 2 demonstrate. Having enough housing to meet it is a good criterion of "enough."

The two components of the definition—the quality of the housing and the household's ability to pay for it—pose very different problems. A physically inadequate unit needs to be repaired or removed from the inventory if it cannot be repaired or would be too expensive to repair. If razing the unit is the cost-effective choice, the question of whether there are other units available for the household is directly relevant. An affordability problem, however, concerns the household's income, not the quality of its housing. Affordability problems can be addressed, and are in fact addressed, in all housing programs. The problems are managed by establishing a maximum rent-income ratio—virtually all programs now have a 30 percent maximum rent-income ratio by statute—and by providing subsidies to cover the remainder of the costs. The voucher directly provides funds for a household to lower its rent-income ratio to 30 percent, while allowing the household to spend a larger share if it chooses; public housing provides operating subsidies based on the household's income and modernization funds to cover major repairs that in the private sector would be covered from tenant rents; the Section 8 program pays private project owners the difference between 30 percent of the tenant's income and the FMR, representing in this case the cost of building and operating the project. The AHS reports on the characteristics of assisted households certainly show a remarkably high incidence of rent burden among assisted households; this, however, is a problem with program management, or possibly with the household responses to the survey, not a flaw in program design for any of the programs.[1]

Other housing priorities could be established. Crowding, for example, has been recognized as a problem since the first decennial Census of Housing in 1940, and it has been regularly reported since then, but addressing this problem has never been part of the national housing goal, even as early as the first official formulation in 1948. Crowded households were included with households having severe physical problems in a category of households that "need to move" in some early worst-case needs reports;[2] more recently, crowding has been treated as a moderate problem, not a severe problem qualifying as a worst-case need. The standard for the type of physical problem deserving priority could also be lowered from "severely inadequate" to "moderately inadequate." The distinction is essentially between housing that probably needs to be replaced and housing that could probably be repaired on a cost-effective basis. While clear in the data, this distinction in reality probably does not offer a hard-and-fast rule. Some units that are counted in either category would turn out to belong to the other—some that are classified as "severely inadequate" could be repaired; some classified as "moderately inadequate" probably should be replaced. That said, the distinction remains valid for policy purposes.

Using the Voucher to Address Housing Needs

The relative importance of the two components of worst-case needs is quite different. The data analysis in chapter 2 concluded that far more households suffered from high rent burdens than from severely inadequate housing. There were 443,000 unassisted very low-income renter households living in severely inadequate housing in 2009, compared to 6.9 million with a rent burden above 50 percent of their income, of whom 6.2 million suffered from only a rent burden. These data, the most recent calculations from HUD's worst-case needs reports, are shown in table 9-1, along with data from other AHS tabulations for 2003 and 2005.

The ability of tenant-based assistance to address the housing quality problems of low-income households depends on the stock of available vacant rental units. Table 9-1 also reports the number of vacant units in each year that are being offered for rent at less than the national average FMR, as estimated by the Census Bureau's Housing Vacancy Survey. The vacancy rate was consistently about 10 percent, and the number of available units about 2.5 million. The 443,000 unassisted families with severely inadequate housing could easily be accommodated within that stock.

TABLE 9-1

THE ABILITY OF TENANT-BASED ASSISTANCE TO SERVE LOW-INCOME RENTERS
LIVING IN SEVERELY INADEQUATE HOUSING, 2003–2009

(Housing Units in 1,000s)

| Income Category | Year | Severely Inadequate | | | Vacant Units Renting for Less than FMR | | |
		Total	Unassisted	FMR	Number	Rate	Excess
Very Low Income	2009	581	443	$889	2,724	9.3%	961
Extremely Low Income	2009	387	228	$889	2,724	9.3%	961
Poor Households	2009	348	N.A.	$889	2,724	9.3%	961
Very Low Income	2005	658	521	$767	2,567	10.0%	1,027
Extremely Low Income	2005	430	318	$767	2,567	10.0%	1,027
Poor Households	2005	392	N.A.	$767	2,567	10.0%	1,027
Very Low Income	2003	614	444	$735	2,463	9.9%	970
Extremely Low Income	2003	401	280	$735	2,463	9.9%	970
Poor Households	2003	325	N.A.	$735	2,463	9.9%	970
Eligible for Assistance	2003	639	488	$735	2,463	9.9%	970

SOURCES: Very Low Income and Extremely Low Income Households: U.S. Department of Housing and Urban Development, Office of Policy Development and Research, *Worst Case Housing Needs 2009: Report to Congress*, February 2011, Tables A-1a and A-3 (2009 data); U.S. Department of Housing and Urban Development, Office of Policy Development and Research, *Affordable Housing Needs 2005: Report to Congress*, May 2007, Tables A-1a and A-3 (2005 data); U.S. Department of Housing and Urban Development, Office of Policy Development and Research, *Affordable Housing Needs: A Report to Congress on the Significant Need for Housing, December 2005*, Tables A-1a and A-3 (2003 data); Poor Households: *American Housing Survey for the United States: 2009*, H150/09, February 2011, Table 4-7, and similarly for earlier years; Households Eligible for Assistance: U.S. Department of Housing and Urban Development, Office of Policy Development and Research, *Characteristics of HUD-Assisted Renters and Their Units in 2003*, May 2008, Table 4; FMRs: Unpublished table provided by U.S. Department of Housing and Urban Development; Vacancy data: U.S. Census Bureau, *Housing Vacancies and Homeownership (HVS/CPS), Annual Statistics*, various years, available for 2009 at http://www.census.gov/hhes/www/housing/hvs/annual09/ann09ind.html and similarly for earlier years, calculated from Tables 2 and 11.
NOTE: NA = not available in source document.

Moreover, they could easily be accommodated and still leave a large number of vacant units. A vacancy rate of 6 percent is the usual dividing line between tight and loose rental markets. As table 9-1 shows, the rental market could accommodate very low-income households in severely inadequate housing and remain loose.

Table 9-1 also reports on the problems of extremely low-income renters, those with incomes below 30 percent of the median, and the problems of renters with incomes below the poverty threshold. As explained in chapter 2, poverty is measured differently from HUD's low-income categories; it is determined on a national basis, while the HUD measures are based on household incomes in individual local housing markets. The national poverty threshold for a four-person household was 29.5 percent of the median household income in 2009, very close to HUD's measure of extremely low income. There are fewer households in these more restrictive income categories living in physically inadequate housing; they could still more easily be served by the voucher.

The table reports the total number of households in each income category living in severely inadequate housing, as well as the number self-identified as not receiving assistance. As discussed in chapter 2, the AHS has had a continuing problem determining which households receive housing assistance, and it has tended to overstate the number, according to program data. The total number of households living in severely inadequate housing certainly includes some assisted households, as shown in table 9-1 and is therefore surely an overestimate of the number of unassisted households with severe problems; correspondingly, the total number of self-identified unassisted renters living in severely inadequate housing probably does not include some households that incorrectly report themselves as assisted, and is therefore probably an underestimate. The precise number of unassisted renters living in severely inadequate housing lies in between.[3] Whatever the correct number may be, clearly those households can be served by the voucher program without creating a "tight" housing market. If all very low-income households in severely inadequate housing in 2009 were to receive vouchers, the vacancy rate would be 7.3 percent; if unassisted very low-income households were to receive vouchers, it would be 7.8 percent.

The problem of determining which and how many households receive housing assistance has been addressed by HUD and the Census Bureau, matching program data with data from the AHS. The most recent analysis, for 2003, is shown in table 9-1, along with the published AHS data from the worst-case needs report for that year. The differences between households eligible for assistance and very low-income households are not large, and the conclusion is the same: the voucher can serve all income-eligible households with severe housing problems.

The table also reports the latest AHS data, from the 2009 survey, for households which are officially counted as poor. Between 2003 and 2009, the number of poor households in severely inadequate housing has fluctuated, rising during 2003–2005 and declining by 2009. Since 2003, the number has increased by 23,000; over the same period, the number of vacant units renting for less than the FMR increased by 264,000. The market became looser for lower-income households. These data, too, argue for the voucher's ability to serve poor households.

The Voucher and Local Markets

The calculations in table 9-1 are for the United States as a whole and use national data. In particular, they use the national average FMR for calculating vacant units and vacancy rates, not the FMRs in individual markets.[4] There has been no recent analysis of local housing markets to investigate whether the local vacancy rates are sufficiently high to serve the local very low-income renters living in severely inadequate housing. The only such analysis covers the period 1987–1990 and appears in the worst-case needs report published in 1992.[5] The analysis includes forty-four large metropolitan areas, those for which there was at the time a metropolitan area survey conducted as part of the AHS.

These areas were surveyed over a four-year period, eleven each year. These forty-four areas contained 50.9 percent of all rental housing, 47.8 percent of all very low-income renters, and 54.4 percent of all households with worst-case housing needs. A total of 217,000 very low-income renters were living in severely inadequate housing in these metropolitan areas, as tabulated in the 1992 worst-case needs report. Nationally, there were about 650,000 in 1987 and about 700,000 in 1989.[6] Table 9-2 reports the number of severely inadequate units in each metropolitan area that exceeded 6 percent of the number of units renting for less than the local FMR, or in other words, the number of households living in severely inadequate housing that could not be served by tenant-based assistance unless the local vacancy rate went below 6 percent, thus creating a tight market for lower-rent housing. In thirty-three of the forty-three metropolitan areas, the stock of vacant housing was sufficient to serve these households without creating a tight market. In the other eleven, there was a total of 95,000 households

TABLE 9-2
THE ABILITY OF TENANT-BASED ASSISTANCE TO SERVE LOW-INCOME RENTERS WITH WORST-CASE NEEDS BY MSA, 1987–1990

(Housing Units in 1,000s)

MSA	Additional Units Needed to Serve Households in Severely Inadequate Housing	
	6% Vacancy Rate	5% Vacancy Rate
New York	52	52
Newark	6	6
Boston	4	0
Rochester	0.5	0
Providence	0.2	0
Hartford	0	0
Buffalo	0	0
Philadelphia	0	0
Pittsburgh	0	0
Milwaukee	5	4
Chicago	0	0
Cincinnati	0	0
Cleveland	0	0
Columbus	0	0
Detroit	0	0
Indianapolis	0	0
Kansas City	0	0
Minneapolis	0	0
St. Louis	0	0
Baltimore	0.3	0
Atlanta	0	0
Birmingham	0	0
Dallas	0	0
Fort Worth	0	0
Houston	0	0
Memphis	0	0
New Orleans	0	0
Norfolk	0	0
Oklahoma City	0	0
San Antonio	0	0
Tampa	0	0
Washington	0	0

(*continued*)

TABLE 9-2

THE ABILITY OF TENANT-BASED ASSISTANCE TO SERVE LOW-INCOME RENTERS
WITH WORST-CASE NEEDS BY MSA, 1987–1990 (*continued*)

(Housing Units in 1,000s)

MSA	Additional Units Needed to Serve Households in Severely Inadequate Housing	
	6% Vacancy Rate	5% Vacancy Rate
Los Angeles	19	9
San Francisco	4	0
Portland	2	2
San Jose	1	1
Orange County	0	0
San Bernardino	0	0
San Diego	0	0
Denver	0	0
Phoenix	0	0
Salt Lake City	0	0
Seattle	0	0
Total	95	74

SOURCE: Calculated from data in U.S. Department of Housing and Urban Development, Office of Policy Development and Research, *The Location of Worst Case Needs in the Late 1980s: A Report to Congress,* Washington, DC, December 1992, Tables 5, 9.

that could not be served without creating a tight market—something less than half the total of very low-income renters living in severely inadequate housing for all forty-four areas. Of these households, 61 percent or 52,000 lived in New York, and 20 percent or 19,000 in Los Angeles, defining both markets broadly to include suburban areas that are part of the Consolidated Metropolitan Statistical Areas.[7] Vouchers could have eliminated the problem of severely inadequate housing for very low-income renters in most of the large metropolitan areas.

The 1992 worst-case needs report considered vacancy rates of 5 and 4 percent, rather than 6 percent. For comparability, table 9-2 also repeats the calculation from the 1992 report for a vacancy rate of 5 percent, with essentially the same conclusion; indeed, the remaining households were even more concentrated in New York and Los Angeles. All but 74,000 households could be served by a voucher, and 68,000 of the remainder were in New York or Los Angeles (again, 52,000 lived in New York).

These data are more than twenty years old. As of 2010 (the latest annual data), the overall rental vacancy rate is higher in thirty-nine of these forty-three metropolitan areas, according to the Census Bureau. Vacancy rates are higher in all of the eleven metropolitan areas where there was a shortage of vacant units to serve households living in severely inadequate housing.[8] Nationally, the rental vacancy rate has been rising for the last twenty years. It ranged between 7 and 7.5 percent during the early 1990s, between 7.5 and 8 percent in the later 1990s, and between 8 and 9 percent from 2000 to 2002; since 2003 it has fluctuated between 9 and 11 percent. It seems likely that a new local market analysis would show more markets and more households that could be served without bringing the local lower-rent vacancy rate below 6 percent—and hence likely that the national housing goal could be met through tenant-based assistance, without building more subsidized housing for the poor.

Conclusion

The last five chapters have compared subsidized production programs and housing vouchers across a variety of dimensions, including their ability to serve households in need, their effect on neighborhoods, and their cost. This chapter sums up the findings and discusses their implications for future housing policy.

The Comparability of Housing Outcomes

The best evidence indicates that both production programs and vouchers do about equally well in enabling low-income families to live in decent housing. There are several reasons for this perhaps counterintuitive conclusion. Households must be willing to move to receive assistance in public housing or privately owned subsidized projects, so that those unwilling to move do not benefit from these programs; among households that are willing to move, about the same proportion move from physically inadequate to decent housing in each program. In addition, some subsidized projects do not meet the program quality standards. Subjective assessments of housing quality indicate that voucher recipients are marginally more satisfied with their home and their neighborhood than public housing residents or residents of privately owned subsidized projects. Finally, relatively few housing units, even among the least expensive segment of the housing stock, are in fact physically inadequate, so that most households that receive subsidies were living in decent housing to begin with.

At the same time, subsidized production programs generally build to a higher quality standard than is required to provide decent housing, or than is available on average in the existing privately owned inventory. In a sense, the choice between production and voucher programs is a choice between providing greater housing improvement for a smaller number of people, or more modest improvement for a larger number.

Advocates of subsidized production programs believe that these programs expand the supply of decent housing, while vouchers at best encourage owners to maintain the quality of existing housing. But the effective supply expansion depends on the extent to which new subsidized housing actually does represent net new housing, rather than simply substituting for private housing that would otherwise be built. The limited research on this question indicates that subsidized privately owned projects do not increase the supply of housing, but instead completely crowd out private unsubsidized housing construction. Public housing seems to represent an increase in the overall stock; but, again, public housing is generally the least satisfactory subsidy program.

The other important housing outcome is affordability, and here the difference between programs is clear. Vouchers bring down the cost of housing quite directly. With vouchers, lower-income households that have been spending most of their income to live in decent housing can reduce their rent burden to manageable proportions. They can also move to housing they consider more satisfactory. Subsidized projects, on the other hand, do not address the affordability problem, unless there is an additional subsidy to bring down the rent. The projects are expensive to build, even when the cost is subsidized (as for example with tax-exempt financing); they cost much more than lower-income households can afford. The high cost of housing production has been recognized for more than thirty years, during which all subsidized production programs have both conditioned the resident's rental payment on income and provided some sort of subsidy to operate the program in addition to subsidizing the construction cost in the first place.

The Lower Cost of Vouchers

Indeed, cost is the most striking difference between the programs. Vouchers are far less expensive than either of the large older subsidy programs, which is one important reason why neither of these subsidy programs is now a source of incremental assistance. If they were to be revived as major programs, public housing and privately owned projects each would cost between 50 to 100 percent more than vouchers on a per-unit basis. Cost differences of this order of magnitude were also the norm when all three types of programs were active. The GAO comparisons discussed in chapter 7 include only active programs, none of which attempts to serve the same market as the voucher; but they report similar differences between the voucher and the broadest currently active production programs, the LIHTC and HOPE VI.

The cost of building subsidized housing is so high that the Millennial Housing Commission, the most recent governmental commission concerned with housing, recognized in its 2002 report that the federal government could not be expected to pay for the full cost of providing new housing for poor families. The commission proposed a 100 percent capital subsidy on new units intended for extremely low-income households, within a mixed-income project in which only 20 percent of the units would be intended for these households; it then acknowledged that even these heavily subsidized units would not be affordable for extremely low-income households without a subsidy to cover part of the operating costs. The commission did not in fact advocate subsidizing operating costs, even though "the program would only serve ELI [extremely low-income] households willing and able to pay more than 30 percent of their incomes for rent."[1] This sounds much like the existing LIHTC, the more so in that the subsidy would be allocated by the same state agencies rather than awarded to specific projects by the federal government. No advocates of either actual or proposed new construction programs seriously expect the government to cover the full cost of subsidizing these projects for the poor.

The high cost of subsidized production has also led policymakers to look for ways to fund this production outside the federal budget process. This has been the great attraction of the Housing Trust Fund; the decade-long effort of its advocates to find an off-budget funding source was detailed in chapter 3. The LIHTC has the advantage of not appearing in the budget as an expenditure, although it is duly reported each year in the president's budget as a "tax expenditure," a reduction in tax revenue resulting from a special exclusion, exemption, or deduction from gross income, or, as in the case of the LIHTC a special credit.[2] Tax expenditures are less visible than appropriations and rarely require annual action by Congress.

Reviving the Rationales for Production Programs

Even though most policymakers and advocates recognize that the problem of substandard housing—the major rationale for subsidizing new projects—has largely been addressed, and also recognize that the cost of the projects is very high, nonetheless many advocates continue to call for building more subsidized projects.[3] They argue that building more projects would forestall rent increases resulting from vouchers; serve categories of households that are not effectively served by the private market or by vouchers; enable low-income households to live in better neighborhoods than they can using vouchers; and help to revitalize declining neighborhoods.[4]

But the evidence does not particularly suggest that subsidized production would achieve any of these objectives, or for that matter that vouchers really cause the problems they are said to cause. Most studies have shown little or no rent inflation resulting from vouchers. Large households are better served in the voucher program than in the production programs, partly because substantial fractions of the units in public housing and Section 8 New Construction are designed for and occupied by elderly couples and individuals; minority households are served about as well by vouchers as by public housing, and far better than by Section 8 New Construction, which started as mainly a program for white elderly households and which has continued to serve this group disproportionately. Voucher holders are not likely to live in high-income neighborhoods, but are widely scattered within metropolitan areas, and they have more opportunities to find better neighborhoods than do residents of public housing and other projects, who have to live where the projects are built. Efforts to locate projects in higher-income areas have not been very successful, and there is no reason to think they would be more successful in a new production program. Finally, while vouchers are not a particularly effective means of promoting community development, neither are production programs; the most recent systematic review of the evidence concludes, "The case for using production of subsidized rental housing as a revitalization tool remains weak."[5]

Emerging Trends in Housing Policy

Amid the day-to-day of program management and policy argument, two possibly significant trends can be observed. Housing assistance is gradually being shifted to serve somewhat higher-income households, and housing programs are being asked to serve other purposes besides housing. Each of these trends has important policy implications.

Housing the Nonpoor. Both HOPE VI and the LIHTC are expressly intended to serve moderate-income as well as low-income families and individuals, and while there is relatively little information about the incomes of residents in these programs, the more widely available data on rents indicate that these programs are much more likely than the older HUD-administered subsidy programs to serve households with a range of incomes. And although the current income limits for the LIHTC are already above those for vouchers and public housing, some advocates and developers are beginning to suggest that they should be increased. The recommendation of the Millennial Housing Commission moves in the same direction. So also did legislative proposals in the later years of the Bush administration to increase the number of households served by the Housing Choice Voucher, without much increasing the total amount appropriated.[6] This step invites public housing authorities to move farther up in the income distribution in offering vouchers, at once reducing the amount of assistance per household and simplifying their own administrative task, since higher-income households are easier to serve.

All these initiatives suggest that housing policy is moving back toward its original emphasis, serving households above the lowest income levels rather than solely the very poorest. For that matter, the subsidy mechanism for the LIHTC is essentially the original public housing subsidy mechanism, with the federal government paying the entire capital cost and the tenant paying the full operating costs. The sponsors of public housing in 1937 were well aware that it would not serve the lowest-income households.[7] Section 221(d)(3) (BMIR) in the 1960s similarly provided a mortgage write-down of construction costs, but no assistance toward covering the owner's remaining mortgage payment and operating costs; Section 236 as originally enacted varied the mortgage write-down by income but only to a point, which was not low enough to reach the low end of the income distribution. The emphasis on serving the poorest, and conditioning assistance on income, dates back only to the 1970s.

Nor would the Millennial Housing Commission's proposed program go as far in addressing the problem of affordability as the voucher, or, for that matter, as either public housing since the advent of operating subsidies more than thirty years ago, or Section 8 New Construction. In this respect, the Housing Trust Fund would do a better job of serving poor households.

A shift back toward the original target population would move housing assistance away from those who most need it. The most recent data show that renters with extremely low incomes (less than 30 percent of area median income, approximately the poverty line) constitute about three-quarters of all subsidized renters, and almost two-thirds of unassisted renters with severe problems. Renters with very low incomes (between 31 and 50 percent of area median income) constitute another 20 percent of assisted households, and also 20 percent of unassisted households with severe problems; renters with low incomes (between 51 and 80 percent of area median income) constitute only 5 percent of assisted households, and only 8 percent of households with severe problems. Looked at from a slightly different perspective, assistance would be shifted away from a population with a high incidence of severe problems (extremely low-income households, at 76 percent) toward populations with much lower incidences of severe problems (very low income at 33 percent, or low income at 7 percent). The people who need housing assistance the most are the poor. Targeting assistance toward households above the poverty line—households with fewer and less severe problems than the poor—is indefensible, however much this shift simplifies program management.

Housing as an Antipoverty Program. Over the last two decades there have been recurring efforts to make use of housing assistance to achieve broader social policy purposes. These efforts began in the mid-1980s with the Project Self-Sufficiency demonstration, intended to help low-income single parents become part of the labor force and work themselves off welfare, and its successors, the Operation Bootstrap demonstration for two-parent families and the full-scale Family Self-Sufficiency program, enacted in 1991 and still in operation. They have continued with the Moving to Opportunity demonstration in the 1990s, intended not only to help low-income parents join the labor force but also to improve the education and the social environment of their children; the Welfare to Work Voucher program, enacted in 2000, has essentially the same goals.

These demonstrations and programs have similar objectives to the original public housing program; they are attempting to fight poverty with housing assistance. But they include other forms of assistance besides housing, such as job training, child care, and transportation subsidies. In addition, they require participants to move into better neighborhoods. "A decent home" is not expected to be enough; "a suitable living environment" is also important, and perhaps substantially more important. The most extensive program evaluations have been the 1981 comparison of Section 8 projects to certificate holders, and the 2011 final report on the Moving to Opportunity demonstration. The former devotes over two-thirds of the text to housing conditions, and the rest to neighborhood demographics; the latter devotes less than 10 percent to housing conditions, not much more than that to neighborhood demographics, and about three-quarters to socioeconomic changes.[8] In general, evaluations have given very little attention to the changes in housing conditions, and much more to the changes in neighborhoods. They rarely attempt to relate changes in housing per se to changes in labor force participation, earnings, or school achievement. It is the improved neighborhoods that are implicitly understood to bring about the desired economic and social changes.

How Well Do the Different Housing Programs Fulfill These Broader Objectives? In 2003 the Brookings Institution Center on Urban and Metropolitan Policy published a guide on housing policy for state and local governments. The report included a matrix gauging the effectiveness of housing programs by policy goals, comparing vouchers and production programs with respect to five broader goals beyond decent and affordable housing. There was little difference between the programs, and little evidence that either vouchers or production was very effective in meeting these goals. No broad objective was met more often than "sometimes." Even that less than enthusiastic assessment was given only once, and only to production programs for special-needs populations that link support services to housing, specifically Section 202 for the frail elderly and Section 811 for the disabled.[9] Such small and highly specialized programs are hardly a relevant model for housing policy in general. And even for these special groups, the role of production programs is limited and to some extent controversial. Among housing advocates for the disabled, a significant minority strongly favors providing only "mainstream vouchers," treating the disabled like all other low-income households, rather than building housing specifically for them; and it has long been recognized that most of the elderly prefer to live in their own homes as long as possible. For other objectives—promoting racial and economic diversity, strengthening families, helping households build wealth, and promoting balanced metropolitan growth—the ratings were "possibly," "rarely," or "generally not."

The evidence since 2003 is at best only marginally more encouraging. The major evaluations of Moving to Opportunity and the Welfare to Work Voucher found little if any evidence of economic and educational improvements that might strengthen families, and some evidence that was negative. Both evaluations found significant but modest evidence of increased racial diversity.[10] (It should be noted, however, that the HUD study of voucher location patterns found voucher recipients spread out in over 80 percent of neighborhoods with affordable housing rather than concentrated in particular neighborhoods; few were living in neighborhoods with high poverty concentrations.[11]) The Family Self-Sufficiency evaluation was more positive but less rigorous, and the program tended to attract participants who were more motivated to succeed.[12] These are all analyses of vouchers in various circumstances, but the recent literature on production programs provides little reason to revise the conclusions for those programs, either.

Summing Up and Looking Ahead

The most important housing problem for the poor is affordability. The voucher addresses that problem directly and at lower cost than any other program. The historically important problem of housing quality is fading as quality improves; vouchers and production programs appear to be about equally effective in moving people from substandard to adequate housing. The voucher is simpler, easier to administer, and a more effective housing program; it achieves the long-standing public policy objectives of decent and affordable housing.

The case for production programs is now being made primarily in terms of their purported ability to serve broader purposes such as neighborhood revitalization. The literature on the subject is sketchy and inconclusive, but suggests that the impact on the neighborhood is if anything more likely to be negative than positive. Vouchers seem to allow recipients to live in better neighborhoods than production programs do; the gap in neighborhood quality between voucher recipients and public housing residents is particularly wide. Thus the repeated calls for new subsidized production programs seem to be the triumph of hope over experience.

Notes

Introduction

1. While at HUD in 1990, I presided over a meeting of representatives from federal agencies which sold houses to the public. There were seventeen agencies represented at the meeting.

Chapter 1: Housing Assistance and the Problems of Poverty

1. For a review of this literature, see Robert Moore Fisher, *Twenty Years of Public Housing* (New York: Harper, 1959), especially chap. 3.

2. S. 165 as reported, Calendar #960, 75th Congress, 1st session; quoted in Milton P. Semer et al., "A Review of Federal Subsidized Housing Programs," in National Housing Policy Review, *Housing in the Seventies: Working Papers* (Washington, DC: U.S. Department of Housing and Urban Development, 1976), 1:98. This paper provides a summary of federal legislation through 1972, with emphasis on the early history of public housing.

3. *U.S. Housing Act of 1949*, Public Law 81-171, sec. 2.

4. Addictive behavior may be an exception—for example, the individual who continues to smoke when the link between smoking and lung cancer is generally accepted by medical scientists. Even then the individual may be making a rational choice in his or her own terms, preferring the immediate pleasure of smoking to the risk of illness or death much later. Substandard housing certainly does not fall into this category; it has never been suggested that there is anything addictive about leaking roofs, cracks in walls, or defective plumbing.

5. Daniel Seligman, "The Enduring Slums," in *The Exploding Metropolis*, ed. *Fortune* editors (Garden City, NY: Doubleday, 1958), 92–114.

6. Jane Jacobs, *The Death and Life of Great American Cities* (New York: Macmillan, 1961).

7. To be precise, two programs of privately owned subsidized projects were created and terminated between 1961 and 1974; a third was enacted in 1974 at the same time as cash assistance, and terminated in 1983. Program chronology is discussed in detail in chapter 3.

8. Daniel M. Wilner et al., *The Housing Environment and Family Life* (Baltimore: Johns Hopkins University, 1962).

9. Stanislav V. Kasl, "Effects of Housing on Mental and Physical Health," in National Housing Policy Review, *Housing in the Seventies: Working Papers* (Washington, DC: U.S. Department of Housing and Urban Development, 1976), 1:296.

10. Richard F. Muth, "The Rationale for Government Intervention in Housing," in National Housing Policy Review, *Housing in the Seventies: Working Papers* (Washington, DC: U.S. Department of Housing and Urban Development, 1976), 1:194.

11. Edwin S. Mills, "Housing Policy as a Means to Achieve National Growth Policy," in National Housing Policy Review, *Housing in the Seventies: Working Papers* (Washington, DC: U.S. Department of Housing and Urban Development, 1976), 1: 209.

12. John C. Weicher, "The Rationales for Government Intervention in Housing: An Overview," in National Housing Policy Review, *Housing in the Seventies: Working Papers* (Washington, DC: U.S. Department of Housing and Urban Development, 1976), 1:181–92.

13. Hugh O. Nourse, "A Rationale for Government Intervention in Housing: The External Benefits of Good Housing, Particularly with Reference to Property Values," in National Housing Policy Review, *Housing in the Seventies: Working Papers* (Washington, DC: U.S. Department of Housing and Urban Development, 1976), 1:243–50.

14. D. J. Dedman et al., "Childhood Housing Conditions and Later Mortality in the Boyd Orr Cohort," *Journal of Epidemiology and Community Health* 55, no. 1 (2001): 10–15. The quotations are from p. 10 and p. 15, respectively. The two housing conditions with significant associations to mortality were "lack of private indoor tapped water supply" (which would classify a housing unit as "substandard" in the United States at that time) and "poor ventilation."

15. Thomas D. Matte and David E. Jacobs, "Housing and Health: Current Issues and Implications for Research and Progress," *Journal of Urban Health: Bulletin of the New York Academy of Medicine* 77, no. 1 (March 2000): 7–25.

16. The American Housing Survey for 2009 reports that less than 0.6 percent of occupied units had signs of rats in the last three months before the interview, and 0.9 percent of those occupied by the poor. Mice were ten times as common but less serious. See U.S. Department of Housing and Urban Development and U.S. Census Bureau, *American Housing Survey for the United States: 2009*, Current Housing Reports H150/09, Washington, DC, March 2011, table 2-7. All of the incidence figures are lower by one-third to one-half compared to 1997, the first year in which "signs of rats" and "signs of mice" were reported separately.

17. U.S. Department of Housing and Urban Development, Office of Policy Development and Research, *Comprehensive and Workable Plan for the Abatement of Lead-Based Paint in Privately Owned Housing: Report to Congress*, Washington, DC, 1990. The data on incidence appear in table 3-2.

18. U.S. Department of Housing and Urban Development and U.S. Census Bureau, *American Housing Survey for the United States: 2009*, Current Housing Reports H150/09, table 2-1.

19. Gary W. Evans and Elyse Kantrowitz, "Socioeconomic Status and Health: The Potential Role of Environmental Risk Exposure," *Annual Review of Public Health* 23 (2002): 321.

20. Ibid.

21. Gary W. Evans, "The Built Environment and Mental Health," *Journal of Urban Health: Bulletin of the New York Academy of Medicine* 80 (December 2003): 536–55.

22. Sandra J. Newman, "Does Housing Matter for Poor Families? A Critical Summary of Research and Issues Still to be Resolved," *Journal of Policy Analysis and Management*, Policy Retrospectives Section, 27 (Autumn 2008), 895–925. The quotations are on p. 918. Newman refers specifically to Evans, "The Built Environment," in support of this conclusion, although earlier in the paper she cites Evans and Kantrowitz, "Socioeconomic Status and Health," as saying the relationship is not consistent.

23. For a full discussion of Kemp's approach, see John C. Weicher, "A New War on Poverty: The Kemp Program to Empower the Poor," in *Reducing Poverty in America: Views and Approaches*, ed. Michael R. Darby (Thousand Oaks, CA: Sage Publications, 1995), 199–223.

24. Lisa Sanbonmatsu et al., *Moving to Opportunity for Fair Housing Demonstration Program: Final Impacts Evaluation* (Washington, DC: U.S. Department of Housing and Urban Development, Office of Policy Development and Research, 2011).

25. J. Anthony Lukas, *Common Ground: A Turbulent Decade in the Lives of Three American Families* (New York: Vintage Books, 1986), 185–94, 405–12; the quotation is from p. 429. Methunion Manor avoided foreclosure only through heavy political lobbying, according to Lukas. It is now a tenant-owned cooperative. Lukas states that seventy of the seventy-three projects located in Boston that were subsidized in this program—Section 221(d)(3)(BMIR)—went into foreclosure (407).

26. This statement is based on my experience as assistant secretary for housing and Federal Housing Administration commissioner at HUD during 2001–2005. The projects were privately owned Section 8 projects, which were being restructured financially as part of a program to preserve them as low-income subsidized housing.

27. George C. Galster, *A Review of Existing Research on the Effects of Federally Assisted Housing Programs on Neighboring Residential Property Values* (Washington, DC: National Association of Realtors, National Center for Real Estate Research, 2002), 25–26.

28. A study of Philadelphia found that subsidizing homeownership has no effect on nearby property values, while a study of New York City found positive impacts, which dissipated over time. Jean L. Cummings, Denise DiPasquale, and Matthew E. Kahn, "Measuring the Consequences of Promoting Inner-City Homeownership," *Journal of Housing Economics* 11, no. 4 (2002): 330–59; Ingrid Gould Ellen et al., "Building Homes, Reviving Neighborhoods: Spillovers from Subsidized Construction of Owner-Occupied Housing in New York City," *Journal of Housing Research* 12, no. 2 (2001): 185–216.

29. Data on the number of mixed-income projects are taken from Jill Khadduri and Marge Martin, "Mixed-Income Housing in the HUD Multifamily Stock," *Cityscape* 3, no. 2 (1997): 33–69.

30. Alex Schwartz and Kian Tajbakhsh, "Mixed-Income Housing: Unanswered Questions," *Cityscape* 3, no. 2 (1997): 71–92; Alastair Smith, *Mixed-Income Housing Developments: Promise and Reality* (Cambridge, MA, and Washington, DC: Joint Center for Housing Studies of Harvard University and Neighborhood Reinvestment Corporation, 2002).

31. Jean L. Cummings and Denise DiPasquale, "The Low-Income Housing Tax Credit: An Analysis of the First Ten Years," *Housing Policy Debate* 10, no. 2 (1999): 251–307; see especially 278–82.

32. Susan J. Popkin et al., *A Decade of HOPE VI: Research Findings and Policy Challenges* (Washington, DC: Urban Institute, 2004), 42–45.

33. Jill Khadduri, "Should the Housing Voucher Program Become a State-Administered Block Grant?" *Housing Policy Debate* 14, no. 3 (2003): 257.

34. Anthony Downs, "Comment," in *Urban Problems and Community Development*, ed. Ronald F. Ferguson and William T. Dickens (Washington, DC: Brookings Institution Press, 1999), 466–67.

35. This occurred in 1935, in a federal government program to build low-income housing directly, under the Public Works Administration. The program itself was terminated later that year, following a court decision ruling that the blanket condemnation proceedings through which the federal government was attempting to acquire land were unconstitutional. For the early history of federal housing programs, see Gilbert A. Cam, "United States Government Activity in Low-Cost Housing, 1932–1938," *Journal of Political Economy* 47 (June 1939): 357–78.

36. See, for example, National Commission on Urban Problems, *Building the American City* (New York: Praeger, 1969). The commission was chaired by former senator Paul Douglas (D–IL) and is often referred to as the "Douglas Commission."

37. The legislation included a total of $13.6 billion for various lower-income housing programs (Public Law 111-5, Title 12), but did not provide money for the Housing Trust Fund, created by statute in July 2008.

38. Stephen Malpezzi and Kerry Vandell, "Does the Low-Income Housing Tax Credit Increase the Supply of Housing?" *Journal of Housing Economics* 11, no. 4 (December 2002): 360–80.

39. Todd M. Sinai and Joel Waldfogel, "Do Low-Income Housing Subsidies Increase Housing Consumption?" *Journal of Public Economics* 89 (December 2005): 2137–2164.

40. For example, New York, Philadelphia, and Washington in the Northeast; Chicago, Cincinnati, St. Louis, and Kansas City in the Midwest. Other such areas include Charlotte, Louisville, and Portland, Oregon.

41. Michael P. Murray, "Subsidized and Unsubsidized Housing Stocks 1935 to 1987: Crowding Out and Cointegration," *Journal of Real Estate Finance and Economics* 18, no. 1 (January 1999): 107–24.

42. Michael P. Murray, "Subsidized and Unsubsidized Housing Starts, 1961–1977," *Review of Economics and Statistics* 65, no. 4 (November 1983): 590–97; Craig Swan, "Subsidized and Unsubsidized Housing Starts," *American Real Estate and Urban Economics Association Journal* 1, no. 2 (Fall 1973): 119–40. Swan's analysis covers the years 1960–1972 and includes public housing as well as privately owned projects, but the large numbers of Section 236 projects dominate the data after 1968.

43. John C. Weicher and Thomas G. Thibodeau, "Filtering and Housing Markets: An Empirical Analysis," *Journal of Urban Economics* 23, no. 1 (January 1988): 21–40.

Chapter 2: Housing Conditions and Problems

1. The two most important assistance programs for owners are the Section 235 program and the Experimental Housing Allowance program, both now defunct.

2. *Cranston-Gonzalez National Affordable Housing Act*, Public Law 101-625, 42 USC 12701, sec. 101.

3. *Housing Act of 1949*, Public Law 171, 81st Congress, 42 USC 14441, sec. 2.

4. *U.S. Housing Act of 1937* as amended, sec. 8(d)(1)(A). This statutory provision was suspended in 1996 for one year and again in 1997 for a second year; it was permanently repealed in 1998 in the *Quality Housing and Work Responsibility Act of 1998*, Public Law 105-276, 42 USC 1437, sec. 514(a). For a brief history of federal preferences, see U.S. Department of Housing and Urban Development, Office of Policy Development and Research, *Rental Housing Assistance—The Crisis Continues: The 1997 Report to Congress on Worst Case Housing Needs*, Washington, DC, April 1998, 25.

5. U.S. Senate, *Departments of Veterans Affairs and Housing and Urban Development, and Independent Agencies Appropriations Act of 1991: Report (to Accompany H.R. 5158)*, Report 101-474, 37.

6. The development of the process of reporting worst-case needs to Congress is summarized in the first such report: U.S. Department of Housing and Urban Development, Office of Policy Development and Research, *Priority Housing Problems and "Worst Case Needs" in 1989: A Report to Congress*, Washington, DC, June 1991, 1.

7. U.S. Department of Housing and Urban Development, Office of Policy Development and Research, *Worst Case Housing Needs 2009: A Report to Congress*, Washington, DC, February 2011.

8. Calculated from U.S. Department of Housing and Urban Development, Office of Policy Development and Research, "1999 & Estimated 2009 Decile Distributions of Family Income by Metropolitan Statistical Areas and Non Metropolitan Counties," http://www.huduser.org/portal/datasets/il/il09/msacounty_medians.pdf. HUD estimates the incomes for any given year for program purposes, in advance; they are not the official income data as reported by the Census Bureau after the end of the year. The HUD projection has been below the official census figure every year from 1997 to 2009 (the latest available census data). Buffalo County, South Dakota, had

a population of about 2,000 in the year 2000, of whom over 80 percent were Native American; the Crow Creek Indian Reservation makes up most of the county.

9. HUD incomes and income limits are calculated for families, rather than for all households, in accord with statutory requirements. The difference between four-person households and four-person families, however, is quite small, about $1,500 in 2009, because nearly all such households are in fact families. The median income is much higher for all families than for all households—$60,088 vs. $49,777 (more than a 20 percent difference) in 2009. This is because a family by definition has at least two persons, and one-person households generally have lower incomes rather than larger ones. The median family size in 2005 was 2.72 persons, and the median household size was 2.19. U.S. Bureau of the Census, *Income, Poverty, and Health Insurance Coverage in the United States: 2009*, P60-238 (Washington, DC: Government Printing Office, 2010).

10. Milton P. Semer et al., "A Review of Federal Housing Subsidy Programs," in U.S. Department of Housing and Urban Development, *National Housing Policy Review, Housing in the Seventies: Working Papers* (Washington, DC: U.S. Department of Housing and Urban Development, 1976), 1:139. This study traces the use of the term in legislation to 1961, but summarizes earlier discussions back to the 1930s.

11. This calculation is based on the number of poor renter households as reported in the American Housing Survey for 2009, taking the median household income from table 2-12 and the data for renters from table 4-12. U.S. Department of Housing and Urban Development and U.S. Census Bureau, *American Housing Survey for the United States: 2009*, Current Housing Reports H150/09, Washington, DC, `March 2011. "Median income" is calculated nationally rather than for individual metropolitan areas and counties. Among extremely low-income households with worst-case needs, about 85 percent are poor, as reported in U.S. Department of Housing and Urban Development, Office of Policy Development and Research, *Worst Case Housing Needs 2009: A Report to Congress*, Washington, DC, February 2011, table A-8; extremely low income in this report is calculated by local market rather than nationally.

12. The most recent changes in the questionnaire were made in 1997 in an effort to obtain more precise information on whether the household received housing assistance. More detailed questions about income were asked, and the wording of questions involving problems with systems were changed to determine whether the problem occurred in the respondent's house, met the more precise definition of the problem, and occurred within the specified time period (e.g., the previous three months). The latter change probably contributed to a reduction in the number of units with severe physical problems from 2.0 to 1.8 million between 1995 and 1997. U.S. Department of Housing and Urban Development, Office of Policy Development and Research, *Rental Housing Assistance—The Worsening Crisis: A Report to Congress on Worst Case Housing Needs*, Washington, DC, March 2000, appendix C, A-23–A-24.

13. This conclusion cannot be directly derived from table 2-2, but if no household suffered both moderate physical problems and crowding, then about 2.9 million of the 3.8 million with less serious problems (73 percent) would have only a rent burden.

For 1999, the most recent year with "rent burden only" reported for households with less serious problems, 2.7 million of 3.9 million (69 percent) had only a rent burden. U.S. Department of Housing and Urban Development, Office of Policy Development and Research, *Trends in Worst Case Needs for Housing, 1978–1999: A Report to Congress on Worst Case Housing Needs*, Washington, DC, December 2003, table A-4.

14. The AHS asks specifically whether a unit is "owned by a public housing authority" or receiving "government subsidy," and whether the household must report its income when its lease is up for renewal. These three categories come close to representing conceptually the categories of HUD-assisted housing. Unfortunately, they are a substantial overcount, compared to HUD administrative program data. The total number of these units in the AHS for 2003 is 6.185 million, compared to 4.279 million in HUD administrative records. Units subsidized through the Rural Housing Service Section 515 program should also fall into the second category, making the total number of units 4.743 million, according to the administrative records of the two agencies. In addition, the AHS reports substantially more public housing units than do HUD records: 1.793 million compared to 1.094 million. The AHS number should match the HUD administrative number. Public housing is the oldest assisted housing program, and the term is sometimes used generically for assisted housing; but the difference seems too large to be explained in this way, and implies a very large discrepancy for units receiving federal subsidy in other programs. HUD has long been concerned about response errors and has revised the questions on housing assistance more than once, most recently in 1997. These serious and well-designed efforts have not yet resolved the discrepancies. For a discussion of the current survey procedure and a description of the changes, see U.S. Department of Housing and Urban Development, *Trends in Worst Case Needs for Housing, 1978–1999*, A-44 to A-45.

15. U.S. Department of Housing and Urban Development, Office of Policy Development and Research, *Characteristics of HUD-Assisted Renters and Their Units in 2003*, Washington, DC, May 2008, 44–48.

16. For more detailed discussion of this problem and suggested solutions, see Committee to Evaluate the Research Plan of the Department of Housing and Urban Development, *Rebuilding the Research Capacity at HUD* (Washington, DC: National Academies Press, 2008), 117–24.

17. U.S. Department of Housing and Urban Development, Office of Policy Development and Research, *Characteristics of HUD-Assisted Renters and Their Units in 2003*, 32, table 2.

18. For discussions of the problem and efforts to resolve it, see ibid., 16–18, and U.S. Department of Housing and Urban Development, Office of Policy Development and Research, *Characteristics of HUD-Assisted Renters and Their Units in 1989*, Washington DC, March 1992, 33–34, appendix 2.

19. E.g., U.S. Department of Housing and Urban Development and U.S. Census Bureau, *American Housing Survey for the United States: 2007*, table 4-19; similar notations appear in earlier AHS reports.

20. U.S. Department of Housing and Urban Development, *Worst Case Housing Needs 2009*, table A-7, reports 1.9 million female-headed families with children having worst-case needs, out of a total of 2.7 million such families with children. There were 9.8 million female-headed families with children. See U.S. Census Bureau, *America's Families and Living Arrangements: 2009*, Washington, DC, January 2010, table 1, http://www.census.gov/population/www/socdemo/hh-fam/cps2009.html.

21. U.S. Department of Housing and Urban Development, *Worst Case Housing Needs 2009,* table A-7. Data for unassisted households by racial and ethnic group, and by location, are not published, but published data for these groups including assisted households with severe housing problems also indicate that units with severe physical problems are similarly infrequent in each group.

22. The numbers in table 2-7 are rounded to the nearest percentage point. Carried to an additional digit, there was a slight increase from 3.1 percent in 1999 to 3.3 percent in 2001, and then a decline to 2.6 percent in 2003. It is also 2.6 percent in 2009.

23. Data for 1974, for families and elderly households only, are consistent with these trends. The share of very low-income renters with worst-case needs rose slightly from 1974 to 1978, but the share with severe physical problems declined. Rent burden has been a growing problem for some twenty years, and physical condition a declining one. U.S. Department of Housing and Urban Development, *Priority Housing Problems and "Worst Case Needs" in 1989*, table 6.

24. The first extensive discussion of affordability in a housing policy context appears in President's Commission on Housing, *The Report of the President's Commission on Housing*, Washington, DC, April 1982, 9–12.

25. U.S. Congress, Joint Committee on Housing, *Housing Study and Investigation: Final Majority Report*, 80th Congress, 2nd session, House Report no. 1564, March 15, 1948, 9.

26. The Joint Committee on Housing was mainly, though not exclusively, concerned with urban housing. The urban-rural distinctions drawn by the committee had no impact on the 1949 goal or later analyses, as the declining importance of farming and the rapid improvement in the quality of farm housing reduced their importance.

27. For a fuller discussion of the change in coverage, see John C. Weicher, *Housing: Federal Policies and Programs* (Washington, DC: American Enterprise Institute for Public Policy Research, 1980), 15–16.

28. For a detailed description and comparison of these measures, see Richard B. Clemmer and John Simonson, "Trends in Substandard American Housing, 1940–1980," *AREUEA Journal* 10 (Winter 1983): 442–64. Clemmer and Simonson concluded that newer definitions set a higher standard for adequate housing; they suggested that the number of inadequate rental units according to the HUD definition should be multiplied by 0.6, and the number of inadequate owner-occupied units should be multiplied by 0.7, for comparability with the usual census definition. Stated alternatively, the HUD measure counted as inadequate 67 percent more rental units, and 43 percent more owner-occupied units, than the usual census definition.

Overall, the HUD measure counted about 57 percent more occupied units as inadequate. Clemmer and Simonson stressed that any adjustment to achieve consistency between the 1970 Census criterion and the post-1973 AHS-based definitions was arbitrary, but they also argued that some adjustment was necessary for consistency. (The current HUD measure used in this book differs in some details from the measure Clemmer and Simonson described and analyzed.)

29. The limited data that carry over from the decennial census to the AHS support the view of continued improvement between 1970 and the mid-1970s, and reinforce the inference that the AHS-based concept of "severely inadequate" sets a higher threshold for "decent housing" than the older decennial census concept of "substandard." The incidence of occupied units without complete plumbing—explicitly part of both criteria—declined from 5.5 percent in 1970 to 2.9 percent in 1975. Similar declines occur for units without complete kitchen facilities for exclusive use (3.1 percent to 2.0 percent), which is part of the "moderately inadequate" AHS criterion, and for units without a telephone (12.7 percent to 10.0 percent).

30. The AHS separately identifies only African American and Hispanic households. Asian American and American Indian households are included in the total but are not enumerated separately. If African Americans and Hispanics are subtracted from the total population of the United States, non-Hispanic whites constitute about 92 percent of the remainder; Asian Americans about 5 percent; American Indians, Alaska natives, and native Hawaiian and Pacific Islanders about 1 percent; "some other race" about 0.2 percent; and persons reporting two or more races about 2 percent. U.S. Bureau of the Census, "Overview of Race and Hispanic Origin 2000," Census 2000 Brief C2KBR/01-1, March 2001, table 10. American Indians in particular probably have a high incidence of housing deficiencies, based on their incomes and the limited information on housing conditions available in the decennial census and occasional special studies.

31. The sources of the data supporting this summary appear in chapter 4.

32. For a review of this literature through 1980, see Weicher, *Housing*, 24–27.

33. For example, Davis, Eastman, and Hua analyzed the change in housing units without complete plumbing between 1960 and 1970 for the central cities of the fifty largest metropolitan areas, but could not study changes in substandard housing; the limited information on dilapidated units that was collected at the end of the 1970 census was not published until their study was completed. Otto A. Davis, Charles M. Eastman, and Chan-I Hua, "The Shrinkage in the Stock of Low-Quality Housing in the Central City: An Empirical Study of the U.S. Experience over the Last Ten Years," *Urban Studies* 11, no. 1 (February 1974): 13–26.

34. See John C. Weicher, Lorene Yap, and Mary S. Jones, *National Housing Needs and Quality Changes During the 1980s* (Washington, DC: Urban Institute, 1980), chap. 9, which analyzes the level of inadequate housing across the sixty large metropolitan areas separately surveyed as part of the AHS in the mid-1970s, as well as changes in substandard housing across the fifty largest metropolitan areas during the 1960s.

35. James L. Sweeney, "A Commodity Hierarchy Model of the Rental Housing Market," *Journal of Urban Economics* 1, no. 3 (June 1974): 288–323; Lawrence Schall, "Commodity Hierarchy Chain Systems and the Housing Market," *Journal of Urban Economics* 10, no. 2 (April 1981): 141–63; James Ohls, "Public Policy Toward Low Income Housing and Filtering in Housing Markets," *Journal of Urban Economics* 2, no. 2 (April 1975): 144–71.

36. See in particular Ralph Braid, "The Effects of Government Housing Policies in a Vintage Housing Model," *Journal of Urban Economics* 16, no. 3 (November 1984): 272–96.

37. Sweeney, "A Commodity Hierarchy Model of the Rental Housing Market." See also James L. Sweeney, "Quality, Commodity Hierarchies, and Housing Markets," *Econometrica* 42, no. 1 (May 1974): 147–67.

38. Alex Anas and Richard J. Arnott, "Dynamic Housing Market Equilibrium with Taste Heterogeneity, Idiosyncratic Perfect Foresight, and Stock Conversions," *Journal of Housing Economics* 1 (March 1991): 2–32. The exception they cite—when the new high-priced housing is built on sites formerly occupied by low-quality housing—is minor, since most new private housing is built on former farmland on the outskirts of metropolitan areas. The exception is relevant for some federal programs, perhaps most notably urban renewal, in which low-quality housing is razed and replaced by high- quality housing in an effort to revive decaying urban neighborhoods. The model provides a theoretical basis for the frequently expressed concern among economists that urban renewal adversely affects the housing conditions of the poor.

39. Weicher and Thibodeau, "Filtering and Housing Markets: An Empirical Analysis."

40. See for example Werner Hirsch and C. K. Law, "Habitability Laws and the Shrinkage of Substandard Rental Housing Stock," *Urban Studies* 16 (February 1979): 19–28; and Donald Vitaliano, "Public Housing and Slums: Cure or Cause?" *Urban Studies* 20 (May 1983): 173–83.

41. Analytically, these patterns need not occur, however. What happens depends on the responsiveness of households to changes in income or changes in prices. If income rises, households may choose to spend a larger share of it on housing, and the rent-income ratio could be higher for higher-income households; conversely, if income falls, households may cut back on their housing more than on other goods and services, and the rent-income ratio could be lower. In economists' terms, the income elasticity of demand may be greater or less than unity. There has been extensive research on the income elasticity of demand for housing, with the general consensus being that it is less than unity; i.e., rent-income ratios fall as income rises. See Edgar O. Olsen, "The Demand and Supply of Housing Services: A Critical Survey of the Empirical Literature," in *Handbook of Urban Economics*, ed. Edwin S. Mills (New York: Elsevier, 1987), 989–1022. Similarly, if the price of housing rises, households may choose to cut back on their housing—move to a smaller unit or one with fewer amenities—and the reduction in quality may more than offset the increase in price, so that the rent-income ratio may be lower when prices rise. This is less likely for housing

than for narrowly defined goods with good substitutes. The price elasticity of demand may be greater or less than unity; if it is less, rent-income ratios will be higher where housing prices are high.

42. The share of renter households consisting of single individuals rose modestly from 35.6 percent in 1978 to 37.7 percent in 2009. This is not large, but by itself would tend to raise rent-income ratios for renters as a whole. The median rent-income ratio for elderly renters was 40 percent in 2009, compared to 29 percent for non-elderly renters. U.S. Department of Housing and Urban Development and U.S. Census Bureau, *American Housing Survey for the United States: 2009*, Current Housing Reports H150/09, Washington, DC, March 2011, table 4-13.

43. Milton Friedman, *A Theory of the Consumption Function* (Princeton, NJ: Princeton University Press, 1957).

44. Median household income is conceptually preferable to median family income, but the household data go back only to 1967. From 1970 on, the changes over the intervals in table 2-10 are quite close to the changes in median family income.

45. Median household income grew at almost the same rate as median family income over each period in the table.

46. The statistical procedure is "hedonic estimation," a form of multiple regression analysis, in which the rents for a large number of housing units are related to the attributes of the housing (number of rooms, number of bathrooms, etc.), in order to estimate the market value of the individual attributes. The value of a unit of a given size and quality can then be computed by adding the estimated values of the individual attributes.

47. Anthony M. J. Yezer, *The Physical Adequacy and Affordability of Housing in America: Measurements Using the Annual Housing Survey for 1975 and 1977*, U.S. Department of Housing and Urban Development, Annual Housing Survey Studies, no. 7, June 1981.

48. For a similar conclusion (but with different policy recommendations), see William G. Grigsby and Steven C. Bourassa, "Section 8: The Time for Fundamental Program Change?" *Housing Policy Debate* 15, no. 4 (2004): 805–34: "Since . . . 1974, the quality of the nation's housing stock has continued to improve, to the point that only a very small percentage of it is severely inadequate" (805). The article notes that quality has improved to the point that the Millennium Housing Commission's report largely ignores it as an issue.

Chapter 3: Housing Assistance Programs: Taxonomy and History

1. U.S. Department of Housing and Urban Development, Chief Financial Officer, "Housing: Housing Payments: Summary of Assisted Units and Outlays," Congressional Justifications for 2011 Estimates, K1–K4, http://hud.gov/offices/cfo/reports/2011/cjs/Housing_Payments_2011.pdf.

2. U.S. Department of Housing and Urban Development, Office of Policy Development and Research, "A Picture of Subsidized Households," United States Summary, http://www.huduser.org/datasets/assthsg/statedata96/hud2us3.txt. This is a database for subsidy programs and is available for 1993, 1996, 1997, 1998, 2000, and 2004–2008 on the HUD USER Web site; see http://www.huduser.org/datasets/ assthsg.html. The figure in the text for privately owned projects includes 0.3 million identified as "other subsidy."

3. Calculations by author from U.S. Department of Housing and Urban Development, Office of Policy Development and Research, "LIHTC Database," available at http://www.huduser.org/portal/datasets/lihtc.html. See also Clarissa Climaco et al., *Updating the Low-Income Housing Tax Credit (LIHTC) Database: Projects Placed in Service Through 2006* (Washington, DC: U.S. Department of Housing and Urban Development), 2009), exhibit C-1; Abt Associates, Inc., "Updating the Low-Income Housing Tax Credit (LIHTC) Database: Projects Placed in Service Through 2007," at http:// www.huduser.org/Datasets/lihtc/tables9507.pdf.

4. U.S. Department of Housing and Urban Development, Office of Community Planning and Development, "HOME Program National Production Report (As Of 6/30/09)," http://www.hud.gov/offices/cpd/affordablehousing/reports/production/ 063009.pdf. HOME has also provided funds for about 375,000 homebuyers and 185,000 homeowners to rehabilitate their homes; these activities are outside the scope of this book. For a discussion of the first ten years of HOME, with emphasis on activities to promote homeownership, see Jennifer Turnham et al., *Study of Homebuyer Activity through the HOME Investment Program* (Cambridge, MA: Abt Associates, Inc., 2004), 3–8.

5. See for example John J. Fialka, "A Tale of Contrasts: Two Buildings Show How Public Housing Slid into Such a Mess," *Wall Street Journal*, February 28, 1995, A1. Despite its title, the story actually refers to two privately owned projects.

6. U.S. Department of Housing and Urban Development, Office of Policy Development and Research, *Characteristics of HUD-Assisted Households and Their Units in 2003*, Washington, DC, May 2008, 34, Table 3. As of 2003, fewer than 4 percent of public housing units had been built after 1985. There has been little construction since 2003.

7. See for example John C. Weicher, *Housing: Federal Policies and Programs* (Washington, DC: American Enterprise Institute for Public Policy Research, 1980), 58–60.

8. Quoted in Milton P. Semer et al., "A Review of Federal Subsidized Housing Programs," in National Housing Policy Review, *Housing in the Seventies: Working Papers* (Washington, DC: U.S. Department of Housing and Urban Development, 1976), 1:102.

9. U.S. Department of Housing and Urban Development, *1967 HUD Statistical Yearbook*, Washington, DC, 264, HAA table 28; *1979 HUD Statistical Yearbook*, Washington, DC, 208, table 66; 210, table 68.

10. U.S. Department of Housing and Urban Development, Office of Policy Development and Research, *Characteristics of HUD-Assisted Renters and Their Units in 1989*, Washington, DC, March 1992, 68, table 2-12.

11. U.S. Department of Housing and Urban Development, Office of Policy Development and Research, *Characteristics of HUD-Assisted Renters and Their Units in 2003*, 94, table 3-12.

12. National Commission on Severely Distressed Public Housing, *Final Report to Congress and the Secretary of Housing and Urban Development* (Washington, DC: U.S. Department of Housing and Urban Development, 1992).

13. Calculated from project data in Henry G. Cisneros and Lora Engdahl, eds., *From Despair to Hope: HOPE VI and the New Promise of Public Housing in America's Cities* (Washington DC: Brookings Institution Press, 2009), appendix B.

14. Susan J. Popkin et al., *A Decade of HOPE VI: Research Findings and Policy Challenges* (Washington, DC: Urban Institute, 2004), 21. There is clearly some imprecision about the numbers. A contemporaneous report by the General Accounting Office (now the Government Accountability Office) stated that 77,000 units had been demolished or were scheduled for demolition as of June 30, 2003, and that 45,000 replacement units were to be built or rehabilitated. U.S. General Accounting Office, *Public Housing: HOPE VI Resident Issues and Changes in Neighborhoods Surrounding Grant Sites*, GAO-04-109, November 2003, 11–12. The HUD budget for FY2010 states that 92,000 units had been demolished as of December 31, 2008.

15. U.S. Department of Housing and Urban Development, "FY 2010 Budget: Road Map for Transformation," 20–21, www.hud.gov/budgetsummary2010.

16. FHA multifamily mortgage insurance began in the 1930s, but the programs were very small until the postwar period. U.S. Department of Housing and Urban Development, *1979 HUD Statistical Yearbook*, 74.

17. Data on Section 221(d)(3)(BMIR) and Section 236 are taken from Congressional Budget Office, "The Potential Loss of Assisted Housing Units as Certain Mortgage-Interest Subsidy Programs Mature," Staff Working Paper, March 1987, table 1, http://www.cbo.gov/doc.cfm?index=6245&type=0; data on Section 8 are taken from Urban Systems Research & Engineering, Inc, *The Costs of HUD Multifamily Housing Programs* (Washington, DC: U.S. Department of Housing and Urban Development, Office of Policy Development and Research, 1982), vol. 1, table 2-2; and Richard Hilton et al., *Evaluation of the Mark-to-Market Program* (Washington, DC: U.S. Department of Housing and Urban Development, 2004), xii.

18. The numbers in this example are not atypical, although the per-unit mortgage was more often in the range of $120,000 to $150,000. The interest rate at which the government borrowed was 3 percent from 1965 on, and the reduction in the mortgage payment was about 40 percent; before that the subsidized rate was tied to the federal borrowing rate, and was about two percentage points below the private market rate, which reduced the mortgage payment by about 25 percent. For simplicity, the numbers in the example exclude the FHA mortgage insurance premium and also escrowed property taxes and insurance.

19. National Commission on Urban Problems, *Building the American City* (New York: Praeger, 1970), 146.

20. U.S. Department of Housing and Urban Development, *1973 HUD Statistical Yearbook*, Washington, DC, 145.

21. Under this program, 5 percent of the funds could be used in BMIR projects rather than unsubsidized projects.

22. See Semer et al., "A Review of Federal Subsidized Housing Programs," 1:121–22; and National Commission on Urban Problems, *Building the American City*, 149–51.

23. Edgar O. Olsen, "Housing Programs for Low-Income Households," in *Means-Tested Transfer Programs in the United States*, ed. Robert Moffitt (Chicago: University of Chicago Press, 2003), 365–441, table 5.

24. The monthly payment on a forty-year $100,000 mortgage amortized at 5 percent (approximately the market rate early in the program) is about $482; amortized at 1 percent, it is about $253.

25. U.S. Department of Housing and Urban Development, *1979 HUD Statistical Yearbook*, 74–79, section IV, table 6.

26. U.S. Department of Housing and Urban Development, Chief Financial Officer, "Housing: Housing Payments," Congressional Justifications for 2011 Estimates, K1–K4.

27. The U.S. Housing Act of 1937 created the public housing program, and Section 8 New Construction was technically a public housing program. The National Housing Act created federal mortgage insurance programs in Title II, and sections 221 and 236 were additions to that act.

28. U.S. Department of Housing and Urban Development, *1979 Statistical Yearbook*, 213 (through FY 1979); unpublished table prepared by the HUD Budget Office and provided by Robert Gray (after FY 1979).

29. U.S. Department of Housing and Urban Development, Chief Financial Officer, "Housing: Housing Payments," Congressional Justifications for 2010 Estimates, M1–M3.

30. Unpublished HUD tabulation. Hilton et al., *Evaluation of the Mark-to-Market Program*, table A.3.1, reports about 800,000 units in or eligible for Mark-to-Market as of late 2003; the Mark-to-Market program was limited to FHA-insured projects.

31. For a comparison of costs as of 1979, see Urban Systems Research and Engineering, Inc., *The Costs of HUD Multifamily Housing Programs*, vol. 1, Summary.

32. Some of these represented conversions from the Rent Supplement program. Conversion to Section 8 was authorized in 1979, and required in 1980; about 70,000 units were converted by 1982. John C. Weicher, "Halfway to a Housing Allowance?" in John C. Weicher, ed., *Maintaining the Safety Net: Income Redistribution Programs in the Reagan Administration* (Washington, DC: American Enterprise Institute for Public Policy Research, 1984), 97–98. Nearly all other units in the Rent Supplement program were converted to Section 8 in the next few years. As of 2009, about 14,000 units remained in the program. U.S. Department of Housing and Urban Development, Chief Financial Officer, "Housing: Rent Supplement Program," Congressional Justifications for 2011 Estimates, L1–L8, http://www.hud.gov/offices/cfo/reports/2011/cjs/Rent_Supplement_Program_2011.pdf.

33. For example, if a project cost $1 million and had a $900,000 mortgage, an investor putting up $10,000, or 10 percent of the equity in the project, could deduct from his or her income the amount of depreciation attributable to $100,000, or 10 percent of the value of the project. In the early years of a project, with accelerated depreciation schedules, the amount of depreciation could be larger than the investment.

34. U.S. Department of Housing and Urban Development, *Housing in the Seventies: A Report of the National Housing Policy Review* (Washington, DC: U.S. Government Printing Office, 1974), 112.

35. Ibid., 119.

36. U.S. Department of Housing and Urban Development, *1967 Statistical Yearbook*, FHA table 21; U.S. Department of Housing and Urban Development, *1979 Statistical Yearbook*, housing table 18.

37. Between 1978 and 1994, HUD had to address a further statutory complication. In selling a defaulted subsidized project, HUD was required to provide subsidies for all units that were previously being subsidized, and to ensure that any unsubsidized units in the project were available and affordable to lower-income households. The subsidy level was based on Section 8, which is more generous with subsidies than Section 236 or other programs, so the sale of the project imposed additional costs on HUD. These requirements were partially relaxed in the Multifamily Property Disposition Reform Act of 1994, but they were an additional important reason for FHA's desire to avoid taking title to a defaulted project. Current law continues to require tenant protection, but with more flexibility.

38. The original program also had a property disposition component. This was used as a way of promoting sales of FHA-owned projects by guaranteeing that project buyers would have a rental income on some of the apartments in the project, with the amount of the subsidy again based on the income of the resident. The programs were sometimes referred to jointly by the acronym LMPD.

39. For a discussion of these programs, see Laurent V. Hodes, *Capital Needs Assessment: Multifamily Rental Housing with HUD-Insured (or Held) Mortgages* (Washington, DC: U.S. Department of Housing and Urban Development, Office of Policy Development and Research, 1992), chap. 4. The data are reported in James E. Wallace et al., *Assessment of the HUD-Insured Multifamily Housing Stock: Final Report, vol. 1, Current Status of HUD-Insured (or Held) Multifamily Rental Housing* (Washington, DC: U.S. Department of Housing and Urban Development, Office of Policy Development and Research, 1993), 2-44–2-45.

40. Hodes, *Capital Needs Assessment*, chap. 4. To my knowledge, there has been no more recent analysis. A later assessment of HUD's multifamily portfolio did not separately report the status of these projects; see Meryl Finkel et al., *Status of HUD-Insured (or Held) Multifamily Rental Housing in 1995: Final Report* (Washington, DC: U.S. Department of Housing and Urban Development, Office of Policy Development and Research, 1999). With the termination of new commitments under Flexible Subsidy in 1996, there has been no interest in further study of the programs.

41. Hodes, *Capital Needs Assessment*, chap. 4.

42. Finkel et al., *Status of HUD-Insured Multifamily Rental Housing in 1995*, chap. 4.

43. Hilton et al., *Evaluation of the Mark-to-Market Program*, table 3.2, reports about 9,000 eligible projects; U.S. Department of Housing and Urban Development, Office of Housing, "M2M Pipeline Summary Report," http://portal.hud.gov/hudportal/documents/huddoc?id=m2mstats.pdf, reports that about 3,400 projects have completed the process as of November 2011.

44. U.S. Department of Housing and Urban Development, *Annual Performance Plan: Fiscal Year 2009*, Washington, DC, 2008, 57.

45. National Low Income Housing Preservation Commission, *Preventing the Disappearance of Low-Income Housing* (Washington, DC: National Corporation for Housing Partnerships, 1988), exhibit 2-5. The commission is also known as the Hills-Reuss Commission, after the cochairs, former HUD secretary Carla A. Hills and former congressman Henry S. Reuss (D–WI).

46. Congressional Budget Office, "Potential Loss of Assisted Housing Units," table 1.

47. Public Law 100-242, Title II. The quotation is from U.S. House of Representatives, *Cranston-Gonzalez National Affordable Housing Act: Conference Report to Accompany S. 566*, Report 101-943, October 25, 1990, 458.

48. Ibid., 466.

49. Emily Achtenberg, "Stemming the Tide: A Handbook on Preserving Multifamily Subsidized Housing," Local Issues Support Corporation, September 2002, 2, at http://www.lisc.org/content/publications/detail/893/.

50. U.S. Department of Housing and Urban Development, *HUD Reinvention: From Blueprint to Action*, Washington, DC, March 1995, 58.

51. *Multifamily Assisted Housing Reform and Affordability Act of 1997*, Public Law 10565, Title V. For a description and analysis of Mark-to-Market, see Hilton et al., *Evaluation of the Mark-to-Market Program*.

52. U.S. Department of Housing and Urban Development, Office of Housing, "M2M Pipeline Summary Report." The data on number of assisted units are taken from "M2M Transactions Report as of November 4, 2011," http://portal.hud.gov/hudportal/documents/huddoc?id=m2mstran.pdf.

53. For more detailed descriptions of Mark-Up-To-Market and Mark-Up-To-Budget, see Achtenberg, "Stemming the Tide," 9–12.

54. Calculated from U.S. Department of Housing and Urban Development, Chief Financial Officer, "Housing: Housing Payments," Congressional Justifications for (Year) Estimates, 1999 to 2010.

55. National Housing Trust, *Changes to Project-Based Multifamily Units in HUD's Inventory Between 1995 and 2003* (Washington, DC: National Housing Trust, 2004) http://www.nhtinc.org/documents/PB_Inventory.pdf. The data exclude the Section 8 Moderate Rehabilitation program; the National Housing Trust calculates the reduction in this program at 51,000 to 67,000 units.

56. Econometrica, Inc., and Abt Associates, Inc., *Multifamily Properties: Opting In, Opting Out and Remaining Affordable* (Washington DC: U.S. Department of Housing and Urban Development, Office of Policy Development and Research, 2006). This study excluded the Section 8 Moderate Rehabilitation program, which is administered within HUD by the Office of Public and Indian Housing, while all the other programs for privately owned assisted projects are administered by the Office of Housing.

57. John C. Weicher, *Privatizing Subsidized Housing* (Washington: The AEI Press, 1997), chap. 5.

58. U.S. Department of Housing and Urban Development, *1973 HUD Statistical Yearbook*, 124.

59. Millennial Housing Commission, *Meeting Our Nation's Housing Challenges: Report of the Bipartisan Millennial Housing Commission Appointed by the Congress of the United States* (Washington, DC: U.S. Government Printing Office, 2002), 95. The commission cites the 207,000 figure without indicating its source. HUD budget data report 227,000 unit reservations in the Section 202/8 program; the difference may be units reserved but not built. U.S. Department of Housing and Urban Development, *1979 HUD Statistical Yearbook*, 213 (through FY 1979); unpublished table prepared by the HUD Budget Office and provided by Robert Gray (after FY 1979).

60. U.S. Department of Housing and Urban Development, Chief Financial Officer, "Housing: Housing Payments: Summary of Assisted Units and Outlays," Congressional Justifications for 2011 Estimates, K1–K4.

61. "Supply-side" housing programs have little if anything in common with "supply-side" economics. The housing programs rely on government funding for a particular commodity, while supply-side economics is concerned with marginal tax rates and their effect on the private production of goods and services in the aggregate, and not with the composition of output.

62. For a detailed explanation of this difference, see Stephen D. Kennedy and Meryl Finkel, *Section 8 Rental Voucher and Rental Certificate Utilization Study: Final Report* (Cambridge, MA: Abt Associates, Inc., 1994), 3–4.

63. To be precise, the tenant pays the larger of 30 percent of net income (after adjustments as specified in the statute), 10 percent of gross income, or the amount designated for housing in any welfare payment received by the tenant. The most common payment is 30 percent of net income.

64. For simplicity, this discussion assumes that the FMR and payment standard are the same. In practice, as discussed earlier, they can and do vary.

65. A different "shopping incentive," formally known by that title, was originally part of the certificate program, with families keeping half of the difference between the FMR and the actual rent. It was repealed in 1980.

66. U.S. Department of Housing and Urban Development, Chief Financial Officer, "Housing: Housing Payments: Summary of Assisted Units and Outlays," Congressional Justifications for 2011 Estimates, K1–K4.

67. Only the first five years were studied in the experiment; the remaining five-year subsidies were provided in order to persuade assisted households to regard the payment as part of their permanent income, as it would be in a full-fledged program, rather than as transitory income.

68. Richard Nixon, "Special Message to the Congress Proposing Legislation and Outlining Administration Actions to Deal with Federal Housing Policy," *Public Papers of the Presidents of the United States*, September 19, 1973, 9, http://www.presidency. ucsb. edu/ws/index.php?pid=3968&st=special+message+to+the+congress&st1=.

69. U.S. Department of Housing and Urban Development, *Programs of HUD*, Washington, DC, 2005, 76; Barbara Sard, "Housing Vouchers Should Be a Major Component of Future Housing Policy for the Lowest Income Families," *Cityscape* 5, no. 2 (2001): 98–99.

70. A number of public housing authorities, including some of the largest ones, were not required to report their use of project-based vouchers to HUD's basic reporting system. These PHAs have been participating in HUD's Moving to Work (MTW) demonstration since 2000. (The demonstration is discussed in chapter 6.) The figure in the text includes over 19,000 from PHAs submitting information to HUD's data system, and about 6,500 from PHAs participating in MTW; it is taken from an unpublished HUD tabulation.

71. HUD also administers a Community Development Block Grant (CDBG), enacted in 1974 as the successor to urban renewal. Community development programs are generally outside the scope of this book, except insofar as they overlap with assisted housing. For an evaluation of urban renewal, see John C. Weicher, *Urban Renewal: Federal Program for Local Problems* (Washington, DC: American Enterprise Institute for Public Policy Research, 1972).

72. Urban Institute, *Implementing Block Grants for Housing: An Evaluation of the First Year of HOME* (Washington, DC: U.S. Department of Housing and Urban Development, Office of Policy Development and Research, 1995), 3–4.

73. The factors are (1) the number of rental units occupied by poor households, adjusted for the rental vacancy rate; (2) the number of occupied rental units that are overcrowded, lack complete kitchen or plumbing facilities, or are occupied by a household with a rent burden greater than 30 percent of income; (3) the number of these units multiplied by the ratio of local housing production costs to national costs; (4) the number of rental units built before 1950 and occupied by poor households; (5) the number of poor families; (6) the population adjusted for per capita income, with poor jurisdictions receiving more money. The first and last factors are each weighted at 10 percent, and the other four each at 20 percent.

74. Originally there were also restrictions on where new construction could be located within a metropolitan area; these were repealed by 1994, when Congress also raised the original per-unit subsidy limit.

75. For an analysis of the difference between block grants and categorical programs in the context of CDBG and urban renewal, see John C. Weicher, "The Fiscal

Profitability of Urban Renewal under Matching Grants and Revenue Sharing," *Journal of Urban Economics* 3, no. 3 (March 1976): 193–208.

76. Office of Management and Budget, "Budget Authority," in Public Budget Database, Budget of the United States Government, Fiscal Year 2012, http://www.white house.gov/sites/default/files/omb/budget/fy2012/assets/budauth.xls, line 3032; and Office of Management and Budget, "Outlays," in Public Budget Database, Budget of the United States Government, Fiscal Year 2012, http://www.whitehouse.gov/omb/budget/fy2011/assets/outlays.csv, line 3482.

77. U.S. Department of Housing and Urban Development, Office of Community Planning and Development, "Home Program National Production Report as of 6/30/09," http://www.hud.gov/offices/cpd/affordablehousing/reports/production/063009.pdf.

78. Urban Institute, *Implementing Block Grants for Housing*, 28; Turnham et al., *Study of Homebuyer Activity through the Home Investment Program*, 3-1–3-3.

79. U.S. Department of Housing and Urban Development, Office of Community Planning and Development, "Home Program National Production Report as of 6/30/09."

80. Turnham et al., *Study of Homebuyer Activity through the Home Investment Program*, p. 3-3.

81. Christopher Herbert et al., *Study of the Ongoing Affordability of HOME Program Rents* (Cambridge, MA: Abt Associates, Inc., 2001), 32–40.

82. The sponsors of the proposed legislation were Reps. William A. Barrett (D–PA) and Thomas L. Ashley (D–OH), and Sen. John Sparkman (D–AL). Rep. Barrett and Sen. Sparkman were the housing subcommittee chairmen in their respective houses, and Rep. Ashley was a recognized authority on housing policy.

83. For an analysis of the block grant concept and discussion of its history, see John C. Weicher, "Housing Block Grants in the United States," *Urban Law and Policy* 4 (September 1981): 269–83.

84. Data on the number of tax credit units is taken from a database maintained by HUD, available at http://lihtc.huduser.org. See Abt Associates, Inc., *Development and Analysis of the National Low-Income Housing Tax Credit Database*, July 1996, exhibits 1-1 and 3-1 (projects through 1994), http://www.huduser.org/Datasets/LIHTC/report.pdf. The database has been updated twelve times; the most recent complete update is Climaco et al., *Updating the Low-Income Housing Tax Credit (LIHTC) Database: Projects Placed in Service Through 2006*. Most of the tables in this report have been updated through 2007: Abt Associates, Inc., "Updating the Low-Income Housing Tax Credit (LIHTC) Database: Projects Placed in Service Through 2007," at http://www.huduser.org/Datasets/lihtc/tables9507.pdf. Most recently, a brief article in HUD's quarterly publication, *U.S. Housing Market Conditions*, updates several of the most important tables through 2009: "New Low-Income Housing Tax Credit Property Data Available," *U.S. Housing Market Conditions*, 2nd quarter 2011 (August 2011), 6-14. Unless otherwise

indicated, all data in the text are taken from calculations by the author from the LIHTC database. All of these recent updates report annual data on project characteristics back to 1995. The HUD User Web site for the LIHTC—http://www.huduser.org/datasets/lihtc.html—includes all of the updates, but not the 1996 Abt report. The best sources of data on the LIHTC for earlier periods are U.S. General Accounting Office, *Tax Credits: Opportunities to Improve Oversight of the Low-Income Housing Program*, GAO/GGD/RCED-97-55, Washington, DC, 1997 (covering 1992–1994); and Jean L. Cummings and Denise DiPasquale, "The Low-Income Housing Tax Credit: The First Ten Years," *Housing Policy Debate* 10, no. 2 (1999): 251–307 (covering 1987–1996).

85.   For a description and evaluation of the LIHTC during its first two years, see ICF Incorporated, *Evaluation of the Low-Income Housing Tax Credit: Final Report* (Washington, DC: U.S. Department of Housing and Urban Development, Office of Policy Development and Research, 1991).

86.   Because the credit is calculated in present value terms, the amount can vary as a percentage of project costs from year to year. Although there were no HUD programs to build subsidized projects in 1986, the Farmers Home Administration had and still has subsidized construction programs that could be used with the tax credit on the 30 percent basis.

87.   Abt Associates, Inc., "Updating the Low-Income Housing Tax Credit (LIHTC) Database: Projects Placed in Service Through 2007," Table 3.

88.   Unless otherwise indicated, the information in this section has been calculated by the author from the LIHTC database.

89.   Larry Buron et al., *Assessment of the Economic and Social Characteristics of LIHTC Residents and Neighborhoods* (Cambridge, MA: Abt Associates, Inc., 2000), 3-32–3-33.

90.   Climaco et al., *Updating the Low-Income Housing Tax Credit (LIHTC) Database: Projects Placed in Service Through 2006*, 68–76.

91.   This paragraph draws on the author's conversation with Denise DiPasquale, January 19, 2008.

92.   Cummings and DiPasquale, "The Low-Income Housing Tax Credit," 291–96, calculate proceeds of 47 cents in 1987, rising to 55 cents by 1995. Kirk McClure, "The Low-Income Housing Tax Credit as an Aid to Housing Finance: How Well Has It Worked?" *Housing Policy Debate* 11, no. 1 (2000): 104–6, calculates that proceeds for Missouri tax credit projects rose from 42 cents in 1987 to 53 cents by 1994, then dropped to 45 cents in 1995, the last year of his data. These figures include the cost of syndication.

93.   Ernst & Young, *Understanding the Dynamics V: Housing Tax Credit Investment Performance*, June 2010, 45.

94.   These figures are taken from the earnings releases of the two GSEs, available at http://www.fanniemae.com/media/pdf/newsreleases/form10k_newsrelease_022609.pdf;jsessionid=0XGE5CSTUI2SRJ2FQSISFGQ, and http://www.freddiemac.com/investors/er/.

95. Alex Frangos, "Losses Stall Affordable Housing Projects," *Wall Street Journal,* March 12, 2008, B1.

96. The best source of information on the Housing Trust Fund is the website of the National Low Income Housing Coalition, www.nlihc.org. NLIHC refers to it as the "National Housing Trust Fund."

97. Up to 10 percent of the trust fund can be spent to support first-time homebuyers or very low-income homeowners. The legislation also allows funds to be spent for "operation" of lower-income housing, which could permit tenant-based assistance. Advocates have argued that the trust fund is intended for one-time capital grants, rather than ongoing operations. National Low Income Housing Coalition, "Frequently Asked Questions," http://www.nlihc.org/doc/FAQ-NHTF.pdf.

98. Technical Analysis Center with Integrated Financial Engineering, Inc., "An Actuarial Review of the Federal Housing Administration Mutual Mortgage Insurance Fund for Fiscal Year 2004," October 19, 2004, 19.

99. See Congressional Budget Office, "Responses to Senator Allard's Questions about the 1999 Actuarial Review of the Federal Housing Administration's Mutual Mortgage Insurance Fund," October 23, 2000, http://www.cbo.gov/doc.cfm?index= 2666&type=0.

100. Integrated Financial Engineering, Inc., "An Actuarial Review of the Federal Housing Administration Mutual Mortgage Insurance Fund for Fiscal Year 2008," October 13, 2008, ii.

101. These statements are based on unpublished FHA data from my term as FHA Commissioner (2001–2005) and earlier years.

102. National Low Income Housing Coalition, "NATIONAL HOUSING TRUST FUND: White House Reiterates Promise to Capitalize the NHTF," *Memo to Members* 14, No. 42 (October 30, 2009).

103. S. 1489 and H.R. 1477, The Preserving Homes and Communities Act of 2011. See National Low Income Housing Coalition, "NHTF Funding Bill Gains Cosponsors," *Memo to Members 16,* No. 19 (May 13, 2011).

104. The one-time nature of the funding is recognized by trust fund advocates. See National Low Income Housing Coalition, "NATIONAL HOUSING TRUST FUND: National Conference Call Reports on New Developments," *Memo to Members* 14, no. 43 (November 6, 2009).

105. National Low Income Housing Coalition. "House Bill Would Abolish NHTF," *Memo to Members 16,* No. 19 (May 13, 2011).

106. The proposed formula was issued by HUD in a proposed rule for comment: *Federal Register,* December 4, 2009, 63938–42. The allocation to individual states has been estimated by the National Low Income Housing Coalition. "NLIHC Updated Estimates of State Allocation Amounts from NHTF for Every Billion Allocated and Invested: February 10, 2011," http://www.nlihc.org/doc/NHTF-state-estimates.pdf. See also U.S. Department of Housing and Urban Development, Office of Policy Development and Research, "Regulatory Impact Analysis for the Housing Trust Fund,"

August 10, 2009, http://www.huduser.org/portal/publications/pdf/5246__RIA_for_
HTF_Proposed_Rule1_final.pdf.

107. Edward L. Glaeser and Joseph Gyourko, *Rethinking Federal Housing Policy: How
to Make Housing Plentiful and Affordable* (Washington, DC: AEI Press, 2008), 166–70,
identify eight states as having counties with barriers to housing construction, with
four having more than two such counties: California, Massachusetts, New Jersey, and
New York. They exclude the District of Columbia from their analysis, but do include
three large suburban counties in Virginia and Maryland.

108. Jane Jacobs, *The Death and Life of Great American Cities* (New York: Macmillan,
1961), 4.

109. See ibid.; and Daniel Seligman, "The Enduring Slums," in *The Exploding
Metropolis*, ed. *Fortune* editors (Garden City, New York: Doubleday, 1958), 92–114,
especially 105–8.

110. A vivid and widely praised account of such a project is provided in Alex Kotlowitz, *There are No Children Here* (New York: Doubleday, 1991), about a family in
Henry Horner Homes in Chicago.

111. Brad Heath, "Housing Agencies Faulted in Audits to Get $300M of Stimulus,"
USA Today, April 7, 2009, http://www.usatoday.com/news/washington/2009-04-
07Stimulus-Housing_N.htm. On PHAs' management problems generally, see Alex
F. Schwartz, *Housing Policy in the United States: Second Edition* (New York: Routledge,
2010), 136–137.

112. U.S. Government Accountability Office, *RECOVERY ACT: Status of States' and
Localities' Use of Funds and Efforts to Insure Accountability*, GAO-10-231, December
2009, 80-81, http://www.recovery.gov/Accountability/Documents/d10231.pdf.

113. Letter from Senator Charles Grassley to HUD Secretary Shaun Donovan, March
15, 2010, http://grassley.senate.gov/about/upload/2010-03-15-Letter-to-HUD.pdf.

114. For the Chicago PHA, see Judy England-Joseph, "Public Housing: HUD's
Takeover of the Chicago Housing Authority," testimony before the Subcommit-
tee on Housing and Community Opportunity, Committee on Banking and Finan-
cial Services, U.S. House of Representatives, GAO/T-RCED-95-222, June 7, 1995.
For the Philadelphia PHA, see Dale Russakoff, "U.S. Seizes Philadelphia Public
Housing Authority; HUD Acts After Political Corruption Charge," *Washington
Post*, May 21, 1992, http://www.encyclopedia.com/doc/1P2-1006736.html. For
the Passaic PHA, see Joseph F. Sullivan, "Passaic Housing Aides Guilty," *New York
Times*, June 13, 1990, http://www.nytimes.com/1990/06/13/nyregion/passaic-
housing-aides-guilty.html.

115. Schwartz, *Housing Policy in the United States*, 133–136; Oscar Newman, *Defensible Space* (New York: Macmillan, 1972).

116. Ronald D. Utt, "The Conservative Critique of HOPE VI," in Henry G. Cisneros
and Lara Engdahl, eds., *From Despair to Hope: HOPE VI and the New Promise of Public
Housing in America's Cities* (Washington: Brookings Institution Press, 2009), chap. 14.

117. Schwartz, *Housing Policy in the United States*, 134.

118. See for example *The Report of the President's Commission on Housing* (Washington, DC: U.S. Government Printing Office, 1982), chap. 1, especially 12–14; U.S. Department of Housing and Urban Development, *HUD Reinvention: From Blueprint to Action*, Washington, DC, March 1995, chap. 3, especially 53–60.

119. Emily Paradise Achtenberg, "Subsidized Housing at Risk: The Social Costs of Private Ownership," in Sara Rosenberry and Chester Hartman, eds., *Housing Issues of the 1990s* (New York: Praeger, 1989), 233.

120. James E. Wallace et al., *Participation and Benefits in the Urban Section 8 Program: New Construction and Existing Housing,* (Cambridge, MA: Abt Associates Inc., 1981), S-2.

121. Schwartz, *Housing Policy in the United States,* 174.

122. See for example Chester Hartman, *Housing and Social Policy* (Englewood Cliffs, NJ: Prentice Hall, 1975), 156.

123. Christopher Swope, "Section 8 Is Broken," *Shelterforce Online,* January/February 2003, http://www.shelterforce.com/online/issues/127/section8.html; Manny Fernandez, "Bias is Seen as Landlords Bar Vouchers," *New York Times,* October 30, 2007.

124. Hartman, *Housing and Social Policy,* 159.

125. Howard Husock, "Let's End Housing Vouchers," *City Journal* 10, no. 4 (Autumn 2000), http://www.city-journal.org/html/10_4_lets_end_housing.html. A collection of such concerns appears in Sarah Churchill et al., *Strategies That Enhance Community Relations in Tenant-Based Section 8 Programs* (Washington, DC: U.S. Department of Housing and Urban Development, Office of Policy Development and Research, 2001).

126. Kathryn P. Nelson and Jill Khadduri, "To Whom Should Limited Housing Resources Be Directed?" *Housing Policy Debate* 3, no. 1 (1992): 35.

Chapter 4: Program Activity and Costs in the Aggregate

1. At a 4 percent interest rate, the total cost over forty years is 2.0 times the development cost; at 5 percent, 2.3 times; at 6 percent, 2.6 times; at 8 percent, 3.3 times.

2. U.S. Department of Housing and Urban Development, *Budget Summary, Department of Housing and Urban Development, Fiscal Year 1997*, Washington, DC, 1996, H-7. Beginning in FY1997, funds for the construction of new public housing (apart from HOPE VI) were combined with modernization funding in the new Public Housing Capital Fund.

3. Public housing bonds were both tax exempt and federally guaranteed, and thus carried very low interest rates. The point of the comparisons does not depend on the precise numbers in the example.

4. U.S. Department of Housing and Urban Development, Office of Policy Development and Research, *Issue Brief: Will It Cost More to Replace Public Housing with Certificates?* Washington, DC, March 1995. The tenant rent contribution is calculated for public housing residents rather than for households with certificates or vouchers, but the incomes of the two groups are close, on average. The most recent

budget data, for FY 2009 and 2010, indicate that the federal government's share is about 65 to 67 percent.

5. Section 811 was created in 1990 in the same act that changed the financing of Section 202, and it is financed in the same way. Before 1990, Section 202 included projects for the disabled as well as the elderly. Before 1975, the direct loan from the U.S. Treasury was the only subsidy for Section 202 projects; there was no subsidy to bring the rent within reach of lower-income elderly. Thus there is no budget authority, or outlay, associated with the program before 1975.

6. A number of budget data sources begin with FY1977. A detailed discussion of the sources of table 4-1 is contained in the appendix to this chapter.

7. See the appendix to this chapter for more detailed discussion of the budgetary treatment for the LIHTC.

8. Details of the imputations are shown in the appendix to this chapter.

9. U.S. Department of Housing and Urban Development. Chief Financial Officer. "Public and Indian Housing: Native American Housing Block Grants," Congressional Justifications for 2010 Estimates, J1–J17, http://hud.gov/offices/cfo/reports/2010/cjs/pih2010.pdf. The allocations for 2004–2007 are reported on page J-5.

10. Jack Kemp was HUD secretary during this period, and as a former member of the House Appropriations Committee understood why the department's budget authority was rising. He often said that he would be judged a very successful HUD secretary if growth in budget authority was the yardstick, but he wouldn't deserve any of the credit for the increase; nor was it the basis on which he should be judged.

11. Budget authority for the LIHTC in table 4-1 is the full amount authorized by Congress; outlays in table 4-4 are reduced to reflect the fact that some tax credit units (consistently about 10 percent) are not intended for low-income households, and that some (declining from about 30 percent in the early years of the program to less than 10 percent since 2002) are used in combination with the Section 515 program of the Rural Housing Service in the U.S. Department of Agriculture.

12. Section 221(d)(3)(BMIR) was not included as a subsidy program, because it did not involve budget outlays. It would add about 35,000 units to the total as of 1965, and another 125,000 as of 1970.

13. Carissa Climaco et al., *Updating the Low-Income Housing Tax Credit (LIHTC) Database: Projects Placed in Service Through 2006* (Washington, DC: U.S. Department of Housing and Urban Development, 2009), 68–72.

14. See for example National Housing Conference, "NHC's First 75 Years" (Washington, DC: National Housing Conference, 2006), a short recapitulation of federal housing policy since the 1930s, which includes a chart of budget authority since 1976 and states: "From a high of more than $100 billion in HUD budget authorizations (figured in 2005 dollars), affordable housing allocations have steadily declined. . . . Allocations have hovered around the $30–$40 billion mark for the past 15 years. . . . Affordable housing has taken a back seat." In fact, the number of assisted households increased by 11 percent between 1991 and 2005.

15. See for example Edward Lazere et al., *A Place to Call Home: The Low Income Housing Crisis Continues* (Washington, DC: Center for Budget and Policy Priorities and Low Income Housing Information Service, 1991).

16. For further discussion, see Anna Kondratas and John C. Weicher, "Is Homelessness a Problem of Housing Policy?" *Jobs and Capital* 4 (Spring 1995): 37–39.

17. The database is available on the OMB Web site at http://www.whitehouse.gov/omb/budget/fy2011/assets/budauth.xls (for budget authority) and http://www.whitehouse.gov/omb/budget/fy2011/assets/outlays.csv (for outlays).

18. Congressional Budget Office, *The Challenges Facing Federal Rental Assistance Programs*, Washington, DC, December 1994, appendix A. The tabulation reports actual data through 1993 and estimates for 1994 and 1995.

19. U.S. House of Representatives, Committee on Ways and Means, *2004 Green Book: Background Material and Data on the Programs Within the Jurisdiction of the Committee on Ways and Means*, Washington, DC, March 2004, sec. 15, table 15-Housing-2, http://waysandmeans.house.gov/media/pdf/greenbook2003/FEDERALHOUSING ASSISTANCE.pdf. The table reports data from 1980 through 2002. Data for 1977 through 1979 are taken from U.S. House of Representatives, Committee on Ways and Means, *1998 Green Book: Background Material and Data on Programs Within the Jurisdiction of the Committee on Ways and Means*, Washington, DC, May 1998, sec. 15, table 15-27.

20. *2004 Green Book*, table 15-Housing-3.

21. A brief history of modernization funding and a description of data sources are in U.S. Department of Housing and Urban Development, Office of Policy Development and Research, *Report to Congress on Alternative Methods for Funding Public Housing Modernization*, Washington, DC, April 1990, I-6–I-14.

22. *2004 Green Book*, table 15-Housing-1.

23. Henry G. Cisneros and Lora Engdahl, eds., *From Despair to Hope: HOPE VI and the New Promise of Public Housing in America's Cities* (Washington, DC: Brookings Institution Press, 2009). The list of HOPE VI projects is Appendix B.

24. National Council of State Housing Finance Agencies, "Housing Credit Utilization Charts," http://www.ncsha.org/resource/housing-credit-utilization-charts.

25. Climaco et al., *Updating the Low-Income Housing Tax Credit (LIHTC) Database: Projects Placed in Service Through 2006*, exhibit 3-13.

26. Abt Associates, Inc., *Development and Analysis of the National Low-Income Housing Tax Credit Database*, July 1996, http://www.huduser.org/Datasets/LIHTC/report.pdf.

27. "New Low-Income Housing Tax Credit Property Data Available," *U.S. Housing Market Conditions*, Second quarter 2011 (August 2011), 6–14.

28. As of 2009, there were 436,000 units in Section 515 projects (Tammye H. Trevino, "Results of the 2009 Multi-Family Housing Annual Fair Housing Occupancy Report" [memorandum], July 14, 2009, available at http://hac.nonprofitsoapbox.com/storage/documents/OccupancyMFH2009.pdf). Table 4-6 shows 128,000 Section 515 units with tax credits, 29 percent of the total.

Chapter 5: The Voucher/Production Debate:
Program Comparisons

1. James E. Wallace et al., *Participation and Benefits in the Urban Section 8 Program: New Construction and Existing Housing* (Cambridge, MA: Abt Associates, Inc., 1981).

2. The interim evaluation is Larry Orr et al., *Moving to Opportunity Interim Impacts Evaluation: Final Report* (Washington, DC: U.S. Department of Housing and Urban Development, 2003); the final impacts evaluation is Lisa Sanbonmatsu et al., *Moving to Opportunity for Fair Housing Demonstration Program: Final Impacts Evaluation* (Washington, DC: U.S. Department of Housing and Urban Development, Office of Policy Development and Research, 2011).

3. U.S. Department of Housing and Urban Development, *Housing in the Seventies: A Report of the National Housing Policy Review* (Washington, DC: U.S. Government Printing Office, 1974), chap. 5.

4. Mireille L. Leger and Stephen Kennedy, *Final Comprehensive Report of the Freestanding Housing Voucher Demonstration* (Washington, DC: U.S. Department of Housing and Urban Development, 1990).

5. Margaret Drury et al., *Lower Income Housing Assistance Program (Section 8): Nationwide Evaluation of the Existing Housing Program* (Washington, DC: U.S. Government Printing Office, November 1978).

6. Gregory Mills et al., *Effects of Housing Vouchers on Welfare Families* (Washington, DC: U.S. Department of Housing and Urban Development, 2006).

7. See for example Raymond J. Struyk and Marc Bendick, Jr., eds., *Housing Vouchers for the Poor: Lessons from a National Experiment* (Washington, DC: Urban Institute Press, 1981); and Katharine L. Bradbury and Anthony Downs, eds., *Do Housing Allowances Work?* (Washington, DC: Brookings Institution, 1981).

8. Orr et al, *Moving to Opportunity Interim Impacts Evaluation,* 27–29; 33–36.

9. Sanbonmatsu et al., *Moving to Opportunity Final Impacts Evaluation,* 51–57.

10. Ibid., 68.

11. The Housing and Community Development Amendments of 1979 required HUD to give priority to households occupying substandard housing and to those involuntarily displaced; the Housing and Urban-Rural Recovery Act of 1983 added another priority category: families paying 50 percent or more of their income for rent. A regulation implementing these priorities was promulgated on January 15, 1988. Until 1990 the law required that 90 percent of available units should go to households in these priority categories, but the National Affordable Housing Act in that year reduced the requirement to 70 percent for public housing and Section 8 projects (not certificates or vouchers).

12. Wallace et al., *Participation and Benefits in the Urban Section 8 Program.*

13. Inadequate housing was measured by a standard developed by CBO; see Congressional Budget Office, "Measures of Housing Need: Findings from the

Annual Housing Survey," in U.S. House of Representatives, Committee on Banking and Urban Affairs, Subcommittee on Housing and Community Development, Task Force on Assisted Housing: *Hearings before the Subcommittee on Housing and Community Development of the Committee on Banking, Finance, and Urban Affairs, House of Representatives, Ninety-Fifth Congress, Second Session*. Washington, DC, 1979, 1570–90.

14. Wallace et al., *Participation and Benefits in the Urban Section 8 Program*, 239.

15. An alternative comparison is to adjust the participation rates for Section 8 New Construction to take account of eligible households that are unwilling to move. Evidence from the tenant-based assistance programs in the late 1980s (discussed later in this chapter) indicates that about 30 percent of participants in those programs were unwilling to move; they are therefore unlikely to participate in project-based programs. Adjusting the rates in table 5-1 to include these households in the denominators yields ratios of 15 percent of the eligible population, and 17 percent of program participants, living in substandard housing originally. These are both lower than the proportions for the certificate program.

16. Leger and Kennedy, *Final Comprehensive Report*, 49–59. The calculation in the study combines success rates by preprogram housing quality for households willing to move (table 3.10) with the proportions of households willing to move that originally lived in different qualities of housing (calculated from table 3.7A).

17. A later utilization study reports success rates for households having a federal preference for assistance because they live in substandard housing; however, homelessness is included as substandard housing and also tabulated separately, and the number homeless is almost identical to the number in substandard housing. Indeed, 4 percent of successful enrollees who remained in their original unit are classified as homeless! See Stephen D. Kennedy and Meryl Finkel, *Section 8 Rental Voucher and Rental Certificate Utilization Study: Final Report* (Washington, DC: U.S. Department of Housing and Urban Development, Office of Policy Development and Research, 1994), 21.

18. Mills et al., *Effects of Housing Vouchers on Welfare Families*, 137–42.

19. Wallace et al., *Participation and Benefits in the Urban Section 8 Program*, S-11, S-12.

20. Ira Lowry, *Experimenting with Housing Allowances* (Cambridge, MA: Oelgeschlager, Gunn and Hain, 1983), 144.

21. See John C. Weicher, "Housing Policy," in *Current Issues in Urban Economics*, ed. Peter Mieszkowski and Mahlon Straszheim (Baltimore: Johns Hopkins University Press, 1978), 469–508, for a review of the literature on the income elasticity of demand in a policy context up to the time that Section 8 was enacted. For subsequent analyses, see Stephen K. Mayo, "Theory and Estimation in the Economics of Housing Demand," *Journal of Urban Economics* 10 (July 1981): 95–116; and Stephen Malpezzi and Duncan Maclennan, "The Long-Run Price Elasticity of Supply of New Construction in the United States and the United Kingdom," *Journal of Housing Economics* 10 (September 2001): 278–306.

22. Joseph S. Friedman and Daniel Weinberg, *The Economics of Housing Vouchers* (Cambridge, MA: Abt Associates, Inc., 1981), summarizes the findings from the Demand Experiment.

23. For a discussion of the problem, see U.S. Department of Housing and Urban Development, Office of Policy Development and Research, *Characteristics of HUD-Assisted Renters and Their Units in 1989*, Washington, DC, March 1992.

24. The data are from U.S. Department of Housing and Urban Development, Office of Policy Development and Research, *Characteristics of HUD-Assisted Renters and Their Units in 2003*, Washington, DC, May 2008. The sample sizes differ for the program categories: about 600 for tenant-based assistance and privately owned projects, and about 300 for public housing. The small sample for public housing in particular suggests that the comparisons should be regarded with caution.

25. Larry Buron et al., *Assessment of the Economic and Social Characteristics of LIHTC Residents and Neighborhoods* (Cambridge, MA: Abt Associates, Inc., 2000), 3-20–3-25.

26. Mills, *Effects of Housing Vouchers on Welfare Families*, 139–42.

27. Buron et al., *Assessment of the Economic and Social Characteristics of LIHTC Residents and Neighborhoods*, 3-22–3-23.

28. The Urban Institute published a number of reports from the panel study on various topics but did not publish a comprehensive or final report. I cite individual reports where relevant. The study ended in 2006.

29. Jennifer Comey, "An Improved Living Environment? Housing Quality Outcomes for HOPE VI Relocatees," Urban Institute, Metropolitan Housing and Communities Center, Brief No. 2, September 2004.

30. Ibid.

31. Larry Buron et al., *The HOPE VI Resident Tracking Study: A Snapshot of the Current Living Situation of Original Residents from Eight Sites* (Washington, DC: Abt Associates, Inc., and Urban Institute, 2002), chap. 2. The eight projects originally contained 4,029 units; as of the study, 773 were available for occupancy and another 489 were being built in projects described as "partially occupied."

32. Ibid., chap. 3. Residents were also asked about some specific problems that are components of the "severely inadequate" criterion. About 5 to 10 percent of residents in each housing category reported "big problems" of each type, and there were few significant differences across housing categories. Voucher holders were significantly more likely to report rats or mice, and those in HOPE VI projects or the homeownership/unsubsidized rental category were significantly less likely. Those in the last category were also significantly more likely to report problems with heating. The differences in specific problems are less pronounced than the improvement ratings.

33. Edward G. Goetz, "Better Neighborhoods, Better Outcomes? Explaining Relocation Outcomes in Hope VI," *Cityscape* 12, No. 1 (2010): 5–31.

34. Sheila Crowley, "HOPE VI: What Went Wrong," in Henry Cisneros and Lora Engdahl, eds, *From Despair to Hope: HOPE VI and the New Promise of Public Housing*

in America's Cities (Washington, DC: Brookings Institution Press, 2009) , chap, 13. The Urban Institute Panel Study was unable to locate 17 percent of original residents. Mary K. Cunningham, "An Improved Living Environment? Relocation Outcomes for HOPE VI Relocatees," Urban Institute, Metropolitan Housing and Communities Center, Brief No. 1, September 2004, 3–4.

35. See U.S. Department of Housing and Urban Development, Office of Policy Development and Research, *Worst Case Housing Needs 2009: Report to Congress,* Washington, DC, February 2011.

36. Strictly speaking, the target ratio is 30 percent of adjusted income, taking account of various statutory and regulatory exclusions from income. These include part or all of unreimbursed medical expenses, child care expenses, and payments for support of a child or former spouse; and specified exclusions for children attending school, for disabled household members, and for any elderly or disabled family.

37. U.S. Department of Housing and Urban Development, Office of Policy Development and Research, *Characteristics of HUD-Assisted Renters and Their Units in 2003.*

38. For detailed discussions of the problem, see U.S. Department of Housing and Urban Development, Office of Policy Development and Research, *Characteristics of HUD-Assisted Renters and Their Units in 1989,* 11–13, 33–34; and U.S. Department of Housing and Urban Development, Office of Policy Development and Research, *Characteristics of HUD-Assisted Renters and Their Units in 1993,* Washington, DC, May 1997, 17–20.

39. U.S. Department of Housing and Urban Development, Office of Policy Development and Research, *A Picture of Subsidized Households—2008,* http://www.huduser.org/picture2008/index.html.

40. Kirk McClure, "Rent Burden in the Housing Choice Voucher Program," *Cityscape* 8, no. 2 (2005): 5–20. The rent burden intervals reported in the paper do not precisely correspond to those established for assisted housing preferences or worst-case needs calculations. Tabulations are provided only for individual characteristics, without cross-classification, so it is not possible to say that high rent burdens were disproportionately found in the rural South, but it seems likely that they were.

41. Christopher E. Herbert et al., *Study of the Ongoing Affordability of HOME Program Rents* (Cambridge, MA: Abt Associates, Inc., 2001), 32–35.

42. U.S. Department of Housing and Urban Development, Office of Community Planning and Development, "HOME Program National Production Report As Of 6/30/09," 2, http://www.hud.gov/offices/cpd/affordablehousing/reports/production/063009.pdf.

43. The Housing and Economic Recovery Act of 2008 added a reporting requirement for characteristics of households occupying tax credit units, including income, race and ethnicity, and whether the household received a voucher (Section 2835(d)). These data were collected for 2009, but not published because of underreporting (also a problem with the data on projects placed in service in that year). "New Low-Income

Housing Tax Credit Property Data Available," *U.S. Housing Market Conditions,* Second quarter 2011 (August 2011), 6–14.

44.   U.S. General Accounting Office, *Tax Credits: Opportunities to Improve Oversight of the Low-Income Housing Program,* GAO/GGD/RCED-97-55, Washington, DC, 1997, 38–41.

45.   Buron et al., *Assessment of the Economic and Social Characteristics of LIHTC Residents and Neighborhoods,* 3-27–3-32.

46.   Jean L. Cummings and Denise DiPasquale, "The Low-Income Housing Tax Credit: An Analysis of the First Ten Years," *Housing Policy Debate* 10, no. 2 (1999): 251–307. Income and rent are discussed on pp. 278–82; the quotation appears on 304.

47.   Carissa Climaco et al., *Updating the Low-Income Housing Tax Credit (LIHTC) Database: Projects Placed in Service Through 2006* (Washington, DC: U.S. Department of Housing and Urban Development, 2009), 68–76.

48.   Conversation with Denise DiPasquale, January 19, 2008.

49.   Francis J. Cronin, "Participation in the Experimental Housing Allowance Program," in *Housing Vouchers for the Poor: Lessons from a National Experiment,* ed. Raymond J. Struyk and Marc Bendick, Jr. (Washington, DC: Urban Institute Press, 1981), 79–106. The percentages were 57 percent in Green Bay and 54 percent in South Bend.

50.   The difference between the Green Bay and the South Bend subsidies occurs because of differences in the cost of standard housing. The comparison with the Food Stamps program is not intended to be exact. Net income is not calculated in the same way in Food Stamps and EHAP, and there are other differences in eligibility, so participation rates can be expected to differ. The food stamp participation rate is reported in U.S. House of Representatives, Committee on Ways and Means, *1998 Green Book: Background Material and Data on Programs Within the Jurisdiction of the Committee on Ways and Means,* Washington, DC, May 1998, 940–41.

51.   Francis J. Cronin and David W. Rasmussen, "Mobility," in *Housing Vouchers for the Poor: Lessons from a National Experiment,* ed. Raymond J. Struyk and Marc Bendick, Jr. (Washington, DC: Urban Institute Press, 1981), 108–10.

52.   Some households said they were "not sure" whether they intended to stay, and some that did not originally intend to move did actually move. The households that changed their mind amounted to about 5 percent of all enrollees. Leger and Kennedy, *Final Comprehensive Report,* 51–54.

53.   Cronin, "Participation," 84–85.

54.   Ibid., 94–100; Lowry, *Experimenting with Housing Allowances,* 129–36. This comparison excludes those households in the Demand Experiment with no housing quality requirement.

55.   As an example, participation in Jacksonville, Florida, one of the smaller EHAP programs, lagged well behind the others. It turned out that the program standard included a requirement for at least eight square feet of kitchen counter space, which relatively few rental units had.

56. Jean MacMillan, *Mobility in the Housing Allowance Demand Experiment* (Cambridge, MA: Abt Associates, Inc., 1980), 82–85; Cronin and Rasmussen, "Mobility," 118–21.

57. The 1985 rate is from Leger and Kennedy, *Final Comprehensive Report*, 11; the 1993 rate, from Kennedy and Finkel, *Section 8 Utilization Study*, 12.

58. Meryl Finkel and Larry Buron, *Study on Section 8 Voucher Success Rates*, vol. 1, *Quantitative Study of Success Rates in Metropolitan Areas* (Washington, DC: U.S. Department of Housing and Urban Development, 2001). Finkel and Buron recomputed the success rates for the two previous studies to match the sample of metropolitan areas.

59. Kennedy and Finkel, *Section 8 Utilization Study*, i–ii; Stephen D. Kennedy and Meryl Finkel, *Report of First Year Findings for the Freestanding Voucher Demonstration* (Washington, DC: U.S. Department of Housing and Urban Development, 1987), 50–51.

60. The 1976 figure is taken from Drury et al., *Lower Income Housing Assistance Program*, xvi; the later figures are from Finkel and Buron, *Study on Section 8 Voucher Success Rates*, 2–10.

61. Jill Khadduri, "Should the Housing Voucher Program Become a State-Administered Block Grant?" *Housing Policy Debate* 14, no. 3 (2003): 243–45.

62. Meryl Finkel et al., *Costs and Utilization in the Housing Choice Voucher Program* (Washington, DC: U.S. Department of Housing and Urban Development, Office of Policy Development and Research, 2003).

63. U.S. Department of Housing and Urban Development, *Annual Performance Plan: Fiscal Year 2009*, February 2008, 69–70, http://www.hud.gov/offices/cfo/reports/pdfs/app2009.pdf.

64. The data are published in U.S. Department of Housing and Urban Development, Office of Policy Development and Research, A Picture of Subsidized Households—2008, http://www.huduser.org/portal/picture2008/index.html.

65. The estimate for the LIHTC in Table 5-5 is interpolated by the author from U.S. General Accounting Office, *Tax Credits*, 39, exhibit 2-1.

66. Cisneros and Engdahl, eds., *From Despair to Hope*, appendix B.

67. Mary Jo Holin et al., *Interim Assessment of the HOPE VI Program Cross-Site Report* (Cambridge, MA: Abt Associates, Inc., 2003); see especially chap. 3.

68. As of 2001, 26 percent of very low-income renters were black, and 18 percent were Hispanic (of any race). U.S. Department of Housing and Urban Development, Office of Policy Development and Research, *Affordable Housing Needs: A Report to Congress on the Significant Need for Housing*, Washington, DC, December 2005, appendix A. The proportions were about the same in 1999. U.S. Department of Housing and Urban Development, *Trends in Worst Case Needs for Housing, 1978–1999: A Report to Congress on Worst Case Housing Needs*, Washington, DC, December 2003, appendix A.

69. President's Commission on Housing, *The Report of the President's Commission on Housing*, Washington, DC, April 1982, 41.

70. Stephen D. Kennedy and James E. Wallace, *An Evaluation of Success Rates in Housing Assistance Programs Using the Existing Housing Stock* (Cambridge, MA.: Abt Associates, Inc., 1983), 23; Kennedy and Finkel, *Report of First Year Findings for the Voucher Demonstration*, 76.

71. Kennedy and Finkel, *Section Eight Utilization Study*, 27–28.

72. Locational differences may have contributed to the 1979 pattern. Minority households were concentrated in metropolitan areas that have lower success rates, but within each area, minorities were as successful as whites. In addition, PHAs in places with large minority populations apparently interpreted the program quality standards more stringently, at least at that time. Kennedy and Wallace, *Evaluation of Success Rates*, 5. In addition, fewer minority households lived in housing that met program standards to begin with, so fewer were able to qualify without moving or upgrading. Households that had to move or upgrade were less likely to participate.

73. As of 2001, 23 percent of very low-income renters were elderly. U.S. Department of Housing and Urban Development, *Affordable Housing Needs 2005*, table A-5.

74. Kennedy and Finkel, *Section Eight Utilization Study*, 27–28.

75. Kennedy and Wallace, *Evaluation of Success Rates*, 97–101.

76. The mean as of 2000 is the only measure available for all of the programs shown in table 5-5. Distributional data are available as of 2003 for voucher recipients, public housing residents, and residents of all privately owned projects combined. Those data show that vouchers and public housing serve large families about equally: 12.2 percent of voucher recipients and 11.4 percent of public housing residents are households with five or more persons, compared to only 6.5 percent of residents of privately owned projects. U.S. Department of Housing and Urban Development, Office of Policy Development and Research, *Characteristics of HUD-Assisted Renters and Their Units in 2003*, table 2.

77. President's Commission on Housing, *Report of the President's Commission on Housing*, 20.

78. See Rand Corporation, *Third Annual Report of the Housing Assistance Supply Experiment* (Santa Monica, California: Rand Corporation, 1977), xiv.

79. Lowry, *Experimenting with Housing Allowances*, 179–85.

80. Stephen D. Kennedy, "What Do We Know About Direct Cash Low Income Housing Assistance?" (paper presented at the American Evaluation Society, Kansas City, MO, October 1986, rev. June 1987), 20–21.

81. Wallace et al., *Participation and Benefits in the Urban Section 8 Program*, 332–40; Kennedy and Finkel, *Report of First Year Findings for the Voucher Demonstration*, 25.

82. Leger and Kennedy, *Final Comprehensive Report*, 88–91. The 10 percent increase for those who stayed applies only to households that did not share their unit before they participated in the program and therefore paid the full rent on the unit. The study does not cross-classify payment of full or partial rent by whether repairs were made; the increase for those paying full rent without any repairs would be the best measure of pure rent inflation.

83. Ibid., 94.

84. Drury et al., *Lower Income Housing Assistance Program*, 64–69.

85. Scott Susin, "Rent Vouchers and the Price of Low-Income Housing," *Journal of Public Economics* 83, no. 1 (January 2002): 109–52.

86. Calculated by the author from information in U.S. Department of Housing and Urban Development and U.S. Bureau of the Census. *American Housing Survey for the United States: 2003,* Current Housing Reports H150/03 (Washington, DC: September 2004). The AHS reports 33.6 million occupied rental units, and an average weight for each unit in the sample of 2,148.

87. U.S. Department of Housing and Urban Development, *Characteristics of HUD-Assisted Households and Their Units in 2003,* 52.

88. Susin's study uses voucher data for 1993. The report on housing assistance for that year does not have the same analysis of misreporting as the report for 2003, but it is clear that the sample does contain relatively few units reported by the interviewees as public housing or in privately owned subsidized projects. U.S. Department of Housing and Urban Development, Office of Policy Development and Research, *Characteristics of HUD-Assisted Renters and Their Units in 1993,* 5-7. This may simply reflect unusually small samples of these units; or it may occur because households did not report assistance status correctly.

89. Deborah J. Devine et al., *Housing Choice Voucher Location Patterns: Implications for Participants and Neighborhood Welfare* (Washington, DC: U.S. Department of Housing and Urban Development, Office of Policy Development and Research, 2003).

90. Several analysts have also concluded that the preponderance of evidence continues to support the judgment that vouchers do not result in rent inflation. See Edward L. Glaeser and Joseph Gyourko, *Rethinking Federal Housing Policy: How to Make Housing Plentiful and Affordable* (Washington, DC: AEI Press, 2008), 116-118; and Jill Khadduri, Kimberly Burnett, and David Rodda, *Targeting Production Subsidies: Literature Review* (Washington, DC: U.S. Department of Housing and Urban Development, Office of Policy Development and Research, 2003), 39–41.

91. Cronin, "Participation," 82–88; Raymond J. Struyk, "Policy Questions and Experimental Responses," in Raymond J. Struyk and Marc Bendick, Jr., eds., *Housing Vouchers for the Poor: Lessons from a National Experiment,* 15–16.

92. Kennedy and Finkel, *Report of First Year Findings for the Voucher Demonstration*, 45–53; Leger and Kennedy, *Final Comprehensive Report*, 62–68.

93. Kennedy and Finkel, *Section 8 Utilization Study,* 12.

94. Finkel and Buron, *Study on Section 8 Voucher Success Rates*, 3–14. Using a vacancy rate for the share of the market available to voucher holders, as estimated by the senior researchers participating in this study, the success rate ranged from 61 percent in very tight markets to 80 percent in loose markets; using the Census Bureau's vacancy rate calculated from the Housing Vacancy Survey for large metropolitan areas, the success rate ranged from 64 percent in tight markets to 71 percent in very loose markets. Neither measure is ideal; the Finkel and Buron figures are

estimates, while the census figures cover the entire market, rather than the lower-rent submarket.

95. Edgar O. Olsen, "A Possible Rationale for Government Intervention in Housing: The Slow Adjustment of the Housing Market to its Longrun Equilibrium Position," in National Housing Policy Review, *Housing in the Seventies: Working Papers* (Washington, DC: U.S. Department of Housing and Urban Development, 1976), 1:455–58. This is consistent with the earliest research on the subject by Richard F. Muth, "The Demand for Non-farm Housing," in *The Demand for Durable Goods*, ed. Arnold C. Harberger (Chicago: University of Chicago Press, 1962), 29–98.

96. John C. Weicher, *Housing: Federal Policies and Programs* (Washington, DC: American Enterprise Institute for Public Policy Research, 1980), 54–55, 66–67.

97. Buron et al., *HOPE VI Resident Tracking Study*, 9.

Chapter 6: The Voucher/Production Debate: Neighborhood Issues

1. The Census Bureau stresses that homogeneity is the basis of the original delineation; over time, tract boundaries are kept as constant as feasible, so the tract may come to include disparate communities within its boundaries. See U.S. Census Bureau, "Census Tracts and Block Numbering Areas," http://www.census.gov/geo/www/cen_tract.html.

2. The four projects are located in Baltimore, Cleveland, Milwaukee, and Charlotte. Mary Jo Holin et al., *Interim Assessment of the HOPE VI Program Cross-Site Report* (Cambridge, MA: Abt Associates, Inc., 2003), chap. 2 (project type), chap. 6 (completion date); appendix D (neighborhood characteristics).

3. Sandra J. Newman and Ann B. Schnare, "'And a Suitable Living Environment': The Failure of Housing Programs to Deliver on Neighborhood Quality," *Housing Policy Debate* 8, no. 4 (1997): 703–41. Newman and Schnare took great care to develop an accurate database for HUD-subsidized programs from program records, as described in the appendix to their paper (730–38). They also included Department of Agriculture assisted housing, which I have omitted from table 6-2. The underclass tract criterion is from Erol Ricketts and Isabell Sawhill, "Defining and Measuring the Underclass," *Journal of the Association of Public Policy Analysis and Management* 7, no. 4 (1988): 316–25.

4. Newman and Schnare do not report the precise incidence of welfare recipients in tracts where 40 percent or more of households have minority heads; instead they report intervals, including 30 to 50 percent. They do report both 40 percent-plus and 30 to 50 percent for public housing projects and recipients of tenant-based assistance; in both cases, about 45 percent of those in the interval are between 40 and 50 percent. I have therefore used 45 percent of that interval to calculate the incidence of welfare recipients in tracts where the minority concentration is 40 percent or more. Newman and Schnare do report the shares in tracts where 80 percent or more are minority-headed households; here, also, the incidence is lowest for certificate and voucher holders (less

than 10 percent), is similar for residents of private developments and welfare recipients (15 to 20 percent), and is high for public housing (between 35 and 40 percent).

5. Carissa Climaco et al., *Updating the Low-Income Housing Tax Credit (LIHTC) Database: Projects Placed in Service Through 2006* (Washington, DC: U.S. Department of Housing and Urban Development, 2009), exhibit 4-14.

6. Larry Buron et al., *Assessment of the Economic and Social Characteristics of LIHTC Residents and Neighborhoods* (Cambridge, MA: Abt Associates, Inc., 2000), p. 3-24.

7. Lisa Sanbonmatsu et al., *Moving to Opportunity for Fair Housing Demonstration Program: Final Impacts Evaluation* (Washington, DC: U.S. Department of Housing and Urban Development, Office of Policy Development and Research, 2011), 57, 62.

8. For example, see Newman and Schnare, "And a Suitable Living Environment," 726, with respect to project-based assistance.

9. Judith D. Feins and Rhiannon Patterson, "Geographic Mobility in the Housing Choice Voucher Program: A Study of Families Entering the Program, 1995–2002," *Cityscape* 8, no. 2 (2005): 21–47. There was a consistently higher probability that those who originally moved would move again within a given period than those who originally did not move, but the difference was small, between three and five percentage points at any point after the household first received a voucher.

10. Ibid., 26–30.

11. Orr et al., *Moving to Opportunity Interim Impacts Evaluation*, 27–37; Sanbonmatsu et al., *Moving to Opportunity Final Impacts Evaluation*, 41, 61.

12. Buron et al., *Assessment of the Economic and Social Characteristics of LIHTC Residents and Neighborhoods*, p. 3-26.

13. Orr et al., *Moving to Opportunity Interim Impacts Evaluation*, chap. 2; Sanbonmatsu et al., *Moving to Opportunity Final Impacts Evaluation*, chap. 1.

14. Peter Dreier and David Moberg, "Moving from the 'Hood': The Mixed Success of Integrating Suburbia," *American Prospect*, December 1, 1995, http://www.prospect.org/cs/articles?article=moving_from_the_hood; David Moberg, "No Vacancy! Denial, Fear and the Rumor Mill Waged a War Against Moving to Opportunity in Baltimore's Suburbs," *Shelterforce* 79 (January/February 1995), http://www.nhi.org/online/issues/79/novacancy.html. The first year of the demonstration was in fact completed; the findings are discussed later in this chapter.

15. Sarah Churchill et al., *Strategies That Enhance Community Relations in Tenant-Based Section 8 Programs* (Washington, DC: U.S. Department of Housing and Urban Development, Office of Policy Development and Research, 2001).

16. Ibid., 28.

17. Ibid., 7–24.

18. Ibid., 40–51.

19. Ira Lowry, *Experimenting with Housing Allowances* (Cambridge, MA: Oelgeschlager, Gunn and Hain, 1983), 206–12.

20. Susan J. Popkin et al., *A Decade of Hope VI: Research Findings and Policy Challenges* (Washington, DC: Urban Institute and Brookings Institution, 2004), 41.

21. See for example Michael H. Schill and Susan M. Wachter, "The Spatial Bias of Federal Housing Law and Poverty: Concentrated Poverty in Urban America," *University of Pennsylvania Law Review* 143 (1995): 1285–1342; and William H. Carter, Michael H. Schill, and Susan M. Wachter, "Polarisation, Public Housing, and Racial Minorities in U.S. Cities," *Urban Studies* 35 (October 1998): 1889–1911.

22. See for example Lance Freeman and William Rohe, "Subsidized Housing and Neighborhood Racial Transition: An Empirical Investigation," *Housing Policy Debate* 11, no. 1 (2000): 67–89. For a summary of the literature on this general topic, see Lance Freeman, "The Impact of Assisted Housing Developments on Concentrated Poverty," *Housing Policy Debate* 14, no. 1 (2003): 103–40.

23. Richard P. Taub, D. Garth Taylor, and Jan D. Dunham, *Paths of Neighborhood Change* (Chicago: University of Chicago Press, 1984). A recent study of several Chicago neighborhoods, however, makes almost no mention of subsidized rental housing as a factor or issue in neighborhood change; see William Julius Wilson and Richard P. Taub, *There Goes the Neighborhood: Racial, Ethnic, and Class Tensions in Four Chicago Neighborhoods and Their Meaning for America* (New York: Knopf, 2006).

24. Jill Khadduri and Charles Wilkins, "Designing Subsidized Rental Housing Programs: What Have We Learned?" (unpublished paper prepared for the Millennial Housing Commission, 2006).

25. Jean L. Cummings and Denise DiPasquale, "The Low-Income Housing Tax Credit: An Analysis of The First Ten Years," *Housing Policy Debate* 10, no. 2 (1999): 268.

26. Ibid., 269–72. Cummings and DiPasquale report data separately for Brooklyn and "Manhattan-Bronx"; whether they are separated or combined does not affect the statement in the text.

27. U.S. General Accounting Office, "Tax Credits: Characteristics of Tax Credit Properties and Their Residents," GAO/RCED-00-51R, January 10, 2000 (letter to HUD Secretary Andrew Cuomo).

28. Newman and Schnare, "And a Suitable Living Environment," 728.

29. Buron et al., *Assessment of the Economic and Social Characteristics of LIHTC Residents and Neighborhoods*, chap. 4. There was a sharp difference between nonprofit and for-profit project sponsors, with the former locating much more frequently in low-income neighborhoods.

30. Climaco et al., *Updating the Low-Income Housing Tax Credit (LIHTC) Database: Projects Placed in Service Through 2006*, exhibit 4-14.

31. U.S. Department of Housing and Urban Development, Chief Financial Officer, "Public and Indian Housing: Revitalization of Severely Distressed Public Housing," Congressional Justifications for 2010 Estimates, N-2, http://www.hud.gov/offices/cfo/reports/2010/cjs/pih2010.pdf.

32. The studies are Sean Zielenbach, "Assessing Economic Change in HOPE VI Neighborhoods," *Housing Policy Debate* 14, no. 4 (2003): 621–55 (eight projects, each "at least 50 percent completed" at the time of the study); Holin et al., *Interim*

Assessment of HOPE VI (thirteen projects, seven completed); U.S. General Accounting Office, *Public Housing: HOPE VI Resident Issues and Changes in Neighborhoods Surrounding Grant Sites*, GAO-04-109, Washington, DC, November 2003 (four projects, with some information for sixteen others; in each of the four, at least 75 percent of the new construction had been completed; among the other sixteen, no construction had been completed in seven, and construction did not begin at the majority of sites until 2000 or later); Valerie Piper and Mindy Turbov, *HOPE VI and Mixed-Finance Developments: A Catalyst for Neighborhood Renewal* (Washington, DC: Brookings Institution, 2005) (four projects, three completed). One project is included in three of these studies, and two others are included in two, resulting in twenty-five different projects across the four studies, excluding the larger set of sixteen projects in the GAO study. At least nine of the projects were completed at the time of the study.

33. Holin et al., *Interim Assessment of HOPE VI*.

34. One study site, San Francisco, included two projects three miles apart.

35. The Brookings study is Piper and Turbov, *HOPE VI and Mixed-Finance Developments*; the comments on the Brookings study appear in Popkin et al., *A Decade of HOPE VI*, 44.

36. U.S. General Accounting Office, *Public Housing: HOPE VI Resident Issues*, 23.

37. Ibid., 23–24.

38. Ibid., 31.

39. Popkin et al., *A Decade of HOPE VI*, 45.

40. Larry Buron et al., *The HOPE VI Resident Tracking Study: A Snapshot of the Current Living Situation of Original Residents from Eight Sites* (Washington, DC: Abt Associates, Inc., and Urban Institute, 2002), 84–92.

41. Holin et al., *Interim Assessment of HOPE VI*, 88–97. Supportive services were also offered to original residents of the projects and residents of the surrounding neighborhoods, but the attitudes of these households were not reported.

42. For summaries and reviews of this research, see George C. Galster, *A Review of Existing Research on the Effects of Federally Assisted Housing Programs on Neighboring Residential Property Values* (Washington, DC: National Association of Realtors, 2002); Lance Freeman and Hilary Botein, "Subsidized Housing and Neighborhood Impacts: A Theoretical Discussion and Review of the Literature," *Journal of Planning Literature* 16 (February 2002): 359–78.

43. George C. Galster, Peter Tatian, and Robin Smith, "The Impact of Neighbors Who Use Section 8 Certificates on Property Values," *Housing Policy Debate* 10, no. 4 (1999): 879–917.

44. George C. Galster et al., *Assessing Property Value Impacts of Dispersed Housing Subsidy Programs: Final Report* (Washington, DC: U.S. Department of Housing and Urban Development, 1999).

45. Ingrid Gould Ellen et al., "Does Federally Subsidized Rental Housing Depress Neighborhood Housing Values?" *Journal of Policy Analysis & Management* 26, Issue 2 (2007): 257–280.

46. Jennifer E.H. Johnson and Beata A. Bednarz, *Neighborhood Effects of the Low Income Housing Tax Credit Program: Final Report* (Washington, DC: U.S. Department of Housing and Urban Development, 2002), cited in Jill Khadduri, Kimberly Burnett, and David Rodda, *Targeting Production Subsidies: Literature Review* (Cambridge, MA: Abt Associates, Inc., 2003), 67.

47. Holin et al., *Interim Assessment of HOPE VI*, 129–40.

48. Khadduri and Wilkins, "Designing Subsidized Rental Housing Programs," 7.

49. Churchill et al., *Strategies That Enhance Community Relations in Tenant-Based Section 8 Programs*, 33.

50. In August 1996 I appeared on the "Ed Graham Show" on MSNBC, on the occasion of the demolition of a public housing project in Newark. When I suggested that tenant-based assistance was the most effective replacement housing for project residents, Mr. Graham's first response was that tenant-based assistance wouldn't happen because white households would object to helping minority households move into their neighborhoods.

51. Rand Corporation, *First Annual Report of the Housing Assistance Supply Experiment* (Santa Monica, CA: Rand Corporation, 1974), 26–27. See also Ira S. Lowry, ed., *The Design of the Housing Assistance Supply Experiment* (Santa Monica, CA: Rand Corporation, 1980), 24–25.

52. Rand Corporation, *Fifth Annual Report of the Housing Assistance Supply Experiment* (Santa Monica, CA: Rand Corporation, 1979), 71–73, and Lowry, *Design of the Housing Assistance Supply Experiment*, 24–25.

53. Larry Ozanne and James Zais, "Communitywide Effects of Housing Allowances," in *Housing Vouchers for the Poor*, ed. Raymond J. Struyk and Marc Bendick, Jr. (Washington, DC: Urban Institute Press, 1981), 227–30.

54. James E. Wallace et al., *Participation and Benefits in the Urban Section 8 Program: New Construction and Existing Housing* (Cambridge, MA: Abt Associates, Inc., 1981), 243–48. There were too few Hispanic households to provide a basis for any conclusions.

55. Orr et al., *Moving to Opportunity Interim Impacts Evaluation*, 36–37; Sanbonmatsu et al., *Moving to Opportunity Final Impacts Evaluation*, 9–10, 60.

56. Gregory Mills et al., *Effects of Housing Vouchers on Welfare Families* (Washington, DC: U.S. Department of Housing and Urban Development, 2006), 68–71.

57. Feins and Patterson, "Geographic Mobility," 8–10.

58. Stephen D. Kennedy and Meryl Finkel, *Section 8 Voucher and Rental Certificate Utilization Study* (Cambridge, MA: Abt Associates, Inc., 1994), 27–28.

59. Arnold R. Hirsch, "Massive Resistance in the Urban North: Trumbull Park, Chicago, 1953–1966," *Journal of American History* 82 (September 1995): 522–50.

60. Wallace et al., *Participation and Benefits in the Urban Section 8 Program*, 121–28.

61. Cummings and DiPasquale, "The Low-Income Housing Tax Credit," 268.

62. Buron et al., *Assessment of the Economic and Social Characteristics of LIHTC Residents and Neighborhoods*, 4–17.

63. Climaco et al., *Updating the Low-Income Housing Tax Credit (LIHTC) Database: Projects Placed in Service Through 2006*, exhibit 4-15.

64. Holin et al., *Interim Assessment of HOPE VI*, 30–31, 35–37.

65. Buron et al., *Assessment of the HOPE VI Resident Tracking Study*, 70.

66. Ibid., 82.

67. Zielenbach, "Assessing Economic Change in HOPE VI Neighborhoods," 632.

68. Orr et al., *Moving to Opportunity Interim Impacts Evaluation*, iv–v.

69. Martin D. Abravanel et al., *Housing Agency Responses to Federal Deregulation: An Assessment of HUD's "Moving to Work" Demonstration* (Washington, DC: Urban Institute, 2004), chap. 7, http://www.hud.gov/offices/pih/programs/ph/mtw/eval report.pdf.

70. U.S. Department of Housing and Urban Development, Office of Policy Development and Research, *Project Self-Sufficiency: An Interim Report on Progress and Performance*, Washington, DC, December 1987, chap. 11.

71. U.S. Department of Housing and Urban Development, Office of Policy Development and Research, "Promoting Self-Sufficiency in Public Housing," Urban Policy Brief no. 3, Washington, DC, August 1996.

72. Robert C. Ficke and Andrea Piesse, *Evaluation of the Family Self-Sufficiency Program: Retrospective Analysis, 1996 to 2000* (Rockville, MD: Westat, 2004), ix–xvi, chap. 3. The study was unable to take account of educational differences between program participants and the control group.

73. Abravanel et al., *Housing Agency Responses to Federal Deregulation*, chap. 7.

74. Orr et al., *Moving to Opportunity Interim Impacts Evaluation*, viii–xv; Sanbonmatsu et al., *Moving to Opportunity Final Impacts Evaluation*, xxvi–xxvii. The quotation is on p. xxvi.

75. Mills, *Effects of Housing Vouchers on Welfare Families*, chap. 4, especially 98–99.

76. Edgar Olsen et al., "The Effects of Different Types of Housing Assistance on Earnings and Employment," *Cityscape* 8, no. 2 (2005): 63–87.

77. Scott Susin, "Longitudinal Outcomes of Subsidized Housing Recipients in Matched Survey and Administrative Data," *Cityscape* 8, no. 2 (2005): 189–218.

78. Janet Currie and Aaron Yelowitz, "Are Public Housing Projects Good for Kids?" *Journal of Public Economics* 75, no. 1 (January 2000): 99–124.

79. Calculated from tables 2-8 and 5-8 in U.S. Department of Housing and Urban Development, Office of Policy Development and Research, *Characteristics of HUD-Assisted Renters and Their Units in 1993*, Washington, DC, May 1997.

80. Sandra J. Newman and Joseph M. Harkness, "The Long-Term Effects of Public Housing on Self-Sufficiency," *Journal of Policy Analysis and Management* 21 (Winter 2002): 21–43.

81. Orr et al., *Moving to Opportunity Interim Impacts Evaluation*, 75–84; Sanbonmatsu et al., *Moving to Opportunity Final Impacts Evaluation*, 80–112.

82. Orr et al., *Moving to Opportunity Interim Impacts Evaluation*, 75–84; Sanbonmatsu et al., *Moving to Opportunity Final Impacts Evaluation*, 113–137. In both evaluations, results were similar for individuals in families that were offered a particular kind of voucher, either the standard voucher that could be used anywhere or the

experimental voucher requiring a move to a low-poverty area, regardless of whether the family did or did not use the voucher.

83. Daniel M. Wilner et al., *The Housing Environment and Family Life* (Baltimore: Johns Hopkins University, 1962); Stanislav V. Karl, "Effects of Housing on Mental and Physical Health," in National Housing Policy Review, *Housing in the Seventies: Working Papers* (Washington, DC: U.S. Department of Housing and Urban Development, 1976), I: 286–304.

84. Sanbonmatsu et al., *Moving to Opportunity Final Impacts Evaluation,* 186–211.

85. Orr et al., *Moving to Opportunity Interim Impacts Evaluation,* 94–98.

86. Michael Lens et al., "Do Vouchers Help Low-Income Households Live in Safer Neighborhoods? Evidence on the Housing Choice Voucher Program," *Cityscape* 13, No. 3 (2011), 135–159.

87. Meagan Cahill, "Using the Weighted Displacement Quotient to Explore Crime Displacement from Public Housing Redevelopment Sites," *Cityscape* 13, No. 3 (2011), 103–134.

Chapter 7: The Voucher/Production Debate: Program Costs

1. U.S. General Accounting Office, *Federal Housing Assistance: Comparing the Characteristics and Costs of Housing Programs,* GAO-02-76, Washington, DC, January 2002. An earlier version of this report is also relevant: U.S. General Accounting Office, *Federal Housing Programs: What They Cost and What They Provide,* GAO-01-901R, Washington, DC, July 18, 2001. This version is in the form of a letter to the relevant congressional committees and a PowerPoint presentation.

2. HOME is excluded because "HOME grants are often used in conjunction with other housing programs." U.S. General Accounting Office, *Federal Housing Assistance,* 7.

3. Millennial Housing Commission, *Meeting Our Nation's Housing Challenges: Report of the Bipartisan Millennial Housing Commission Appointed by the Congress of the United States* (Washington, DC: U.S. Government Printing Office, 2002). The capital grant recommendation is on p. 37; the recommendation to replace some public housing projects is on pp. 46–47; it is part of a broader recommendation to "transform and revitalize the public housing program," and its main thrust is rehabilitating and managing the existing public housing inventory (43–49). There is also a recommendation to expand HOPE VI (46), which appears to be different from the recommendation to replace some public housing projects.

4. Edgar O. Olsen, "The Cost-Effectiveness of Alternative Methods of Delivering Housing Subsidies" (Working Paper 351, Thomas Jefferson Center for Political Economy, University of Virginia, Charlottesville, December 2000), http://www.virginia.edu/economics/papers/olsen/costeffectivenesssurvey.pdf.

5. Based on my experience as senior policy official responsible for Section 202 and Section 811 in 2001–2005, I believe that these programs have relatively large

administrative staffing requirements, because they are competitive grant programs, and each individual proposal must be evaluated and ranked against all others in its market area. HOPE VI is also a competitive program, with a smaller number of larger projects to be evaluated. The same is true for the LIHTC, but most of the costs are incurred at the state level. The HUD staff managing the voucher program is relatively small.

6. U.S. General Accounting Office, *Federal Housing Assistance*, 24n22. The HUD estimate is based on studies of capital needs for both public housing and privately owned subsidized projects, which are discussed in the next section of this chapter. The HUD recommendation of $1,000 per unit per year appears in the agency comments on p. 84 of the GAO report.

7. The GAO report makes no mention of these costs, and I am not aware of any data on them.

8. Jean L. Cummings and Denise DiPasquale, "The Low-Income Housing Credit: An Analysis of the First Ten Years," *Housing Policy Debate* 10, no. 2 (1999): 251–307.

9. Mary Jo Holin et al., *Interim Assessment of the HOPE VI Program Cross-Site Report* (Cambridge, MA: Abt Associates, Inc., 2003).

10. U.S. General Accounting Office, *Federal Housing Assistance*, 48; Holin et al., *Interim Assessment of HOPE VI*, 16–28.

11. U.S. General Accounting Office, *Federal Housing Assistance*, 45–46.

12. James E. Wallace et al., *Participation and Benefits in the Urban Section 8 Program: New Construction, Existing Housing* (Cambridge, MA: Abt Associates, Inc., 1981).

13. Ibid., 226, citing an earlier Abt study by Stephen K. Mayo et al., *Housing Allowances and Other Rental Housing Assistance Programs—A Comparison Based on the Housing Allowance Demand Experiment, Part 2: Costs and Efficiency* (Cambridge, MA: Abt Associates, Inc., 1979; rev. 1980), 122.

14. Mayo et al., *Housing Allowances and Other Rental Housing Assistance Programs*, 137.

15. James E. Wallace et al., *Assessment of the HUD-Insured Multifamily Housing Stock: Final Report, vol 1, Current Status of HUD-Insured (or Held) Multifamily Rental Housing* (Washington, DC: U.S. Department of Housing and Urban Development, Office of Policy Development and Research, 1993), exhibit 2.13; and Meryl Finkel et al., *Status of HUD-Insured (or Held) Multifamily Rental Housing in 1995: Final Report* (Washington, DC: U.S. Department of Housing and Urban Development, Office of Policy Development and Research, 1999). exhibit 3.3.

16. U.S. Department of Housing and Urban Development, Chief Financial Officer, Congressional Justifications for 2012 Estimates, "Public and Indian Housing: Tenant-Based Rental Assistance," http://portal.hud.gov/hudportal/documents/huddoc?id=PH_Opera_fund_2012.pdf, H-1—H-25.

17. This is the average across "all reported cities" (about 400) for a two-bedroom apartment in an elevator building, which seems closest to the traditional public housing program in terms of unit size, structure type, and location. See U.S. Department of Housing and Urban Development, Office of Public and Indian Housing, "2011 Unit

Total Development Cost (TDC) Limits," http://portal.hud.gov/hudportal/documents/huddoc?id=DOC_8094.pdf, an attachment to PIH notice 2010-20 (HA), issued May 24, 2010.The year 1995 was about the last time the estimate would have been used for actual public housing construction, but development costs have been updated in most years since then.

18. U.S. Department of Housing and Urban Development, Chief Financial Officer, Congressional Justifications for 2012 Estimates, "Public and Indian Housing: Public Housing Operating Fund" http://portal.hud.gov/hudportal/documents/huddoc?id=PH_Opera_fund_2012.pdf, J-1—J-16.

19. Abt Associates, Inc., *Capital Needs in the Public Housing Program: Revised Final Report* (Cambridge, MA: Abt Associates, Inc., 2010), 18–21.

20. Ibid.

21. Ibid., 22–24.

22. Ibid., 34–37. Including expenditures for lead-paint abatement, energy efficiency, and modifications for accessibility for the disabled, the total is $25.6 billion.

23. A further complication results from the administration's efforts to shift from a system of paying according to the number of leased units to a "budget-based" system with incentives for PHAs to maximize the number of assisted households (and thus reduce the payment per household). I am indebted to Barbara Sard and Douglas Rice of the Center for Budget and Policy Priorities for information on the implications of the change in the accounting structure.

24. John W. Cox, "Statement on the Impacts of Late Housing Assistance Payments on Tenants and Owners in the Project-Based Rental Assistance Program," U.S. House of Representatives, Committee on Financial Services, Subcommittee on Housing and Community Opportunity, October 17, 2007, http://financialservices.house.gov/hearing110/ htcox101707.pdf. Cox was chief financial officer at HUD at the time.

25. Lawrence J. Lipton, "Testimony on Late Payments Under Section 8 Project-Based Contracts," U.S. House of Representatives, Committee on Financial Services, Subcommittee on Housing and Community Opportunity, October 17, 2007, http://financialservices.house.gov/hearing110/htlipton101707.pdf.; Douglas Rice and Barbara Sard, "Decade of Neglect Has Weakened Federal Low-Income Housing Programs: New Resources Required to Meet Growing Needs," Center for Budget and Policy Priorities, Washington, DC, February 24, 2009, table 1, http://www.cbpp.org/files/2-24-09hous.pdf.

26. Finkel et al., *Status of HUD-Insured Multifamily Rental Housing in 1995*. Finkel and her coauthors were analysts at Abt Associates, which conducted the study under contract to HUD.

27. Ibid., exhibit 3-1. The 1995 figures were $10,100 for mean revenue, $7,400 for federal subsidies, and $2,600 for tenant rent payments. The earlier Abt study had lower figures for revenue and subsidies, and higher for rent payments. See Wallace et al., *Assessment of the HUD-Insured Multifamily Housing Stock, Final Report*, exhibit 2.11.

28. I have calculated this ratio from data in Larry Hodes, unpublished HUD memorandum, December 22, 1993, 17. This memorandum has been made public. The sample of projects used for the analysis in the Hodes memorandum is the sample employed in the earlier Abt study, that is, Wallace et al., *Assessment of the HUD-Insured Multifamily Housing Stock.*

29. Finkel et al., *Status of HUD-Insured Multifamily Rental Housing in 1995*, exhibits 2-2, 2-7. The 1995 figures were $3,200 for backlog and $1,100 for accrual. The earlier study calculated substantially smaller costs for backlog (about one-third as much) and modestly smaller accrual costs. See Wallace et al., *Assessment of the HUD-Insured Multifamily Housing Stock*, 2-11–2-22.

30. Ernst & Young Kenneth Leventhal Real Estate Group, "E&Y Survey: Results" (handout, May 2, 1996), exhibit V. The number in the text combines the Ernst & Young categories of immediate deferred maintenance, short-term capital backlog, replacement and cash reserves (an offset), and long-term capital backlog. The first three categories are the amounts needed so the project can obtain uninsured mortgage financing; the long-term backlog is also needed to replace the used life of components of the property (20). The cost is divided almost in half between the first three categories and the long-term backlog.

31. Unpublished tabulations by David A. Vandenbroucke, reported in Edgar O. Olsen, "Getting More from Low-Income Housing Assistance," available at http://www.brookings.edu/research/papers/2008/09/low-income-housing-olsen, 13.

32. Vandenbroucke did not distinguish between Section 236 and Section 8 projects in his calculations.

33. U.S. Government Accountability Office, *Rental Housing Assistance: Policy Decisions and Market Factors Explain Changes in the Costs of the Section 8 Programs*, GAO-06-405, Washington, DC, April 2006. The analysis of the contribution of these factors appears on pp. 31–37. GAO actually cites "changes in market rents" as the first factor (31), but uses the FMR as the market rent, even though the FMR increased much more rapidly than the rent component of the CPI. With respect to the third factor, average household income increased by 14.9 percent over the period, compared to 10.5 percent for voucher recipients.

34. U.S. Department of Housing and Urban Development, "24 CFR Part 888—Fair Market Rents for Fiscal Year 2001 for Certain Areas: Proposed Rule," *Federal Register*, October 6, 2000, p. 60084.

35. U.S. Department of Housing and Urban Development, Office of Policy Development and Research, unpublished tabulation.

36. U.S. Government Accountability Office, *Rental Housing Assistance: Policy Decisions and Market Factors*, 60–64.

37. President's Commission on Housing, *The Report of the President's Commission on Housing*, Washington, DC, April 1982, chap. 3. The commission further reported that 85 percent of public housing units had annual costs below the FMR (43). This was not the most appropriate comparison, for several reasons. The commission included

public housing debt service but excluded modernization, and used FMRs to measure the cost of the certificate program, omitting the tenant rent contribution. Although the 85 percent number is subject to question, however, the qualitative conclusion was probably valid.

38. John C. Weicher, *Privatizing Subsidized Housing* (Washington, DC: AEI Press, 1997), 16.

Chapter 8: The Voucher/Production Debate: Program Efficiency

1. This conceptual framework and the measurement of program efficiency date back to the National Housing Policy Review of the early 1970s. See U.S. Department of Housing and Urban Development, *Housing in the Seventies: A Report of the National Housing Policy Review* (Washington, DC: U.S. Government Printing Office, 1974), chap. 4.

2. Richard K. Green and Stephen Malpezzi, *A Primer on U.S. Housing Markets and Housing Policy* (Washington, DC: Urban Institute Press, 2003), 98. The ellipses reflect the omission of "high administrative costs," which is properly a component of administrative efficiency.

3. Edgar O. Olsen and David H. Barton, "The Benefits and Costs of Public Housing in New York City," *Journal of Public Economics* 20 (April 1983): 299–332.

4. For more information, see U.S. Census Bureau, "New York City Housing and Vacancy Survey," http://www.census.gov/hhes/www/housing/nychvs/nychvs.html.

5. U.S. Department of Housing and Urban Development, *Housing in the Seventies*, chap. 4. Many of the methodological specifics of the analyses were not fully discussed in the report but appeared in a technical appendix that was never published. Olsen conducted the analysis of public housing, and he describes his methodology in some detail in Edgar O. Olsen, "The Cost-Effectiveness of Alternative Methods of Delivering Housing Subsidies" (Working Paper No. 351, University of Virginia, Charlottesville, December 2000), 4–17, http://www.virginia.edu/economics/papers/olsen/costeffectivenesssurvey.pdf.

6. Frank De Leeuw and Sam H. Leaman, "The Section 23 Leasing Program," in U.S. Congress, Joint Economic Committee, *The Economics of Federal Subsidy Programs, Part 5—Housing Subsidies* (Washington, DC: U.S. Government Printing Office, 1972), 642–59.

7. Stephen K. Mayo et al., *Housing Allowances and Other Rental Assistance Programs—A Comparison Based on the Housing Allowance Demand Experiment, Part 2, Costs and Efficiency* (Cambridge, MA: Abt Associates, Inc., 1980). As the title suggests, these cities were selected because they were two of the major sites for the Experimental Housing Allowance program; some 2,400 households in each city were given vouchers under various formulas, and information about their housing choices was collected and analyzed. Analysis of the other programs in these cities contributed to understanding the effectiveness of the voucher program.

8. Ibid., 76–82, 142–43.

9. James E. Wallace et al., *Participation and Benefits in the Urban Section 8 Program: New Construction and Existing Housing* (Cambridge, MA: Abt Associates, Inc., 1981).

10. The dollar figures are taken from table 7-3. The market value of an assisted housing unit was calculated from two alternative hedonic indices; I have used the values derived from the Housing Management Survey conducted by Abt, which identified households that would receive assistance before they moved into their assisted unit, and which collected detailed information on the attributes and the quality of the original unsubsidized unit and the rent. This is the measure most often cited in the Abt study; see for example, Wallace et al., *Participation and Benefits in the Urban Section 8 Program*, executive summary, especially S-10–S-14. The alternative indices were based on the AHS; the results were similar.

11. Ibid., S-14.

12. Mereille L. Leger and Stephen D. Kennedy, *Final Comprehensive Report of the Freestanding Housing Voucher Demonstration* (Cambridge, MA: Abt Associates, Inc., 1990), 137–49.

13. See John C. Weicher, "The Voucher/Production Debate," in *Building Foundations: Housing and Federal Policy*, ed. Denise DiPasquale and Langley C. Keyes (Philadelphia: University of Pennsylvania Press, 1990), 263–92, especially 286–88. In my judgment, the controversy was purely political. By the early 1980s, both Republican and Democratic administrations had accepted the certificate program as a major subsidy program; the voucher, enacted in 1983 as a demonstration, had been proposed by a Republican administration and did not become an accepted program among Democrats until the Clinton administration.

14. Gregory S. Burge, "Do Tenants Capture the Benefits from the Low-Income Housing Tax Credit Program?" *Real Estate Economics* 39, no. 1(Spring 2011): 71-96.

15. For analyses using program data, see Michael P. Murray, "The Distribution of Tenant Benefits in Public Housing," *Econometrica* 43, no. 4 (July 1975): 771–88; Jarjisu Sa-Aadu, "Alternative Estimates of Direct Tenant Benefit and Consumption Inefficiencies from the Section 8 New Construction Program," *Land Economics* 60, no. 2 (May 1984): 189–201; Richard B. Clemmer, "Measuring Welfare Effects of In-Kind Transfers," *Journal of Urban Economics* 15, no. 1 (January 1984): 46–65; and Robert M. Schwab, "The Benefits of In-Kind Government Programs," *Journal of Public Economics* 27, no. 2 (1985), 195–210. For an analysis using survey data on renters, see Olsen and Barton, "Benefits and Costs of Public Housing in New York City."

16. A number of these studies calculated more than one measure of efficiency, using different statistical techniques; the table includes the result preferred by the author of the study. Clemmer, "Measuring Welfare Effects of In-Kind Transfers," reports four measures, ranging from .67 to .92; Sa-Aadu, "Alternative Estimates of Direct Tenant Benefit and Consumption Inefficiences," reports two, .62 and .67; Murray, "Distribution of Tenant Benefits," reports two, .81 and .84; Schwab, "Benefits of In-Kind Programs," reports two, .63 and .77.

17. E.g., Olsen and Barton, "Benefits and Costs of Public Housing in New York City," table 9; Murray, "Distribution of Tenant Benefits," table 5; Sa-Aadu, "Alternative Estimates of Direct Tenant Benefit and Consumption Inefficiences," table 2.

18. The normal housing expenditure is calculated from hedonic analysis of rent and housing characteristics for unsubsidized lower-income households, and from the rent paid and the characteristics of the housing occupied by program participants before they received assistance. For a detailed description, see Wallace et al., *Participation and Benefits in the Urban Section 8 Program*, 1:212–14, 325–27.

Chapter 9: Is There Enough Housing?

1. U.S. Department of Housing and Urban Development, Office of Policy Development and Research, *Characteristics of HUD-Assisted Households and Their Units in 2003*, Washington, DC, May 2008; the earlier reports in this series, for 1989, 1991, and 1993, document the same phenomenon.

2. U.S. Department of Housing and Urban Development, Office of Policy Development and Research, *The Location of Worst Case Needs in the Late 1980s: A Report to Congress*, Washington, DC, December 1992, 29–33; U.S. Department of Housing and Urban Development, Office of Policy Development and Research, *Worst Case Needs for Housing Assistance in the United States in 1990 and 1991: A Report to Congress*, Washington, DC, June 1994, 16–19.

3. The published AHS reports do not cross-tabulate housing quality by assistance status for poor households.

4. HUD's 2005 worst-case needs report does not tabulate the actual number of vacancies below the local FMRs. The report does state that there were 21.997 million units with rents below the local FMRs as of 2003. See U.S. Department of Housing and Urban Development, Office of Policy Development and Research, *Affordable Housing Needs: A Report to Congress on the Significant Need for Housing*, Washington, DC, December 2005, 43, exhibit 4-6. This figure is close to the 21.432 million below the national average FMR of $735, which suggests that the national average calculations in table 9-2 are reasonable approximations. The 1996 worst-case needs report, however, states a vacancy rate for units renting for less than the local FMRs of 7.4 percent in 1993. U.S. Department of Housing and Urban Development Office of Policy Development and Research, *Rental Housing Assistance at a Crossroads: A Report to Congress on Worst Case Housing Needs*, Washington, DC, March 1996, 44, table 7. This figure is markedly below the 9.2 percent rate calculated from the national average FMR of $555. At the lower vacancy rate, there were 1.542 million vacant units renting for less than the FMR, compared to 470,000 very low-income renters living in severely inadequate housing. If these households received tenant-based assistance, the resulting vacancy rate would have been 5.1 percent, a somewhat tight market but not an impossibly tight one.

5. U.S. Department of Housing and Urban Development, Office of Policy Development and Research, *The Location of Worst Case Needs in the Late 1980s.*

6. The precise national numbers are affected by a change in weights for the individual observations in the AHS after the 1990 decennial census. Using weights derived from the 1980 census, the number of unassisted very low-income renters living in severely inadequate housing was 690,000; using weights derived from the 1990 Census, the number was 716,000. U.S. Department of Housing and Urban Development, Office of Policy Development and Research, *Priority Housing Problems and "Worst Case" Needs in 1989: A Report to Congress*, June 1991, table 5; and U.S. Department of Housing and Urban Development, Office of Policy Development and Research, *Rental Housing Assistance at a Crossroads*, table A-5. There are similar inconsistencies in the vacancy rates. The first report indicates a vacancy rate of 6.6 percent among units with rents below the local FMR in 1989, based on the AHS; the third report indicates a vacancy rate of 9 percent among units affordable to very low-income households, based on the 1990 census. See U.S. Department of Housing and Urban Development, Office of Policy Development and Research, *Priority Housing Problems and "Worst Case" Needs in 1989*, table 8; and U.S. Department of Housing and Urban Development, Office of Policy Development and Research, *Worst Case Needs for Housing Assistance in the United States in 1990 and 1991*, table 8.

7. Calculated from data in U.S. Department of Housing and Urban Development, Office of Policy Development and Research, *Location of Worst Case Needs in the Late 1980s*, table 5, table 9.

8. The Census Bureau as part of the Housing Vacancy Survey publishes annual rental vacancy rates. Data since 1986 are available at U.S. Census Bureau, "Housing Vacancies and Homeownership," table 6 (for 2005 to 2010), table 6a (for earlier years), http://www.census.gov/hhes/www/housing/hvs/annual10/ann10ind.html.

Conclusion

1. Millennial Housing Commission, *Meeting Our Nation's Housing Challenges: Report of the Bipartisan Millennial Housing Commission Appointed by the Congress of the United States* (Washington, DC: U.S. Government Printing Office, 2002), 37–39. The quotation is on p. 38.

2. Tax expenditures generally are described in Office of Management and Budget, *Analytical Perspectives, Budget of the United States Government, Fiscal Year 2012*, Washington, DC, 2011, chap. 17, and in similar sections of previous budgets.

3. See for example William G. Grigsby and Steven C. Bourassa, "Section 8: The Time for Fundamental Program Change?" *Housing Policy Debate* 15, no. 4 (2004): 805–34, which asserts that "the portion of the stock that is estimated to be seriously inadequate has dropped to such a low figure that the [Millennial Housing

Commission's] recent report largely ignores housing-quality issues. . . . The physical quality of housing has improved dramatically" (807–8). See also Jill Khadduri and Charles Wilkins, "Designing Subsidized Rental Housing Programs: What Have We Learned?" (unpublished paper prepared for the Millennial Housing Commission, 2002), which states that "very few [households] live in substandard housing units" (3).

4. These four rationales appear in Grigsby and Bourassa, "Section 8," 829; and Khadduri and Wilkins, "Designing Subsidized Rental Programs," 7. Grigsby and Bourassa add "increas[ing] homeownership," which is outside the scope of this book. I note here that homeownership is being addressed through the use of vouchers to make monthly mortgage payments and even down payments for home purchase, and that homeownership has in the past proven difficult and expensive to promote through subsidized production programs, notably Section 235.

5. Khadduri and Wilkins, "Designing Subsidized Rental Programs," 7.

6. See for example HUD's 2008 Congressional Budget Justifications, which proposed to remove the cap on the number of households that can be served; to base administrative fees—the income of the PHAs—on the number of households served rather than the total dollar amount of assistance; and to reduce the fund allocation in future years if PHAs fail to spend all their funds in a given year. These incentives all serve to encourage PHAs to serve more households above the extremely low-income category. U.S. Department of Housing and Urban Development, Chief Financial Officer, "Public and Indian Housing: Tenant-Based Rental Assistance," Congressional Justifications for 2008 Estimates, C-2, http:// www.hud.gov/offices/cfo/reports/2008/cjs/part1/pih/tbdassistance.pdf. Similar though somewhat less specific language also appears in the FY2009 congressional justifications; see U.S. Department of Housing and Urban Development, Chief Financial Officer, "Public and Indian Housing: Tenant-Based Rental Assistance," Congressional Justifications for 2009 Estimates, C1–C2, http://www.hud.gov/offices/cfo/reports/2009/cjs/pih1.pdf.

7. For a summary of the congressional debate on income limitations, see Milton P. Semer et al., "A Review of Federal Subsidized Housing Programs," in National Housing Policy Review, Housing in the Seventies: Working Papers (Washington, DC: U.S. Department of Housing and Urban Development, 1976), 1:101–3.

8. James E. Wallace et al., Participation and Benefits in the Urban Section 8 Program: New Construction and Existing Housing (Cambridge, MA: Abt Associates Inc., 1981); Lisa Sanbonmatsu et al., Moving to Opportunity for Fair Housing Demonstration Program: Final Impacts Evaluation (Washington, DC: U.S. Department of Housing and Urban Development, Office of Policy Development and Research, 2011). These calculations exclude executive summaries, reference lists, etc.

9. Brookings Institution Center on Urban and Metropolitan Policy and the Urban Institute, Rethinking Local Affordable Housing Strategies: Lessons from 70 Years of Policy and Practice (Washington, DC: Brookings Institution and Urban Institute, 2003). In addition to Section 202 and Section 811, the report cited Housing for Persons with AIDS (HOPWA), which lies outside the scope of this study.

10. Sanbonmatsu et al., *Moving to Opportunity Final Impacts Evaluation;* Gregory Mills et al., *Effects of Housing Vouchers on Welfare Families* (Washington, DC: U.S. Department of Housing and Urban Development, 2006).

11. Deborah J. Devine et al., *Housing Choice Voucher Location Patterns: Implications for Participant and Neighborhood Welfare* (Washington, DC: U.S. Department of Housing and Urban Development, Office of Policy Development and Research, 2003). Although this analysis was published almost a year before the Brookings program comparison, it is not mentioned there. In light of the HUD study, the Brookings conclusion that vouchers only "possibly" promote economic diversity "if recipients can find units in diverse neighborhoods" seems too lukewarm.

12. Robert C. Ficke and Andrea Piesse, *Evaluation of the Family Self-Sufficiency Program: Retrospective Analysis, 1996 to 2000* (Rockville, MD: Westat, 2004).

References

Abravanel, Martin D., et al. *Housing Agency Responses to Federal Deregulation: An Assessment of HUD's "Moving to Work" Demonstration*. Washington, DC: Urban Institute, 2004. http://www.hud.gov/offices/pih/programs/ph/mtw/evalreport.pdf.

Abt Associates, Inc. *Capital Needs in the Public Housing Program: Revised Final Report*. Cambridge, MA: Abt Associates, Inc., 2010.

———. *Development and Analysis of the National Low-Income Housing Tax Credit Database*. July 1996. http://www.huduser.org/Datasets/LIHTC/report.pdf.

———. "Updating the National Low-Income Housing Tax Credit Database: Projects Placed in Service Through 2007." Washington, DC: U.S. Department of Housing and Urban Development, 2010. http://www.huduser.org/Datasets/lihtc/tables9507.pdf

Achtenberg, Emily. "Stemming the Tide: A Handbook on Preserving Multifamily Subsidized Housing." Local Issues Support Corporation, September 2002. Available at http://www.lisc.org/content/publications/detail/893/.

Achtenberg, Emily Paradise. "Subsidized Housing at Risk: The Social Costs of Private Ownership," in *Housing Issues of the 1990s*, edited by Sara Rosenberry and Chester Hartman, 227–67. New York: Praeger, 1989.

Anas, Alex, and Richard J. Arnott. "Dynamic Housing Market Equilibrium with Taste Heterogeneity, Idiosyncratic Perfect Foresight, and Stock Conversions." *Journal of Housing Economics* 1 (March 1991): 2–32.

Bradbury, Katharine L., and Anthony Downs, eds. *Do Housing Allowances Work?* Washington, DC: Brookings Institution, 1981.

Braid, Ralph. "The Effects of Government Housing Policies in a Vintage Housing Model." *Journal of Urban Economics* 16, no. 3 (November 1984): 272–96.

Brookings Institution Center on Urban and Metropolitan Policy and the Urban Institute. *Rethinking Local Affordable Housing Strategies: Lessons from 70 Years of Policy and Practice*. Washington, DC: Brookings Institution and Urban Institute, 2003.

Burge, Gregory S. "Do Tenants Capture the Benefits from the Low-Income Housing Tax Credit Program?" *Real Estate Economics* 39, no. 1(Spring 2011): 71-96.

Buron, Larry, et al. *Assessment of the Economic and Social Characteristics of LIHTC Residents and Neighborhoods*. Cambridge, MA: Abt Associates, Inc., 2000.

————. *The HOPE VI Resident Tracking Study: A Snapshot of the Current Living Situation of Original Residents from Eight Sites*. Washington, DC: Abt Associates, Inc., and Urban Institute, 2002.

Cahill, Meagan. "Using the Weighted Displacement Quotient to Explore Crime Displacement from Public Housing Redevelopment Sites." *Cityscape* 13, No. 3(2011): 103–134.

Cam, Gilbert A. "United States Government Activity in Low-Cost Housing, 1932–1938." *Journal of Political Economy* 47 (June 1939): 357–78.

Carter, William H., Michael H. Schill, and Susan M. Wachter. "Polarisation, Public Housing, and Racial Minorities in U.S. Cities." *Urban Studies* 35 (October 1998): 1889–1911.

Churchill, Sarah, et al. *Strategies That Enhance Community Relations in Tenant-Based Section 8 Programs*. Washington, DC: U.S. Department of Housing and Urban Development, Office of Policy Development and Research, 2001.

Cisneros, Henry G., and Lara Engdahl, eds. *From Despair to Hope: HOPE VI and the New Promise of Public Housing in America's Cities*. Washington, DC: Brookings Institution Press, 2009.

Clemmer, Richard B. "Measuring Welfare Effects of In-Kind Transfers." *Journal of Urban Economics* 15, no. 1 (January 1984): 46–65.

————, and John Simonson. "Trends in Substandard American Housing, 1940–1980." *AREUEA Journal* 10 (Winter 1983): 442–64.

Climaco, Carissa, et al., *Updating the Low-Income Housing Tax Credit (LIHTC) Database: Projects Placed in Service Through 2006*. Washington, DC: U. S. Department of Housing and Urban Development, 2009.

Comey, Jennifer. "An Improved Living Environment? Housing Quality Outcomes for HOPE VI Relocatees." Urban Institute, Metropolitan Housing and Communities Center, Brief No. 2, September 2004.

Committee to Evaluate the Research Plan of the Department of Housing and Urban Development. *Rebuilding the Research Capacity at HUD*. Washington, DC: National Academies Press, 2008.

Congressional Budget Office. *The Challenges Facing Federal Rental Assistance Programs*. Washington, DC, December 1994.

————. "Measures of Housing Need: Findings from the Annual Housing Survey." In U.S. House of Representatives, Committee on Banking and Urban Affairs. Subcommittee on Housing and Community Development, Task Force on Assisted Housing, *Hearings before the Subcommittee on Housing and Community Development of the Committee on Banking, Finance, and Urban Affairs, House of Representatives, Ninety-Fifth Congress, Second Session*. 1570–90. Washington, DC, 1979.

————. "The Potential Loss of Assisted Housing Units as Certain Mortgage-Interest Subsidy Programs Mature." Staff working paper, March 1987.

————. "Responses to Senator Allard's Questions about the 1999 Actuarial Review of the Federal Housing Administration's Mutual Mortgage Insurance Fund." October 23, 2000. http://www.cbo.gov/doc.cfm?index=2666&type=0.

Cox, John W. "Statement on the Impacts of Late Housing Assistance Payments on Tenants and Owners in the Project-Based Rental Assistance Program." U.S. House of Representatives, Committee on Financial Services, Subcommittee on Housing and Community Opportunity, October 17, 2007. http://financialservices.house.gov/hearing110/htcox101707.pdf.

Cronin, Francis J. "Participation in the Experimental Housing Allowance Program." In *Housing Vouchers for the Poor: Lessons from a National Experiment*, edited by Raymond J. Struyk and Marc Bendick, Jr., 79–106. Washington, DC: Urban Institute Press, 1981.

———, and David W. Rasmussen. "Mobility." In *Housing Vouchers for the Poor: Lessons from a National Experiment,* edited by Raymond J. Struyk and Marc Bendick, Jr., 108–10. Washington, DC: Urban Institute Press, 1981.

Crowley, Sheila. "HOPE VI: What Went Wrong." In *From Despair to Hope: HOPE VI and the New Promise of Public Housing in America's Cities*, edited by Henry G. Cisneros and Lara Engdahl, 229–47. Washington, DC: Brookings Institution Press, 2009.

Cummings, Jean L., and Denise DiPasquale. "The Low-Income Housing Tax Credit: An Analysis of the First Ten Years." *Housing Policy Debate* 10, no. 2 (1999): 251–87.

Cummings, Jean L. and Matthew E. Kahn. "Measuring the Consequences of Promoting Inner-City Homeownership." *Journal of Housing Economics* 11, no. 4 (2002): 330–59.

Cunningham, Mary K. "An Improved Living Environment? Relocation Outcomes for HOPE VI Relocatees." Urban Institute, Metropolitan Housing and Communities Center, Brief No. 1, September 2004.

Currie, Janet, and Aaron Yelowitz. "Are Public Housing Projects Good for Kids?" *Journal of Public Economics* 75, no. 1 (January 2000): 99–124.

Davis, Otto A., Charles M. Eastman, and Chan-I Hua. "The Shrinkage in the Stock of Low-Quality Housing in the Central City: An Empirical Study of the U.S. Experience over the Last Ten Years." *Urban Studies* 11, no. 1 (February 1974): 13–26.

De Leeuw, Frank, and Sam H. Leaman. "The Section 23 Leasing Program." In *The Economics of Federal Subsidy Programs, Part 5—Housing Subsidies*, U.S. Congress, Joint Economic Committee, 642–59. Washington, DC: U.S. Government Printing Office, 1972.

Dedman, D. J., et al. "Childhood Housing Conditions and Later Mortality in the Boyd Orr Cohort." *Journal of Epidemiology and Community Health* 55, no. 1 (2001): 10–15.

Devine, Deborah J., et al. *Housing Choice Voucher Location Patterns: Implications for Participants and Neighborhood Welfare*. Washington, DC: U.S. Department of Housing and Urban Development, Office of Policy Development and Research, 2003.

DiPasquale, Denise, and Langley C. Keyes, eds. *Building Foundations: Housing and Federal Policy*. Philadelphia: University of Pennsylvania Press, 1990.

Downs, Anthony. "Comment." In *Urban Problems and Community Development*, edited by Ronald F. Ferguson and William T. Dickens, 466–67. Washington, DC: Brookings Institution Press, 1999.

Dreier, Peter, and David Moberg. "Moving from the 'Hood': The Mixed Success of Integrating Suburbia." *American Prospect*, December 1, 1995. http://www.prospect.org/cs/articles?article=moving_from_the_hood.

Drury, Margaret, et al. *Lower Income Housing Assistance Program (Section 8): Nationwide Evaluation of the Existing Housing Program*. Washington, DC: U.S. Government Printing Office, November 1978.

Econometrica, Inc., and Abt Associates, Inc. *Multifamily Properties: Opting In, Opting Out and Remaining Affordable*. Washington DC: U.S. Department of Housing and Urban Development, Office of Policy Development and Research, 2006.

Ellen, Ingrid Gould, et al. "Building Homes, Reviving Neighborhoods: Spillovers from Subsidized Construction of Owner-Occupied Housing in New York City," *Journal of Housing Research* 12, no. 2 (2001): 185–216.

———. "Does Federally Subsidized Rental Housing Depress Neighborhood Housing Values?" Working Paper 05-03, New York University Furman Center for Real Estate and Social Policy, New York, 2005.

England-Joseph, Judy. "Public Housing: HUD's Takeover of the Chicago Housing Authority." Testimony Before the Subcommittee on Housing and Community Opportunity, Committee on Banking and Financial Services, U.S. House of Representatives, GAO/T-RCED-95-222. June 7, 1995.

Ernst & Young. *Understanding the Dynamics V: Housing Tax Credit Investment Performance*, June 2010.

Ernst & Young Kenneth Leventhal Real Estate Group. "E&Y Survey: Results." Handout, May 2, 1996.

Evans, Gary W. "The Built Environment and Mental Health." *Journal of Urban Health: Bulletin of the New York Academy of Medicine* 80 (December 2003): 536–55.

———, and Elyse Kantrowitz. "Socioeconomic Status and Health: The Potential Role of Environmental Risk Exposure." *Annual Review of Public Health* 23 (2002): 303–331.

Federal Home Loan Mortgage Corporation. "Freddie Mac Reports Fourth Quarter and Full-Year 2008 Financial Results." March 26, 2009. http://www.freddiemac.com/investors/er/.

Federal National Mortgage Association. "Fannie Mae Reports Fourth-Quarter and Full-Year 2008 Results." February 26, 2009. http://www.fanniemae.com/media/pdf/newsreleases/form10k_newsrelease_022609.pdf;jsessionid=0XGE5CSTUI2SRJ2FQSISFGQ.

Feins, Judith D., and Rhiannon Patterson. "Geographic Mobility in the Housing Choice Voucher Program: A Study of Families Entering the Program, 1995–2002." *Cityscape* 8, no. 2 (2005): 21–47.

Fernandez, Manny. "Bias is Seen as Landlords Bar Vouchers." *New York Times*, October 30, 2007.

Fialka, John J. "A Tale of Contrasts: Two Buildings Show How Public Housing Slid into Such a Mess." *Wall Street Journal*, February 28, 1995, A1.

Ficke, Robert C., and Andrea Piesse. *Evaluation of the Family Self-Sufficiency Program: Retrospective Analysis, 1996 to 2000*. Rockville, MD: Westat, 2004.

Finkel, Meryl, and Larry Buron. *Study on Section 8 Voucher Success Rates*. Vol. 1, *Quantitative Study of Success Rates in Metropolitan Areas*. Washington, DC: U.S. Department of Housing and Urban Development, 2001.

Finkel, Meryl, et al. *Costs and Utilization in the Housing Choice Voucher Program*. Washington, DC: U.S. Department of Housing and Urban Development, Office of Policy Development and Research, 2003.

————. *Status of HUD-Insured (or Held) Multifamily Rental Housing in 1995: Final Report*. Washington, DC: U.S. Department of Housing and Urban Development, Office of Policy Development and Research, 1999.

Fisher, Robert Moore. *Twenty Years of Public Housing*. New York: Harper, 1959.

Frangos, Alex. "Losses Stall Affordable Housing Projects." *Wall Street Journal*, March 12, 2008.

Freeman, Lance. "The Impact of Assisted Housing Developments on Concentrated Poverty." *Housing Policy Debate* 14, no. 1 (2003): 103–140.

————, and Hilary Botein. "Subsidized Housing and Neighborhood Impacts: A Theoretical Discussion and Review of the Literature." *Journal of Planning Literature* 16 (February 2002): 359–78.

————, and William Rohe. "Subsidized Housing and Neighborhood Racial Transition: An Empirical Investigation." *Housing Policy Debate* 11, no. 1 (2000): 67–89.

Friedman, Joseph S., and Daniel Weinberg. *The Economics of Housing Vouchers*. Cambridge, MA: Abt Associates, Inc., 1981.

Friedman, Milton. *A Theory of the Consumption Function*. Princeton, NJ: Princeton University Press, 1957.

Galster, George C. *A Review of Existing Research on the Effects of Federally Assisted Housing Programs on Neighboring Residential Property Values*. Washington, DC: National Association of Realtors, National Center for Real Estate Research, 2002.

————, Peter Tatian, and Robin Smith. "The Impact of Neighbors Who Use Section 8 Certificates on Property Values." *Housing Policy Debate* 10, no. 4 (1999): 879–917.

Galster, George C., et al., *Assessing Property Value Impacts of Dispersed Housing Subsidy Programs: Final Report* (Washington, DC: U.S. Department of Housing and Urban Development, 1999).

Glaeser, Edward L., and Joseph Gyourko. *Rethinking Federal Housing Policy: How to Make Housing Plentiful and Affordable*. Washington, DC: AEI Press, 2008.

Goetz, Edward G. "Better Neighborhoods, Better Outcomes? Explaining Relocation Outcomes in Hope VI," *Cityscape* 12, No. 1 (2010): 5-31.

Grassley, Charles. Letter of Senator Charles Grassley to HUD Secretary Shaun Donovan, March 15, 2010, http://grassley.senate.gov/about/upload/2010-03-15-Letter-to-HUD.pdf.

Green, Richard K., and Stephen Malpezzi. *A Primer on U.S. Housing Markets and Housing Policy*. Washington, DC: Urban Institute Press, 2003.

Grigsby, William G., and Steven C. Bourassa. "Section 8: The Time for Fundamental Program Change?" *Housing Policy Debate* 15, no. 4 (2004): 805–34.

Hartman, Chester. *Housing and Social Policy*. Englewood Cliffs, NJ: Prentice Hall, 1975.

Heath, Brad. "Housing Agencies Faulted in Audits to Get $300M of Stimulus." *USA Today*, April 7, 2009. http://www.usatoday.com/news/washington/2009-04-07Stimulus-Housing_N.htm.

Herbert, Christopher, et al. *Study of the Ongoing Affordability of HOME Program Rents*. Cambridge, MA: Abt Associates, Inc., 2001.

Hilton, Richard, et al. *Evaluation of the Mark-to-Market Program*. Washington, DC: U.S. Department of Housing and Urban Development, 2004.

Hirsch, Arnold R. "Massive Resistance in the Urban North: Trumbull Park, Chicago, 1953–1966." *Journal of American History* 82 (September 1995): 522–50.

Hirsch, Werner, and C. K. Law. "Habitability Laws and the Shrinkage of Substandard Rental Housing Stock." *Urban Studies* 16 (February 1979): 19–28.

Hodes, Laurent V. *Capital Needs Assessment: Multifamily Rental Housing with HUD-Insured (or Held) Mortgages*. Washington, DC: U.S. Department of Housing and Urban Development, Office of Policy Development and Research, 1992.

Holin, Mary Jo, et al. *Interim Assessment of the HOPE VI Program Cross-Site Report*. Cambridge, MA: Abt Associates, Inc., 2003.

Husock, Howard. "Let's End Housing Vouchers." *City Journal* 10, no. 4 (Autumn 2000). http://www.city-journal.org/html/10_4_lets_end_housing.html.

ICF Incorporated. *Evaluation of the Low-Income Housing Tax Credit: Final Report*. Washington, DC: U.S. Department of Housing and Urban Development, Office of Policy Development and Research, 1991.

Integrated Financial Engineering, Inc. "An Actuarial Review of the Federal Housing Administration Mutual Mortgage Insurance Fund for Fiscal Year 2008." October 13, 2008.

Jacobs, Jane. *The Death and Life of Great American Cities*. New York: Macmillan, 1961.

Johnson, Jennifer E. H., and Beata A. Bednarz. *Neighborhood Effects of the Low Income Housing Tax Credit Program: Final Report*. Washington, DC: U.S. Department of Housing and Urban Development, 2002.

Kasl, Stanislav V. "Effects of Housing on Mental and Physical Health." In *Housing in the Seventies: Working Papers*, National Housing Policy Review, 1:286–304. Washington, DC: U.S. Department of Housing and Urban Development, 1976.

Kennedy, Stephen D. "What Do We Know About Direct Cash Low Income Housing Assistance?" Paper presented at the American Evaluation Society, Kansas City, MO, October 1986, rev. June 1987.

———, and Meryl Finkel. *Report of First Year Findings for the Freestanding Voucher Demonstration*. Washington, DC: U.S. Department of Housing and Urban Development, 1987.

———. *Section 8 Rental Voucher and Rental Certificate Utilization Study*. Cambridge, MA: Abt Associates, Inc., 1994.

Kennedy, Stephen D., and James E. Wallace. *An Evaluation of Success Rates in Housing Assistance Programs Using the Existing Housing Stock*. Cambridge, MA.: Abt Associates, Inc., 1983.

Khadduri, Jill, "Should the Housing Voucher Program Become a State-Administered Block Grant?" *Housing Policy Debate* 14, no. 3 (2003): 235–69.

———, Kimberly Burnett, and David Rodda. *Targeting Production Subsidies: Literature Review*. Washington, DC: U.S. Department of Housing and Urban Development, Office of Policy Development and Research, 2003.

———, and Marge Martin. "Mixed-Income Housing in the HUD Multifamily Stock." *Cityscape* 3, no. 2 (1997): 33–69.

———, and Charles Wilkins. "Designing Subsidized Rental Housing Programs: What Have We Learned?" Unpublished paper prepared for the Millennial Housing Commission, 2002.

Kondratas, Anna, and John C. Weicher. "Is Homelessness a Problem of Housing Policy?" *Jobs and Capital* 4 (Spring 1995): 37–39.

Kotlowitz, Alex. *There are No Children Here*. New York: Doubleday, 1991.

Lazere, Edward et al., *A Place to Call Home: The Low Income Housing Crisis Continues*. Washington, DC: Center for Budget and Policy Priorities and Low Income Housing Information Service, 1991.

Leger, Mireille L., and Stephen Kennedy. *Final Comprehensive Report of the Freestanding Housing Voucher Demonstration*. Washington, DC: U.S. Department of Housing and Urban Development, 1990.

Lens, Michael et al. "Do Vouchers Help Low-Income Households Live in Safer Neighborhoods? Evidence on the Housing Choice Voucher Program." *Cityscape* 13, No. 3(2011): 135-159.

Lipton, Lawrence J. "Testimony on Late Payments Under Section 8 Project-Based Contracts." U.S. House of Representatives, Committee on Financial Services, Subcommittee on Housing and Community Opportunity, October 17, 2007. http://financialservices.house.gov/hearing110/htlipton101707.pdf.

Lowry, Ira S., ed. *The Design of the Housing Assistance Supply Experiment*. Santa Monica, CA: Rand Corporation, 1980.

———. *Experimenting with Housing Allowances*. Cambridge, MA: Oelgeschlager, Gunn and Hain, 1983.

Lukas, J. Anthony. *Common Ground: A Turbulent Decade in the Lives of Three American Families*. New York: Vintage Books, 1986.

MacMillan, Jean. *Mobility in the Housing Allowance Demand Experiment*. Cambridge, MA: Abt Associates, Inc., 1980.

Malpezzi, Stephen, and Richard K. Green. *A Primer on U.S. Housing Markets and Housing Policy*. Washington, DC: Urban Institute Press, 2003.

Malpezzi, Stephen, and Duncan Maclennan. "The Long-Run Price Elasticity of Supply of New Construction in the United States and the United Kingdom." *Journal of Housing Economics* 10 (September 2001): 278–306.

Malpezzi, Stephen, and Kerry Vandell. "Does the Low-Income Housing Tax Credit Increase the Supply of Housing?" *Journal of Housing Economics* 11, no. 4 (December 2002): 360–80.

Matte, Thomas D., and David E. Jacobs. "Housing and Health: Current Issues and Implications for Research and Progress." *Journal of Urban Health: Bulletin of the New York Academy of Medicine* 77, no. 1 (March 2000): 7–25.

Mayo, Stephen K. "Sources of Inefficiency in Subsidized Housing Programs: A Comparison of U.S. and German Experience." *Journal of Urban Economics* 20, no. 2 (September 1986): 229–49.

———. "Theory and Estimation in the Economics of Housing Demand." *Journal of Urban Economics* 10 (July 1981): 95–116.

———, et al. *Housing Allowances and Other Rental Housing Assistance Programs—A Comparison Based on the Housing Allowance Demand Experiment, Part 2, Costs and Efficiency*. Cambridge, MA: Abt Associates, Inc., 1979; rev. 1980.

McClure, Kirk. "The Low-Income Housing Tax Credit as an Aid to Housing Finance: How Well Has It Worked?" *Housing Policy Debate* 11, no. 1 (2000): 91–114.

———. "Rent Burden in the Housing Choice Voucher Program." *Cityscape* 8, no. 2 (2005): 5–20.

Millennial Housing Commission. *Meeting Our Nation's Housing Challenges: Report of the Bipartisan Millennial Housing Commission Appointed by the Congress of the United States*. Washington, DC: U.S. Government Printing Office, 2002.

Mills, Edwin S. "Housing Policy as a Means to Achieve National Growth Policy." In *Housing in the Seventies: Working Papers*, National Housing Policy Review, 1:202–14. Washington, DC: U.S. Department of Housing and Urban Development, 1976.

Mills, Gregory, et al. *Effects of Housing Vouchers on Welfare Families*. Washington, DC: U.S. Department of Housing and Urban Development, 2006.

Moberg, David. "No Vacancy! Denial, Fear and the Rumor Mill Waged a War Against Moving to Opportunity in Baltimore's Suburbs." *Shelterforce* 79 (January/February 1995). http://www.nhi.org/online/issues/79/novacancy.html.

Murray, Michael P. "The Distribution of Tenant Benefits in Public Housing." *Econometrica* 43, no. 4 (July 1975): 771–88.

———. "Subsidized and Unsubsidized Housing Starts, 1961–1977." *Review of Economics and Statistics* 65, no. 4 (November 1983): 590–97.

———. "Subsidized and Unsubsidized Housing Stocks 1935 to 1987: Crowding Out and Cointegration." *Journal of Real Estate Finance and Economics* 18, no. 1 (January 1999): 107–24.

Muth, Richard F. "The Demand for Non-farm Housing." In *The Demand for Durable Goods*, edited by Arnold C. Harberger, 29–98. Chicago: University of Chicago Press, 1962.

———. "The Rationale for Government Intervention in Housing." In *Housing in the Seventies: Working Papers*, National Housing Policy Review, 1:192–202. Washington, DC: U.S. Department of Housing and Urban Development, 1976.

National Commission on Severely Distressed Public Housing. *Final Report to Congress and the Secretary of Housing and Urban Development.* Washington, DC: U.S. Department of Housing and Urban Development, 1992.

National Commission on Urban Problems (Douglas Commission). *Building the American City.* New York: Praeger, 1969.

National Council of State Housing Finance Agencies. "Housing Credit Utilization Charts." http://www.ncsha.org/resource/housing-credit-utilization-charts.

National Housing Conference. *NHC's First 75 Years.* Washington, DC: National Housing Conference, 2006.

National Housing Policy Review, *Housing in the Seventies: Working Papers.* Washington, DC: U.S. Department of Housing and Urban Development, 1976.

National Housing Trust. *Changes to Project-Based Multifamily Units in HUD's Inventory Between 1995 and 2003.* Washington, DC: National Housing Trust, 2004. http://www.nhtinc.org/documents/PB_Inventory.pdf.

National Low Income Housing Coalition. "Frequently Asked Questions." http://www.nlihc.org/doc/FAQ-NHTF.pdf.

———. "NLIHC Updated Estimates of State Allocation Amounts from NHTF for Every Billion Allocated and Invested: February 10, 2011." http://www.nlihc.org/doc/NHTF-state-estimates.pdf.

———. "NATIONAL HOUSING TRUST FUND: National Conference Call Reports on New Developments." *Memo to Members* 14, no. 43 (November 6, 2009).

———. "NATIONAL HOUSING TRUST FUND: White House Reiterates Promise to Capitalize the NHTF." *Memo to Members* 14, no. 42 (October 30, 2009).

———. "House Bill Would Abolish NHTF." *Memo to Members* 16, no. 19 (May 13, 2011).

———. "NHTF Funding Bill Gains Cosponsors." *Memo to Members* 16, no. 19 (May 13, 2011).

National Low Income Housing Preservation Commission. *Preventing the Disappearance of Low-Income Housing.* Washington, DC: National Corporation for Housing Partnerships, 1988.

Nelson, Kathryn P., and Jill Khadduri. "To Whom Should Limited Housing Resources Be Directed?" *Housing Policy Debate* 3, no. 1 (1992): 1–55.

Newman, Oscar. *Defensible Space.* New York: Macmillan, 1972.

Newman, Sandra J. "How Housing Matters: A Critical Summary of Research and Issues Still to be Resolved." "Does Housing Matter for Poor Families? A Critical Summary of Research and Issues Still to be Resolved," *Journal of Policy Analysis and Management,* Policy Retrospectives Section, 27 (Autumn 2008), 895–925.

———, and Joseph M. Harkness. "The Long-Term Effects of Public Housing on Self-Sufficiency." *Journal of Policy Analysis and Management* 21 (Winter 2002): 21–43.

———, and Ann B. Schnare. "'And a Suitable Living Environment': The Failure of Housing Programs to Deliver on Neighborhood Quality." *Housing Policy Debate* 8, no. 4 (1997): 703–41.

Nixon, Richard. "Special Message to the Congress Proposing Legislation and Outlining Administration Actions to Deal with Federal Housing Policy." *Public Papers of the Presidents of the United States*, September 19, 1973. http://www.presidency.ucsb.edu/ws/index.php?pid=3968&st=special+message+to+the+congress&st1=.

Nourse, Hugh O. "A Rationale for Government Intervention in Housing: The External Benefits of Good Housing, Particularly with Reference to Property Values." In *Housing in the Seventies: Working Papers*, National Housing Policy Review, 1:243–250. Washington, DC: U.S. Department of Housing and Urban Development, 1976.

Office of Management and Budget. *Analytical Perspectives, Budget of the United States Government, Fiscal Year 2012*. Washington, DC, 2011.

———."Budget Authority." Public Budget Database, Budget of the United States Government, Fiscal Year 2012. http://www.whitehouse.gov/sites/default/files/omb/budget/fy2012/assets/budauth.xls.

———. "Outlays." Public Budget Database, Budget of the United States Government, Fiscal Year 2012. http://www.whitehouse.gov/sites/default/files/omb/budget/fy2012/assets/outlays.xls.

Ohls, James. "Public Policy Toward Low Income Housing and Filtering in Housing Markets." *Journal of Urban Economics* 2, no. 2 (April 1975): 144–71.

Olsen, Edgar O. "The Cost-Effectiveness of Alternative Methods of Delivering Housing Subsidies." Paper Presented at Thirty-First APPAM Research Conference, October 2009. http://www.virginia.edu/economics/Workshops/papers/olsen/CESurvey2009.pdf.

———. "The Demand and Supply of Housing Services: A Critical Survey of the Empirical Literature." In *Handbook of Urban Economics*, edited by Edwin S. Mills, 989–1022. New York: Elsevier, 1987.

———. "Getting More from Low-Income Housing Assistance," available at http://www.brookings.edu/research/papers/2008/09/low-income-housing-olsen.

———. "Housing Programs for Low-Income Households." In *Means-Tested Transfer Programs in the United States*, edited by Robert Moffitt, 365–441. Chicago: University of Chicago Press, 2003.

———. "A Possible Rationale for Government Intervention in Housing: The Slow Adjustment of the Housing Market to its Longrun Equilibrium Position." In *Housing in the Seventies: Working Papers*, National Housing Policy Review, 1:455–58. Washington, DC: U.S. Department of Housing and Urban Development, 1976.

———, and David H. Barton. "The Benefits and Costs of Public Housing in New York City." *Journal of Public Economics* 20 (April 1983): 299–332.

———, et al. "The Effects of Different Types of Housing Assistance on Earnings and Employment." *Cityscape* 8, no. 2 (2005): 63–87.

Orr, Larry, et al. *Moving to Opportunity Interim Impacts Evaluation: Final Report*. Washington, DC: U.S. Department of Housing and Urban Development, 2003.

Ozanne, Larry, and James Zais, "Communitywide Effects of Housing Allowances." In *Housing Vouchers for the Poor: Lessons from a National Experiment*, edited by Raymond J. Struyk and Marc Bendick, 207–33. Washington, DC: Urban Institute Press, 1981.

Piper, Valerie, and Mindy Turbov. *HOPE VI and Mixed-Finance Developments: A Catalyst for Neighborhood Renewal*. Washington, DC: Brookings Institution, 2005.

Popkin, Susan J., et al. *A Decade of HOPE VI: Research Findings and Policy Challenges*. Washington, DC: Urban Institute, 2004.

President's Commission on Housing. *The Report of the President's Commission on Housing*. Washington, DC, April 1982.

Rand Corporation. *Fifth Annual Report of the Housing Assistance Supply Experiment*. Santa Monica, CA: Rand Corporation, 1979.

———. *First Annual Report of the Housing Assistance Supply Experiment*. Santa Monica, CA: Rand Corporation, 1974.

———. *Third Annual Report of the Housing Assistance Supply Experiment*. Santa Monica, California: Rand Corporation, 1977.

Rice, Douglas, and Barbara Sard. "Decade of Neglect Has Weakened Federal Low-Income Housing Programs: New Resources Required to Meet Growing Needs." Washington, DC, Center for Budget and Policy Priorities, February 24, 2009. http://www.cbpp.org/files/2-24-09hous.pdf.

Ricketts, Erol, and Isabell Sawhill. "Defining and Measuring the Underclass." *Journal of the Association of Public Policy Analysis and Management* 7, no. 4 (1988): 316–25.

Russakoff, Dale. "U.S. Seizes Philadelphia Public Housing Authority; HUD Acts After Political Corruption Charge." *Washington Post*, May 21, 1992. http://www.encyclopedia.com/doc/1P2-1006736.html.

Sa-Aadu, Jarjisu. "Alternative Estimates of Direct Tenant Benefit and Consumption Inefficiencies from the Section 8 New Construction Program." *Land Economics* 60, no. 2 (May 1984): 189–201.

Sanbonmatsu, Lisa et al., *Moving to Opportunity for Fair Housing Demonstration Program: Final Impacts Evaluation*. Washington, DC: U.S. Department of Housing and Urban Development, Office of Policy Development and Research, 2011.

Sard, Barbara. "Housing Vouchers Should Be a Major Component of Future Housing Policy for the Lowest Income Families," *Cityscape* 5, no. 2 (2001): 89–110.

Schall, Lawrence. "Commodity Hierarchy Chain Systems and the Housing Market." *Journal of Urban Economics* 10, no. 2 (April 1981): 141–63.

Schill, Michael H., and Susan M. Wachter. "The Spatial Bias of Federal Housing Law and Poverty: Concentrated Poverty in Urban America." *University of Pennsylvania Law Review* 143 (1995): 1285–1342.

Schwab, Robert M. "The Estimation of the Benefits of In-Kind Government Programs." *Journal of Public Economics* 27, no. 2 (1985), 195–210.

Schwartz, Alex F. *Housing Policy in the United States: Second Edition*. New York: Routledge, 2010.

————, and Kian Tajbakhsh. "Mixed-Income Housing: Unanswered Questions." *Cityscape* 3, no. 2 (1997): 71–92.

Seligman, Daniel. "The Enduring Slums." In *The Exploding Metropolis*, edited by *Fortune* editors, 92–114. Garden City, NY: Doubleday, 1958.

Semer, Milton P., et al. "A Review of Federal Subsidized Housing Programs" In *Housing in the Seventies: Working Papers*, National Housing Policy Review, 82–144. Washington, DC: U.S. Department of Housing and Urban Development, 1976.

Sinai, Todd M., and Joel Waldfogel. "Do Low-Income Housing Subsidies Increase Housing Consumption?" *Journal of Public Economics* 89 (December 2005): 2137–2164.

Smith, Alastair. *Mixed-Income Housing Developments: Promise and Reality.* Cambridge, MA, and Washington, DC: Joint Center for Housing Studies of Harvard University and Neighborhood Reinvestment Corporation, 2002.

Struyk, Raymond J. "Policy Questions and Experimental Responses." In *Housing Vouchers for the Poor: Lessons from a National Experiment*, edited by Raymond J. Struyk and Marc Bendick, Jr. Washington, DC: Urban Institute Press, 1981.

————, and Marc Bendick, Jr., eds. *Housing Vouchers for the Poor: Lessons from a National Experiment.* Washington, DC: Urban Institute Press, 1981.

Sullivan, Joseph F. "Passaic Housing Aides Guilty." *New York Times*, June 13, 1990. http://www.nytimes.com/1990/06/13/nyregion/passaic-housing-aides-guilty.html.

Susin, Scott."Longitudinal Outcomes of Subsidized Housing Recipients in Matched Survey and Administrative Data." *Cityscape* 8, no. 2 (2005): 189–218.

————."Rent Vouchers and the Price of Low-Income Housing." *Journal of Public Economics* 83, no. 1 (January 2002): 109–152.

Swan, Craig. "Subsidized and Unsubsidized Housing Starts." *American Real Estate and Urban Economics Association Journal* 1, no. 2 (Fall 1973): 119–40.

Sweeney, James L. "A Commodity Hierarchy Model of the Rental Housing Market." *Journal of Urban Economics* 1, no. 3 (June 1974): 288–323.

————. "Quality, Commodity Hierarchies, and Housing Markets." *Econometrica* 42, no. 1 (May 1974): 147–67.

Swope, Christopher. "Section 8 Is Broken." *Shelterforce Online*, January/February 2003. http://www.shelterforce.com/online/issues/127/section8.html.

Taub, Richard P., D. Garth Taylor, and Jan D. Dunham. *Paths of Neighborhood Change.* Chicago: University of Chicago Press, 1984.

Technical Analysis Center with Integrated Financial Engineering, Inc. "An Actuarial Review of the Federal Housing Administration Mutual Mortgage Insurance Fund for Fiscal Year 2004." October 19, 2004.

Trevino, Tammye H. "Results of the 2009 Multi-Family Housing Annual Fair Housing Occupancy Report" (memorandum), July 14, 2009, available at http://hac.non profitsoapbox.com/storage/documents/OccupancyMFH2009.pdf.

Turnham, Jennifer, et al. *Study of Homebuyer Activity through the HOME Investment Program.* Cambridge, MA: Abt Associates, Inc., 2004.

U.S. Bureau of the Census. *America's Families and Living Arrangements: 2010*. Washington, DC, November 2010.

———. "Census Tracts and Block Numbering Areas." http://www.census.gov/geo/www/cen_tract.html.

———. "Housing Vacancies and Homeownership." 2010. http://www.census.gov/hhes/www/housing/hvs/annual10/ann10ind.html.

———. *Income, Poverty, and Health Insurance Coverage in the United States: 2009*. Washington, DC, September 2010.

———. "New York City Housing and Vacancy Survey." http://www.census.gov/hhes/www/housing/nychvs/nychvs.html.

———. "Overview of Race and Hispanic Origin 2000." Census 2000 Brief C2KBR/01-1. March 2001.

U.S. Congress. House. *Cranston-Gonzalez National Affordable Housing Act: Conference Report to Accompany S. 566*. Report 101-943. October 25, 1990.

U.S. Congress. House. Committee on Ways and Means. *1998 Green Book: Background Material and Data on Programs Within the Jurisdiction of the Committee on Ways and Means*. Washington, DC, May 1998.

———. *2004 Green Book: Background Material and Data on the Programs Within the Jurisdiction of the Committee on Ways and Means, March 2004*. http://waysandmeans.house.gov/Documents.asp?section=813.

U.S. Congress. Joint Committee on Housing. *Housing Study and Investigation: Final Majority Report*. 80th Congress, 2nd session, March 15, 1948. House Report no. 1564.

U.S. Congress. Joint Economic Committee. *The Economics of Federal Subsidy Programs, Part 5—Housing Subsidies*. Washington, DC: U.S. Government Printing Office, 1972.

U.S. Congress. Senate. *Departments of Veterans Affairs and Housing and Urban Development, and Independent Agencies Appropriations Act of 1991: Report (to Accompany H.R. 5158)*, Report 101-474.

U.S. Department of Housing and Urban Development. *Annual Performance Plan: Fiscal Year 2009*. Washington, DC, February 2008.

———. *Budget Summary, Department of Housing and Urban Development, Fiscal Year 1997*. Washington, DC, 1996.

———. "FY 2010 Budget: Road Map for Transformation." www.hud.gov/budgetsummary2010.

———. *Housing in the Seventies: A Report of the National Housing Policy Review*. Washington, DC, 1974.

———. *HUD Reinvention: From Blueprint to Action*. Washington, DC, March 1995.

———. *Programs of HUD*. Washington, DC, 2005.

———. "24 CFR Part 888—Fair Market Rents for Fiscal Year 2001 for Certain Areas: Proposed Rule." *Federal Register*, October 6, 2000.

———. "24 CFR Part 93—Housing Trust Fund: Allocation Formula; Proposed Rule." *Federal Register*, December 4, 2009: 63938–42.

————. *1967 HUD Statistical Yearbook.* Washington, DC.

————. *1976 HUD Statistical Yearbook.* Washington, DC.

————. *1979 HUD Statistical Yearbook.* Washington, DC.

U.S. Department of Housing and Urban Development. Budget Office. Unpublished table. 1997.

U.S. Department of Housing and Urban Development. Chief Financial Officer. "Budget Authority by Program, Comparative Summary, Fiscal Years 2001–2003." Congressional Justifications for 2003 Estimates. http://www.hud.gov/about/budget/fy03/cjs/part_1/summary/budgetauthority.pdf.

————. "Budget Authority by Program, Comparative Summary, Fiscal Years 2010–2012." Congressional Justifications for 2012 Estimates. http://portal.hud.gov/hudportal/documents/huddoc?id=budget_authority_2012.pdf.

————. "Housing: Housing Payments: Summary of Assisted Units and Outlays." Congressional Justifications for 2010 Estimates, M1–M3. http://www.hud.gov/offices/cfo/reports/2010/cjs/hsg2010.pdf.

————. "Housing: Housing Payments: Summary of Assisted Units and Outlays." Congressional Justifications for 2011 Estimates, K1–K4. http://www.hud.gov/offices/cfo/reports/2011/cjs/Housing_Payments_2011.pdf.

————. "Housing: Rent Supplement Program." Congressional Justifications for 2009 Estimates, J1–J5, http://www.hud.gov/offices/cfo/reports/2009/cjs/hsg1.pdf.

————. "Overview of New and Cross-Cutting Initiatives: Public and Indian Housing: Transforming Rental Assistance." Congressional Justifications for 2012 Estimates. http://portal.hud.gov/hudportal/documents/huddoc?id=Transform_R_Assis_2012.pdf.

————. "Public and Indian Housing: Native American Housing Block Grants." Congressional Justifications for 2010 Estimates. http://hud.gov/offices/cfo/reports/2010/cjs/pih2010.pdf.

————. "Public and Indian Housing: Public Housing Operating Fund." Congressional Justifications for 2012 Estimates, J-1—J-16. http://portal.hud.gov/hudportal/documents/huddoc?id=PH_Opera_fund_2012.pdf,

————. "Public and Indian Housing: Revitalization of Severely Distressed Public Housing." Congressional Justifications for 2010 Estimates, N1–N9. http://www.hud.gov/offices/cfo/reports/2010/cjs/pih2010.pdf.

————. "Public and Indian Housing: Tenant-Based Rental Assistance." Congressional Justifications for 2008 Estimates. http://www.hud.gov/offices/cfo/reports/2008/cjs/part1/pih/tbdassistance.pdf.

————. "Public and Indian Housing: Tenant-Based Rental Assistance." Congressional Justifications for 2009 Estimates, C1–C22. http://www.hud.gov/offices/cfo/reports/2009/cjs/pih1.pdf.

————. "Public and Indian Housing: Tenant-Based Rental Assistance." Congressional Justifications for 2012 Estimates, H1–H25. http://portal.hud.gov/hudportal/documents/huddoc?id=Tenant_BR_Assis_2012.pdf.

U.S. Department of Housing and Urban Development. Office of Community Planning and Development. "HOME Program National Production Report (As Of 6/30/09)." http://www.hud.gov/offices/cpd/affordablehousing/reports/production/063009.pdf.

U.S. Department of Housing and Urban Development. Office of Housing. "M2M Pipeline Summary Report." http://portal.hud.gov/hudportal/documents/huddoc?id=m2mstats.pdf.

———. M2M Transactions Report as of November 4, 2011," http://portal.hud.gov/hudportal/documents/huddoc?id=m2mstran.pdf.

U.S. Department of Housing and Urban Development. Office of Policy Development and Research. *Affordable Housing Needs: A Report to Congress on the Significant Need for Housing.* Washington, DC, December 2005.

———. *Affordable Housing Needs 2005: Report to Congress.* Washington, DC, May 2007.

———. *Characteristics of HUD-Assisted Renters and Their Units in 1989.* Washington, DC, March 1992.

———. *Characteristics of HUD-Assisted Renters and Their Units in 1993.* Washington, DC, May 1997.

———. *Characteristics of HUD-Assisted Renters and Their Units in 2003.* Washington, DC, May 2008. http://www.huduser.org/Publications/pdf/Hud_asst_renters_report_p2.pdf.

———. *Comprehensive and Workable Plan for the Abatement of Lead-Based Paint in Privately Owned Housing: Report to Congress.* Washington, DC, 1990.

———. "FY 2009 HUD Income Limits: Briefing Material," April 20, 2009, at http://www.huduser.org/portal/datasets/il/il09/IncomeLimitsBriefingMaterial_FY09.pdf.

———. *Issue Brief: Will It Cost More to Replace Public Housing with Certificates?* Washington, DC, March 1995.

———. "LIHTC Database," available at http://www.huduser.org/portal/datasets/lihtc.html.

———. *The Location of Worst Case Needs in the Late 1980s: A Report to Congress.* Washington, DC, December 1992.

———. "New Low-Income Housing Tax Credit Property Data Available." *U.S. Housing Market Conditions* 2011, Second quarter (August 2011): 6-14.

———. "1999 & Estimated 2009 Decile Distributions of Family Income by Metropolitan Statistical Areas and Non Metropolitan Counties," http://www.huduser.org/portal/datasets/il/il09/msacounty_medians.pdf.

———. A Picture of Subsidized Households. United States Summary. http://www.huduser.org/datasets/assthsg/statedata96/hud2us3.txt.

———. A Picture of Subsidized Households—2008. http://www.huduser.org/portal/picture2008/index.html.

———. Picture of Subsidized Households for 2004–2007. http://www.huduser.org/portal/picture/query.html.

————. *Priority Housing Problems and "Worst Case Needs" in 1989: A Report to Congress.* Washington, DC, June 1991.

————. *Project Self-Sufficiency: An Interim Report on Progress and Performance.* Washington, DC, December 1987.

————. "Promoting Self-Sufficiency in Public Housing." Urban Policy Brief no. 3, Washington, DC, August 1996.

————. "Regulatory Impact Analysis for the Housing Trust Fund," August 10, 2009, http://www.huduser.org/publications/pdf/5246__RIA_for_HTF_Proposed_Rule1_final.pdf.

————. *Rental Housing Assistance at a Crossroads: A Report to Congress on Worst Case Housing Needs.* Washington, DC, March 1996.

————. *Rental Housing Assistance—The Crisis Continues: The 1997 Report to Congress on Worst Case Housing Needs.* Washington, DC, April 1998.

————. *Rental Housing Assistance—The Worsening Crisis: A Report to Congress on Worst Case Housing Needs.* Washington, DC, March 2000.

————. *Report to Congress on Alternative Methods for Funding Public Housing Modernization.* Washington, DC, April 1990.

————. *Trends in Worst Case Needs for Housing, 1978–1999: A Report to Congress on Worst Case Housing Needs.* Washington, DC, December 2003.

————. *2009 Worst Case Housing Needs of People with Disabilities*, March 2011.

————. *Worst Case Housing Needs 2007: A Report to Congress.* Washington, DC, May 2010.

————. *Worst Case Housing Needs 2009: Report to Congress.* Washington, DC, February 2011.

————. *Worst Case Needs for Housing Assistance in the United States in 1990 and 1991: A Report to Congress.* Washington, DC, June 1994.

U.S. Department of Housing and Urban Development, Office of Public and Indian Housing, "2011 Unit Total Development Cost (TDC) Limits," http://portal.hud.gov/hudportal/documents/huddoc?id=DOC_8094.pdf, an attachment to PIH notice 2010-20 (HA), issued May 24, 2010.

U.S. Department of Housing and Urban Development and U.S. Census Bureau. *American Housing Survey for the United States: 2003.* Current Housing Reports H150/03. Washington, DC: September 2004.

————. *American Housing Survey for the United States: 2005.* Current Housing Reports H150/05. Washington, DC, August 2006.

————. *American Housing Survey for the United States: 2007.* Current Housing Reports H150/07. Washington, DC, September 2008.

————. *American Housing Survey for the United States: 2009.* Current Housing Reports H150/09. Washington, DC, March 2011.

U.S. General Accounting Office. *Federal Housing Assistance: Comparing the Characteristics and Costs of Housing Programs.* GAO-02-76. Washington, DC, January 2002.

————. *Federal Housing Programs: What They Cost and What They Provide.* GAO-01-901R. Washington, DC, July 18, 2001.

———. *Public Housing: HOPE VI Resident Issues and Changes in Neighborhoods Surrounding Grant Sites.* GAO-04-109. November 2003.

———. *Tax Credits: Characteristics of Tax Credit Properties and Their Residents.* GAO/RCED-00-51R. January 10, 2000.

———. *Tax Credits: Opportunities to Improve Oversight of the Low-Income Housing Program.* GAO/GGD/RCED-97-55. Washington, DC, 1997.

U.S. Government Accountability Office. *Rental Housing Assistance: Policy Decisions and Market Factors Explain Changes in the Costs of the Section 8 Programs.* GAO-06-405. Washington, DC, April 2006.

———. *RECOVERY ACT: Status of States' and Localities' Use of Funds and Efforts to Insure Accountability,* GAO-10-231. Washington, DC, December 2009, 80-81.

Urban Institute. *Implementing Block Grants for Housing: An Evaluation of the First Year of HOME.* Washington, DC: U.S. Department of Housing and Urban Development, Office of Policy Development and Research, 1995.

Urban Systems Research & Engineering, Inc. *The Costs of HUD Multifamily Housing Programs.* Washington, DC: U.S. Department of Housing and Urban Development, Office of Policy Development and Research, 1982.

Utt, Ronald D. "The Conservative Critique of HOPE VI." In *From Despair to Hope: HOPE VI and the New Promise of Public Housing in America's Cities,* edited by Henry G. Cisneros and Lara Engdahl, chap. 14. Washington, DC: Brookings Institution Press, 2009.

Vitaliano, Donald. "Public Housing and Slums: Cure or Cause?" *Urban Studies* 20 (May 1983): 173–83.

Wallace, James E., et al. *Assessment of the HUD-Insured Multifamily Housing Stock: Final Report. Vol. 1, Current Status of HUD-Insured (or Held) Multifamily Rental Housing.* Washington, DC: U.S. Department of Housing and Urban Development, Office of Policy Development and Research, 1993.

———. *Participation and Benefits in the Urban Section 8 Program: New Construction and Existing Housing.* Cambridge, MA: Abt Associates, Inc., 1981.

Weicher, John C., "The Fiscal Profitability of Urban Renewal under Matching Grants and Revenue Sharing." *Journal of Urban Economics* 3, no. 3 (March 1976): 193–208.

———. "Halfway to a Housing Allowance?" In *Maintaining the Safety Net: Income Redistribution Programs in the Reagan Administration,* edited by John C. Weicher, 92–118. Washington, DC: American Enterprise Institute for Public Policy Research, 1984.

———. "Housing Block Grants in the United States." *Urban Law and Policy* 4 (September 1981): 269–83.

———. *Housing: Federal Policies and Programs.* Washington, DC: American Enterprise Institute for Public Policy Research, 1980.

———. "Housing Policy." In *Current Issues in Urban Economics,* edited by Peter Mieszkowski and Mahlon Straszheim, 469–508. Baltimore: Johns Hopkins University Press, 1978.

————. "A New War on Poverty: The Kemp Program to Empower the Poor." In *Reducing Poverty in America: Views and Approaches*, edited by Michael R. Darby, 199–223. Thousand Oaks, CA: Sage Publications, 1995.

————. *Privatizing Subsidized Housing*. Washington, DC: AEI Press, 1997.

————. "The Rationales for Government Intervention in Housing: An Overview." In *Housing in the Seventies: Working Papers*, National Housing Policy Review, 1:181–92. Washington, DC: U.S. Department of Housing and Urban Development, 1976.

————. *Urban Renewal: Federal Program for Local Problems*. Washington, DC: American Enterprise Institute for Public Policy Research, 1972.

————. "The Voucher/Production Debate." In *Building Foundations: Housing and Federal Policy*, edited by Denise DiPasquale and Langley C. Keyes, 263–92. Philadelphia: University of Pennsylvania Press, 1990.

————, and Thomas G. Thibodeau. "Filtering and Housing Markets: An Empirical Analysis." *Journal of Urban Economics* 23, no. 1 (January 1988): 21–40.

Weicher, John C., Lorene Yap, and Mary S. Jones. *National Housing Needs and Quality Changes During the 1980s*. Washington, DC: Urban Institute, 1980.

Wilner, Daniel M., et al. *The Housing Environment and Family Life*. Baltimore: Johns Hopkins University Press, 1962.

Wilson, William Julius, and Richard P. Taub. *There Goes the Neighborhood: Racial, Ethnic, and Class Tensions in Four Chicago Neighborhoods and Their Meaning for America*. New York: Knopf, 2006.

Yezer, Anthony M. J. *The Physical Adequacy and Affordability of Housing in America: Measurements Using the Annual Housing Survey for 1975 and 1977*. U.S. Department of Housing and Urban Development, Annual Housing Survey Studies no. 7, June 1981.

Zielenbach, Sean. "Assessing Economic Change in HOPE VI Neighborhoods." *Housing Policy Debate* 14, no. 4 (2003): 621–55.

About the Author

John C. Weicher is Director of Hudson Institute's Center for Housing and Financial Markets. From 2001 to 2005 he served as Assistant Secretary for Housing and Federal Housing Commissioner at the U.S. Department of Housing and Urban Development. He previously served as Assistant Secretary for Policy Development and Research at HUD, and as Chief Economist at both HUD and the Office of Management and Budget.

He has managed research programs at the Urban Institute and the American Enterprise Institute, where he held the F.K. Weyerhaeuser Chair in Public Policy Research. During 2007–2008 he chaired the National Research Council's Committee to Evaluate HUD's Research Plan; he has also been a member of the Millennium Housing Commission, the Census Advisory Committee on Population Statistics, and the Committee on Urban Policy of the National Research Council. He was President of the American Real Estate and Urban Economics Association in 1982, and received the Association's Career Achievement Award in 1993. He currently serves on the Advisory Committee on Economic Inclusion of the Federal Deposit Insurance Corporation, and the Editorial Advisory Board of *Cityscape*.

Weicher holds an A.B. from the University of Michigan and a Ph.D. in economics from the University of Chicago. He is the author or editor of fourteen books, and the author of numerous popular and scholarly articles on housing and urban issues. He has testified before Congressional committees on more than 40 occasions.